Humana Festival 2007
The Complete Plays

Humana Inc., headquartered in Louisville, Kentucky, is one of the nation's largest publicly traded health benefits companies, with approximately 11.3 million medical members. Humana offers a diversified portfolio of health insurance products and related services—through traditional and consumer-choice plans—to employer groups, government-sponsored plans, and individuals.

The Humana Foundation was established in 1981 as the philanthropic arm of Humana Inc. It is a private foundation that supports and nurtures charitable activities that promote healthy lives and healthy communities.

Humana Festival 2007
The Complete Plays

Edited by
Adrien-Alice Hansel and Julie Felise Dubiner

Playscripts, Inc.
New York, NY

Published by Playscripts, Inc.
325 West 38th Street, Suite 305
New York, New York, 10018
www.playscripts.com

Cover design by Matt Dobson
Text design and layout by Erin Detrick

First Edition: April 2008
10 9 8 7 6 5 4 3 2 1

LCCN: 95650734
ISSN: 1935-4452

ISBN-13: 978-0-9709046-3-8

Contents

FANTASTIC – ONE-WOMAN SHOW W/ BARBIE DOLLS

NICE GENDER-BLIND PIECE ABOUT THE "RIGHT" TO DO THIS STUPID THING

INTERESTING, A LITTLE FAR FETCHED, SOME GOOD WRITING

TWO MEN IN PRISON – HAUNTING

Acknowledgments

The editors wish to thank the following persons for their invaluable assistance in compiling this volume:

Jennifer Bielstein
Cathy Culliver
Matt Dobson
Diana Grisanti
Leslie Hankins
Charles Haugland
Devon LaBelle
Jessica Leader
Marc Masterson
Cara Pacifico
Jeffrey S. Rodgers
Zan Sawyer-Dailey
James Seacat
Wanda Snyder
Amy Wegener

Beth Blickers
Val Day
Morgan Jenness
Joyce Ketay
Carl Mulert
Antje Oegel
Bruce Ostler
Mark Christian Subias
Chris Till
Derek Zasky

Actors Theatre of Louisville Staff
Humana Festival 2007

Artistic Director .... Marc Masterson
Managing Director .... Jennifer Bielstein

ADMINISTRATION
Budget and Management
General Manager .... James Roemer
Assistant General Manager .... Jeffrey S. Rodgers
Systems Manager .... Dottie Krebs
Accounting Manager .... Peggy Shake
Accounting Assistant .... Shirley Bruce

Business Office
Executive Secretary .... Wanda Snyder

Communications
Director .... James Seacat
Marketing Manager .... Cathy Culliver
Media & Publicity Coordinator .... Kyle Shepherd
Group Sales Manager .... Sarah Peters
Festival/Events Coordinator .... Katherine Bilby
Outbound Sales Manager .... Lynda Sylvester
Communications Associate .... Leslie Hankins
Group Sales Assistant Manager .... J. Stephen Smith
Graphics Coordinator .... Matt Dobson
Mail Services .... Alan Meyer

Development
Director .... Christen McDonough Boone
Manager of Foundation & Government Relations ...... Michael K. Brooks, Jr.
Manager of Patron Relations .... Trish Pugh Jones
Manager of Corporate Relations .... Jamie Grider Paradis
Coordinator .... David Clark

Ticket Sales
Director .... Kim McKercher
Senior Box Office Manager .... Saundra Blakeney
Training & Technology Manager .... Steve Clark
Subscriptions Manager .... Julie Gallegos
Customer Service .... Gretchen Abrahamsen, Chris Bryant,
Kristy Kannapell, Julia Leist,
Cara Pacifico, Kae Thompson

Operations

Director ....Mike Schüssler-Williams
Maintenance Staff ....Bruce Foley, Richard Graham, Allan Reed
Receptionist ....Dot King
Housekeeping Staff.. Gregory McClure, Darrell Mudd,
Jennifer Shaw, Alex Simon, LaTonya Yarbo

Volunteer and Audience Relations

Director .... Allison Hammons
House Managers... Amy Attaway, Amanda Comstock,
Ian Frank, Darnell Johnson,
Leah Roberts, Kyle Sawyer-Dailey
Coat Check Attendants........ Jennifer Burks, Nathaniel Nobbe, Cory Vaughn

ARTISTIC AND PRODUCTION

Production Manager...Frazier W. Marsh
Associate Director .... Zan Sawyer-Dailey
Artistic Manager.. Emily Ruddock
Production Stage Manager .... Paul Mills Holmes
Resident Stage Manager...Debra Anne Gasper
Company Manager... Ashleigh Pugh
Arts Administration Fellow..Ian Frank

Resident Designers

Scenic Designer... Paul Owen
Costume Designer ....Lorraine Venberg
Properties Director..Mark Walston
Lighting Designer ....Brian J. Lilienthal
Sound Designer... Matt Callahan

Literary

Director of New Play Development....................................Adrien-Alice Hansel
Resident Dramaturg ....Julie Felise Dubiner
Playwright-in-Residence...Naomi Wallace
Literary Assistants..............................Joanna K. Donehower, Kyle J. Schmidt

Education

Interim Director..Katie Blackerby
Interim Associate Director...Jess Jung
Playwriting in the Schools Coordinator ....Lee Look

Design and Technology

Technical Director..Michael J. Bowen
Assistant Technical Director...Justin Hagovsky
Technical Production Assistant...Rebecca Price
Shop Foreman .... Alexis Tucker

Lead Carpenter .... Pierre Vendette
Carpenters ....Javan Roy-Bachman*, Braden Blauser,
          Noah J. Johnson, Nick Passafiume, Marshall Spratt
Journeyman Carpenter ....Amy Jonas*
Deck Carpenter .... Emily Meyer
Stage Operations Supervisor.................................... Corey B. Harrison
Design Assistant.. Brenda Ellis
Scenic Charge .... Kieran Wathen
Scenic Artists ....Sabra Crockett, Margie Fall
Props Master.. Doc Manning
Props Soft Goods Artisan ....Deanna Hilleman
Props Carpenter ....Joe Cunningham
Props Artisans .... William Griffith, Eric Hart, Scott Rygalski
Props Journeyman ....Elizabeth Clark
Costume Shop Manager.. Margret Fenske
Costume Crafts..Shari Cochran
Draper......................................Shana Lincoln, Barbara Niederer
First Hands.............................. Karen Merrill, Mary Lee Younger
Stitchers .... Jessica Allison, Lorie Baltes,
          Nina Rosenberg, Brandie Purvis
Costume Journeyman...Susan Neason*
Design Assistants ....Stacy B. Squires, Rebekah Trigg
Wig Master.. Marty Kopulsky
Wardrobe Master .... Paul M. C. Thompson
Bingham Wardrobe Mistress..Patti Luther
Media Technologist ....Jason Czaja
Sound Engineer... Paul Doyle
Associate Sound Designer.. Benjamin Marcum
Sound Technicians.................Jessica Collins, David M. Romich, Adam Smith
Lighting Supervisor...Paul Werner
Assistant Lighting Supervisor .... Nick Dent
First Electrician .... Derek Easton
Deck Electrician...Lauren Scattolini
Board Operators/ Swing Electricians .... Rob Brodersen, Kat Seaton
Lighting Journeyman...Danielle Clifford

*Paul Owen Fellow

Apprentice/Intern Company
Director ....Will MacAdams
Associate Director .... Monica Francisco

Apprentices
Timo Aker, Sean Andries, Katie Barton, Loren Bidner, Eleanor Caudill, Maurine Evans, Kristen B. Jackson, Rafael Jordan, Jane Lee, Nicole Marquez, Jake Millgard, Michael Judson Pace, Zachary T. Palamara, Phil

Pickens, Zarina Shea, Zdenko Slobodnik, Jeff Snodgrass, Ashley Spearman, Angela Sperazza, Mark Stringham, Emily Tate Frank, Biz Wells

Interns

Apprentice/Intern Company	Andrew Jessop
Communications	Julia Curiel, Nathaniel Nobbe
Education	Megan Alexander
Festival	Ashley Cease
Literary	Diana Grisanti, Cara Pacifico
Scenic	Jim Knapp, Alan Perez
Scenic Design	Megan McKinney, Nick Passafiume
Stage Management	Amy Kellett, Kristy Matero, Mary Spadoni, Silka Phyllis Werness
Properties	Jennifer Burks

Special Thanks

Actors Theatre's company doctors:

Dr. Andrew Mickler, F.A.C.S.
Dr. Edwin Hopson, DC, CSCS
Dr. April Hopson, DC
Dr. Bill Breuer, MCH, DC, FAPHP

Actors Theatre of Louisville was founded in 1964 by Richard Block in association with Ewel Cornett. Jon Jory was Producing Director from 1969 to 2000.

Alexander Speer, Executive Director, ended his 40-year tenure at Actors Theatre in 2006.

Foreword

The celebration of theatrical imagination contained in this Humana Festival anthology of 2007 dances across a broad spectrum of styles and content. This diversity of voices is an expression of the vitality running through the American Theatre in the present moment, as more and more theatres embrace the exhilaration of producing new work and more and more playwrights rise to the opportunity. Many of these writers are brand new to the Humana Festival, and we have been inspired by their fresh perspectives.

Our desire now is to move these plays out into the world and help them find a home—in the imagination of the readers of this book and ultimately on other stages. Several of these plays have already moved to second and third productions, and the variety of venues is as varied as the plays themselves. Second productions of new plays are sometimes hard to come by, but we have been working on expanding the partnerships that make them possible. This book is part of that effort.

So here they are in their eccentric glory: comedy, drama, social critique, edgy ensemble work; plays both personal and political. There are plays of the moment and plays that have a chance of standing the test of time. We love them all and welcome your collaboration in the next phase of their existence.

—Marc Masterson
Artistic Director
Actors Theatre of Louisville

Editors' Note

"In a very real way, living with earthquakes cannot help but diminish us, by reducing our lives to a biological afterthought... Yet if we open our minds we may, paradoxically, find ourselves enlarged. Human life, after all, is only ephemeral on its own terms, when we consider it independent of everything else. Place it in a context, in conjunction with something larger, and it immediately takes on a more complicated shape. Eternity is right in front of us, if we allow ourselves to see."

—David Ulin, *The Myth of Solid Ground*

David Ulin conceives of geological time as small movement over eons punctuated by sudden, unpredictable change. Naomi Iizuka takes this concept as the backbone for her examination of eight intersecting lives in her drama *Strike-Slip*, but Ulin's observation about the ways a larger context refigures life on a human scale just as easily embraces the full compliment of offerings at the 2007 Humana Festival of New American Plays.

Of the hundreds of plays Actors Theatre reads each year, we strive to find the six full-length plays, a commissioned full-length anthology and handful of ten-minute plays that will chart a diverse range of experience, theatrically and thematically. This year, Actors Theatre was pleased to partake in the year-long, world-wide premiere of Suzan-Lori Parks' *365 Days/365 Plays* as well. So what happenstance could connect these plays, which range from internet psychodrama to a comedy about football and the end of the world, to bracing and idiosyncratic examinations of the bachelor/ette party or Barbie and Big Oil? Our short answer is the great writers, the exquisitely considered questions about what it is to live in this culture of ours, and the intense work of artistic, production and administrative staffs that carry off this annual theatrical feat with deceptive ease. There is a larger answer too, one that we can approach once we have the distance to consider these plays in their collective context: Each play is indeed only distinct on its own terms. Placed in the context of each other, a complex overlapping of theme and thought, of cultural references and of a larger yearning for connection threads through the plays from the 31st Humana Festival.

"A city like Los Angeles has many centers of the universe, and there are these unexpected links among the different centers," says Iizuka of her play *Strike-Slip*. These unexpected links are central to the dramaturgy of Iizuka's play, as its eight characters, connected by family ties, love and coincidence, collide with each other in the expanse of urban Los Angeles. In writing about a city straddling physical and cultural fault lines, Iizuka explores both the isolation of the metropolis and the relentless energy that keeps its characters converging in each other's lives, leaving the audience with the god's-eye view with which to see how interwoven these isolated lives truly are.

dark play or stories for boys by Carlos Murillo explores loneliness and attachment in a darker key, taking its cue from a true story of a teenager's near-fatal internet attraction. "As individuals we all have a need, a desire, for belonging," says Murillo. "And there's a fear of expressing that desire in the real world. I see it in my students. They believe you're not supposed to feel, you should be skeptical. Yet despite that pose, I think people really crave meaning and understanding, but to admit it would mean taking an emotional risk." Murillo explores this desire for intimacy without vulnerability as teenaged Nick starts making up fictional identities out of boredom. But when the teenager he meets online starts to fall for the character Nick's created, he has to face the issues of love, intimacy and betrayal that follow in real life.

"At any given time, there are 36 people on Earth, chosen...by God to carry all the pain of the world... I know, I know what you're thinking. I had the same thought. 36? That seems hardly enough. I mean back in Biblical times, maybe... But now, I mean baby boomers, billions in China, surely we need more—" So claims an overworked social worker in Ken Weitzman's *The As If Body Loop,* a play which ultimately finds its transcendence in the collisions of football, a team of Jewish ecstatics who bear the pain of the world, and the shared physiological experience of seeing suffering and feeling it as your own. "I found the idea that there are 36 people who carry the pain of the world incredibly moving," says Weitzman, "and the As If Body Loop concept is about the power of being a witness. In my mind, they are different ways of challenging the idea that we are individuals only." As his characters map out their interdependence, they unearth their own latent powers to hold each other up, and through each other, a small part of the world.

Craig Wright further anatomizes the nature of connection and knowledge in his terse drama *The Unseen,* which follows two men imprisoned by a totalitarian regime and mercilessly tortured for unknown crimes. When an enigmatic new prisoner arrives and begins—potentially—to communicate with them in code, the men make different decisions about where to place their faith, what to do with their doubts and how to spend the ever-shrinking time they have left. As Wright puts it, "There's no way to ignore the fact that there are billions of people who don't think what you believe is true, and it becomes radically obvious that the work of being human together suddenly has less to do with proving our claims and more to do with listening to each other's claims, looking for that moment where we realize we're on the same journey. That's the trick: It's not that we don't have the same answers; we don't even have the same questions! But we do have a few things in common." And it is in these commonalities that empathy starts to grow between each man's approach to the universe, forming a partnership that comforts each in the transient span of their individual lives.

When Something Wonderful Ends, Sherry Kramer's one-woman show, finds its main character trying to make sense of her mother's death by connecting the ephemera from her childhood—the Barbies she must pack up as her family sells her girlhood home—with her growing realization of the global consequences of her personal oil dependency. Kramer's character fights her fears of insignificance with humor and stories of a mother whose love for the world was so fierce that her daughter has to save it to become worthy of her. This character's effervescent personality rings through the play, as does her deep belief that we hold all the power we need to take real responsibility for the world. In packing up her childhood, she grieves for her mother, while finally growing into the kind of woman her mother always wanted her to become.

Batch, a collaboration between New Paradise Laboratories and playwright Alice Tuan, explores the bonds of friendship and marriage, bonds that shift as the night before a wedding unfolds. Part bacchanal, part boxing match, part exploration of the nature of transformation, *Batch* carries a community through the strange and sacred process of becoming married. The piece is the second in a series of works that New Paradise Laboratories is creating about rite-of-passage parties. As co-creator and director Whit MacLaughlin, Artistic Director of NPL, frames the piece, "When we get married, we say, in one way or another, 'I'm getting married forever'. We're trying to rise out of our little moment of time and speak to our future selves. In that context, the bachelor party becomes very interesting because we're revving up to make one of the few transcendental statements of our lives: I do." *Batch* connects the mundane to the transcendent, ricocheting from mythic past to dance-beat present, in a fractured story of the power of ritual to reconsecrate commitment.

The call of the open road has reverberated since the founding of our nation: in the wind in our hair and promise of a new life around the corner, or in the legacy of land taken, communities divided and the increasingly guarded borders behind which Americans drive. As in previous years, *The Open Road Anthology* is a multi-author collaboration, commissioned by Actors Theatre for the resident Apprentice Acting Company. Written by Constance Congdon, Kia Corthron, Michael John Garcés, Rolin Jones, A. Rey Pamatmat and Kathryn Walat, with music by GrooveLily, *The Open Road Anthology* travels the American landscape by car, by plane, by foot and by song. Comic and thought-provoking, the play embraces the yearning for freedom, the joy of a good backbeat and the way you can only know home by learning who you are once you've left.

The three ten-minute plays that comprised the 2007 Humana Festival's evening of shorts are likewise diverse and resonant. Marco Ramirez's *I am Not Batman.* (winner of the 2007 Heideman Award) introduces us to a storytelling kid who imagines himself strong, nimble—*mythic*—enough to save himself and his father from a street fight, or at least from the loneliness of a world with too little of everything but imagination. *Mr. & Mrs.* by Julie Marie Myatt explores the comic side of connection—the moment after till death do we part when each newlywed starts counting the moments to parting. *Clarisse & Larmon*, Deb Margolin's breathtaking tragedy about a middle-aged couple coping with the news of their son's death, explores the impossibility of severing the bond between a child and the bodies who created him.

Each play from this year's Humana Festival explores the world beyond the context of a single life, and in concert with each other, this collection of plays represents a gathering of thought and experiment about the nature of our contemporary society. These artists have asked thoughtful questions about commitment and isolation, about the world created by the media and about the world in which we live. The great undertaking of the Humana Festival itself is an exercise in interdependence, built on the work of the entire staff of Actors Theatre, brought into being by the vision and sustained support of the Humana Foundation. Furthermore, the festival creates a national audience for these plays—itself a corrective to the sense of separation and remoteness of an individual life or community. These plays find their next reverberant home in the anthology of plays you now hold.

—*Adrien-Alice Hansel and Julie Felise Dubiner*

STRIKE-SLIP
by Naomi Iizuka

BIOGRAPHY

Naomi Iizuka's plays include *Anon(ymous)*; *At the Vanishing Point* (2005 Humana Festival); *36 Views*; *Language of Angels*; *Polaroid Stories* (1997 Humana Festival); *War of the Worlds* (2000 Humana Festival, co-written with Anne Bogart and SITI Company); *Aloha, Say the Pretty Girls* (1999 Humana Festival); *Tattoo Girl*; and *Skin*. Her plays have been produced at Actors Theatre, The Children's Theatre Company, The Kennedy Center, Huntington Theatre Company, Portland Center Stage, Berkeley Repertory Theatre, The Public Theater, Geva Theatre Center, Campo Santo, CalShakes and Brooklyn Academy of Music; workshopped at Mark Taper Forum, Geva Theatre Center, Sundance Theatre and The Playwrights' Center's PlayLabs Festival; and published by Playscripts, Inc., Dramatic Publishing and Overlook Press. Ms. Iizuka is a member of New Dramatists and the recipient of an Alpert Award, Whiting Award, Stavis Award, PEN Center/USA West Award for Drama, Rockefeller MAP grant, NEA/TCG Artist-in-Residence grant, McKnight Fellowship and Princeton's Hodder Fellowship.

ACKNOWLEDGMENTS

Strike-Slip premiered at the Humana Festival of New American Plays in March 2007. It was directed by Chay Yew with the following cast and staff:

LEE SUNG CHO	Nelson Mashita
FRANK RICHMOND	Keith Randolph Smith
RAFAEL GUTTIEREZ	Justin Huen
ANGIE LEE	Ali Ahn
VIVIANA RAMOS	Romi Dias
RACHEL MORSE	Heather Lea Anderson
DAN MORSE	Tim Altmeyer
VINCE LEE	Hanson Tse
Scenic Designer	Paul Owen
Costume Designer	Christal Weatherly
Lighting Designer	Deb Sullivan
Sound Designer	Andre Pluess
Properties Designer	Ron Riall
Fight Director	Lee Look
Stage Manager	Debra Anne Gasper
Production Assistant	Melissa Miller
Dramaturg	Julie Felise Dubiner
Assistant Dramaturg	Cara Pacifico
Casting	Judy Bowman Casting
Directing Assistant	Amanda Boekelheide

CAST OF CHARACTERS

(In order of appearance:)

LEE SUNG CHO, Korean, fifties, born and raised in Korea, owner of a small market in downtown Los Angeles

FRANK RICHMOND, African-American man in his forties

RAFAEL GUTTIEREZ, Mexican-American, seventeen years old, second generation American, born and raised in Los Angeles

ANGIE LEE, Korean-American, seventeen years old, first generation American, born and raised in Los Angeles

VIVIANA RAMOS, Mexican-American, late thirties, first generation American, born and raised in Los Angeles, a real estate agent

RACHEL MORSE, Caucasian, late thirties, a creative writing teacher

DAN MORSE, Caucasian, late thirties, a seismic analyst and associate professor at Cal Tech

VINCE LEE, Korean-American, early twenties, first generation American, born and raised in Los Angeles

PLACE
Los Angeles.

TIME
Act 1 takes place now over a 24-hour period.
Act 2 takes place over a 24-hour period one year later.

"An earthquake of consequence is never an isolated event."
—Charles Richter, *Elementary Seismology*

3

Ali Ahn and Justin Huen
in *Strike-Slip*

31st Annual Humana Festival of New American Plays
Actors Theatre of Louisville, 2007
Photo by Harlan Taylor

STRIKE-SLIP

ACT I
Scene 1

Mid-morning. A market in downtown Los Angeles. LEE SUNG CHO is behind the counter watching a Korean language drama on a tiny television. FRANK RICHMOND enters.

RICHMOND. Hey.

> (*Pause.*)

Hey. A pack of Marlboro Lights.

> (LEE *retrieves a pack of cigarettes.*)

I said lights.

> (LEE *retrieves another pack.*)

No not that one. I want the box.

> (LEE *retrieves another pack.*)

No. Box.

LEE. No more.

RICHMOND. Say again.

LEE. No more. Out.

RICHMOND. All right just give me that one then. And give me six quick picks.

> (LEE *retrieves the tickets.*)

Anybody ever win around here? Anybody ever strike it rich?

> (LEE *doesn't respond.*)

I asked you a question.

> (LEE *rings up the cigarettes and the scratchers.*)

LEE. Ten sixty-three.

> (RICHMOND *gives* LEE *money.* LEE *gives back change.*)

RICHMOND. I gave you a ten and a five.

LEE. Ten and a one.

RICHMOND. Man you can't count. I gave you a ten and a five.

LEE. You gave me one.

RICHMOND. That's a lie.

LEE. I not lie.

RICHMOND. Man, what do you think, I'm stupid?

LEE. You gave me a ten and a one.

RICHMOND. That's bullshit.

LEE. Not bullshit.

RICHMOND. What did you say to me?

LEE. Here, take.

> (LEE SUNG CHO *pushes the money back at* RICHMOND.)

RICHMOND. Don't fuckin throw money at me.

LEE. I want you get out.

RICHMOND. I ain't gonna say it but one more time. I gave you a ten and a five. You owe me.

LEE. Not five. One.

RICHMOND. What do you think I am? You think you can just stand there and lie to my face? Who do you think you're dealing with?

LEE. Get out of my store.

RICHMOND. What do you think I am?

LEE. Get out.

> (LEE SUNG CHO *retrieves a gun.*)

RICHMOND. I'll be back.

> (RICHMOND *takes back his change and goes.* LEE *puts down the gun.*)

Scene 2

Morning. A bus stop in downtown Los Angeles. The sound of street vendors, transistor radio music, and traffic like the ocean. RAFAEL GUTTIEREZ *has his hands over* ANGIE LEE's *eyes.*

RAFAEL. What do you see?

ANGIE. Tiny dots, hundreds of them, thousands even. And they're moving, they're like moving in different directions. And they're all different colors all at once: red and orange. Yellow and green. Blue. Chartreuse.

RAFAEL. Chartreuse?

ANGIE. What?

RAFAEL. Where do you get a word like that?

ANGIE. I don't know. It's just a word.

> (ANGIE *pushes* RAFAEL'S *hands away.*)

RAFAEL. Chartreuse.

ANGIE. Shut up.

RAFAEL. That's funny.

> (ANGIE *punches* RAFAEL *in the arm.*)

Ow!

ANGIE. That didn't hurt.

RAFAEL. Yeah, it did.

ANGIE. No it didn't.

RAFAEL. How do you know? I'm telling you it did.

ANGIE. Really?

RAFAEL. What'd I say?

ANGIE. I'm sorry. Rafi? I didn't mean it. (*Beat.*) Rafi?

RAFAEL. Aaah! Psych!

ANGIE. I hate you.

RAFAEL. No cause it did, it did kinda hurt.

ANGIE. Liar.

RAFAEL. I'm serious.

ANGIE. I don't want to hear it.

RAFAEL. No cause see, you hit like a guy.

ANGIE. I do not.

RAFAEL. That's a good thing. Like most girls, they go (*Swatting the air.*) "I hate you. I hate you." You ain't like that. You're just like (*Throwing a left upper cut.*) Thwack. You hit hard, girl. You should be like a girl boxer.

ANGIE. I'm not going to be some girl boxer.

RAFAEL. No? What are you going to be?

ANGIE. I don't know. (*Beat.*) A doctor maybe. A pediatrician.

RAFAEL. Yeah? Well that's cool.

ANGIE. You think it's dumb.

RAFAEL. No I don't. Taking care of little kids, like when they get really sick and they can't even say what's wrong, or if they get hurt, and you make them better, that's tight. I think it's cool, you know, you got a plan. I think that's cool.

ANGIE. Everybody has a plan.

RAFAEL. Not everybody. Some people, they just kinda— (*Beat.*) I don't know. A lot of people, they don't think like that. They just end up where they end up. That's how it is for them.

(*Beat. An expensive car drives by.*)

ANGIE. Look at that car. That's a nice car. Who drives a car like that, I wonder.

RAFAEL. Some rich person, that's who.

ANGIE. What do you think it'd be like to drive a car like that?

RAFAEL. How would I know?

ANGIE. I bet it's amazing. All-leather interior and surround sound. And the ride, I bet the ride is like out of this world. Sometimes I see a car like that, and it's so nice, it's all new and nice, and it's like—perfect. And I wonder what it'd be like to be that person, to be that person who gets to drive that car and live that life.

RAFAEL. What do you care about people you don't even know? Who cares?

ANGIE. I'm just talking.

RAFAEL. It's not like we can afford that kinda car. It's not like we're ever gonna have that kinda bank.

ANGIE. It's just something I wonder about.

RAFAEL. Yeah? Well it's a waste of time.

ANGIE. I just wonder. I just— Nothing. Never mind.

(*The sound of traffic.* ANGIE *and* RAFAEL *sit in silence a while.*)

RAFAEL. Sometimes I think what it'd be like if we could just keep going. Like get on the freeway and just go till we got to like the ocean, and then get on a boat or something and just keep going, just keep sailing till we got to like Fiji.

ANGIE. Fiji?

RAFAEL. Or wherever. Someplace else.

ANGIE. We could do that. Just take off.

RAFAEL. Yeah?

ANGIE. Yeah. Take off and go someplace where nobody'd know who we were, and we could like change our names and make new lives for ourselves and be these other people, these whole other people.

RAFAEL. That'd be cool.

ANGIE. Yeah, it would. (*Beat.*) Look we shouldn't be ditching. I got a midterm in English tomorrow.

RAFAEL. So? Come on. We could go down to the beach, go to Santa Monica or something.

ANGIE. No, Rafi, we should go.

RAFAEL. Is that what you want?

ANGIE. It's not about that.

RAFAEL. What's it about then?

ANGIE. I don't know. It's not about what I want. It's not that simple.

RAFAEL. Yeah it is. What do you want? Angie?

ANGIE. I don't know what I want. (*Beat.*) I don't know.

(RAFAEL *and* ANGIE *kiss. The traffic goes by.*)

Scene 3

Late morning. Sound of unseen children playing outside. The empty living room of a house for sale in Santa Monica. RACHEL *and* DAN MORSE, *and* VIVIANA RAMOS, *their real estate agent.*

VIVIANA. It's a very nice property: three bedrooms, two baths, a bonus room. It goes on the market tomorrow and it's going to be snapped up in no time. In this area—well I don't need to tell you, houses in this price range, they're just isn't the inventory. If you're interested, we're going to have to come up with a very aggressive bid and then we're going to have to move on it fast.

RACHEL. I love the garden. It's so beautiful.

VIVIANA. They did a nice job with the landscaping. It has that English garden feel with the roses and the wisteria. It's very nice.

DAN. When was the house built?

VIVIANA. 1929, but of course it's been updated over the years. The master bath was redone and the French doors off the family room, that's all new. The kitchen needs a little work, but it's a nice size lot. You could always add on if you wanted to.

RACHEL. It's so pretty, so bright.

VIVIANA. It has very good light and a very nice flow.

RACHEL. Dan? What do you think?

DAN. It's nice. It's really nice.

VIVIANA. The school district in this area is first-rate. I don't know if you and Mr. Morse have children.

RACHEL. No, not yet, but we'd like to. We've been talking about it.

VIVIANA. So what do you do, Mr. Morse?

RACHEL. My husband is a seismologist.

VIVIANA. That's fascinating. Do you work for that agency? I forget the name. It's the one they always have on the news when there's an earthquake. It looks like they're all sitting in a little underground bunker somewhere, and they have that machine they use—I forget the name.

DAN. No, I don't.

RACHEL. My husband teaches at Caltech. He actually, he just got tenure.

VIVIANA. Congratulations. That's wonderful. But from Santa Monica, that's quite a commute you're looking at.

DAN. My wife has her heart set on being by the ocean.

VIVIANA. The air is so much better. So much cleaner and cooler.

RACHEL. I've just always dreamed of living by the ocean.

DAN. I know you have. I like being by the ocean, too.

VIVIANA. Seismology. Wow. I can't get over that. That's so neat.

RACHEL. People are always asking Dan if he knows when the big one's going to hit, if there's any way to predict.

VIVIANA. And what do you tell them, Mr. Morse?

DAN. That it doesn't work that way.

RACHEL. It's a different conception of time, people don't always understand that. You're looking at windows of time that are, you know, a hundred years, a thousand years, and that's just, well that's the kind of time frame you're dealing with. And you're dealing with things that are happening miles and miles below the earth's surface, where you can't see, you can't really measure in the same way, so it's very hard to say exactly when something like that, when it will happen.

DAN. My wife is the expert.

RACHEL. No, I'm not.

DAN. She can tell you everything you ever wanted to know, whether she knows what she's talking about or not.

RACHEL. I'm just trying to explain. I don't really know all that much about it.

VIVIANA. Well you'll be happy to know this house is retrofitted and completely up to code.

DAN. It doesn't make much of a difference, but I appreciate the effort.

VIVIANA. You sound like a fatalist, Mr. Morse.

DAN. You have to be to live in this city, don't you think.

VIVIANA. I don't know about that. I'm more of an optimist, I guess.

DAN. That must be nice, to be that way.

VIVIANA. I think you have to be an optimist to do what I do.

DAN. Why? Because you sell dreams? Isn't that what your card says?

VIVIANA. Something like that, yes.

DAN. So what's the price tag on this dream?

VIVIANA. Eight hundred and fifty thousand.

DAN. So what do you think? Is that the fair market price for a dream?

VIVIANA. I guess it depends on what your dream is.

RACHEL. It's such a nice place. So light, so bright. I love how light it is. And the garden, I love the garden. It's so quiet and peaceful. It's so peaceful.

DAN. I think we should keep looking.

RACHEL. No.

DAN. Rachel—

RACHEL. I don't want to keep looking. This is the one. I'm sure. Dan? I don't want to keep looking. I don't want that. Dan?

DAN. (*Beat.*) OK.

RACHEL. Really?

DAN. Yeah. Let's do it.

(RACHEL *hugs* DAN.)

VIVIANA. So will we be making an offer?

DAN. Yes. Yes.

VIVIANA. Good. Great. I'll meet you back at the office and we can sign the papers.

(VIVIANA *exits*. RACHEL *exits*. DAN *remains*.)

Scene 4

Afternoon. The sound of traffic. FRANK RICHMOND *and* VINCE LEE *in an empty back alley in downtown Los Angeles.*

RICHMOND. You're late. I don't appreciate waiting for you in some alley smells like garbage and piss.

VINCE. I hit traffic.

RICHMOND. You need to manage your time better, my friend.

VINCE. I'm not your friend.

RICHMOND. You're right. I misspoke. You're my associate.

VINCE. Look I got your message. I'm here. I don't have all day.

RICHMOND. You're a busy man. I'm a busy man, too. I just want to know everything's set. I don't want to find out come tomorrow there's some kinda problem, some kinda screw up.

VINCE. I told you already. I'm meeting them tonight like I said. It's all set.

RICHMOND. I went by the store today, see if you were there.

VINCE. You're wasting your time. I'm never there.

RICHMOND. Now see that, that's an untruth. I know for a fact, what you said just now is not true. I seen you in there. I seen you stocking shelves, sweeping up. Your pops got you working hard.

VINCE. Are we done?

RICHMOND. See now, when you lie to me like that, that makes me think I can't trust you. It makes me have all kinds of little doubts, and I don't like that, cause that kinda thing, that just chews you up.

VINCE. I help out sometimes.

RICHMOND. That's what a good son does, right? Cause you're a good son. Isn't that right?

VINCE. Look, I gotta go.

RICHMOND. It's safer, two people. Him there all by himself, he could get jacked. Wasn't there a guy got killed right near there. One shot in the back. They say it was an inside job. They say his own people had a beef with him.

VINCE. I wouldn't know about that.

RICHMOND. I like your pops. He's a badass. He don't mess around. I like that. Tell me, what's his cut?

VINCE. He doesn't have a cut. He's not part of it.

RICHMOND. Now see, I find that hard to believe. I say to myself: is Vince telling me another untruth? Is Vince lying to my face?

VINCE. I'm telling you how it is. Are we finished?

RICHMOND. Yeah. For now.

> (VINCE *goes.* RICHMOND *remains. The city goes from afternoon to night. The buildings empty out. The traffic dwindles. The streetlights go on. The sounds of night begin.*)

Scene 5

Dusk. A market in downtown Los Angeles. The sound of a Korean language drama on the TV. ANGIE *is reading.* LEE SUNG CHO *is cutting melon for fruit salad trays. He watches* ANGIE.

LEE. What you read?

ANGIE. Nothing. It's just a book.

LEE. What book?

ANGIE. It's called *Sister Carrie.*

LEE. Who write?

ANGIE. It's by Theodore Dreiser.

LEE. What it's about?

ANGIE. I don't know. It's like some girl goes to the city, and she gets this job, and then she meets this man, and they fall in love, and then he steals this money.

LEE. Why he steal the money?

ANGIE. I don't know. He just does. He's a good person but it's like things happen. They just happen and he can't stop them. It's like random in a way. I don't know. It's hard to explain.

LEE. What mean random?

ANGIE. Random means like, for no reason. When something happens and there's no reason.

LEE. Always a reason. Maybe you don't know, you don't see, because you just one person.

ANGIE. I think sometimes things just happen.

LEE. If you believe no reason, how you do anything? How you supposed to live? If you believe no reason, how you supposed to live?

ANGIE. You just do.

LEE. That make no sense. Always a reason. You just don't see, so you don't know. (*Beat.*) What happen to them?

ANGIE. I haven't finished yet.

LEE. You read that one for school?

ANGIE. Yeah. It's a classic.

LEE. What that mean?

ANGIE. Classic: *Yet-nal-gut-gat-chi, gwan-ship-juk-in-gut. Moout-in-ga gwan-ship-juk-in-gut—*

LEE. Yeah yeah yeah, I understand.

ANGIE. You want me to help?

LEE. No.

ANGIE. Are you sure? Let me help. It'll go faster.

LEE. No. You work hard. You study. School your job.

(LEE *looks at* ANGIE. *He keeps looking at* ANGIE.)

ANGIE. What?

LEE. You look like your mother. Your face is like your mother's face. *Umma-nun joe-un yujah-yut-suh.* She was good wife, good mother.

ANGIE. I don't remember.

LEE. What you mean you don't remember?

ANGIE. Just what I said. I don't remember.

LEE. How you not remember?

ANGIE. I just don't. It's been a long time.

LEE. It not long time.

ANGIE. I look at her photograph and it's like I don't even feel anything. I can't remember her voice. I can't remember the sound of her voice.

LEE. You don't know what you talk about.

ANGIE. I'm just saying I don't remember her. I wish I did, but I don't. I don't remember.

LEE. You don't know what you talk about. Don't say stupid things. Better not to say anything. Better to be quiet.

ANGIE. I'm just telling you the truth.

LEE. *Jo-young-heh. Neh-ga jo-young-hee-ha-la-go het-ji.*

ANGIE. Speak English.

LEE. *Uh-dduk-geh gi-uk-ul moot-ha-ni? Uh-dduk-geh?*

ANGIE. Speak English. Why can't you just speak English? Just speak English.

(LEE *slaps* ANGIE. *Pause.*)

LEE. Nothing else to say.

(ANGIE *returns to reading her book.* LEE *watches her.*)

Scene 6

Early evening. The sound of traffic and Latin music. RACHEL *smokes on a small terrace in a rental apartment in Silver Lake. She uses a dish as an ashtray. She looks out at the lights on Sunset Boulevard and in the hills above.* DAN *opens the sliding doors.*

RACHEL. Hey.

DAN. Hey.

RACHEL. You done?

DAN. Yeah. I was just finishing up some e-mails.

RACHEL. It's warm tonight. It feels like Santa Anas. The air is like electric. Do you feel it?

DAN. Yeah, I do. You shouldn't smoke, you know.

RACHEL. I know. I shouldn't do a lot of things.

DAN. I just, I care about you, that's all.

(DAN *rubs* RACHEL's *shoulders.*)

RACHEL. That feels nice. Over more.

DAN. There?

RACHEL. More.

DAN. How's that?

RACHEL. Perfect.

DAN. How was class?

RACHEL. Good, it was good. I did this exercise. It's a kind of memory exercise. You try to go back and remember the sound of a thing, like a TV in the next room or the sound of the ocean, it could be anything, and what you do, what you try to do: you rebuild the memory starting with the sound. And it's so strange where your mind goes, the things you remember, things you haven't thought about in years. I found myself thinking about this fire that happened when I was a kid, in the canyon where we lived. The sound, the way it sounded, it was like bones breaking, and this kind of whistling, like a high-pitched whistling. I remember that. It spread so fast until the flames were just a few yards from the house, and then all of a sudden, the wind changed course, and this wall of fire, it just swung around, and we were safe. All the houses around us, they burned to the ground, but ours was left completely untouched. What do you call that? Fate? Was that fate that our house was spared?

DAN. You know, I'm not sure I believe in fate.

RACHEL. Luck.

DAN. I'm not sure I believe in that either.

RACHEL. What's left to believe in?

DAN. That the wind changed direction.

RACHEL. A butterfly in China.

DAN. A high pressure system over the Pacific. A temperature shift in the Gulf Stream. I think it's about pattern recognition. If you can see the pattern, you see that fate or luck, it's just a chain reaction of quantifiable events. You just have to be able to see it.

RACHEL. They accepted our bid. She called on my cell while you were inside.

DAN. That's great.

RACHEL. I'm so happy. It'll be so nice to have a place of our own, to have a home. I'm sick of renting, throwing all that money away, never feeling like the place belongs to me. It'll be different now, it'll all be different. Here. I want to show you something.

> (RACHEL *reaches into her pocket and takes out a small object wrapped in a handkerchief. She gives it to* DAN. *He unwraps it.*)

It's a *mezuzah*. We never had one growing up. My family—well, like your family—we just never—well I don't know—we just didn't do stuff like that. I just thought with the new house, it would be nice to put one up. I don't know. It's OK if you don't want to. I just thought it might be, I don't know, I thought it might be nice.

DAN. Rachel—

RACHEL. Yeah? What? What is it, Dan?

DAN. Nothing. Listen, I need to go back to my office.

RACHEL. Now?

DAN. I left some papers I need for my lecture tomorrow.

RACHEL. Can't you just deal with it in the morning?

DAN. No I can't. I won't have time. I have a faculty meeting right before my class. I really need to get those papers tonight. I won't be long.

> (DAN *kisses* RACHEL, *and goes.* RACHEL *lights up another cigarette. She smokes.*)

Scene 7

Mid-evening. The sound of sprinklers. A garage in a house in Highland Park. RAFAEL lifts weights on a bench press. VIVIANA comes in.

VIVIANA. I sold a house today.

RAFAEL. Congratulations. You can buy me some new clothes.

VIVIANA. It doesn't work that way, *mijo*, light of my life. I hate to be the one to break the news. Someday you're going to support me. That's how it works.

RAFAEL. Yeah? How am I going to do that?

VIVIANA. You're gonna get a job.

RAFAEL. Yeah right. At Jiffy Lube.

VIVIANA. A good job.

RAFAEL. Like what?

VIVIANA. Like a lawyer. Like a businessman. Maybe a job in sales.

RAFAEL. Sales? What am I going to sell?

VIVIANA. I don't know. You figure it out. *No se lo que vas a vender.* You can sell shoes.

RAFAEL. I'm not going to sell shoes.

VIVIANA. It doesn't matter what. *Mira*, you can sell anything, all the nails and screws that hold this place together, the wires in the wall that you can't see, everything there is, somebody makes it and then somebody else sells it. Things you don't even think about, somebody's selling. You just gotta know what people want and what they're willing to pay. You'd be good at it.

RAFAEL. Why? Cause I take after you?

VIVIANA. Yeah you take after me. You count your blessings you take after me. *(Beat.)* How was school?

RAFAEL. OK.

VIVIANA. You got homework?

RAFAEL. No.

VIVIANA. How is that?

RAFAEL. I just don't, OK?

VIVIANA. You look at that application?

RAFAEL. I'm not going to get into Berkeley.

VIVIANA. You don't know that.

RAFAEL. I know. I don't have the grades, I don't have the scores.

VIVIANA. You can't think that way.

RAFAEL. Mom, please.

(RAFAEL *stops lifting weights and changes his sweaty shirt.*)

VIVIANA. *Tienes que ser* more positive. You have so much going for you. You have no idea.

RAFAEL. Just stop OK, stop.

(VIVIANA *sees RAFAEL has a new tattoo of the word ANGIE.*)

VIVIANA. *Á ver.* Angie? *Qué es eso?*

RAFAEL. Nothing.

VIVIANA. When did you get that?

RAFAEL. I don't know. I forget.

VIVIANA. Who's Angie?

RAFAEL. She's just some girl I know.

VIVIANA. Just some girl? She's not just some girl. Don't lie to me. Don't disrespect me like that.

RAFAEL. She's just someone I know, OK?

VIVIANA. Fine, you don't want to tell me, that's fine. (*Beat.*) I don't like how you're all tatted up. I don't like that. It's low-class and ugly.

RAFAEL. You don't know what you're talking about.

VIVIANA. I know what I see. You think how you look, you think that's cool? Who are you supposed to be? Like your father? You want to be some thug like your father? You think being some tatted up *vato*, you think that's cool?

RAFAEL. Don't start.

VIVIANA. I expect more from you.

RAFAEL. I don't want to hear this.

VIVIANA. You have everything going for you. Don't screw it up. Don't sell yourself short. Don't get some stupid girl knocked up and throw it all away, don't do yourself like that. You hear me, you hear what I'm saying to you? I'm talking to you.

RAFAEL. I'm not like him OK? I'm nothing like him. And I'm not like you either.

(RAFAEL *goes.* VIVIANA *remains.*)

Scene 8

Late evening. The interior of Griffith Park. VINCE *is waiting, listening to hip-hop.* DAN *appears.* VINCE *turns the music off.*

DAN. Vince?

VINCE. (*Beat.*) Yeah. (*Beat.*) I thought you weren't going to show.

DAN. I've never been to this side of the park before. I got a little turned around.

VINCE. (*Beat.*) You parked over there?

DAN. Yeah.

VINCE. Me too. You can follow me.

(VINCE *turns his iPod back on. An explosion of music.* VINCE *exits.* DAN *follows.*)

Scene 9

Late evening. A market in downtown Los Angeles. The sound of a Korean language drama on the TV. ANGIE is behind the counter reading her book. LEE SUNG CHO breaks down boxes with box cutters. He stacks them and ties them with twine. He opens the back door of the store. He lifts the boxes.

LEE. Close door, close behind me. Lock. You hear what I said? Hey.

ANGIE. Yes.

(*LEE goes out the back door. ANGIE puts her book in her backpack, takes her backpack and starts to go. FRANK enters the store.*)

RICHMOND. Your brother around?

ANGIE. No.

RICHMOND. Where is he?

ANGIE. I don't know.

RICHMOND. You don't know or you won't say.

ANGIE. He's not here. I don't know where he is.

RICHMOND. Are you telling me the truth? I hope you are. I really do. Cause if you're not, we're gonna have ourselves a problem.

(*ANGIE tries to go past RICHMOND. RICHMOND blocks her.*)

Listen up. I got a message for your brother. You tell him I don't appreciate when people don't return my calls. You tell him that don't fly with me. Tell him he better call Frank or he ain't gonna like what happens. You tell him that.

(*RICHMOND goes. ANGIE waits. And then ANGIE exits into the night. The sound of traffic, the sound of garbage trucks, the sound of voices and fights breaking out, the sound of glass shattering, the sound of a hundred thousand TVs and radios in different apartments throughout the city, the thumping of a bass.*)

Scene 10

Late night. RACHEL sits on the small terrace of her and Dan's apartment. She dials a number on her cell phone.

RACHEL. Mom? Did I wake you? I'm sorry…. Yeah, no everything's fine. Yeah, we got it. I know. I can't wait. (*Beat.*) Yeah, we've been discussing it. That's the plan…. Mom, we've talked about this already. It just hasn't been the right time. We want to be ready. We want to be in a place in our lives…. No, I know, I know that. Mom, this isn't helping, OK? (*Beat.*) No, he's not listening. He's not even here. No, he had to go back to the office. Yeah, he left some papers he needed for tomorrow. Mom, it's fine. He'll be back soon. Listen, I should probably let you get some sleep…. OK. I will. I love you, too. Goodnight.

(RACHEL *hangs up. The sound of the city grows louder and louder.*
RACHEL *sweeps the ashtray off the table with a single motion. It falls and
shatters.*)

Scene 11

*Late night. A motel off the freeway. The sound of an action sequence: automatic
gunfire, explosions, cars crashing.* VINCE *lies in bed, watching an action movie
on TV. A flickering, ghostly TV light illuminates the room.* VINCE's *cell
phone starts ringing. He looks at the incoming number and doesn't pick up.*
DAN *enters from the bathroom.*

DAN. What are you watching?

VINCE. I don't know. It's like it takes place in the future, but it's also like it
takes place now. It's like the way it is now, except everything is different, the
same in a way, but different.

DAN. Is that the main guy?

VINCE. Yeah.

DAN. What's his story?

VINCE. I don't know. He's kinda messed up.

DAN. Messed up how?

VINCE. I don't know. Like something happened to him, like a long time
ago, I don't know what it is. Something bad, and now he's messed up. He
can't get close to people. He's not like them. It's like he's contaminated or
something. It's like he has this thing inside of him, and everything he
touches, he fucks up. He doesn't mean to, but he does. He fucks it all up. He
fucks everything up.

(DAN *and* VINCE *kiss for a long time.* DAN *pulls away.*)

DAN. Look I should go.

VINCE. Right. OK.

DAN. It's late and I have a long day—

VINCE. You don't have to explain.

DAN. No I just, I don't want you to think—

VINCE. It's cool. I should go too. I got some stuff I need to take care of.
My Dad has this store. I gotta help him open up in a couple of hours.

DAN. Yeah? What kinda store?

VINCE. It's just like a little market.

DAN. Whereabouts?

VINCE. Why? You gonna come visit?

DAN. No. I don't know. It's none of my business. I'm just—I don't know.

VINCE. It's off Second, down by Toy Town. Skid row. You know where
that's at?

DAN. Yeah.

VINCE. Yeah? You work down there?

DAN. No, but I know the area. Listen, do you have a number? You know what, never mind. I understand. I don't know what I was thinking.

VINCE. Here. Give me your phone.

(DAN *gives* VINCE *his phone.* VINCE *programs his number into* DAN's *phone and gives back the phone.*)

VINCE. Call me.

DAN. Yeah, I will.

(DAN *goes.* VINCE *remains.*)

Scene 12

Late night. A rooftop in downtown Los Angeles. Traffic on a nearby freeway sparkles, an endless stream of headlights. ANGIE *and* RAFAEL. RAFAEL *touches* ANGIE's *palm.*

ANGIE. *Son-ppa-lak.*

RAFAEL. *Son-ppa-lak.*

(RAFAEL *touches* ANGIE's *face.*)

ANGIE. *Ul-gool.*

RAFAEL. *Ul-gool.*

(RAFAEL *touches* ANGIE's *eyes.*)

ANGIE. Noon.

RAFAEL. Noon.

(RAFAEL *touches* ANGIE's *mouth.*)

ANGIE. *Eep.*

RAFAEL. *Eep.*

(RAFAEL *touches* ANGIE's *lips.*)

ANGIE. *Eep-sool.*

RAFAEL. *Eep-sool.*

(RAFAEL *and* ANGIE *kiss.* ANGIE *pulls away.*)

ANGIE. Why do you want to learn Korean? It's not like you're not going to remember. You're going to forget.

RAFAEL. No I'm not. (*Touching* ANGIE's *palm.*) *Son-ppa-lak.* See? I remember.

ANGIE. Not bad. (*Beat.*) I like this place. You feel like you're on top of the world. It's like you can see the whole city down below and it's all like twinkling. Look at all those cars. They look so tiny from up here. Think about all those people just like in their own little worlds. Like they don't even think about what's out there. It's like they're trapped, you know. And they think that's all there is. It's like their worlds are so small and they never even wonder what else there is out there.

RAFAEL. (*Beat.*) What? What is it?

ANGIE. Nothing.

RAFAEL. No. You're like, you're like thinking about something. It's cool. Just say it.

ANGIE. Rafi, I want to go away.

RAFAEL. What do you mean?

ANGIE. I mean I want to go away.

RAFAEL. Like go where?

ANGIE. I don't know. Fiji—

RAFAEL. Fiji?

ANGIE. It doesn't matter. It doesn't matter where. Just somewhere else, anywhere else. Let's just go, Rafi, just you and me.

RAFAEL. Angie, you know I want that. You know that. I want that more than anything. After we graduate, we can take off. I promise. We can go anywhere—

ANGIE. No. Now, tonight. I want to go tonight.

RAFAEL. Tonight? Where are we gonna go tonight?

ANGIE. It doesn't matter. Somewhere else. Somewhere far away. It doesn't matter where. Rafi, please.

RAFAEL. Angie—

ANGIE. What? Say it. Just say it.

RAFAEL. Listen. Listen to me—

ANGIE. No don't.

RAFAEL. Angie—

ANGIE. No I don't want to hear it.

RAFAEL. Come on.

ANGIE. No, cause we talk about these things, we talk about all these things. And you tell me this stuff, you tell me that you love me, you tell me that we're going to have this life, that we're gonna go and have this whole life together, but you don't mean it. You don't mean any of it.

RAFAEL. That's not true. You don't know. You read your books and you go to school and you don't know how it is.

ANGIE. You asked me what I want and I'm telling you.

RAFAEL. You need money to live. You can't just go. You can't just leave with the clothes on your back. Not in real life.

ANGIE. I can get money.

RAFAEL. Where?

ANGIE. It doesn't matter.

RAFAEL. Angie—

ANGIE. What?

RAFAEL. It's not just that.

ANGIE. What then? What's stopping you?

RAFAEL. I can't just leave, Angie. I can't do that.

ANGIE. Fine. Do what you want.

> (ANGIE *starts to go.*)

RAFAEL. Angie. What are you doing, where are you going, wait.

> (RAFAEL *stops her.*)

What's wrong with you? Did somebody do something to you? Did somebody hurt you? Who hurt you, Angie? Tell me who.

ANGIE. Why? What are you going to do about it?

RAFAEL. I will kill anyone who hurt you.

ANGIE. No, see, don't say things you don't mean. That's your problem. You're like a kid.

RAFAEL. I'm not a kid. I'm a grown man.

ANGIE. A grown man does what he says he's gonna do. A grown man doesn't talk just to hear himself talk. It's like you say things, but you don't mean them.

RAFAEL. That's not true.

ANGIE. You don't even know what I have to live with. You have no idea.

RAFAEL. Angie, please. I love you.

ANGIE. If you love me, then let's go. Let's go tonight.

RAFAEL. Angie—

ANGIE. Cause otherwise we're done. It's over. You're never gonna see me again. (*Beat.*) Yeah? Is that how it's gonna be? All right then.

> (ANGIE *starts to go.*)

RAFAEL. Wait. Angie, wait. We'll go. We'll leave tonight.

ANGIE. For real?

RAFAEL. Yeah. Just go back home. Get your stuff together. I'll meet you there. It's going to be OK.

> (RAFAEL *and* ANGIE *kiss.* ANGIE *goes.* RAFAEL *remains.*)

Scene 13

Late night. Downtown Los Angeles. RICHMOND *dials a number on his cell phone. No one answers. The sound of a distant siren.* RICHMOND *moves on.*

Scene 14

Late night. The sound of a distant siren. A small terrace in a rental apartment in Silver Lake. DAN *picks up pieces of the broken dish.* RACHEL *appears.*

RACHEL. It broke.

(DAN *continues to pick up the pieces.*)

Leave it.

(DAN *continues to pick up the pieces.*)

I said leave it. Where were you?

DAN. I told you. I had to go back to the office.

RACHEL. Do you know what time it is?

DAN. Listen, Rachel, I can't do this with you right now.

RACHEL. What do you think I am?

DAN. Do you want me to leave? Is that what you want?

RACHEL. I'm asking you a question. Because I'm having trouble understanding. I go through everything I know, everything I think I know, but I can't make it fit, it won't fit.

DAN. I can't deal with this. I'm going. Don't wait up for me.

(DAN *exits.*)

RACHEL. Where are you going? I'm asking you a question. Answer my question. Answer me.

(RACHEL *remains.*)

Scene 15

Pre-dawn. A market in downtown Los Angeles. The sound of a distant siren. ANGIE *opens the cash box, and removes the cash.* LEE SUNG CHO *enters. He sees* ANGIE *taking the cash.*

LEE. What do you do?

ANGIE. *Apa—*

LEE. What do you do?

(LEE *strikes* ANGIE. *She drops the cash box.* LEE *strikes her. She tries to get away.* LEE *tries to strike her again.* VINCE *enters.* ANGIE *grabs* LEE's *arm and slaps him.*)

LEE. I give you everything. Everything I have I give to you. How can you do this? You make me so ashame.

(LEE *goes.* ANGIE *turns and sees* VINCE.)

VINCE. What were you thinking?

ANGIE. Don't even talk to me.

VINCE. (*Taking out his wallet.*) Look, how much do you need?

ANGIE. Oh now you're gonna be my big brother? Is that's how it's gonna be? I don't need anything.

(VINCE *offers* ANGIE *money.*)

VINCE. Take it. Just take it.

(*Beat.* ANGIE *takes the money.*)

You should've just come to me.

ANGIE. Yeah right. You don't even see how you are. You come and go whenever you feel like it. You do whatever it is you do.

VINCE. Don't worry about what I do.

ANGIE. All you think about is yourself. That's how it's always been. You're never around. I'm the one that's here. I'm the one that's gotta deal with everything, not you. (*Beat.*) Some guy came by looking for you.

VINCE. What guy?

ANGIE. Just some guy.

VINCE. What did he want?

ANGIE. You tell me. You think I don't know things, but I do.

VINCE. You know the parts you see.

ANGIE. I see things you don't even realize. I see all kinds of things.

VINCE. OK look, it's late. You should just get some sleep.

ANGIE. I can't. I got a friend meeting me here in a little while and then I'm taking off.

VINCE. What do you mean you're taking off?

ANGIE. Just like I said.

VINCE. Angie—

ANGIE. What? You're gonna say something to me about how I live my life? You? Look, you worry about your own life. Let me worry about mine.

(ANGIE *goes.* VINCE *remains.*)

Scene 16

Early morning, before dawn. A house in Highland Park. RAFAEL *packs a bag.* VIVIANA *enters and watches him.* RAFAEL *retrieves a handgun, loads it, studies it.*

VIVIANA. What are you doing with that?

RAFAEL. Nothing.

VIVIANA. That's your father's gun.

RAFAEL. I know.

VIVIANA. You going somewhere?

RAFAEL. No.

VIVIANA. Don't lie. Don't lie to me. What do you need that for?

RAFAEL. Protection.

VIVIANA. Protection? You think that's going to protect you? You really think that, huh? You have no idea. *No sabes nada.*

RAFAEL. Momma, please. You don't understand.

VIVIANA. You think I don't understand? I understand more than you will ever know. I've been down this road already with your father. I'm not going down it again.

RAFAEL. Momma, I'm not like him. Momma, please—

(RAFAEL *goes to* VIVIANA. *He embraces her. She holds him tight.*)

VIVIANA. Before you were born, you had a hole in your heart. They showed me pictures of you, when you were inside of me. They were all gray and blurry, like those pictures you see from outer space, like photographs of some far off galaxy. I thought you were going to die. That's what the doctors said. But you didn't die, and I thought it was a kind of miracle.

(VIVIANA *pulls away.*)

Sometimes I think it would've been better if you had. It would've been better than watching you throw your life away like a piece of garbage. You walk out that door now and you don't need to come back. That's it.

RAFAEL. Momma, don't say that.

VIVIANA. You walk out that door and you're dead to me.

RAFAEL. Please don't say that.

VIVIANA. It'll be like you was never born.

RAFAEL. Is that what you want?

VIVIANA. You got a choice. I'm giving you a choice.

RAFAEL. Then I'm dead to you.

(RAFAEL *goes.* VIVIANA *remains.*)

Scene 17

Dawn. A market in downtown Los Angeles. The sound of a Korean language drama. Light up on LEE SUNG CHO behind the counter. He hears a sound in the doorway. He looks up.

LEE. You. What I tell you? What I say? I tell you not to come back here. Get out. Get out.

(LEE SUNG CHO *retrieves his gun. He shoots. An unknown assailant returns fire. Blinding light. Chaos. Darkness. The sound of a distant siren.*)

Scene 18

Mid-morning. Fluorescent light on DAN MORSE. *A room in a police station in downtown Los Angeles.* FRANK RICHMOND *is listening.*

DAN. When I arrived, the door was unlocked and open and I went inside and I could tell right away that something was wrong, I could feel it in the air. And then I saw him. He was on the floor. At first I thought maybe he had fallen, but then I saw the blood. There was so much blood.

RICHMOND. Tell me something: what were you doing in Toy Town at that hour?

DAN. I got off on the wrong exit and then I guess I just, I got lost. I was trying to find somebody who could give me directions so I could get back.

RICHMOND. And you were you coming from where?

DAN. I was just driving. I drive sometimes when I can't sleep.

RICHMOND. Yeah? Where do you go?

DAN. All over. Different places.

RICHMOND. It's a big city.

DAN. Yes. (*Beat.*) Look, if there nothing else, detective, I really need to get going. My wife is waiting for me outside.

RICHMOND. (*Giving* DAN *his card.*) I think we're done for now. Here's my card. If you remember anything else, give me a call.

DAN. Yeah, OK.

RICHMOND. (*Beat.*) Yes, Mr. Morse?

DAN. It's just that when I saw you before, when you came into the store and you had a gun, I didn't know. I mean I had just seen this man and he had been shot and I saw you, and I guess I, well I just didn't realize. I thought you were some kind of—I don't know. I don't know what I thought. I guess I just thought you were somebody else.

RICHMOND. Who did you think I was?

DAN. I don't know. Just someone different. It's hard to explain.

RICHMOND. In what I do, I count on people looking at me and seeing whatever it is they see. Drive safe, Mr. Morse. We'll be in touch.

(DAN *goes.* RICHMOND *remains. Blackout.*)

End of Act I

ACT II
Scene 19

Morning. A darkened lecture hall at a university. DAN speaks at a lectern with a small light.

DAN MORSE. It starts miles below the surface. There's a fault between two rock planes and the movement of these rock planes causes a friction or a strain that grows over time until the pressure becomes so great there's finally a rupture. The sudden release creates seismic waves that radiate outwards creating a string of smaller seismic disturbances in an interlocking network of related fault lines. Most major faults on the North American continent are what we call strike-slip faults which refers to the way in which parallel rock planes slide past each other in a horizontal or sideways motion. Though scientists have tried to track the movements leading up to a major seismic event, there are often no clear patterns. The challenge we face is to construct a paradigm for events that do not appear to conform to any discernible model of cause and effect, and that happen without any kind of advanced warning. We have in the past relied on what we thought to be indicators in the landscape: topographical anomalies visible to the human eye or sound waves caused by vibrations inside the earth. We have tried to extrapolate from past seismic events looking for recurring patterns, but what we have found in recent years is that we are dealing with faults we never even took into account, faults we thought were dormant, faults we never even knew existed. And so we're left trying to make sense of phenomena which defy our customary models of quantification and analysis. We're left with a series of variables that come together in violent, seemingly random and discontinuous ways across fault lines we have, it seems, radically and fatally misunderstood. This is the challenge we now face. And we think it's a question for science, but perhaps it's more a question for philosophers. Perhaps it's more a question of how we live our lives in the face of uncertainty, how we understand our relationship to a larger and indifferent universe in which we play the smallest part.

(The sound of a bell tower on campus ringing the hour.)

DAN. All right we're out of time. The problems are posted, small groups meet Friday. I'll see you all on Monday.

(DAN gathers his lecture notes and goes.)

Scene 20

Morning. The buzzing of a prison door opening. A visitor's room in a prison facility on the outskirts of Los Angeles. VINCE sits on one side of a Plexiglas partition. LEE enters and sits on the other side. They pick up phone receivers.

VINCE. I'm sorry I'm late. I would've gotten here sooner, but I had some stuff at the store to take care of.

LEE. You remember to talk to insurance man?

VINCE. Yeah.

LEE. And you talk to the wholesaler like I told you—

VINCE. Yeah.

LEE. Sometime he don't come when he say he gonna.

VINCE. *Apa*, I know. I'm taking care of it. (*Beat.*) Are you eating enough? You need to eat.

LEE. I eat.

VINCE. Listen, *apa*, I talked to the lawyer about filing those papers I was telling you about. I'm sending him some stuff today.

LEE. I no want you to talk to lawyer no more.

VINCE. But, *apa*—

LEE. No. No more lawyer. (*Beat.*) He was eighteen years old. He just boy. So young. What I do? What I do?

VINCE. *Apa*, it's gonna be OK.

LEE. No. Not OK. Never OK. (*Beat.*) No lawyer. No more. (*Beat.*) How your sister?

VINCE. She's good. She's gonna come see you real soon. It's just been hard with everything.

LEE. You don't need to explain.

VINCE. *Apa*—

LEE. You better go now. Before it get too late.

VINCE. Listen, *apa*, I don't want you to worry. You don't need to worry. I'm taking care of everything. I won't let you down.

(*VINCE touches the Plexiglas. LEE hangs up the phone and goes. VINCE hangs up the phone and goes.*)

Scene 21

Morning. The sound of traffic. RICHMOND is eating in a fast-food Vietnamese restaurant in downtown Los Angeles. He's standing at the counter eating a bowl of noodle soup with chopsticks. VINCE enters the restaurant.

RICHMOND. You're late. You're always late.

VINCE. Sorry.

RICHMOND. You know this place? It used to be a Japanese restaurant. I used to come in here all the time and have the teriyaki bowl. Now it's—I don't know what the hell it is—Vietnamese, I think. Things change. (*Beat.*) How long has it been, Vince? A year? Has it been a year? Man o man, time flies. I just retired. I don't think you knew that.

VINCE. No.

RICHMOND. It's a new day. All that bullshit I used to have to deal with, guys jamming you up cause they can, saying shit about you soon as you turn your back, never giving you the respect you deserve. I'm done. It's somebody else's problem now. (*Beat.*) I never did get a chance to thank you. Without you flipping like you did on all your old buddies, I would never have made that last bust. Got a little bronze-plated medal. Got my picture taken with the mayor. Twenty-five years on the force and that's what I get. A handshake and a smile.

VINCE. Look I'm here. What do you want?

RICHMOND. Now is that any way to talk to an old friend?

VINCE. We're not friends.

RICHMOND. Man, I'm the best friend you ever had. I saved your ass. If it wasn't for me, you'd be sitting in Lompoc right now doing federal time and you know it, too. The weight you were moving? It's a gift you're walking around a free man. (*Beat.*) How's your pops?

VINCE. Fine.

RICHMOND. That's a tragedy, boy. Old man shoots some random kid for no good reason. Then again, maybe it wasn't so random after all. Maybe that kid was someone you knew. Maybe he was coming after you, and your pops maybe he knew that. Now that would be a cross to bear, knowing you was the reason your pops was doing hard time. I don't know how you live with yourself knowing something like that.

VINCE. Are we finished?

RICHMOND. Almost. One last thing. Turns out some of that last shipment went missing, just a little bit off the top. I didn't say nothing and nobody asked, but the way I see it, somebody somewhere is sitting on a whole lot of cocaine. You wouldn't know anything about that, would you?

VINCE. No.

RICHMOND. Come on, Vince. You can tell me.

VINCE. I don't know. You're the cop. Or you used to be. You figure it out.

(VINCE *goes.* RICHMOND *remains.*)

Scene 22

Morning. The sound of traffic. The side of a freeway. ANGIE *is pregnant.* RACHEL *approaches her.*

RACHEL. Are you OK? Are you all right?

ANGIE. Yeah, I'm fine.

RACHEL. Are you sure? This is crazy. Look at you.

ANGIE. I said I'm fine.

RACHEL. OK. (*Beat.*) We're OK. I'm shaking. My hands area shaking. My heart is beating so fast right now. I don't even want to think what could've happened. We could've been killed. Do you realize that? Look at my car. Look at your car. Oh my God, oh my God. What were you doing? What were you thinking? You just came out of nowhere.

ANGIE. I didn't see you.

RACHEL. How could you not see me? I was right there. I was right next to you. How could you not see me? Were you looking? Were you just not looking?

ANGIE. I'm sorry OK? I'm sorry.

RACHEL. I don't care. I don't care that you're sorry. You think saying I'm sorry makes it better? It doesn't. It's just words people say. It doesn't mean anything. (*Beat.*) Oh God. What am I doing? Listen—

(RACHEL *reaches out to* ANGIE. ANGIE *withdraws from her.*)

ANGIE. Don't.

RACHEL. (*Beat.*) I'll need your insurance information.

ANGIE. Fine. It's, uh, it's in the car. I'll go get it.

(ANGIE *goes.* RACHEL *waits. The sound of traffic.*)

Scene 23

Morning. A real estate office in West Hollywood. VIVIANA *sits at a desk with a framed photograph.*

VIVIANA. Mrs. Morse?

RACHEL. Yes. Forgive me. I'm just a little—I don't know. I guess I'm just a little out of it.

VIVIANA. Well I'm just about done with this paperwork. Even with closing costs, you're going to be walking away with a nice profit. I'm glad it worked out. Sometimes it doesn't.

RACHEL. I didn't think it would sell so fast.

VIVIANA. You and your husband got in and out just at the right time.

RACHEL. We didn't plan it that way.

VIVIANA. Well you're lucky then.

RACHEL. Yeah. I guess.

(RACHEL *notices the photograph on* VIVIANA's *desk.*)

Is that your son?

VIVIANA. Yes. When he was little.

RACHEL. He was a beautiful little boy.

VIVIANA. Yes. Yes he was.

RACHEL. Is that his brother and sister?

VIVIANA. No, those are his cousins. He's my only one.

RACHEL. I've always wanted to have children. I wanted that so much, but it just, it didn't work out that way. Where is he now?

VIVIANA. My son? He's uh, he's a freshman at UC Berkeley.

RACHEL. That's great, that's a great school.

VIVIANA. He's a smart kid, a good kid. I tell him he can do anything. There's nothing he can't do.

RACHEL. You must be very proud of him.

VIVIANA. Yes. Yes I am. If you would just sign here and here.

RACHEL. Oh, right.

(RACHEL *signs the papers.*)

VIVIANA. I'm also going to need your husband's signature on these. I'll just give these to you now and you can give them to him. Tell me, will you and your husband be looking for other properties in this area?

RACHEL. You know we're actually, we're not together anymore.

VIVIANA. Oh. I see. I'm sorry.

RACHEL. Please don't be. It's fine, it's really, it's fine. Sometimes I think it's as if everything in my life up to this point, it's as if one thing just led to the next. I went to school, I met Dan, we got married. I thought my life would be a certain way. I took it for granted. I'm sorry, I don't know what's wrong with me today. I should go. I have a class on the other side of town and with traffic…I appreciate everything you've done. You've been so great, you really have.

(RACHEL *starts to go.*)

VIVIANA. Listen, I can get those papers to Mr. Morse if you'd like.

RACHEL. No, that's OK. I'll do it. Thank you.

(RACHEL *goes.*)

Scene 24

Late morning. A UPS store. Muzak. Packing materials. DAN is in line waiting to mail a package. VINCE enters with a large manila envelope.

DAN. Vince?

VINCE. Hey. (*Beat.*) What are you, uh…

DAN. Books. I'm going on sabbatical next semester. Yeah, I'm uh, I'm going up to Alaska, to do some research, and so I'm mailing myself some books. There's a lot of volcanic activity up there. Geologically, it's a relatively young part of the planet. I study that kinda thing. (*Beat.*) I still have your number in my phone.

VINCE. Look, you don't have to—

DAN. No I, I should've called.

VINCE. It doesn't matter. (*Beat.*) I should go.

DAN. Right. Right. Look, maybe I'll give you a call sometime.

VINCE. Yeah. Give me a call sometime.

(VINCE *exits.*)

Scene 25

Morning. A garage in Boyle Heights. RAFAEL *is a mechanic. He's working on the engine of a car. He checks his clipboard.* RICHMOND *joins him.* RAFAEL *gives him the clipboard and a pen.*

RAFAEL. If I could get your cell phone number…. How've the brake pads been feeling?

RICHMOND. Fine just fine. Where's Hector at?

RAFAEL. Hector? He, uh, left.

RICHMOND. What do you mean he left? Hector is the guy I work with here. He's the only one I trust to work on my car.

RAFAEL. Well he's gone. Hector don't work here no more.

RICHMOND. Did he say where he went to?

RAFAEL. Why?

RICHMOND. I'm just asking.

RAFAEL. No, he didn't say.

RICHMOND. So you're the new guy?

RAFAEL. Yeah.

RICHMOND. I hope you know what you're doing.

RAFAEL. I do. It's a nice car.

RICHMOND. Pontiac GTO.

RAFAEL. She's a beauty.

RICHMOND. Yeah, she is. I take good care of her.

RAFAEL. Where do you get a car like that?

RICHMOND. You got to have luck and you got to have cash.

RAFAEL. Just like that huh?

RICHMOND. Just like that.

RAFAEL. You make it sound easy.

RICHMOND. It's not that hard really. I guess it just depends on who you are.

RAFAEL. You mean whether or not you're lucky.

RICHMOND. I mean whether or not you got the cash.

RAFAEL. Yeah? And where do you get the cash?

RICHMOND. Are you asking me what I do for a living? Is that the question?

RAFAEL. Yeah, I guess.

RICHMOND. I used to be a cop. I'm retired now.

RAFAEL. Is that right?

RICHMOND. You got something to say about that?

RAFAEL. It just surprises me is all.

RICHMOND. That I was a cop? That surprises you?

RAFAEL. I just wonder how you afford a car like this on a cop's salary, that's all.

RICHMOND. Come again, (*Reading his name tag.*) Raoul?

RAFAEL. It's Rafael.

RICHMOND. Oh OK. Rafael. I'll try and remember that. Next time I get my oil changed, I'll ask for Rafael.

RAFAEL. I guess I just want to know how does someone like you get the cash.

RICHMOND. Someone like me? What is that supposed to mean?

RAFAEL. You know.

RICHMOND. No, I don't think I do. Why don't you illuminate me, Rafael.

RAFAEL. Come on, man. Why you gotta act like that?

RICHMOND. Act like what?

RAFAEL. I just look at someone like you and I think you ain't that different from me. How is it you got what you got?

RICHMOND. Maybe cause I ain't like you. Maybe cause I work harder. Maybe cause I'm smarter. Maybe cause luck shines down on me in a way that you will never know cause you just don't have what that is, because you will never have what that is.

RAFAEL. Man, who do you think you are?

RICHMOND. I'll tell you who I am, Rafael. I'm the fuckin customer and you're the fuckin grease monkey who rotates my fuckin tires. You have a problem with that?

RAFAEL. Fuck you.

RICHMOND. OK see, now, you just chose to mess with the wrong person. Cause I tell you what: I'm going to walk right over there to your manager and I'm going to personally see to it that they fire your ass right here on the spot.

RAFAEL. Go ahead.

RICHMOND. You think I'm kidding?

RAFAEL. Do it, man. See if I care.

(RICHMOND *walks away.*)

RAFAEL. Fuck you, man. Fuck you.

(RAFAEL *looks at the clipboard and tears off the pink sheet with* RICHMOND's *contact information.* RAFAEL *goes.*)

Scene 26

Late morning. LEE *reads aloud part of something he wrote.*

LEE. I come from Busan in Korea. Busan is big city in south, by the ocean. When I was little boy, my father, he used to take me fishing on pier. We catch fish, big one, I don't know name in English. My father tell me story of blind man and his daughter. He tell me all kind of story. My father was good man. Sometime we don't even talk. We just wait. We watch ship come in, small fishing boat and big tanker from America. And I remember I think, maybe someday I go to America. This is what I remember.

(LEE *finishes reading.*)

Scene 27

A community room in a prison facility. RACHEL *has been listening.*

RACHEL. That's wonderful, Sung.

LEE. I don't want you call me Sung.

RACHEL. We're only supposed to use first names.

LEE. I don't care. You call me Mr. Lee.

RACHEL. OK. Sure absolutely. What I was going to say was that I love the image of you and your father standing on the pier fishing. That's a very evocative image.

LEE. What that mean? Evocative?

RACHEL. That the way you write it, I can really picture the grown man and the little boy. It's like you're drawing a picture with your words. What's the story of the blind man and his daughter?

LEE. You don't know that one?

RACHEL. No.

LEE. It's famous story. Everybody in Korea know this story.

RACHEL. What's it about?

LEE. Take too long to explain.

RACHEL. Do you have a son?

LEE. Yes. I have.

RACHEL. Have you ever taken him fishing? Off Santa Monica Pier maybe? My Dad used to take us when I was little.

LEE. I don't want to talk about fishing no more.

RACHEL. OK. (*Beat.*) Well, I guess it's just you and me today. I thought maybe there might be some latecomers, but that's all right, we'll just keep going. What do you say?

LEE. Why you come here?

RACHEL. Excuse me?

LEE. Why you come teach people like me. You know, bad people. Why you do that?

RACHEL. I don't think you're bad, Mr. Lee.

LEE. You think what you think. I don't care what you think. I'm asking you.

RACHEL. I guess I find it rewarding.

LEE. You feel sorry.

RACHEL. No.

LEE. You rich white lady feel sorry.

RACHEL. I don't think that's fair, Mr. Lee. I think that everybody has a story. I'm interested in people's stories.

LEE. Some people maybe they have no story. Some people, maybe their story finish.

RACHEL. I don't believe that.

LEE. Yeah? You don't know. (*Beat.*) I have son and daughter. I take them fishing when they was little. We go to San Pedro, by the docks. It was happy time. They all grown up now. (*Beat.*) You too nice.

RACHEL. That may be.

LEE. (*Beat.*) You know, there's a story about girl and she go to the city and bad things happen. You know that one?

RACHEL. I'm not sure I do.

LEE. It's…classic.

RACHEL. I don't know. Do you remember the title?

LEE. No. Don't remember.

RACHEL. Maybe it'll come to you.

LEE. What about you? What your story?

RACHEL. Me? Oh I don't know, Mr. Lee.

LEE. You the teacher. You say everyone have story. What your story?

RACHEL. You know what, I'm pretty ordinary. Nothing much to tell.

LEE. Where your family come from?

RACHEL. Well, from all over. Germany, Russia, Poland, Lithuania—

LEE. Too many places. How you know where you come from if you come from so many places?

RACHEL. Well that's a good point. I guess, well, I grew up here.

LEE. Your family, they no talk about where they come from?

RACHEL. Not so much. I think when they came to America, it was just so hard, you know, they didn't have time to look back.

LEE. (*Beat.*) Yeah, I understand.

RACHEL. (*Beat.*) We should do some writing, Mr. Lee, before our time is up.

LEE. I don't know what to write.

RACHEL. Maybe if you wrote about your mother.

LEE. Too long time. I don't remember.

RACHEL. You must remember something. Maybe the sound, the sound of her voice, a story she used to tell you or maybe a song she used to sing. Try to think back. Try to remember.

> (ANGIE *looks at her pregnant body in a mirror. She touches her belly. She sings a song to her unborn baby.* LEE *hums the melody of a song he remembers from his boyhood. It's the same song that* ANGIE *sings to her unborn child.*)

Scene 28

Late morning. ANGIE *and* RAFAEL's *apartment in Echo Park.* ANGIE *is looking in the mirror.* RAFAEL *enters.*

RAFAEL. What are you doing?

ANGIE. Nothing. Why are you home so early?

RAFAEL. Uh, they let some of us go for the day. It was a light day. What about you?

ANGIE. I'm waiting for a ride to work.

RAFAEL. What do you mean? What happened to the car?

ANGIE. I had an accident.

RAFAEL. What kind of accident?

ANGIE. I wrecked it.

RAFAEL. What?

ANGIE. You heard me.

RAFAEL. What do you mean you wrecked the car? Angie? Goddamnit, Angie, I'm asking you a question.

ANGIE. Just what I said.

RAFAEL. How bad?

ANGIE. Bad.

RAFAEL. Like how bad? Angie? Angie, I'm talking to you.

ANGIE. Like I wrecked it, OK? Like it's totaled. What do you want me to say?

RAFAEL. How did it happen?

ANGIE. I don't want to talk about it.

RAFAEL. Angie, we don't have insurance.

ANGIE. I know that. You think I don't know that?

RAFAEL. What are we supposed to do?

ANGIE. Maybe if you had a job where you actually made some money—

RAFAEL. I have a job—

ANGIE. Maybe every little thing wouldn't be like the end of the world. Maybe we wouldn't have to be worried all the time.

RAFAEL. I'm doing what I can.

ANGIE. It's not enough.

RAFAEL. What are you saying?

ANGIE. It's like no matter what, we come out short at the end of the month. It's like one bad thing happens and it all gets shot to hell.

RAFAEL. And that's my fault?

ANGIE. We're having a baby.

RAFAEL. I know that.

ANGIE. How are we going to manage?

RAFAEL. We'll manage.

ANGIE. How? (*Beat.*) Look, I'll ask my brother for money.

RAFAEL. I don't want you asking him for money.

ANGIE. What am I supposed to do?

RAFAEL. We don't need his money. I make money.

ANGIE. It's not enough. And you're dreaming if you think it is.

RAFAEL. Why would you say something like that?

ANGIE. You know, you didn't even ask me if I was OK. I'm fuckin eight months pregnant and you didn't even ask me if I was OK.

RAFAEL. Angie—

ANGIE. No, see, cause it didn't even occur to you. It wasn't even part of how you were thinking.

RAFAEL. That's not true.

ANGIE. Yeah, it is. It's like I don't even know who you are. It's like I look at you and I don't even know who you are anymore.

RAFAEL. Angie, please—

(ANGIE's *cell phone rings. She answers it.*)

ANGIE. Yeah, OK. I'll be right down.

(ANGIE *hangs up.*)

RAFAEL. Angie, I'm sorry.

ANGIE. I got nothing left to say to you.

(ANGIE *goes.* RAFAEL *remains.*)

Scene 29

Late morning. DAN *and* RACHEL MORSE's *house in Santa Monica.*
It's empty. DAN *enters. He looks around the empty room. Moments later*
RACHEL *enters.*

RACHEL. I'm sorry I'm late. I hope I didn't keep you waiting.

DAN. No, I just got here.

RACHEL. Thanks for meeting me on such short notice.

DAN. Sure, of course. It feels strange being here.

RACHEL. Yeah.

DAN. It feels so empty.

RACHEL. Yeah.

DAN. It's really good to see you, Rachel.

RACHEL. Yeah, good to see you, too. (*Retrieving papers from her bag.*) Before I forget, you need to sign these. If you can drop them off with the realtor to-day, that would be great.

DAN. I can do that.

RACHEL. Good. Great. Well then I think that's pretty much it.

DAN. So how've you been?

RACHEL. Good, really good. Teaching, writing, you know. I don't think I told you, but I've been looking into adoption. I've started the paperwork.

DAN. That's great, Rachel. I know how much you've wanted this. You'll be a wonderful mother. I always knew you would be.

RACHEL. I don't know if you got the divorce papers…

DAN. Yeah. Yeah, I did. Rachel, listen, we don't have to do this. We don't have to go through with this. I know how hurt and angry you are, but it doesn't have to be the way it was. It can be different.

RACHEL. It's never going to be different.

DAN. Rachel, please.

RACHEL. No, Dan. No.

DAN. All I ever wanted, I just wanted for you to be happy.

RACHEL. Happy? You wanted me to be happy? Is that what you wanted? (*Taking the mezuzah from her purse.*) Here, take it.

DAN. Rachel—

RACHEL. Just take it. You can put it up in your new place. Or just throw it away. I don't care what you do with it. I don't want it.

DAN. Rachel, please—

RACHEL. You know, I think maybe it would be best if we just not see each other for a while. I think that would be best. The thing is, this is the thing, I loved you. That's the stupid thing. I loved you.

(RACHEL *goes. The sound of traffic*.)

Scene 30

Noon. A back alley in Echo Park. RAFAEL *is examining the wrecked car. He pulls back the warped fender. He finds a plastic package of cocaine. He feels around and finds another. He cuts open one of the packages. He tastes the powder. He carefully tapes the package back up and puts it back.* VINCE *enters.*

VINCE. Man, is that your car?

RAFAEL. Uh, yeah.

VINCE. What happened?

RAFAEL. Angie got in an accident.

VINCE. Is she OK?

RAFAEL. Yeah. Yeah, she's fine.

VINCE. Where did you get that car from? Did you just buy it or something?

RAFAEL. No I—I got it on loan.

VINCE. What do you mean you got it on loan?

RAFAEL. This guy Hector I used to work with, he had to go out of town. He asked me to watch his car for him.

VINCE. What are you gonna tell him?

RAFAEL. Nothing. He's dead.

VINCE. What?

RAFAEL. Yeah.

VINCE. How'd he die?

RAFAEL. He got shot. I don't know all the details. I heard about it from the guys at work.

VINCE. So you just kept the car?

RAFAEL. I figure he didn't need it no more. Vince, what are you doing here?

VINCE. I wanted to see if maybe you'd to talk to Angie about visiting our Dad. I think it'd mean a lot to him. She won't listen to me. She listens to you.

RAFAEL. I'll talk to her.

VINCE. Thanks, man. I owe you one.

RAFAEL. (*Beat.*) Hey, Vince, listen, can I ask you something? It's kind of a crazy question. No, you know what, never mind.

VINCE. What?

RAFAEL. Nah, forget it.

VINCE. What? What is it, Rafi?

RAFAEL. It's just a crazy question. I'm just, I'm just curious. If you were like gonna sell a kilo of coke, how much would you sell it for? Like hypothetically, I mean.

VINCE. Why do you want to know that?

RAFAEL. I'm just wondering.

VINCE. Yeah? Why would you wonder about something like that?

RAFAEL. I don't know. I just do. So are you gonna answer my question?

VINCE. About six thousand. Listen, Rafi, you're a good guy. I don't want to see you do something stupid. These people are for real. If you start something you can't finish—

RAFAEL. I'm a grown man. I can handle my own business.

VINCE. That's not what I mean.

RAFAEL. I got some things I need to take care of now.

VINCE. Rafi—

RAFAEL. Good to see you, Vince. I'll see you around.

(*VINCE goes. RAFAEL takes the pink slip with* RICHMOND's *contact information out of his pocket. He unfolds the paper. He dials a number on his cell phone.*)

Scene 31

Early afternoon. A doctor's office in Century City. An examination room. VIVIANA *is finishing dressing.* ANGIE *enters. She is a nurse's assistant. She has a name tag. She carries a large envelope.*

ANGIE. Ms. Ramos?

VIVIANA. Yes?

ANGIE. These are your X-rays. You need to take these with you when you go see the doctor.

VIVIANA. Do you know what these mean?

ANGIE. The doctor will go over it all with you.

VIVIANA. But I'm asking you.

ANGIE. You'll have to talk to the doctor.

VIVIANA. I'm not going to get in to see a specialist for at least a month, maybe more. I know you see these X-rays all the time. If there's something wrong, if there's some kind of problem, you can tell. I just want to know one way or another.

ANGIE. I'm not even a nurse. I'm just like a medical assistant.

VIVIANA. But you know. Don't act like you don't. I know you know what these mean, and you're just gonna stand there and not tell me anything?

ANGIE. Your doctor will know what to do.

VIVIANA. You think so? Maybe he won't. Maybe it'll be too late.

ANGIE. You can't think like that.

VIVIANA. I'm supposed to have trust, right? Faith. (*Beat.*) I'm sorry. It's just it's hard not knowing. I feel a lump in my breast and because I don't do the exams every month like you're supposed to, I don't know how long it's been there. It could've been there for years. (*Beat.*) So when are you due?

ANGIE. Next month.

VIVIANA. You're gonna have a boy.

ANGIE. How do you know?

VIVIANA. I can tell by how you're carrying. With boys, you kinda stick out. Why? What does your mom think?

ANGIE. I don't know. She died when I was little.

VIVIANA. What did she die of?

(ANGIE *doesn't answer.*)

VIVIANA. Oh, I see. (*Beat.*) Is your dad, is he still— ?

ANGIE. Yeah. Yeah, he is.

VIVIANA. He must be so happy to be a grandfather. You gotta know how happy you've made him. It's like after all those years of working so hard, he can look at his grandson and know that all that sacrifice, that it was worth it. He can look at that little boy and know that a part of him is gonna live on. It's a comfort to know that you're gonna live on. I think family, it's so important. It's maybe the most important thing. People, they don't realize. They say things they can't back. They turn away from the people that love them most and for nothing. For nothing. (*Beat.*) I'm scared. I'm really scared.

(ANGIE *approaches* VIVIANA. *Two strangers embrace. An awkward embrace.* ANGIE *goes.*)

Scene 32

Early afternoon. VIVIANA *is in a real estate office in Santa Monica.* DAN *enters.*

DAN. Oh good, I'm so glad I caught you. I came by earlier but they said you were out.

VIVIANA. Yes, I had another appointment.

DAN. (*Giving* VIVIANA *the papers.*) Rachel said you wanted the papers today. I have them with me. They're all signed.

VIVIANA. Great. Thank you. I'll get these to the buyer's agent right away.

DAN. Are you OK?

VIVIANA. Yeah, I'm fine. Why do you ask?

DAN. You just seem…I don't know. It's probably just me. It's a really good price. I was amazed when Rachel told me how much over the asking price we got. Listen, I may be in the market for another property. I'm thinking a condo, something smaller, low maintenance. I think I still have your card somewhere.

VIVIANA. You know, I don't know, I don't know if I'm still going to be working here.

DAN. Oh?

VIVIANA. Yeah, I've been thinking of making some changes in my life. I've been doing this a long time. I think it's time for a change.

DAN. What would you do?

VIVIANA. I don't know. Lie on a beach somewhere. Listen to the waves. Just stop moving for a little while. Just be still. You know, my whole life, I've lived maybe a half an hour from the ocean and I can count on one hand the number of times I've been. How does a person live that close to the ocean and never go? That's crazy, that's just…crazy. Don't you think, Mr. Morse?

DAN. Yeah, I can see that. Listen, I should let you get on with your day. Best of luck to you, wherever you end up.

VIVIANA. You, too, Mr. Morse.

(DAN *goes.*)

Scene 33

Early afternoon. A deserted lot by the Los Angeles river. RAFAEL *is patting down* RICHMOND. RAFAEL *has a gun tucked in his waistband.*

RICHMOND. You know how hard it was to find this place? The middle of goddamn nowhere. Smells like some kinda toxic dump. Look, I ain't wearing no wire. What am I gonna wear a wire for?

(RAFAEL *finishes.*)

That's a big gun. I sure hope you know how to shoot.

RAFAEL. I know how to shoot.

RICHMOND. Good, that's good. So, tell me, Rafael: why me?

RAFAEL. I see the car you drive. I know how much cops make.

RICHMOND. So you just assumed, huh? Maybe I just invested wisely. Maybe I got some mutual funds. Maybe I'm diversified. You see a brother in a nice car and you automatically think—

RAFAEL. Look, you wanna talk or you wanna do this?

(RAFAEL *takes out a plastic bag of cocaine from his knapsack.* RICHMOND *takes it, opens it, tastes the contents.*)

RICHMOND. So how much you got total?

RAFAEL. Eighty keys.

RICHMOND. Is that right? I'll give you four hundred gs.

RAFAEL. Five hundred.

RICHMOND. Four fifty.

RAFAEL. Four eighty.

RICHMOND. Alright. So when are we doing this?

RAFAEL. Today.

RICHMOND. Today? I can't get that kinda money just like that.

RAFAEL. Well then you're out of luck, I guess.

(RAFAEL *starts to go.*)

RICHMOND. What's the big rush? Come on, man. It ain't like that kinda money is easy to come by. I need time to get it all together. Come on, man. (*Beat.*) Alright. Fine. Today. I can do it later today. So we gonna meet back here or what?

RAFAEL. No. We'll meet in San Pedro. There's a warehouse just past Pier 17. We'll meet there.

RICHMOND. I don't know where that is.

RAFAEL. You'll figure it out. We'll meet at six.

RICHMOND. Six? Are you kidding me? That's rush hour. You know what the traffic is going to be like at that hour.

RAFAEL. Be there at six or I'm gone.

(RAFAEL *goes.* RICHMOND *remains.*)

Scene 34

Late afternoon. A bar in Palos Verdes. Music plays. There's a movie playing on the bar TV. The sound is turned down low. VIVIANA *is sitting at the bar drinking. She watches the movie.* RICHMOND *sees her. He goes to her.*

RICHMOND. You know the story?

VIVIANA. I wasn't really watching.

RICHMOND. You think things work out?

VIVIANA. Probably not. They never do.

RICHMOND. Rough day?

VIVIANA. I'm sorry. I'm just spouting off. Don't listen to me.

RICHMOND. No, no, spout away. I'm Frank. (*Beat.*) You don't want to tell me your name. I bet it's a beautiful name, too, just like the lady whose name it is.

VIVIANA. Listen, Frank, I don't think I'm looking for the same thing you're looking for.

RICHMOND. What do you think I'm looking for?

VIVIANA. I think you're looking for a lady friend, and I'm sure there are many ladies who want to be your friend. I'm just not one of them.

RICHMOND. Oooh, shot down, shot down in flames. (*Beat.*) So, tell me, what's a girl like you doing in a gin joint like this?

VIVIANA. A gin joint?

RICHMOND. Yeah, you know, *Casablanca.*

VIVIANA. Yeah I know *Casablanca.*

RICHMOND. "Of all the gin joints…"

VIVIANA. Oh right right. OK, Frank, a piece of advice: for a pick-up line to work, the lady shouldn't have to think that hard.

RICHMOND. You had to think hard about that?

VIVIANA. You're a funny guy.

RICHMOND. I try. I like old movies. I guess you don't.

VIVIANA. No, I do. I like old movies.

RICHMOND. Like what?

VIVIANA. I like those old-fashioned disaster movies.

RICHMOND. What? Like *The Towering Inferno?*

VIVIANA. Yeah, like that or *The Poseidon Adventure.*

RICHMOND. *Godzilla?*

VIVIANA. Oh my God, my son used to love *Godzilla.*

RICHMOND. It's great. With all that bad dubbing, people's mouths moving when they're not supposed to be talking, and then they're talking and their mouths aren't moving, and you're like what is going on?

VIVIANA. Exactly.

RICHMOND. *Godzilla's* great.

VIVIANA. What do you think that is? What is it about seeing the end of the world played out like that?

RICHMOND. Some people think that with movies like *Godzilla*, that the Japanese were trying to work out their memories of the war. Like all those disaster movies they made, it was like they were trying to come to terms with the atomic bomb, how something like that could happen, that kind of destruction where everything you know and everyone you love, they're just gone. One day you wake up and they're gone.

VIVIANA. How do you know all that?

RICHMOND. I told you I like old movies.

VIVIANA. What are you? Please don't tell me you're an actor.

RICHMOND. No. I'm, uh, self-employed. What do you do?

VIVIANA. Me? I'm a real estate agent.

RICHMOND. Is that right? I'm thinking I might be in the market for something. A little place just south of the border, Ensanada maybe, Costa Rica, right on the water, a couple of palm trees, maybe a little swimming pool.

VIVIANA. Sounds nice.

RICHMOND. You could come with me. You think I'm kidding, but I'm not.

VIVIANA. You just met me.

RICHMOND. So?

VIVIANA. So that's not how people do things.

RICHMOND. How do people do things?

VIVIANA. They go out for coffee, they have dinner, they get to know each other. There's rules, you know.

RICHMOND. Yeah? Well now the way I see it, some people spend their whole lives playing by the rules and for what? Sometimes you gotta just take that leap. An opportunity presents itself and you gotta seize it. Isn't this the land of opportunity? Isn't that what people say?

VIVIANA. Yeah, they do.

RICHMOND. Listen, I got to go take care of something. I won't be long. And then I'll come back and we'll celebrate.

VIVIANA. Celebrate what?

RICHMOND. The start of something new.

(*An old song comes on the juke box.*)

You hear that? I like this song.

VIVIANA. Me too.

RICHMOND. It's old school. Can I have this dance?

VIVIANA. You have to go.

RICHMOND. I got time for one last dance.

VIVIANA. I'm a terrible dancer.

RICHMOND. That's OK. All you got to do is follow me.

(RICHMOND *and* VIVIANA *dance.*)

Scene 35

Six months later. A community room in a prison facility on the outskirts of Los Angeles. LEE is lost in thought. RACHEL approaches him.

RACHEL. Mr. Lee? Mr. Lee, it's me. I'm a little early, I guess.

LEE. You come back.

RACHEL. Of course I'd come back. We have writing to do.

LEE. Yes. Yes. (*Beat.*) Where you go?

RACHEL. I went on a trip. Here, I want to show you something.
(*RACHEL takes out photographs.*)
LEE. Who this?
RACHEL. That's my new baby.
LEE. This your baby?
RACHEL. She's adopted. From China. I went to China to get her and bring her back. That's why I was away for so long.
LEE. She look like my daughter when she was baby. Big cheek, very serious. You know my daughter she just had baby.
(*ANGIE appears holding a baby.*)
Little boy. She name Hyun-Ki. Hyun-Ki Guttierez.
RACHEL. That's a wonderful name.
LEE. It's good name. She bring him to see me. She say he look like me. Hard to tell, I think. Maybe so. (*Beat.*) You remember story I told you about? Story of blind man and his daughter. You remember?
(*ANGIE begins to sing a song to her baby. It's the same song from before, an old Korean song she remembers from her childhood.*)
LEE. In Korea, we call Tale of Shimchung. At the end, the blind man, he hear his daughter's voice. He think she drown, but she not drown. She come back from dead. He now a poor beggar and she now a queen, but she never forget him. And one day he come to castle where she live, and he hear her voice, and he turn and he see her. Even though he blind, he see.
(*The sound of the ocean. It grows.*)

Scene 36

Sunset. The future. A beach. Blue ocean. The sky is shot through with color, streaks of crimson, fuschia, tangerine. ANGIE holds her baby and sings to him. DAN appears. ANGIE stops singing.

DAN. How old?
ANGIE. Six months.
DAN. Boy or girl?
ANGIE. Boy. Do you have kids?
DAN. No. No, I don't. My boyfriend, he talks about it, but I don't know.
ANGIE. It's hard, I think, to raise kids in LA.
DAN. Oh well, we live up in Alaska actually. I'm just down here visiting my folks. Look at that sunset.
ANGIE. I know. It's amazing.
DAN. It's the smog.
ANGIE. What?

DAN. The pollution in the air, that's what makes it look so…

ANGIE. Psychadelic?

DAN. Yeah, exactly. (*Beat.*) So how is it being a mom?

ANGIE. It's great. I'm just trying to figure out how to balance everything. I just went back to school part-time, you know, but a part of me just wants to spend all day with the baby. Each day he does something and it just blows me away. My husband says I shouldn't worry. He says I should just take my time.

DAN. What does he do?

ANGIE. My husband? He owns his own garage and body shop. If you ever need your car fixed: Guttierez and Son.

DAN. I'll remember that. It sounds like you guys, like you're really doing well. Sometimes, when you're young and you're just starting out, well it can be rough.

ANGIE. We just, we caught a lucky break is all. So what do you do?

DAN. I'm a seismologist.

ANGIE. No kidding.

DAN. Yeah.

ANGIE. I'm not even going to ask you.

DAN. No, it's OK. I just won't be able to tell you the answer. It could be tomorrow, it could be a hundred years from now.

ANGIE. We just bought this new house and I think about that kinda stuff, like is it going to survive if the big one hits.

DAN. *When. When* it hits. It's going to happen. It's just a matter of time. People don't want to think that way, but that's how it is. It's like we get so caught up in our lives and we forget how small we are, how everything can change in an instant, at the moment we least expect it. And we think we can prepare, that there's something we can do, we actually think that. Or that there's some kind of grand design we can't see—I'm sorry, I shouldn't even—

ANGIE. No it's, it's fine.

DAN. (*Beat. Taking the mezuzah from his pocket.*) Here, wait, I have this thing. I would love for you to have it.

ANGIE. What is it?

DAN. It's called a *mezuzah.* It's a little box and inside there's a little piece of paper with a blessing. You put it on a doorframe in your home and it protects your family.

ANGIE. That's so lovely, but I can't…

DAN. No, please, I'd really like for you to have it. I've been carrying it around with me. I was going to throw it in the ocean, but it's not that easy, you know, to throw things in the ocean. They kinda wash back and then some old guy with one of those metal detectors comes along and picks it up and, well, I'd rather you have it than some old guy with a metal detector. Please. Keep it.

(ANGIE *takes the mezuzah.*)

ANGIE. Thank you. I'm Angie.

DAN. Dan.

ANGIE. Nice to meet you, Dan. I should go. My husband is waiting.

DAN. Yeah, I should get going too.

ANGIE. Safe travels.

DAN. Yeah. You too.

(ANGIE *exits.* DAN *remains. The sun sets over a vast ocean. Darkness falls.*)

End of Play

WHEN SOMETHING WONDERFUL ENDS

a history lesson
a one woman, one Barbie play

by Sherry Kramer

BIOGRAPHY

Sherry Kramer is the author of more than 15 plays that have been produced here and abroad. Plays include: *David's RedHaired Death, The Wall of Water, What A Man Weighs, Things That Break, The World at Absolute Zero, The Mad Master, The Long Arms of Jupiter* (a croquet performance piece), *The Bay of Fundy, The Law Makes Evening Fall, A Permanent Signal, The Master and Margarita* (a singing-theatre work with Margaret Pine), and *Napoleon's China* (a play with music with Ann Haskell and Rebecca Newton). Selected Productions: Yale Repertory Theatre, NY's Second Stage, the Woolly Mammoth Theatre, Soho Repertory Theatre, Ensemble Studio Theatre, and the Theatre of the First Amendment. She has been awarded the Weissberger Playwriting Award, the Jane Chambers Playwriting Award, the L.A. Women in Theatre New Play Award, a New York Drama League Award, the Marvin Taylor Award, and is the recipient of a National Endowment for the Arts Fellowship, a New York Foundation for the Arts Fellowship, a McKnight National Fellowship, a Pew Charitable Trust/Playwrights Center Residency, and a commission from the Audrey Skirball-Kenis Theatre Project. She was the first national member of New Dramatists, and is a Core Member of the Playwrights' Center in Minneapolis. She holds MFAs from the Iowa Writers' Workshop and the Iowa Playwrights' Workshop. She teaches playwriting at Bennington College, The Michener Center for Writers at the University of Texas, Austin, and the Iowa Playwrights' Workshop, where she was previously head of the workshop. Her plays have been published by TCG, Vintage Books, and are available from Broadway Play Publishing.

ACKNOWLEDGMENTS

When Something Wonderful Ends premiered at the Humana Festival of New American Plays in March 2007, in a co-production with InterAct Theatre (Seth Rozin, Artistic Director). It was directed by Tom Moore with the following cast and staff:

WOMAN	Lori Wilner
Scenic Designer	Paul Owen
Costume Designer	Lorraine Venberg
Lighting Designer	Brian J. Lilienthal
Video Designer	Jason Czaja
Properties Designer	Mark Walston
Stage Manager	Michele Traub
Dramaturg	Carrie Hughes
Assistant Dramaturg	Diana Grisanti
Casting	Andrew Zerman
Directing Assistant	Kyle J. Schmidt

When Something Wonderful Ends was developed at PlayLabs, Polly Carl, Artistic Director; The Bay Area Playwrights Festival, Amy Mueller, Artistic Director; and the Ojai Playwrights Conference, Bob Egan, Artistic Director.

The author wishes to thank Seth Rozin, Adrien-Alice Hansel and Marc Masterson for their courage and faith and everyone at ATL for making working there a luminous experience; Linda Gehringer, Jeri Lynn Cohen, Melissa Kievman, and Jayne Wenger for their contributions to the play, their generosity, and their grace; Victor D'Altorio for his passionate work on the early drafts of this play; and Tom Moore for his wisdom, his vision, and the enduring gifts of a joyful collaboration.

CAST OF CHARACTERS

ONE WOMAN

A Midwestern Reform Jewish baby boomer. She has black curly hair.

ONE BARBIE

A 1964 near mint Bubble Cut Brunette.

The part was originally written for a mint condition, 1964 Redhead Swirl Ponytail Barbie, #850. The Swirl Ponytail Barbie has an unusual ponytail, which is caught in back with a yellow ribbon. Once taken down, as most little girls did immediately, it was almost impossible to return to its former swirly glory, and could never be mint condition again.

The role was recently re-written, however, for a Bubble Cut Brunette, near mint.

Barbies in less than mint condition are of course also invited to audition.

SET

There is a large, antique desk, one like a school teacher might have used years ago, one of those substantial rectangles of wood, lots of desktop space. There is a big old fashioned roll-up map stand, with several maps of the Middle East. The cover, or top sheet of the roll up maps, is white, and photographs can be projected on it.

There are titles in the play, which should be presented in any way compatible with that of a 6th grade classroom presentation in 1964. They might be projected, they might be on large sheets of paper on a huge flip-pad, they might be written by the actress on a blackboard, they might be presented in three or four different ways.

There are Barbie clothes and a Barbie Dream Car. There is a 1964 Brunette Barbie, still in her box, and 59 vintage Barbie outfits. A pile of unmatched Barbie shoes. A smaller pile of Ken clothes. A vintage Barbie Dream House. And a lot of Ziploc bags. Throughout the play, as appropriate, the actress sorts Barbie clothes, and puts them in Ziploc bags.

There are packing boxes, and evidence of things other than Barbie clothes being packed. The set might look pretty cluttered when the audience sits down. Or the desk might be the only thing they see.

CANDY

The actress hands out Brach's cinnamon discs to audience members as they enter the theatre. Or perhaps the ushers do it. But it would be better if the actress did it. If handing out wrapped candies before a performance makes your house management uneasy you might want to include this in the turn-off-your-cell phone speech:

> Please unwrap and enjoy the cinnamon candies now—or put them aside for after the show. Please do not unwrap them during the show, even if you do it painfully slowly, excruciatingly slowly, as if you were a deer in headlights who thinks that if he doesn't move you can't see him. Of course you can see him. He's right there. It doesn't matter how long he doesn't move, he's not going to disappear. It doesn't matter how sloooowly you unwrap your candy.

We can all hear you. Thank you.

For my mother and father

Lori Wilner
in *When Something Wonderful Ends*

31st Annual Humana Festival of New American Plays
Actors Theatre of Louisville, 2007
Photo by Harlan Taylor

OMETHING WONDERFUL ENDS

Title: *When Something Wonderful Ends*

WOMAN. When something wonderful ends, everybody wants to know how it happened. "How did it come to this," they like to say. And "Why didn't we see it coming in time." They like saying that, a lot. And then they get tired of saying it. The bewildered common comfort they got out of saying it wears off, and they get busy looking for something else to say. They get busy trying to figure out how the end of this wonderful something started so they can say, "Ah, now I *see* how it came to this. I *see* why nobody saw it coming." They like saying this about a million times more than they liked saying they didn't see. They think seeing, and knowing, are going to change things.

Here's the good news. I *know* how it came to this. I *know* why we didn't see it coming. I even know the exact moment the end started and where I was at the time.

I was at the Toy Box on the Plaza, Springfield, Missouri's first shopping center, situated five miles south of downtown, on historic Route 66. Now, spending money at a shopping center five miles south of downtown meant that the downtown, finding itself the road not taken, would one day, soon, wither and fade, so the Age of Enlightenment wasn't the only thing dying at this moment, the downtown was too—and not emblematically, but physically, it was really and truly and specifically dying because I was buying a dress. A dress with a name. A dress called Enchanted Evening. Okay, my mother was buying it for me. I was ten years old, so my mother put me in the car. In the front seat, of the car. The world looked different back then, the un-Ralph Nader changed world, no car seats, not even any seat belts, you could run the hell all over the car. When we took family trips in the station wagon, Mom and Dad took a little mattress and spread it out in the back and then it was nap time, party time, the three of us kids, all the way to Cape Cod three times and Miami Beach twice. Oh, and there were cigarette ads everywhere before Nader changed the world. Remember how great cigarette commercials looked? Sexy women, manly men? My mother smoked Herbert Tarytons, the most elegant pack of cigarettes in the world. White background, and no design but this lovely regal blue crown. I don't think the Tarytons killed her. Of course, you can't be sure of much of anything nowadays. So, anyway, my mother plopped me into the car, and drove us from our house in Brentwood, Springfield's very first subdivision, to the Toy Box on the Plaza, where I was allowed to pick out, from a whole wall of boxes filled with unimaginable delight—one outfit.

(I bring out Enchanted Evening.)

This is Enchanted Evening. I think it cost a dollar fifty. A Barbie only cost three seventy-five. I know because I still have the box.

(I bring out my Barbie, still in the box. I take my Barbie out of the box.)

This is a Bubble Cut Brunette Barbie, a model made between 1962 and 1964. She is a basic Barbie, nothing really rare about her. Solid, unremarkable, excellent condition but not exactly mint.

(I dress Barbie in Enchanted Evening.)

Enchanted Evening is a classic Barbie outfit. A pink satin evening gown with a huge, full, round train, the skirt gathered up tight at the waist with a pink rose, which causes it to start off as a tight sheath, then falls in graceful folds that create an elegant drape. A great look, especially if you don't actually have to walk in it. It's from the Golden Age of Barbie, 1959-65. It is one of the most valuable of all the Barbie outfits I have—worth three thousand dollars, NRFP—Never Removed From Package, or three hundred fifty dollars, MC—mint condition, with *all* the accessories. These include—

(I hold up each one as I mention them.)

—a white fur stole lined with pink satin. Sparkly pink plastic shoes. Pearls. Pearl earrings. And opera length gloves. And you can forget about the big money if it's not mint—twenty bucks on eBay, if it's missing an earring or is worn or discolored in any way.

My Enchanted Evening is not worn. It is mint. It's almost as if I'd never played with it. None of my Barbie clothes—and I have fifty-nine outfits, virtually everything manufactured by Mattel from 1960 to 1965—none of these fifty-nine outfits—with the exception of a corduroy jumper with felt poodle appliqué called Friday Night Date which is stained and discolored and may actually belong to Sara Thomas, from across the street—none of my outfits show any sign of being worn at all. Enchanted Evening looks as good as the day I bought it. March 4, 1964.

And this is how I discovered that that very day was the start of the end of something wonderful. I was driving back to Springfield to start the long process of packing up my parents' home. I put a book on tape into my CD player, a history book about the U.S. and the Middle East. It astonished me. I realized that while I had been acquiring Enchanted Evening, serial number 783, for my bubble cut Barbie, serial number 750, at the *exact same moment*, in 1964, a SOFA, S-O-F-A, or Status Of Forces Agreement, had just been made the official law of the land. Not this land. Iran. SOFAs were common, we signed then whenever our troops were stationed in foreign lands, but the results of this one weren't. This SOFA started the cascade of events that lifts the Ayatollah Khomeini, until then a mild mannered cleric minding his own Islamic business, into a rabid dog of rage, launching his career as the official

Islamist godfather of hate until he passes the baton to Osama, though not directly, we'll get to that, who launches two planes into the Twin Towers, one into the Pentagon, and one into the ground. Which then launches America's attack on Iraq. Which then—well, we're just at *that* which then.

Title: The Which Then

Here's what the which-then looks like, from my point of view, the place from which I am packing up the house and sorting my Barbie clothes and watching America's dream go bad.

I am on my way to the cemetery, to put some gladiolas on my mother's grave. It's a frail, magical ritual, my mother brought flowers to her mother's grave, and now I'm doing it for her. It's a little bit like performing a miracle—doing something beautiful for the dead. It's impossible, of course, to do anything for the dead, still, as I drive away from the cemetery, every single time I feel the willfulness of the miracle, I see that the impossible is ordinary and everyday and right in front of me, just around the tiny corners of this world there is always this possibility of contact with the unseen, with the divine, and then it hits me, double barreled, this sudden *ache* hits me, because this miracle is not enough, it changes nothing, the miracle occurs, "Woman does something for the dead" is the headline, the headline runs every time, and nothing changes. I pull out of the cemetery and that's it. Miracle over.

I have a Picture of the Miracle.

> (*I show a picture of the gladiolas at my mother's grave. I'm guessing this will be on the screen.*)

My mother died a few months before 9/11, so I have over six years of pictures like this. It's some sort of documentary impulse, I've always had it, yesterday I found all my old scrapbooks—here's one I made when I was twelve, not about ponies or trips to the beach, but about the first and most important controversy of my life—

> (*I pull the scrapbook out of a box, it has flowers cut out of foil wrapping paper on the front.*)

"JOHN LENNON CLAIMS THE BEATLES ARE MORE POPULAR THAN JESUS."

> (*I open it to a couple pages showing newspaper clippings about the controversy. Then I open the scrapbook to a page where the lyrics to "All You Need Is Love" are carefully, lovingly cut out of different colors of foil wrapping paper and pasted onto separate pages, or cut like a paper-doll chain out of a continuous piece of paper.*)

When you cut out the words "All You Need Is Love"—

(And I don't sing, I say the lyrics, dead-pan, as I turn each page or pull out the chain.)

All you need is love *(Next page or segment.)* All you need is love, love. *(Next page or segment.)* Love is all you need and paste it into a scrapbook with sacred photos of Paul, John, George and Ringo—

(I close, and re-pack the scrapbook.)

—that scrapbook is transformed into a magical tome that throbs with a power only a 12-year-old girl can know.

(And show a few more pictures of flowers.)

I'm not twelve any longer. I know a photo doesn't have a lot of power. These aren't miracles after all, they're just pictures of miracles. Small miracles, that don't have the power to transform the world beyond the cemetery gates.

Most of the other graves in the cemetery have artificial flowers on them. I think that the flowers I put on my mother's grave are better than the artificial ones people put on the graves of their loved ones, nearby. I think that the miracle *I* make is better then the miracle *they* make.

And I think this: that anytime a person puts *their* miraculous ritual with their dead above somebody *else's* miraculous ritual with theirs, means the start of something very unfine. In my case, the unfineness manifests itself in a little arrogant smug smallness. This arrogant smug smallness does two things. It files down some of the finer points of my soul, and this filing down process, it's cumulative, it's catastrophic, it will show up in twenty years as a dull, dead place at my very center—but that's life, you know? That's the way life and time accrue. And the other thing it does is put me squarely in a vast historical context. My grieving heart has landed me smack dab in the center of a ritual that has had some of the ugliest unintended consequences the world has ever known. Miraculous rituals with the dead are the very heart of all religious belief—especially now that we don't spend a lot of time appeasing the weather and the crop gods.

One of the sadder things about life on this planet is that about half of all the rotten things people do to each other start off as miracles they're trying to do for their dead. Filling up the pyramid of someone you love with lots of nice things to eat in the next life—thoughtful. Burying seven thousand slaves alive to help them around the house on the other side—not. I slipped a piece of wrapped candy into my mother's hand, as we left her. A Brach's cinnamon disc—her favorite candy, my favorite candy. Giving her a token—a little sweet to bribe the gods, or tip the boatman, seemed terribly significant at the time. And not just significant—but necessary. Because when your mother dies, and you are, in some way that makes no sense at all and all the sense in the world, dragged pretty far along with her into that other place—you understand that *anything* is possible. You *understand the point of religion*—to issue the passports and publish the train schedules and arrange the passage that is the transformation of the living into the dead. In the end, *all* religion is basically just a construct to organize what happens after. To hold back the night. The Reform Jewish night, by the way, is incredibly long and completely dark, because Reform Jews don't believe in heaven or hell.

The fear of death is the thing that drives all our drives.

Of course, the modern age has a new kind of drive. This kind.

    (I take out Barbie's Dream Car.)

This is Barbie's Dream Car.

That's its actual name, the Dream Car. When you put Barbie in it, you dreamed about the day you'd be behind the wheel. But the thing about driving in your dreams is—you never run out of gas. Because running out of gas—as U.S. policy in the Middle East for the past 50 years will attest to—is a nightmare. A nightmare about oil—about oil and America, the Miracle Nation.

Title: America, the Miracle Nation

You know, we Americans are pretty arrogant. We think we invented the car, right? This may be why we think our drive is better than anybody *else's* drive. Why we think we're the owners and operators of the modern age. We live here, in this miracle of a nation—and it is a miracle, or close to it, an Enlightenment nation. I think that most Americans have forgotten, or never really understood, that before America, there was no such thing as a nation where church and state were separate. Where would the power and authority to rule, where would it come from, if it didn't come from God? Like I said, most Americans don't get this. In the old worlds, governments were a franchise arrangement, God was always the *owner*—we were the just the *operators*.

Not in America. In America we're the owners, and it was always a Mom and Pop store. God was just a shareholder at the very best, and he owned a *minimal* amount of stock. Sundays. He owned Sundays. And a few Catholic schools. He did not have the controlling shares in a country for the first time in history.

The Enlightenment had invented America shortly after it invented a new benign but non-interventionalist God, and a new way of believing in him: Deism. Most religions ask you to use your relationship with other people to prove something to God, to climb on top of other people to get to him—Deism didn't. It made a blueprint for a new kind of country. America is the child of Deists like Tom Jefferson, who was the intellectual child of the most famous Deist of all, David Hume, whose writings directly inspired the Declaration and the Constitution. And David Hume's nickname, for anyone who is interested in these things, was The Great Infidel. Just so you know who your Daddy is.

Once America existed, the world changed, from a vertical world to a horizontal one. "We the people" versus "the glory of God." The world you make is very different *up* versus *across.* The different use of your fellow human beings, in a vertical or a horizontal world, is night and day.

Title: The Ladder

The problem with vertical countries is that while they are engaged in a very *vertical* relationship with God, it gets played out *horizontally*—and this is what fundamentalism *is,* vertical laws, horizontal enforcement. All those rules come from the frustration that comes when you can't climb up the air and be one with your god. So you get busy making a ladder, and you've got to build it using the raw materials at hand, which turn out to be the guy standing next to you. So, vertical countries are desperately trying to transform the horizontal world into a vertical stairway to heaven, *using the other guy.*

Mostly, Americans live fully in the horizontal world. Yes, we climb over each other, but we don't do it for God. We do it for ourselves. We didn't wipe out our Infidels for religious reasons—the Indians were just in the way of our appetite, our huge, unstoppable greed, and after we wiped them out, the word Infidel became a word with virtually no meaning. Oh, our missionaries still use the word, and I heard it a lot when I was growing up, because Springfield, Missouri, is one of the main assembly lines for the American missionary trade, and is the headquarters of the Assemblies of God. It is also the place where John Ashcroft was born. We are the home of Baptist Bible College, Central Bible College and Evangel College. Hard working people from all over America scraped their money together and sent their children to Springfield, MO, where they were expected to take bible classes, get married and go out to spread God's word. Some of them needed to get part-time jobs to help pay for their education, doing housework.

We were one of the best houses for a Baptist Bible Girl to work. Not only were my parents prominent, upstanding members of the business community, but we were Jewish. We were, to vertical religious sects obsessed with proselytizing, Trainer Infidels. The girls could practice their missionary work right here in Springfield while making minimum wage.

This is the way to picture my Barbie and me, during these years. I'm dressing my Barbie in Red Flare.

(*I dress Barbie in Red Flare.*)

Red Flare is a bright red coat, which flares, with white satin lining. It also has a matching red hat and a clutch purse with a gold closure.

Meanwhile Denise, a sweet girl from a small town near Denver, wearing a pastel sweater and three inches below the knee wool skirt, is dusting and mopping the floor near by. God has firm and unshakable notions about a woman's knees, so there were strict dress codes at Baptist Bible College. This was not a problem. The BBC girls loved strict codes and rules, they were brought up loving them, that's how you *know*, when you're a vertical, how much you love God, by how much you love His *rules*. And when you're young, and pretty, you're just bursting to love. So. Picture Denise dusting and singing a song about Jesus *just* loud enough for me to make out every word, and soft enough that my mother can't hear.

The BBC girls had to be clever. My parents wouldn't allow them to try to convert their children, so they could never talk openly to us about Christ. But my *mother* was fair game. And in between the mothering they got *from* her and the cleaning they did *for* her, they proselytized *full time*. They weren't expected to actually convert her. They *were* expected to try. The ones who loved her—and many of them did—tried the hardest. There was one who never stopped writing her long letters begging her to accept Christ as her savior. Like clockwork those letters arrived, for thirty-five years. I was the one who had to call and let them know Mom had died. I think it was an impossible thought for most of them. They had last seen her in the late 60's or 70's, in the full flush of her beauty and power. She seemed unstoppable to most everyone who met her. Mostly, she seemed blessed. We never expect the blessed to die before us. It always comes as a surprise.

When I told Denise and the others about Mother, every single one of them assured me that she was in heaven. I didn't say anything. Mother would have gently, patiently corrected them, she wouldn't have passed up an educational opportunity like this. But I wasn't in an educational mood.

Title: God 2.0

My mother never passed up a chance to tell the people in Springfield what was good about Judaism. She expected us kids to do the same. Of course, you didn't want to spend all day doing it, so she condensed it down to the three most important points. Here were the improvements that made Judaism an important upgrade in religion, that made it a kind of God 2.0.

First: There was just one God. This made worship so much more efficient, like central heating, it put the same god everywhere in your house at once, and it cut down on system conflicts.

Second: No more human sacrifice. You could no longer get to heaven by killing an unbeliever. Almost everything that we call "value" stems from this one upgrade, this first official step toward valuing the other as we value ourselves. I think it's the reason we react so violently to the practice of suicide bombers, a throwback to pagan sacrifice that unsettles us down to the bottom of our souls. Even the rewards of the sacrifice give us the creeps—the Islamic dream of heaven—with the seventy-two virgins? That would be young girls, without experience? Has anybody else noticed that this Islamic heaven is a weekend at a pedophilia convention in Morocco? No? No one's noticed this? I guess it's just me.

And last, but not least, the third great patch on the religion program goes like this: The afterlife is no longer the primary focus of this one. Judaism marks the end of other worldly mindedness.

Of course, it wasn't a clean un-install. It turns out that we need our dead. This is why the lack of an operational afterlife was the deal breaker when it came to Judaism, even though to my way of thinking it should have been circumcision. I remember arguing with my brother about it when we were in high school. I insisted that circumcision was barbaric and aesthetically unpleasing. My brother, ignoring the reference to the pleasing part, and in any case having nothing more to lose…reminded me that it was a sacred covenant, that God gave the Jews the Torah, the great book of our people, and they in return got circumcised. I pointed out that they might have been better off going to a lending library. But without an afterlife with its solid hell and palpable heaven, Judaism would always have limited appeal. If we'd had a plausible exit strategy, we would probably be living in a Jewish world. But we held firm. The Jewish world is like Vegas—what happens here, stays here.

The lack of hell created many problems for the Midwestern Reform Jewish child. I cannot tell you the pity with which I was regarded by my classmates at Eugene Field Elementary School. For I was not saved. On a dozen different occasions, girls in my class actually wept over this. Beverly King, who sat in front of me for years because of alphabetical supremacy, cried more than once. I did not believe in heaven and consequently would not be going there. Explaining to these decent, religious, and not stupid girls that I didn't have to be saved because there was no afterlife *at all*—well, it wasn't hard. It was impossible. What was the point of living if you couldn't get into heaven? What was the point of being good if being bad didn't send you to hell? The children I grew up with lived in a world so uncomprehendingly vertical to me—I lived somewhere else. Our worlds looked the same from the outside—but on the inside, where all the real things happened, all the reasons were different. I was sorry for them, because they believed in heaven. I was jealous of them, because they believed in heaven. But my mother said we didn't need heaven. My mother said we don't need heaven because we have heaven on earth.

(I spin Barbie, making her Red Flare flare.)

My mother's favorite color was red. Red was inevitable in my mother's life because it was practically *illegal* in my grandmother's. My grandmother dressed herself and her home in dusky roses and pale, silken shades of Prussian blue. My mother, who didn't know how *not* to fall in love every second of her life, she was continually falling in love with her husband, her children, her house, her country—well, that kind of passion for the world—is red. My mother didn't have a red coat, as far as I can remember, but that is probably the only red thing she didn't have. She had a red convertible, *several* red rooms filled with red sofas, red chairs, a red fireplace, a red kitchen—okay, it was a cross between salmon and red, but it was almost red. Red shoes and red handbags and red paintings, and her favorite artist was Red Grooms. She and my father collected about a dozen of his paintings. And now they're all about to go on the moving van with my father to independent living, and this house, where I grew up, is getting sold. That's why the Barbies had to come out of the closet where my childhood has been taking its long, long sleep. Why I'm driving myself insane, researching the outfits, discovering the names, like "Ski Queen", or "Dinner at Eight", or "Tennis, Anyone?", sorting the accessories, matching them to the outfit, finding out the going price, putting each outfit in a Ziploc bag with a piece of paper with the name of the outfit, and then—well, that's the then I don't know.

(*I remember the jingle that accompanied Barbie ads in the 60's. I sing it.*)

Mix and match it's fun to choose
What Barbie wears is up to you
There are sweaters and skirts and slacks and shoes
There are lots of styles from which to choose

Oh my God, I can't believe I remember that.

My mother held on to these, all these years. Sometimes I think I should keep them too—but I know I can't. I don't have the room. Tomorrow I'm going to take them over to the guy who's fencing the rest of my childhood on eBay. Maybe it's right that my fifty-nine vintage Barbie outfits join the stream, the great moving river of memory and fetish and greed that the internet has made out of the artifacts of the American dream.

Title: Hit and Run 1

It's hard, if you're an American, to think that America is not different, because we've been taught that we're the Good Guys. We're the forces of the Enlightenment. Slavery, eradicating the Indians, these were things that filed down the finer points of the American soul, hell, these were *crimes* that rubbed off Prime Soul Acreage. But the American experiment was and is about trying to do it right. To make this the land of dreams for everybody. We had a few things that were really screwed up, but we were working on them. And then something made us take all our screwed-up-ness—our greed and our racism—abroad.

America is built on abundance, the kind of abundance that is either the product of divine providence or luck so stupendous it might as well be divine. What other country is protected from almost everybody else by oceans, crowded from coast to coast with rivers and timber and lush, fertile soil, and under the earth filled with coal and silver and gold. The perfect country—except for one fatal flaw. God gave us a land, with more of almost every natural resource in the world than He gave anybody. God gave America more of everything—except for one thing...a thing He apparently didn't know we'd need so much of. Oil.

We used to think we had plenty. We used to think the fun in Texas and Oklahoma would never end. In the 40s, what was more American than a gushing oil well? Well, other than a car, that is. Here's a shocker: Barbie's Dream Car is an Aston Martin.

(I put Barbie into her Dream Car.)

An English car. I know, I know, but James Bond drove an Aston Martin, and the whole double o seven thing was huge back then. English cars, by the way, never ran on English oil—there isn't any. So the Brits had been drilling for oil in the Middle East since the 20s.

Then came World War II. The Brits and the Russians are in trouble. In order to save the world, we have to get supplies to the Russians, and the only route we can use, that isn't impassable during the winter snows is the Persian corridor. But to get to the Persian corridor, you need to go through Iran.

(I pull down a pre-World War II map of the Middle East and the Soviet Union, and indicate the Persian corridor.)

This means that Iran has to stay in Allied hands. So in 1942, that's where we put it. The Shah was being a little too friendly with Germany anyway, so we just kick him out, politely, but kick him out we do, we remove the ruler of a country—of course, regime changing during war is not called regime changing, it's called what it really is, war, but during war it's okay, it's sanctioned, it's expected, so our hands are still semi-clean on the regime changing charge. And then we turn Iran into—like—a Wal-Mart super-center, the biggest Wal-Mart in the world, we fill it up with tanks, and guns, and jeeps, tons of them, millions of tons of them, baby we roll back the prices, this shit we're sending—it's free, it's supermarket sweep for the Russians, and to keep Iran happy, we give her tons and tons of non-military stuff like lampshades and clothing and flatware and such. And the biggest problem we have, as the occupiers of Iran? Traffic accidents. Traffic accidents caused by military vehicles. Hundreds of Iranians killed by Allied soldiers. An American diplomat explains the fatalities like this: "The reflexes of the Iranians are relatively slow."

Title: *No Communication With the Dead*

After she died, my mother did not contact us. This seemed unfair. Everybody I knew who'd lost someone they loved had these stories of the way their mother or brother or husband had contacted them from beyond the grave. I knew that if anyone loved her family enough to bridge the worlds, my mother did. She had already tried to stay with us, after she'd died. When we left the hospital, they were wheeling her body along behind us, on its way to the hearse. Turn after turn on the way across courtyards and hallways and parking lots, we'd lose her, the stretcher was slower than we were, but the attendants knew the short cuts, and sure enough there she'd be. As if we were still a family of five. And then when we couldn't get my sister a ticket to Springfield for the funeral on the same plane as my father and my brother and me (my mother had died in Florida, the funeral was in Springfield), the first seat we *could* get her turned out to be on the same plane my mother's body was coming on. That's the way she was. My mother didn't ever want to be alone.

When I went to the airport to pick up my sister, I brought one of my nieces along for company. We picked up my sister, and then I decided that we should at least meet my mother, even if we couldn't take her home. I asked a scruffy looking baggage handler where her coffin would be, and he said because of construction detours we'd never make it to the cargo area, but he'd go with us, to help us find the way. It was 10:30, eleven o'clock at night, his lunch break, and he considered briefly, before getting into the car, calculating if he would get back in time to avoid losing his job. He did the math, then shrugged and climbed in. He had had a mother, once, too.

As he got in, a kind of joyriding thrill ran through the car. I looked at my niece. She was numb with terror, she was fourteen years old, how many times had it been drummed into her head, never get into a car with a stranger, and here I'd just invited one in. Of course, as all America would soon discover after September 11, the intense aliveness that slices through you after the one who loves you best is dead makes every single moment just vibrate with resonance. The vivid clarity that comes after death—how the important things assume their true size and dimension, crowding out the unimportant things so easily—makes anything possible. Anything except the one impossible thing you truly want.

The baggage handler not only got us to the cargo area, he was our Virgil, he pounded on three different doors, went into places clearly marked NO ADMITTANCE, he did all the lesser impossible things for us that we never could have done. He called and got someone to open a door for us at the *exact moment* the box that contained my mother in her coffin came off the transport and was carried into the cargo area. My mother had gotten off the plane, we had put a strange man in our car, and we had met her. We had not made her wait. The person you're picking up at the airport always knows how much you love them by whether you're there on time or not. It was one of the early miracles, one of the first things we did for our dead.

We waited with her coffin until the people from the funeral home came. We watched as they took her away. Then we took our guide back to the main airport. He was forty-five minutes over his lunch break, but he didn't care. He had taken us to see our mother, out of love for his own. He had been performing his own miracle for the dead.

Anyway, it gradually became clear to me that if my mother hadn't contacted us, it was not out of an inability to do so. Because if defying all the laws of man and God and nature were all that were necessary, if will and love were all it took to communicate with those you left behind after death, she would have been talking to us non-stop. We would hardly have even known she was gone. No, it was a choice. My mother did not *believe* in communication with the dead, and since she always had the courage of her convictions, she was keeping still. It shouldn't have surprised me that she refused to contact us from the other side. Just because she was dead was no reason to let down her standards.

Standards are a funny thing. They are the way we have of believing in things, out loud.

Title: A Better World

I have a cousin, and this cousin has no children. And so, this cousin feels that not adding to the population of the planet is a more than ample contribution to the conservation of its precious resources. Consequently, the washing machine in her house runs twelve hours a day, the house is always lit up like a Christmas tree, televisions flicker away in empty rooms, heat and air-conditioning blast through wide open windows spring, summer, winter and fall. When confronted about this waste, these violent squanderings of air and water and fossil fuels, my cousin merely says "I have no children who will do laundry, no grandchildren who will do laundry, no great-grandchildren who will do laundry—think of all the generations of laundry that are not going to be done because of me. So it's only fair—I get to do all the laundry I want."

When did we stop wanting a better world? Is it the movies that did it to us? Did we stop wanting a better world because it's so much easier to get one there? So much easier to go to the gym, which feels really good, right, than use the movement of our bodies to build a house or a road or a city. Have we forgotten what good is? Have we forgotten what it costs? Take power, for instance. We've ignored the costs of it for years, but now the bill is coming due, now it's time to feel every single watt of power we're paying for with our souls, every single watt that's polluting our air and our water and our foreign policies, raping and pillaging like we're on Mr. Toad's Wild Ride.

Title: The Golden Gimmick

And we've been on that ride since World War II, a war we won with our oil as much as with American blood and guts. We used so much of our oil to save the world, in fact, that it put a serious dent in our oil reserves. So after the war we're in the Persian Gulf right alongside the English and the French, pumping out Middle Eastern oil. It's 1950. The Iranian pedestrians with the slow reflexes who were crushed under Allied wheels are long dead and forgotten by us, but not, of course, by the Iranians. Harry Truman is at the wheel of America, and this is what he does to keep us driving. He encourages a bloodless coup that deposes the president of another nation. We're not at war now, so this is regime changing, pure and simple. We, the forces of freedom and democracy, help regime change Syria, a country with no beef at all with ours, merely because it is the only way we can get a pipeline constructed across it. The ousted president? Shukri Quwatli. A man nobody even remembers, a man whose name has been all but erased from the history books and from history.

And our President does one other thing to make sure the oil will keep flowing. He promises Saudi Arabia that if they are ever attacked by the Soviet Union, the U.S. will come to their aid. This is the first in a string of unprecedented promises that will turn American forces into the Saudis' personal army. This is the moment that starts the cascade of events that will transform the armies of the greatest superpower the world has ever known into a global oil protection service.

It is also the moment when the Saudis realize that Standard Oil has been robbing them blind, carpet bagging them, giving them an unbelievably tiny royalty, less than 10%s. The Saudis say, from now on—50-50. Or no deal.

Standard Oil did not take this lying down. It was all so unfair. They'd been the only ones who'd believed there was any oil at all in Saudi Arabia. And then the unbelievable irony—the Saudi reserves turned out to be the richest in the world. Historians call Standard Oil's sixty-year lease on Saudi oil fields "the greatest material prize in human history." The Saudi reserves are the Helen of Troy of the modern world, launching a billion ships, cars and trucks. Standard Oil had been allowed to exploit this treasure unregulated for years. Now the golden goose was about to get cooked. If they raised the price of gas to cover their increased costs, Detroit would have built smaller cars, Americans would have stopped using so much oil. And if they didn't raise the price, if they took the cut in profits? Well, that was unthinkable too. So Standard Oil went crying to Uncle Sam.

And what did Uncle Sam do? Did he make the Saudis back down? Did he tell Standard oil to grow up and accept that the days of Astounding, Almost Criminal Profits were over, that they were going to have to settle for just, say, Astronomical ones from now on? No. Our government came up with a third party to foot the bill—the American people. From now on, Standard Oil could deduct from their U.S. taxes the amount they paid in royalties to the Saudi government. This meant that we, the American people, essentially paid Standard Oil to make a profit selling us gas, gas that was artificially, deceptively cheap. Artificially cheap gas seems like a good idea—but this was the loophole that created our addiction to oil, destroyed our mass transit system, and has driven our foreign policy for over fifty years. It was called the Golden Gimmick. It reminds me of the names of my Barbie outfits.

Title: Here's What I Was Doing

Here's what I was doing in 1950, when the Golden Gimmick first gave Standard oil the Midas Touch: Nothing. I wasn't born yet. Barbie wasn't either. Her parents, whose name was Handler, wouldn't conceive of her for several years, coincidentally around the same time my parents conceived me. Here the similarities between me and Barbie end.

Barbie was modeled on the German Lilli doll, a quasi-pornographic toy intended for adult men. This fact is no surprise to any little girl who has actually played with a Barbie, as the nasty possibilities are endless and inevitable. The naked Barbie begs to be fondled. The Handlers, toy manufacturers on vacation in Germany, saw the Lillis, and thought, hmmm, maybe American girls would like a doll that looked like a real woman. So they brought a few Lillis home and found a designer, named Jack Ryan. Now Jack wasn't just any old toy designer. He was a playboy who'd been married to Zsa Zsa Gabor, and during the Cold War he designed the bodies of Hawk and Sparrow missiles. Talk about the right man for the job. Work on the Barbie—named for the Handler's daughter, Barbara—went swiftly. There was one little snag. After the first prototypes were designed, they were sent to Japan to be fabricated. The Japanese factory workers repeatedly added nipples, which caused frustration as the American team working on the doll was forced to file them down. Finally Jack sent a model back with the nipples smoothed away, and the Japanese toymakers got the hint.

Like Ken's tiny androgynous genital bulge—whose size was completely dictated by the ergonomics of the zippers in his pants, and not prudery, Barbie's dimensions were similarly enforced. If Barbie were a real person, her measurements would be 40-18-32. The closest living human with those proportions is—

> (*I ask the audience if they can imagine who this would be. Chances are, they'll say "Dolly Parton."*)

—yes, Dolly Parton, except Dolly is a tiny little thing. Barbie, if made to scale, would be over six feet tall. But Barbie's bizarre, impossible body is not an insult to all actual women—it's a necessity. When Barbie is dressed, the elastic and cloth around her waist is just as thick and bulky as the elastic and cloth would be on a skirt around ours, but Barbie is one-hundredth our size. So the huge, impossible breasts balanced on the tiny waist stacked on top of a sliver of hips is not about body hatred or female form revulsion, even though it would later become, probably, a cause of it. It was all about the clothes. It was about the drape of the cloth, the flow of the line, the look of the design.

In 1995, Islamic fundamentalists in Kuwait issued a Fatwa against Barbie.

(I hold my hands out, as if they are scales, and lay Barbie down in one. Then I "weigh" each one.)

Barbie, Salman Rushdie. Barbie, Salman Rushdie. It's difficult, but not impossible, to do the math.

Title: Unintended Consequences

In preparation for putting my parents' house on the market, my brother comes to Springfield for the weekend to pack up the things he's taking. We're at breakfast, and I've just read, that very morning, about how we helped create the Taliban and Al Qaeda by having the Saudis give money to the CIA's clandestine campaign in Afghanistan. This meant that we, the Great Infidels, created the pipeline that funneled Saudi "charitable contributions" to militant Islamists and fathered the most violent extremist groups the world has ever known. If this were fiction, it would be called irony. In real life, of course, it's called tragedy.

Anyway, I tell my brother about this. And he just shakes his head, dismissing this demonstration of cause and effect, because we don't live in a cause and effect world, anymore, because in a cause and effect world, the person or institutions who cause the cause have to take responsibility for the effect. And nobody takes responsibility now. So my brother just shakes his head, and says the great new Get Out of Jail Free Card of the 21st century. He says, "Unintended consequences. We can't be held *responsible* for unintended consequences." And I have to stand there, with my mouth hanging open. And I have to say, as ponderously and assholically as I can: "But there's nothing *but* unintended consequences. So if we're not responsible for them, what *are* we responsible *for*?" But he's not listening to that. He doesn't have to. Nobody in America has to listen to anything they don't agree with anymore. The final battle between Faith-Based and Reality-Based America was fought on November 2, 2004, Faith won, the Age of Reason vanished, and now nobody has to worry when facts and a little thing like reality contradict what they want to believe.

Title: On My Way to the Cemetery

I am on my way to put some flowers on my mother's grave when I see a funeral procession coming from the opposite direction.

I see that it is not an ordinary funeral—there is a long line of people standing along the route, waving American flags. It is a military funeral. Someone's son has died in the war in Iraq. Someone's son will lie in the ground in the Springfield National Cemetery, which now borders the Jewish Cemetery on two sides. Someone's son has died in a land far away and will lie under the ground, a few feet from my mother. And he has died for something so big, and in the end, so small. He has died because we lack the political will to produce a widely consumable and cost effective alternative to petroleum. If we had spent the billions and billions developing an alternative, instead of policing and protecting the Middle East...

Title: Imagine a Different Path

Imagine a different path. Say we hadn't treated the Middle East like our very own fossil fuel piñata. Say our government hadn't help create an entire economy dependent on artificially cheap oil. We would have developed alternative technologies. We wouldn't have destroyed our rail system, and deserted our inner cities. No car on earth would exist that got eight miles to the gallon.

Every one of our dreams, every one of our sorrows, every moment of our lives is plugged into the grid that's been betraying the America we thought we belonged to for years. We're in bed with a monster. A molester. And the terrible shame is—we like it. We like what happens when we plug into the current. When the juice starts to flow. The old cliché that power corrupts, and absolute power corrupts absolutely has a whole new meaning now. And when do we feel the most powerful? When we're behind the wheel of a car.

Title: Hit and Run 2

I really would like to keep my Dream Car. I don't know how much it's worth. I can't find it listed in any of my Barbie books. It's nowhere near mint. Apparently, I played with it a lot, and it's many miles shy of NRFP. Curious that a plaything only really has value if it has never been played with. But I did.

(I put Barbie in her car. I show off the broken-off fender.)

Because at some point, we can see that Barbie has had a little fender bender. Barbie must have hit something. Something…or *someone*. Barbie has had a little hit and run.

Our country did too. It's 1964, and we're about to sign a SOFA in Iran that will make hatred for America in the Middle East blossom, and begin to bear the fruit we are tasting now. And I am at the Toy Box, on the Plaza, carefully, tenderly taking Enchanted Evening off the shelf like it's the Holy Grail, blissful, and oblivious, my life nested like a pearl, dead center in the magic oyster bed of the baby boom.

Our servicemen are stationed in Iran in 1964 to pander to the Shah and keep our access to his oil. Unfortunately, the Iranians' slow reflexes have not gotten any quicker since 1943, and once again, our military personnel are hitting and killing them. Of all the insults to Iranian order and tradition, it is the Americans' disregard for their safety that outrages the Iranian people the most. And then America and the Shah's government sign the SOFA, which means that U.S. military personnel suspected of breaking local laws are court-martialed by the U.S. military, instead of being tried in local courts.

When the Iranian people hear that American servicemen are now beyond the reach of Iranian law, they go wild. An unknown Shiite cleric named Ayatollah Ruhollah Khomeini makes an impassioned speech. He says that the Shah and his government have "Reduced the Iranian people to a level lower than that of an American dog. If someone runs over a dog belonging to an American, he will be prosecuted. But if an American cook runs over the Shah, the head of state, no one will have the right to interfere with him."

The entire country rallies about Khomeini, secular and Shiite alike, and suddenly, he is a national hero. It takes almost no time at all for the Shah to arrest and deport him. He flees to Paris, where he will spend fifteen years in exile, honing his hatred for America and the West to a fine, white point.

Title: Oil Made America What She Is Today

Imagine an America built without cheap, abundant oil, and you are no longer imagining America. No malls, no suburbs, no Home Depots. We naively cling to the belief that our hybrid cars will save us. But getting a Prius is not going to get you off the hook.

Don't get me wrong. It *definitely* is the only way to go. If every car on the road were a hybrid, our chances of avoiding Global Nuclear War go way up. It just doesn't change the fact that unless you're living naked in a hut in a glade somewhere, your life, and the oil flow, are enmeshed. You're married, baby. You're in bed with oil, and signs like "Not in our Name" protesting the Gulf 2003 war mean you're an idiot. And the next time you start to get all enraged about the fact that the Bushes are in bed with the Saudi Royal Family, remember that you are too. The Bushes are just accruing more capital while they're lying there. It's in your name the second you take a pill, use a computer, or get dressed. It's in your name when you buy a toy for your child or put her cheerios in a Ziploc bag. It's in your name when you touch anything that doesn't grow out of the earth or have a face and unless you grew or raised those things, they got processed or wrapped or transported by oil. Not in My Name? That's a fairy tale we're way too old to believe in.

Oil is more than the engine that runs our economy. It *is* our economy. No oil, no America. Peak production of oil will occur as early as 2010 and as late as 2030. Some experts believe it is peaking right now. That means that half of all the oil on earth is already gone. That's why every country who is addicted to oil, and China is now pushing ahead of us to the front of that line, every petrochemically addicted country will soon start acting the way addicts act when the supply runs out—committing unspeakable crimes to get hold of what's left.

It's a shame petrochemicals aren't more like gold, isn't it? In the old days, you'd just melt your idols down and make new ones when a new God came to town. You can recycle plastic, but you can't turn it back into oil. Think of the billions of Barbies out there—billions and billions of them. We could run the country for a year, if we could just get the oil back by melting a billion little household goddesses down.

Title: Once I Lived in Barbie's House

I lived in Barbie's house once. I lived there for several months. I don't mean in my mind, in my fantasy. I mean in her actual house, a small two story cottage in a gorgeous New England town. The Handlers bought it for their daughter Barbara in the 70s, after her messy divorce.

The house was next door to an artists' colony, and when I lived there the colony had just bought it, and was in the process of colonizing it. Barbara lived there for ten unhappy years. Alcohol was involved in this unhappiness, and often. Guns also played their part. During the colony's early years we never tired of doing the Barbie Bullet Above the Refrigerator re-enactment. The story we told went like this: He came home drunk. Barbie was waiting for him, drunker.

I imagine she was wearing, when she got home from the bar that night, a western cowgirl outfit—tight jeans, red high-heeled hand tooled cowboy boots, and a fringed suede jacket. I don't have this Barbie outfit, by the way. I wish I did. Fringe was the first clothes drying system, evolved by Native Americans as a brilliant method for wicking moisture away from the body of the garment, to dry the shirt out. There was no drying Barbie out, however.

(*I dress Barbie in Nighty Negligee.*)

She changed into Nighty Negligee, stock number 965, manufactured in 1962, as soon as she got home, hoping that her current Ken would walk in the door and the clouds of pink chiffon would encircle them in a floating sea of pastel love. He didn't, so she kept drinking. She hugged her little stuffed dog—

(*I hold up the dog.*)

—an adorable pink pup with blue ears and a black pearl nose—close to her cool, perfect breasts which are just barely visible beneath the teasing peek-a-boo pink folds, and she drinks some more.

Hours later, half passed out on her empty bed, she hears his car pull up in the drive. The rage wells up inside her. She grabs a gun from the bedside table. Still clutching her little pink dog, she staggers to the top of the stairs. Ken crashes in through the back door. She floats—or so it would seem to someone watching her in her billowing, sleep wrinkled sad chiffon—she floats down the stairs and aims. She fires. The shot goes wild, it lodges above the refrigerator, where the bullet will remain, a source of entertainment for colonists in years to come. She fires again. This time her aim is true, and it lodges in his knee. He goes down. He screams. She screams. No one hears the shots or the screaming because there's no one living next door, the artists colony isn't there yet, it's 1979, Americans are listening to the Bee Gees and flocking to the first *Star Trek* movie, while in Iran the Shah's regime has crumbled, and the Ayatollah Khomeini's followers are storming the U.S. Embassy in Tehran. Barbie drops the gun, calls 9-1-1, and crumples in a puddle of pink on the floor to await the police.

She does not look so good in her mug shot. Barbie is pushing 40, and the years have not been all that kind to her. To her body, yes, the breasts still perky, the legs still perfect. It's her face that shows the drink and the disappointment and the years.

A china doll, barring an accident, holds its looks. Put it on a shelf, it will look the same 40 years later as it did when you put it there. Not a Barbie. Maybe the plastic we make now will last for centuries, but we were just learning how to use petrochemicals to make things like Barbie dolls, and a lot of the soft plastics we made then degrade. Barbie's body is still great—made of a slightly different, harder kind of plastic. It's the face that shows the ravages of time. The lipstick is smeary and looks clumsily applied, missing in places. Across the nose and cheeks, there is a thick greasy smear. The eye makeup is also eroding; the bright blue eye shadow running into the smudged eyeliner. The 40-year-old Barbie doll, with rare exceptions, looks exactly the way the 40-year-old drunken, lipstick smeared Barbara looked that night.

Title: The House of Saud Is Falling Down

I've matched as many Barbie shoes as is humanly possible, and still have about a dozen pairs left. The shoes were always the problem with Barbie. For one thing, they always fell off. The dog was always getting them, or your mother was sucking them up in the vacuum cleaner. If you played with other girls, you never could keep track of whose shoes were whose.

I watch TV while I sort my Barbie outfits. We have two huge TV's, one in the family room—which has a red fireplace and red furniture, and one in the red room, which has…I'll leave that to your imagination. It's hard to understand that the house will be sold, that another family will live here. My parents built it, and even when everybody else in the neighborhood moved out and bought houses in the newer subdivisions, they never dreamed of moving away. Every time she drove up the street, my mother would look at it, and say, as if it were a brand new thought, as if she were discovering it for the first time: "It's a nice house." Every single time. Lately, whenever I drive up the street, just before I turn into the driveway, I hear her say it, so I say it with her. It's a nice house.

It's a Sunday, and while I randomly put the remaining shoes into bags with outfits they couldn't possibly go with, I watch "Face the Nation." They're talking about the monarchy in Saudi Arabia, the trouble it's in, and how quickly it, and its stabilizing influence, could go. One of the guests says that the House of Saud has already begun to fall. Within four years, she says, there will be a coup, the royal family will be out, and Saudi Arabia will not be called Saudi Arabia anymore.

And then it hits me. Saudi Arabia is called Saudi the way George Forman's Grill is called George Forman's. Because it belongs to the Saudi Family.

It is one of the great ironies of the 2003 war and ongoing occupation that we really didn't go to war to have access to Iraq's oil fields. We went to retain our access to Saudi Arabia's. Saddam Hussein in power destabilized the Middle East, threatened Saudi Arabia's monarchy, and made our relations with the house of Saud and its oil precarious. So—Hussein had to go. The research I did made it clear—the plans to regime change Iraq were in the works long before 9/11.

Title: We Have to Believe That It's Oil

Of course, the thing about research is—when you're searching for a clear, unobstructed way to understand something, you tend to find it. And you just ignore the facts that clutter up the view. But the research I did made one thing abundantly clear: We can save ourselves. We can save the world. All we lack is the political will. All we lack is the courage to jump off the runaway stagecoach before it goes over the cliff. You've seen that movie since you were a kid. You know what happens if you don't jump in time.

We have to believe that it's oil. Because if we don't, we won't change. We won't sacrifice. We won't jump in time. I know that to say that everything that's wrong with what we do abroad is because of oil is sloppy thinking, at worst. At best, it's selective thinking—true, but not complete. But sometimes you're falling and you need somebody to throw you something. You need a rope. A rope's not very wide. But it's easier to throw than, say, an entire marble staircase. And oil is the only rope I know of that can get the job done.

You know all that deck furniture we've been rearranging on the Titanic? You know what I'm talking about. Your 401Ks, your children's college funds, your hours at the gym, your non-surgical facelift? You really think any of that's going to make a difference when the Saudi oil stops flowing?

And I have no right at all to preach to anyone about any of this.

I have an SUV.

Ten years ago I was driving to the store for a gallon of milk and got hit by a teenager, and some deck furniture impulse made me go out and buy something big, something huge, something—titanic, something that I thought would be unsinkable, in a car crash sort of way. Never mind that SUV's aren't safer for the occupants, just more dangerous for those in the cars they hit, I *felt* safer. It isn't even a big SUV, as SUVs go—it's a Pathfinder. And I love that Pathfinder.

But. The Pathfinder has to go. I'm putting an ad in the newspaper. Someone else can use it to destroy the world. I'm letting it go.

Let me say again. I love my Pathfinder. I really, really do. I spend a lot of time, moving from place to place in it. I'm like a lot of people, who spend more time in their cars than they do in bed. I think most people spend more time in their cars than they do in love.

I don't take the Pathfinder when I go to the cemetery.

I use my dad's car sometimes, but usually I ride my bike or walk. The cemetery is so close to our house, it's almost impossible to go anywhere without passing it. It's over six years, I know I should stop going there, I know it's time to move on. I move on in my own way. I move on from spring flowers like peonies and phlox to summer flowers like lilies and lisianthus to fall flowers like cosmos and mums. Each time, a small miracle. It's an ancient ritual, who knows how long we've been doing it, bringing flowers to our dead. Who knows when one day it will work. When the small miracles build up, a hundred billion, a billion billion small, every day miracles. Someday, not for me, but for somebody, the miracle will work.

Title: Petro-Regime

The facts are these: We don't live in a democracy anymore. We live in a petro-regime. Which wouldn't be *so* bad, except we live on the wrong side of it. We live at the bottom of the flow.

Is there hope? Of course there is. Sometimes, even when I get really scared, I calm myself down by thinking about Greed. I think we can count on it. Greed is what got us into this mess, and greed is what can get us out of it. I have hopes that some really smart, *really* greedy people are right now cooking up how they can make a fortune in the new "post-petroleum economy." If they hurry, they might even be able to come up with an alternative to oil before global warming kills us all. Yes, I think we can count on greed. But that's just an indication of how scared I am.

My brother comes to down to Springfield again with one of his daughters. We divide up the linens, the silver, the crystal. I say to him, "Do you know what we're doing in the Middle East, do you know we've been regime changing for years?" I'd grown up, like a lot of people, believing that until the Vietnam War, America had been the world's official Knight in Shining Armor, flying in like Superman to make right and vanquish wrong. When I start telling my brother that when it came to the Middle East, we'd pretty much traded in our Good Guy white hat for something, if not black, at least dark grey, when I give him the facts and the dates, the incredible things we've done, in the name of oil, for over fifty years—I expect him to register, if not shock, at least righteous indignation.

But he doesn't. Instead, he just says, patiently, as if I'd asked him why night follows day, "We needed the oil, Sherry. We had to protect our access to it." This scares me. I say, "But the oil's not *ours*." This scares *him*. He looks at me like *I'm* crazy. I look at him like *he's* crazy. And then I go get him some more bubble wrap for the sterling silver punch bowl.

Title: I've Been Scared For a Long Time

I've been scared for a long time. I've been scared since the Israeli Olympic team was slaughtered in 1972. Since that day, I have never found myself in a room with more than ten Jews without checking for alternative exits, calculating the height of the windows, and identifying objects that could serve as possible weapons in a crisis. Imagine how hard it is to shop at Zabar's under these conditions. When I walk into a temple or synagogue, I still do a quick calculus on the bullet deflecting density of prayer books and pew backs. I keep an eye out for old, frail people and children to fling out of harm's way. I feel ridiculous, but I feel justified. 1973—3 Americans killed in the Israeli lounge at the Athens airport in a grenade attack. 1974—bombs bring down TWA 841 on its way from Tel Aviv to NY.

1979. There's a revolution in Iran. The Shah is overthrown, which means the Ayatollah Khomeini, who has been in exile in France since 1964, returns triumphantly to Tehran. He immediately whips resentment against the United States into rabid anti-Americanism. Then President Carter makes an incredible political blunder. He responds with compassion to the Shah's request to come to America for treatment of his advanced cancer. Anti-Americanism spikes as rumors spread that the Shah's illness is just a sham, dreamed up to mask a CIA plot to return the Shah to power

November 5, 1979. The U.S. embassy in Tehran is seized by Islamist militants. They take fifty-two hostages. Frantic embassy employees, shredding madly up until the last second, manage to destroy the most sensitive documents, just before they're overrun.

No one dreamed the occupation, a symbolic gesture, would last more than a week. But Khomeini has been waiting for this moment, stewing in a juice of hatred for the U.S. since 1964. He publicly endorses the seizure of the embassy. And then one of the occupying militants, who has been staring at the piles of shredded documents, gets a brilliant idea. Expert carpet weavers are brought in, women who magically weave the shredded paper back into documents. Documents which seem to imply that the U.S. *is* plotting the Shah's return. The hostage crisis goes from weeks to months, months to over a year.

I was living in LA during the crisis. I had a friend named Jeff who owned a luxury condo, and we used to get high, and take ice sculptures—he always kept three or four in his freezer, a mermaid, a clamshell, a giant lobster—and go down to the Jacuzzi, turn on the jets and watch the sculptures bob and disintegrate. Jeff worked for Rand, the government think tank in Santa Monica. He was a super brain, an MIT boy, he was paid a huge salary because he was on the hottest team Rand had, working on something of vital interest to the U.S. government: how we would continue to get an uninterrupted supply of oil when World War III broke out in the Middle East. Not if. When.

It is difficult to be scared when you are thoroughly baked, watching a mermaid bob in a Jacuzzi. But I managed. And I wasn't alone. In homes all across the country, Americans were starting to ask, "How did it come to this?" And "Why didn't we see it coming in time?" And they were starting to ask something else, too: "Why do they hate us so much?" But when Khomeini took control of our Embassy, he was only picking up where he had left off in 1964. America was his enemy. This was obvious. Except over here. Suddenly, it seemed to Americans, we were hated. *Suddenly*, as if from nowhere.

Think of that hate like a string of pearls. Think of America, putting one after the other in place. Start with the Status of Forces Agreement that enrages and creates the power of Khomeini in 1964.

String your way here from that.

Title: *One of the Last Things*

One of the last things we do for our dead is pick out the clothes their body will wear in the casket. I picked out a blue two-piece dress for my mother—it wasn't super dressy, but it was nice enough. If it were a Barbie outfit, it would have had a name like—Lunch with Midge at the Olive Garden. It had a little pattern on it, white anchors. Mom wore it a lot. She felt comfortable in it. She had prettier things, but I picked it for that.

I also picked out—a bra. Underwear. A slip. Hose—but they told me, no shoes. No need for shoes. The coffin is closed from the waist down. Wherever the dead are going, they will not be walking there. And—a pair of earrings. Jewelry is chief among a woman's treasures. And to bury your mother with treasure seems right. I stood there, for a long time, in front of her jewelry box. I tried to pick what I thought she would want. It's hard to understand, at that moment, in particular, when you are touching the things that your mother wore next to her body, it's hard to understand that it doesn't really matter, anymore, to her. That these things no longer matter to the dead. You go through your mother's closet, through the dresser, the shelves, her jewelry box. It is a small stack, a very small pile of things, you hold it in your hands and you feel how small. Then you hand it to the people at the funeral parlor. It's hard. It's hard because there is no miracle about it at all. It feels less like a miracle than just about anything you know.

If I were picking out clothes for Barbie to be buried in, I'd put her in this.

(*I take out Senior Prom.*)

This was my favorite Barbie outfit. It came in another color, but it seems I passed up the rare, practically priceless apricot and marigold version, and instead bought the common, easy to find emerald green and sapphire blue one. Its name is Senior Prom.

(*I dress Barbie in Senior Prom.*)

I wouldn't be going to my Senior Prom. I would be asked, of course, Greg, the boy next door, asked me, but it was a standing rule in our house—no dating non-Jews. And there weren't any Jews at Glendale High School, except my brother, my sister, and me. Greg took somebody else.

After Mother died there was a package from Greg, he lives in Minnesota now. In it were four envelopes, he didn't know all our different addresses, so he sent them all together to Daddy. He'd sent each one of us a letter, my father, my sister, my brother. Me. A man I had not exchanged a word with in over 30 years wrote me about my mother. About the way she looked, handing a plate of cookies over the backyard fence. I think that in the end, it's the kindnesses you remember the longest, about a person. About a moment. About a dress. About a funeral. About an unlived prom.

(*I take out the box Barbie came in, start to put her away. But as I put the lid on the box I stop. I take her out of the box, and put her, wearing Senior Prom, into her Dream Car.*)

When something wonderful ends, you look desperately for the thing you could have done to stop it. My mother died, in an instant, from something so small. From a hole the size of a pinprick, they say it was probably a congenital weakness, always there, waiting, in her brain. That there was nothing we could have done. It's hard to understand that a life can drain out, so quickly. That the life of someone you love can slip away as fast, and as impossible to stop as the flickering lives of the images of people dying on TV vanish, in a war, far away.

Title: *When Something Wonderful Ends*

It was a bitter spring day when we buried my mother. It could have been warm and beautiful, but it was not.

The three of us children each spoke about my mother. I told a story about Henry James. Someone asked him for advice, about how to live in the world. He said, "You only have to know three things. One. You must always be kind. Two. You must always be kind. Three. You must always be kind."

Our mother's kindness was the earth on which we stood. We never doubted its power or its constancy, it was unconditional, like her love. She never doubted for an instant that goodness had the power to change the world.

When something wonderful ends, we need to know why it happened. If we know why it happened, there's a chance we can do something about taking better care of all the something wonderfuls we still have left.

Let's grow up. Let's put the toys, all the toys, away.

(*I start packing up all the Barbie clothes that are left and put them away.*)

Let's reclaim our lost soul acreage. Our government has failed us, is failing us, and will continue to fail us. Until we make it clear we're willing to change, to sacrifice. The thing about change is, it hurts. It hurts every day. It doesn't get necessarily better. That's not something we're used to. We're used to the Dream Life lived in the Dream Car. In the day, we're resplendent in Red Flare. In the evening, we knock 'em dead in Enchanted Evening. At night, we slip into Nighty Negligee, and if our Dream Date doesn't show up, on *our* terms, the way *we* want him—we take out our gun and start shooting. It's time we got it through our heads—there are no more dream dates where energy is concerned, and we are never again getting into a car that uses petrochemicals without understanding that it is a gun, and it is pointed at our heads.

Change is a kind of miracle. You have to believe in it first, before it can exist. In order for it to happen, you have to act like it already has. That's where the vertical nations have the edge on us. They aren't afraid of paying for the things they've decided are good. They know about the unseen, and how to act like it's the realest thing in the room.

They know how to believe in miracles.

My mother did too. She knew about the miracle of everyday life, of knowing what matters and what does not. Her only regret in life was that she was not much of a writer. She talked all the time about writing her autobiography, though. She already had the title. My mother could not bear to leave us, but we had all grown up and moved away from Springfield. We all assumed that she would outlive my father, and that when she died, and was buried next to him, there would be no one here after her. The title of her autobiography was: *No One To Tend My Grave.*

I have tried to tend it. With both hands, and a full heart, while the world ends, I have tried to tend her grave. I have tried to make a miracle. Just a small one, I admit that. But that's the point of the ritual, after all. It's why we need our dead, what we use them for. The great miracles of all the religions of the world are always accomplished standing on the graves of the dead.

> (*I put the Dream Car, with Barbie in it, into a large box. I close the box. All the Barbie toys are packed away.*)

It's time we grew up, and learned to tend our graves. Our dead, the 9/11 dead, the Iraqi war dead, both sides. Let us claim them all for ours. And honor them, as it is our right and obligation to do.

Let us honor them by making a miracle. Let the miracle we do for our dead be that we save the world.

> (*Something happens to the light. Maybe it's golden and magical. I don't know. Then, dozens of pictures of the flowers on my mother's grave, in a progression, six years of flowers:*
>   *spring, summer, fall,*
>   *spring, summer, fall,*
>   *spring, summer, fall,*
> *ripple across the stage.*)
> (*Fade to blackout.*)

End of Play

CLARISSE AND LARMON
by Deb Margolin

BIOGRAPHY

Deb Margolin is a playwright, performance artist and founding member of Split Britches Theater Company. She is the author of eight full-length solo performance pieces, which she has toured throughout the United States, and is the recipient of a 1999-2000 OBIE Award for Sustained Excellence of Performance. In February of 2001, PS122 presented Ms. Margolin's play *Three Seconds in the Key*, a meditation on illness, love and basketball, and the play was premiered officially under the auspices of New Georges at Baruch Performing Arts Center in April of 2004. Ms. Margolin has been artist-in-residence at Hampshire College and University of Hawaii and Zale writer-in-residence at Tulane University, and is currently an Associate Professor of Playwriting and Performance in Yale University's Theater Studies Program. A book of Ms. Margolin's performance pieces and plays, entitled *Of All The Nerve: Deb Margolin SOLO*, was published in 1999 by Cassell/Continuum Press. She was awarded the 2005 Richard H. Brodhead Prize for Teaching Excellence at Yale University, and the 2005 Kesselring Playwriting Prize.

ACKNOWLEDGMENTS

Clarisse and Larmon was presented in a non-Equity production for 5 performances as a part of the IGNITE Festival under the auspices of Synapse Productions in October 2006, starring Kathleen Chalfant and Shawn Eliot. The play had its world premiere in the Humana Festival of New American Plays in March 2007. It was directed by Jessica Burgess with the following cast and staff:

CLARISSE	Romi Dias
LARMON	Keith Randolph Smith
SOLDIER	Timo Aker
Scenic Designer	Paul Owen
Costume Designer	Susan Neason
Lighting Designer	Paul Werner
Sound Designer	Benjamin Marcum
Properties Designer	Doc Manning
Fight Director	Lee Look
Stage Managers	Michael D. Domue, Debra Anne Gasper
Production Assistant	Melissa Miller
Dramaturg	Joanna K. Donehower
Assistant Dramaturg	Diana Grisanti

CAST OF CHARACTERS

CLARISSE
LARMON
SOLDIER

Romi Dias and Keith Randolph Smith
in *Clarisse and Larmon*

31st Annual Humana Festival of New American Plays
Actors Theatre of Louisville, 2007
Photo by Harlan Taylor

CLARISSE AND LARMON

Lights up on LARMON *and* CLARISSE, *a tattered, middle-aged couple sitting at a nondescript wooden table. A* SOLDIER *is standing at attention before them. A photograph, unseen by the audience, is on the table at which* CLARISSE *and* LARMON *are seated. The room is like a small interrogation room: undecorated, spare, small and green in cast.*

CLARISSE. This is all you have?

SOLDIER. Yes. Yes, I'm afraid so.

LARMON. There was no other...evidence? No other...

SOLDIER. No, I'm afraid not.

LARMON. Why couldn't you have brought...brought...given us...the actual...part...instead of this...this photograph?

SOLDIER. I'm afraid it would have been...

CLARISSE. Why are you so *afraid* of everything?

SOLDIER. Pardon me, ma'am?

CLARISSE. You're afraid this and you're afraid that and you're afraid the other thing!

SOLDIER. Ma'am...

LARMON. Clarisse, it's just a figure of speech.

SOLDIER. I understand, sir; she's upset...

LARMON. That's no excuse!

CLARISSE. I'm not upset!

LARMON. All we have is this knee, shin, ankle and foot, and not even the real knee, shin, ankle or foot, just a *picture* of them, and that's all we have left, and you're NOT UPSET?

CLARISSE. No.

LARMON. We are bereft and aggrieved and we've lost everything and all we have is this bargain basement snapshot of the lower part of one of his legs...

CLARISSE. Left leg, in case you hadn't noticed...

LARMON. ...and you are not upset? You are not disturbed?

CLARISSE. You are yelling at me as if I've said something. I have not said anything.

LARMON. Well, say something!

CLARISSE. You make it sound so easy to say things!

SOLDIER. I am terribly sorry for your loss, sir. Madam. I will leave you alone now. Here is a photograph of me, and on the other side is a telephone number. Please don't hesitate to call me with any questions you may have.

(CLARISSE *takes photo of soldier and drops it on the floor.* CLARISSE *and* LARMON *stare at him. He salutes and exits, stage left.* CLARISSE *and* LARMON *stare at photograph of leg before them in silence.*)

CLARISSE. Why do you suppose...

LARMON. I can't...

CLARISSE. I don't...

(Silence.)

(They laugh.)

LARMON. Look...

CLARISSE. Look at what?

LARMON. Look at the decline of his toes, the way they go down so evenly in height, like climbing down a mountain, or a hill, or a flight of stairs.

CLARISSE. I think they look like a xylophone, like the different notes of the xylophone.

(Silence.)

LARMON. When you consider the whole thing, it looks like Italy.

CLARISSE. You only say that because they always told us in school that Italy is shaped like a boot.

LARMON. They told us that because it's true.

CLARISSE. It may be true, but that may or may not be why they told us that.

LARMON. What, dear?

CLARISSE. People have many different reasons for telling you things. Their being true is often not the reason.

LARMON. Of course. The truth is just an option.

CLARISSE. Look at his knee.

LARMON. What about it?

CLARISSE. He knelt on that knee. Knelt comes from the word knee.

LARMON. Yes! I never thought of that!

CLARISSE. I like it when parts of the body get turned into verbs!

LARMON. But in the past tense, it's always easier, because the body part is further away!

CLARISSE. Do you think so?

LARMON. Tell me some more body parts like that!

CLARISSE. Armed comes from the word arm and palmed from the word palm and muscled from the word muscle and headed from the word head and minded from the word mind.

LARMON. Yes! And did you hear about the woman who backed into an airplane propeller?

CLARISSE. No.

LARMON. *Disaster!* Haha!

(*Pause.*)

CLARISSE. He knelt...

LARMON. From the word knee...

CLARISSE. ...and made me pray for that lobster you killed.

LARMON. Bessie Behemoth.

CLARISSE. Why did you name that lobster? Why did you name it?

LARMON. I was just having fun.

CLARISSE. It upset the boy.

LARMON. I know. I'm sorry.

CLARISSE. He knelt and prayed for the soul of that lobster.

LARMON. Of Bessie. Yes.

CLARISSE. And then he apologized to things for throwing them in the garbage can.

LARMON. Did he?

CLARISSE. Yes. And he'd tell them what a beautiful thing it would be to go in the garbage! How it was the beginning of a long journey, on trucks, to open landfills, through fire and into eternity.

LARMON. He described all of that?

CLARISSE. Yes.

LARMON. Well maybe he was prescient.

CLARISSE. It sounds like a description of being condemned to Hell.

(*Silence.*)

This knee. This shin, this foot. They were inside my body once.

LARMON. Clarisse dearest...

CLARISSE. They always say putting things back in the earth is a return to where things came from, but he came from Me. From my body. He didn't come from some briar patch, or golf course, he came from ME. They should put him back...

LARMON. Dearest Clarisse...he wouldn't fit anymore...

CLARISSE. He wouldn't fit...

LARMON. I...I was thinking...when that...when that...man...was here, that...man...I was thinking: shouldn't they have covered it up...shouldn't it have been covered up, at least, with a blanket or a sheet or...or...something...wouldn't it have been more dignified...

CLARISSE. Yes! Yes it would have!

LARMON. But then I was thinking...the human body is so indecipherable when it's under something.

CLARISSE. That's why they cover it

LARMON. You mean so it looks like nothing!

CLARISSE. That's right! It looks like nothing!

LARMON. So then we would have seen nothing.

CLARISSE. Yes.

LARMON. That would have been torture. I yearn to see him.

CLARISSE. I know you do.

LARMON. But he's gone.

CLARISSE. And we have nothing.

LARMON. Nothing but this leg.

CLARISSE. This *picture* of a leg.

LARMON. *His* leg.

CLARISSE. Is it his?

LARMON. Let's look.

(*They stare at the photo.*)

What do you see?

CLARISSE. Well, nothing really, just the kneecap, the shin with a bit of calf peeking around, the foot.

LARMON. The metatarsal arch.

CLARISSE. Which is that?

LARMON. (*Indicating.*) This here, this swell and the corresponding part under the foot.

CLARISSE. Did his look like that? His foot?

LARMON. I don't know why, but I can't remember. I'm trying to remember his feet.

CLARISSE. It might be easier if we had a picture of both feet. Two feet when put together remind of you of the person.

LARMON. Perhaps we should call that man; maybe he has another photograph of the other foot.

CLARISSE. If he'd had a photograph of the other foot, wouldn't he have left it?

LARMON. Not necessarily.

CLARISSE. Why? Why would he not have left whatever he had?

LARMON. Maybe he wanted to make it as easy as possible for us.

CLARISSE. It isn't easy to leave us with so little.

LARMON. He may not have known. He may have thought the less the better.

CLARISSE. How could anyone be so stupid.

LARMON. Dear, you are just upset.

CLARISSE. I am not upset.

LARMON. (*Returning to photograph.*) And look at all that hair! Look at it all! He was very manly! He had very hairy legs!

CLARISSE. When he was a baby I used to soap his shins and he would kick his little feet and laugh. I bathed him in the birdbath in the summers!

LARMON. Did you? I never knew that!

CLARISSE. Yes! He loved it! When it was warm and it was hot I would do that! And there were beautiful birds, one of them had a flaming red head and polka dotted wings in black and white. He was very powerful, a bossy, powerful bird.

LARMON. How very nice, Clarisse!

CLARISSE. He was a boy the birds would allow to touch them. He held each bird in the palms of his hands and he kissed them.

LARMON. You're just being romantic.

CLARISSE. He put feathers under my pillow. All different kinds.

LARMON. Clarisse…

CLARISSE. It's true, Larmon.

LARMON. Who knows what's true?

CLARISSE. Don't be silly.

LARMON. Let us say only true things about the dead, Clarisse, only true things.

CLARISSE. The expression is actually: let us say only *good* things about the dead. *Nil nisi bonum de mortuis.* Nothing but good things about the dead.

LARMON. They meant *kind* things, not *false* things. There is always something kind to say. That doesn't make them false.

CLARISSE. When you can only say kind things, and no unkind things, you leave a lot out, and that is false.

LARMON. What unkind things are there to say about the boy?

CLARISSE. He's dead.

(*Silence.*)

LARMON. I'll pay you for every true thing. I'll make you rich at our little funeral; every true thing you say about the boy I'll pay you.

CLARISSE. Is truth such a luxury, then?

LARMON. Yes, Clarisse dear, let's pretend it's very expensive. I'll pay you for every true thing you say at our little funeral.

CLARISSE. How much? How much will you pay me?

LARMON. One hundred. I'll pay you one hundred for every true thing you say.

CLARISSE. But how will you know if it's true?

LARMON. I will know.

CLARISSE. But what if you think it isn't true and it is?

LARMON. Then we'll call the man in the photograph.

CLARISSE. Does it have to be big or can it be small?

LARMON. It doesn't matter.

CLARISSE. Alright.

LARMON. Please begin.

CLARISSE. Alright. He died overseas.

LARMON. One hundred.

CLARISSE. He died in war.

LARMON. Two hundred.

CLARISSE. He...he...he wrote us letters sometimes.

LARMON. Three hundred.

CLARISSE. The letters were factual and lacking tenderness and he said he could hear screaming all the time and he said one time he thought guys were horsing around but they were being beheaded.

LARMON. Four hundred.

CLARISSE. He farted very loudly and thought it was funny.

LARMON. Five hundred.

CLARISSE. He...was in pieces. Not many people are in pieces.

LARMON. Seven hundred. For two true things.

CLARISSE. When he was little he couldn't be trusted around flowers. He ate them.

LARMON. Eight hundred.

CLARISSE. He was dead before he died, something already killed him.

LARMON. What does that mean?

CLARISSE. Will you pay me or not?

LARMON. Explain what that means.

CLARISSE. He hated his father.

LARMON. *I won't pay for that!*

CLARISSE. He was already dead!

LARMON. Let's stop this now, Clarisse.

CLARISSE. You've paid for it, Larmon. You've paid for it.

LARMON. Let's call that terrible man in the photograph. Look on the back and get the number. Tell him we're angry. Tell him we're very angry and we want our son back.

CLARISSE. Larmon, I'm sorry...

LARMON. Tell him, Clarisse. I'll tell him. Get the photograph and let's call him. The phone number is on that paper. Tell him he took our son and we want him back. Tell him they seduced our boy. Like in the *Odyssey*. Tell him our son is on the water and sirens are singing and we insist that they return him. I'll tell them. Get the number, Clarisse. Those damned damned liars! Those stupid men who believe in Other Stupid Men!

CLARISSE. Think, Larmon, think! Why would he even go? Why would he even want to go away? It's not that man's fault or his picture, Larmon. It's not that man's fault. He's too stupid for anything to be his fault. Why did the boy go away? Who would go where there is nothing but dying all day and praying you won't all night? We didn't give him anything, he didn't think he was anything, he thought he could become hairy feet and manly legs when he was away, he hated you, Larmon, he was able to hate those foreigners because he hated you.

LARMON. You just need to blame his death on someone you know!

CLARISSE. I need nothing!

LARMON. He did not hate me! They told him it was...

CLARISSE. Did you ever notice his legs before? How hairy and manly they were? Did you ever notice his legs before, Larmon?

LARMON. I...there were...I had many fishing trips with him...

CLARISSE. Now here is his leg.

LARMON. It's probably not his! They're liars!

CLARISSE. Now here is his leg. Let us admire his hairy manly leg and his metaphysical arch.

LARMON. Metatarsal.

(*Silence. They stare at the photograph once again.*)

Look at his ankle.

CLARISSE. There's no hair at all around a one-inch radius from the bone.

LARMON. I wonder why that is.

CLARISSE. The bone is so commanding, so majestic. The bone is the palace of a King, and the hairs are peasants, walking backwards away from the Great One's presence.

LARMON. You are so whimsical today.

CLARISSE. There's a shadow on the big toe.

LARMON. *His* big toe.

CLARISSE. It must be a bruise.

LARMON. A shame, really, the photo is not in color.

CLARISSE. I think it's better, dear.

LARMON. Why better?

CLARISSE. It just is. And another bruise on the shinbone.

LARMON. *His* shinbone. It must have been an explosion.

CLARISSE. You think so?

LARMON. Yes. A big explosion.

CLARISSE. I'm so sorry for him.

LARMON. Don't be sorry for him, don't be sorry for him.

CLARISSE. Let's bury him.

LARMON. Bury him...

CLARISSE. Let's bury him back where he came from.

LARMON. Clarisse...

CLARISSE. (*Taking photograph and crumpling it and tearing it.*) Let's bury him back where he came from.

LARMON. (*Grabbing for the photograph.*) Stop it! Give me that!

CLARISSE. Please, Larmon, please...

> (CLARISSE *gets up from the table after crushing and tearing photograph into a small ball of ruined pieces. She stands stiffly and quietly, then reaches into her clothing, under her skirt, inside her underpants, and begins stuffing the pieces into her crotch. When all the pieces are inside her skirt and panties, she stops, exhausted.* LARMON *rises slowly, comes over to her, kneels down and puts his face where the photograph is. LIGHTS FADE DOWN VERY SLOWLY.*)

End of Play

BATCH
AN AMERICAN BACHELOR/ETTE PARTY
SPECTACLE IN SIX SEXES

conceived by Whit MacLaughlin and Alice Tuan
with text by Alice Tuan
created by New Paradise Laboratories

Batch
an american bachelor/ette party spectacle
in six sexes

Conceived by Whit MacLaughlin and Alice Tuan

With Text by Alice Tuan

With Additional Text by:
Mary McCool, Matt Saunders, McKenna Kerrigan, Lee Ann Etzold, Jeb Krieger, Aaron Mumaw and Whit MacLaughlin.

Created by New Paradise Laboratories

BIOGRAPHIES

Alice Tuan is the author of *Last of the Suns* (Ma-Yi Theater Company, Berkeley Repertory Theatre), *Ikebana* (East West Players), *Some Asians* (Perishable Theatre, UMASS Amherst), *Manilova* (New Georges), *The Roaring Girle* (Foundry Theatre) and the hypertext play *Coastline* (Serious Play! Theatre Ensemble, The Edinburgh Fringe). *Ajax (por nobody)*, presented by New York's Flea Theater and performed at the Melbourne Fringe in September 2001, is archived in The Billy Rose Collection at Lincoln Center and was recently published in the anthology *New Downtown Now*. Her short plays *F.E.T.C.H.* and *Coco Puffs* were seen at previous Humana Festivals. Ms. Tuan received an emerging artist notice from New York's Colbert Award for Excellence as well as Los Angeles's Richard E. Sherwood Award. She holds an M.F.A. in Creative Writing from Brown University and is based in Los Angeles.

Whit MacLaughlin is the Obie Award-winning artistic director of Philadelphia's New Paradise Laboratories (NPL). Founded in 1996, NPL has performed in venues such as Ontological Theater and P.S. 122 in New York City, the Walker Art Center in Minneapolis and The Andy Warhol Museum in Pittsburgh. Mr. MacLaughlin also directs freelance around the country. He is the recipient of a 2002 Pew Charitable Trust Fellowship in Performance Art. His work with NPL includes *The Fab 4 Reach the Pearly Gates*, depicting the Beatles at the end of time; *This Mansion is a Hole*, a deconstruction of the philosophies of Hugh Hefner; *Rrose Selavy Takes a Lover in Philadelphia*, an examination of Philadelphia's utopian history; and *Prom*, an anthropological work for young adults.

94

ACKNOWLEDGMENTS

Batch: An American Bachelor/ette Party Spectacle premiered at the Humana Festival of New American Plays in March 2007. It was directed by Whit MacLaughlin with the following cast and staff:

Round 1 and Beyond:
Betsy Competitive (the bride) .... McKenna Kerrigan
Matty Jay (former maid of honor) .... Jeb Kreager
Betty Lee (the soon-to-be maid of honor) .... Lee Ann Etzold
Becky Steem .... Matt Saunders
Maya Faye .... Aaron Mumaw
Mary Bette .... Mary McCool

Round 2 and Beyond:
Taggis (the groom) .... Aaron Mumaw
Chet (best man) .... Matt Saunders
Smoak (in a jacket) .... Jeb Kreager
Lars .... Lee Ann Etzold
Mike .... Mary McCool
Wesley .... McKenna Kerrigan

Also:
Accomplices: Marie A. Antoinette, Special K, Punch, Punch and Punch; The Saynads, Myclops, Dancers and a Taxi Cab Driver

Scenic Designer .... Matt Saunders
Costume Designer .... Rosemarie McKelvey
Lighting Designer .... Brian J. Lilienthal
Sound Designer .... Whit MacLaughlin
Video Designer .... Jorge Cousineaeu
Properties Designer .... Ron Riall
Stage Manager .... Nancy Pittelman
Production Assistant .... Danielle Teague-Daniels
Dramaturg .... Adrien-Alice Hansel
Assistant Dramaturg .... Diana Grisanti
Directing Assistant .... Joanna K. Donehower

Batch was commissioned by the Actors Theatre of Louisville, and was originally performed at the Connection, a nightclub in Louisville, KY.

"No worthy problem can be solved on its original plane of conception."
—Einstein as quoted by George Saunders

The Company
in *Batch*

31st Annual Humana Festival of New American Plays
Actors Theatre of Louisville, 2007
Photo by Harlan Taylor

DIRECTOR/CO-CREATOR'S NOTE

Batch: An American Bachelor/ette Party Spectacle is a reinvention of the Greek Satyr Play, both literally (there are satyrs in it!) and derivationally. It is part of a series of pieces created with my company, New Paradise Laboratories. The first piece in the series is called *Prom* and was developed in collaboration with the Children's Theatre Company of Minneapolis as a pilot project for their teen theatre initiative. The third piece is tentatively called *Mort* and will explore the phenomenon of Funeral Parties. It goes without saying that the series has as its primary subject three types of American rite-of-passage parties.

All three pieces eschew traditional dramaturgical development and spring from what you might call "party logic"—the specific hopes, dreams, and narrative structure of the party experience. There is a measure of traditional character development in both *Batch* and *Prom* in addition to an odd time sense, but neither are character dramas, per se. After all, what happens in them and at parties? You go to a party for a purpose, holding some vision of a special social environment as a possibility; maybe you get a bit intoxicated, and every once in a while the sky opens up and you go home having a truly extraordinary experience. Every once in a while. Otherwise, parties can range in quality from humdrum to diverting, but one kinda hopes for the transcendental.

I have always been intrigued, like most theatre people, with the specter of the Greek festival play experience. It's an old saw, but we assume that the Greek plays had a celebratory function, were sprung from dance, and that most of the audience would have been familiar with the subject matter of the plays. The fun, the dash, the panache, the power of the plays came from the *way* that the familiar stories were told. And I've always been obsessed with the way that the Greek play experience was organized symphonically to marshal the energies of prophesy and mythology in the service of some sort of collective experience.

We have striven to lasso some of that sort of energy with *Batch*. In performance, it's almost like a crazy, delirious dream-dance. And it springs from a common experience—most of us have attended a pre-nup party or, maybe, have purposely NOT attended. The piece trades on an audience's preconceptions of these parties. I would say that *Batch* really comes to life as an "experience" rather than as a play. I applaud Alice, our intrepid playwright, for trying to wrestle it onto the page. *Batch* truly was a mind-boggling collaboration, and like much of my favorite theatre, it exists primarily in the memories of the beholders.

One last spin: I am quite excited by the fact that *Prom* was created for young audiences. *Batch* was available to those old enough to gain entry to a piece with a light X rating. The pieces, oddly, seem to fit together into a mosaic that is often disallowed in contemporary culture, late childhood into early adulthood, but which, in reality, describes a continuity that is very much at the heart of life itself: growth, sex, and the mysterious transformation of youth into adulthood and social responsibility.

—Whit MacLaughlin

Batch
an american bachelor/ette party spectacle in six sexes

Four screens surround a square stage with an underneath. There is a hole in the corner where batches of folk enter and exit vertically.

The screen world is depicted in Courier.

BRIDE **PREAMBLE**

BETSY *stands alone, live. She imperceptibly turns.*

The screens,
like an orbit,
focus onto TAGGIS—
walking,"walking"with BETSY.
Her fingers are crossed behind her back.
She regards him.
They continue to "walk" together.
Claudine Longet sings "The Look of Love".

The guests arrive and set up camera and pose.

TAGGIS's image fades from the screens.

Former moth **1. Selecting a Date and Time**

MATTY. So when…

BETTY LEE. Oh wait! *Soon to be moth*

(BETTY LEE *flips camera on and:*

We see the party from the Onstage Cam,
standing like cake icons.)

ANNOUNCER. (*Voice over.*) BACHELORETTE PARTY: A PRE-NUPTUAL AGREEMENT WHERE YOU PLAN A GOODBYE TO ALL YOUR FORMER AND FUTURE LOVERS!

(*Ding!*)

BETTY LEE. (*About video-ing.*) For posterity.

MATTY. …so when are you available, then?

(*Pause.*)

BETSY. Well…

MATTY. It's still on, isn't it?

BETTY LEE. Of course it's on!

99

BECKY STEEM. Of course it's on…

MATTY. I just can't tell anymore.

BECKY STEEM. …Like a Catholic's condom, it's on.

    (MAYA *enters. The veil of maya is upon us.*)

MARY BETTE. Maya

MAYA. Hello everybody. Sorry I'm late.

MARY BETTE. Might not even be happening.

MAYA. Really.

BECKY STEEM. It will happen…

MARY BETTE. I'm not so sure.

BECKY STEEM. …like a black girl in the White House, it will happen.

MAYA. You kill it, Mary Bette?

MARY BETTE. No, Maya.

BETTY LEE. Shush you two. It will happen.

MATTY. Because we should proh-bably have it within the week since, since the, the, the 'wedding' itself is, is in, in a, in a week (?), that's what you said yes, Betsy? 'In, like, a week'?

MARY BETTE. Not even a date yet.

MAYA. What's the point.

MATTY. Oh I don't know, I don't know anymore.

BETSY. We're not really doing this are we?

    (*The party nods in unison. Ding!*
    She collapses.

    Betsy lays unconscious on the screen.

    They pick her up.)

MATTY. I'm still Maid of Honor, right? —Betsy?

BETTY LEE. I've compiled a list of themes—Greek, Egyptian, or Roman…

MATTY. I'm not…I'm not…I'm not…

BETTY LEE. …western, oriental or southern…village people, monster truck or traditional American…

MATTY. I'm not the Maid of Honor anymore, Betsy? Betsy? Betsy?

2. Choose a Theme

MARY BETTE. So what *is* the theme, Betty Lee?

BETSY. I don't need a theme.

MATTY. O Betsy

BETTY LEE. There's a spa option

MATTY. We'll get you good and scrubbed

MAYA. Who's paying?

MATTY. Well

BETTY LEE. Well

BETSY. I don't think this should cost any…

MARY BETTE. If we go to the mall—

BETTY LEE. Something *special* for God's sake. Our Betsy, our darling favorite Betsy, is deciding to *marry* (*Bleetingly.*)

BECKY STEEM. A man even

MATTY. And what's wrong with that?

BECKY STEEM. I didn't say anything about wrong—

MATTY. Your tone did.

(BETSY *wonders how she is gonna get through her friends.*)

BECKY STEEM. What *have* you got there, Matty Jay?

MATTY. It's a condom corsage.

MARY BETTE. You consider Taggis a 'man?'

MAYA. His equipment says so.

MARY BETTE. That shit can be strapped on, shit. Betsy just turns into whatever fits her moment. Can't face the music, she just switches tunes.

(MARY BETTE *kisses* BETSY *deeply.*)

MAYA. Enough. (*Watches more.*) Enough, Mary Bette.

MARY BETTE. By any means necessary, right Betsy?

MAYA. I completely support whatever decision you make, Bets.

(BETSY *is grateful to* MAYA *through her eyes.*

MAYA *shoots* BETSY *with the Onstage Cam.*)

BETSY. And what are the other options?

(*Ding! She collapses.*

BETSY *lays unconscious.*

The party sets her up again.)

3. Location

BETTY LEE. Well there's the winery—

MATTY. Who'd drive?

BETTY LEE. Or the park for a picnic.

MATTY. I don't trust those grills.

BETTY LEE. Or the skating rink.

MATTY. You all skate?

BECKY STEEM. The skating rink is not just for skating.

MATTY. What is it for, Becky Steem: *hooking out?*

MAYA. I thought this was supposed to be a 'hot' affair

MARY BETTE. With Betsy's oh so cold now —

BETSY. Mary Bette.

> (*Pause.*)

BETSY. It was a choice.

MARY BETTE. Straight up.

> (*Pabdul.*)

BETSY. *Idiots.* It's real.

MARY BETTE. So versatile, you are, Betsy?

BETSY. It's not gonna be like any marriage anyone could ever have dreamed of.

MATTY. How about the Busch Brewery?

BETSY. We've never even kissed yet.

MAYA. It's true.

MARY BETTE. Yeah right.

MATTY. They give away a free—

BETSY. We've never touched.

ALL. *What!?*

MARY BETTE. O please!

BETTY LEE. It's true.

MATTY. They give away a free pitcher for parties larger than 5.

BETTY LEE. Who will drive?

MATTY. We'll get a limo.

BETTY LEE. Who will pay?

MAYA. My daddy has a boat.

MATTY. You all swim?

MARY BETTE. And there are other fish in the sea.

BETTY LEE. Remember: our goal is to have fun, blow off steam and create fond memories—not nightmares—for you, Betsy Competitive.

BETSY. (*Looking at* BECKY.) Whose steam are we blowing?

> (*POW!*
> *All but* BETSY *collapse.*
> BETSY *has a sort of victory dance.*)

BETSY. (*Sings.*) *not gonna be like any other marriage, do do do do do do*

> (The CHORUS, comprised of the 6 performers
> in neutral gaze, look on.)

4. Poll

Onstage Cam.

MAYA. We should definitely get a stripper.

ALL. YES! OO! HOO!

MAYA. Two of 'em!

MARY BETTE. No, THREE!

BETSY. Not necessarily

MATTY. Where would we call?

BECKY STEEM. With epic cocks.

ALL. BECKY STEEM!

MATTY. Becky Steem? Where would we call?

BETSY. NO no no no no no...

BECKY STEEM. That's what she wants. Look in her eyes.

BETSY. Sure, Becky Steem: if you know of any, bring 'em all along.

BECKY STEEM. I will.

BETTY LEE. Well I have a menu of men here, so *many* delicious dishes, ladies!

MARY BETTE. Well if you think about it—

BECKY STEEM. O well there you go thinking about it.

MARY BETTE. It *is* the one thing that Taggis would load his gun for.

MAYA. No, darling. He'd *watch*.

(*Yo ho! The* BATCH'ETTES *cackle.*)

BETTY LEE. It'll be fun.

BETSY. Well what have you got planned, Betty Lee?

(*BECKY STEEM shoots BETTY LEE's menu with Onstage Cam.*)

BETTY LEE. Appetizer! Entrée! SWEETS! And Mary Bette can make her special PUNCH.

BETSY. What else?

BETTY LEE. It'll be a fucking buffet!

MATTY. Icebreaker games for sure.

BETSY. No no no.

MARY BETTE. Like 'What Am I'?

BETSY. No no no.

(*Closeup on MARY BETTE:*)

MARY BETTE. Where everybody gets a slip of paper they can't see, with a phrase like *virgin*, or *blowjob*, or *wife-icide*, all pinned up on their backs? And then everyone has to ask everyone else what they are?

(BETSY *convulses, and then vomits into the hole.*)

MATTY. Or how about Pin the Privates on the Pinup, where everyone gets an anatomically correct construction-paper penis to pin up on the pinup, after you're all blindfolded and spun around?

MAYA. I never got how that was an icebreaker.

BETTY LEE. But we already know each other.

MATTY. Do we?

MARY BETTE. What is wrong with you?

(*Pause.*)

MARY BETTE. What about you, Betsy?

(BETSY's *mind is elsewhere…pondering other screens.*)

MAYA. Bets?

(*A low drone of muffled gambling.* APPARITIONS *play elsewhere.*)

BECKY STEEM. O this isn't about Betsy Competitive here. This is about how we get together, get funny, get drunk, get sloppy, get hard, get off, get sad, and then get better, right Betsy Competitive?

(BETTY LEE maneuvers the Onstage Cam.)

BETTY LEE. GET TOGETHER

MATTY. GET FUNNY

MARY BETTE. GET DRUNK

MAYA. GET SLOPPY

BECKY STEEM. (*In* SPECIAL K's *voice.*) GET HARD

BETTY LEE. GET OFF

MATTY. GET SAD

MARY BETTE. GET BETTER

MAYA. GET GOTTEN

ALL. GET! GET! GET! GET! GET!

(BETTY LEE *approaches* BETSY COMPETITIVE *with Onstage Cam.*)

BETTY LEE. What *do* you want, Betsy? *What do you want?*

(*Light beams down.*

The screens awaken with onstage biz.

The gals enjoy a feast upon BETSY.

BETSY *gives into the feast.*)

BETSY. The party…starts…right…now.

(One by one the BATCH'ETTES *chute down into the hole.*

Onstage Cam sees a bit of the hole and the path walked on the stage. BETSY walks by.

BETSY's *Hoop, arms rounded, fingers ringing.*
TAGGIS *watches from the hole.*
A hand from the hole reaches for the Onstage Cam and:

We go down under, catching a glimpse of
BETSY's Hoop and into the next party,
raucous and hooting.

BETSY *jumps down into the hole.)*

5. Performance of Man.

Screens show a rowdy hotel room. The
articles-of-confederation sort of bachelor
party.

All 6 of 'em. The male counterparts of the
batch'ettes. Could be the 1950's, the neo-
now of it.

The whole world bumps up, one, two, three times.
A cooler pops up from the hole.
TAGGIS *is delivered up to the roof.*
The rest of the party arrives atop the roof.

ANNOUNCER. (*Voice over.*) BACHELOR PARTY: A DRUNKEN
BLOWOUT WHERE YOUR BEST FRIENDS KNOCK YOU
SENSELESS! (*Ding!*)

(LARS *feelin' the swing of his balls,* MIKE *and* CHET *scattin' a lil dance.*
SMOAK *and* WESLEY *swing* TAGGIS.

Onstage Cam captures the action.)

CHET. Another toast to Taggis—Tits and all!

ALL. Tits and ALL!

MIKE. (*Titty-twists* TAGGIS.) Here, here Taggis

LARS. Tits and all, Taggy!

WESLEY. Here, here.

(MIKE *delivers beers from the cooler to* LARS/Betty Lee,
WESLEY/Betsy, CHET/Becky Steem, SMOAK/Matty Jay, *and
himself,* MIKE/Mary Bette.)

MIKE. Lars! Wesley! Chet! Smoak! I'm Mike!

TAGGIS. I juss wan na say—

(*Searching for anything—*)

SMOAK. Totally.

MIKE. That's deep, man.

CHET. To the men Betsy's loved
To the men Betsy's kissed;
And her heartfelt apologies
To the men she's missed.

ALL. We'll all miss you, Betsy!

> (*They toast. Crash into underground.*
> *The party winds* TAGGIS *up.*)

SMOAK. PULL!

> (...SMOAK *socks* TAGGIS.)

ALL. Yeah!

> (TAGGIS *lurches up from the ground.*)

MIKE. (*Shadowboxing* TAGGIS.) C'mon, Taggis, you and me, one on one.

> (TAGGIS *socks one to the party*
> *The whole party collapses.*
> *He socks another.*)

LARS. Jolly good shot, Taggy!

WESLEY. Fucking ringer, that Taggis.

SMOAK. Hold it hold it hold it hold it—

> (*They all six shadow box/dance a coupla turns, and within a moment, it's*
> *fucked-up violent but without suffering,* Jackass *style.*
> TAGGIS *socks another to the party.*)

TAGGIS. YESSSSSSS- - - - - - - - - -I - - - - - - mmmm - - - - - thuhhhh - - -
- - - - - -champion - - - - - bosssing

> (*His arms are raised in victory.*
> *The party dogtracks and thumb-brushes around him,* CHET *jackhammers*
> *atop* TAGGIS's *head.*)

6.

> TAGGIS *is bounced three times and lifted onto a chair.*

SMOAK. I've got one.

> (*They stand around* TAGGIS.)

SMOAK. Time is never wasted when you're wasted all the time.

TAGGIS. Ma-ree-udge iza wunnerful in-sit-oo-tion, but who wansta live in
un in-sit-oo-tion?

> (TAGGIS *challenges gravity.*)

ALL. Whoa.

CHET. So then ditch her, Taggis.

LARS. Don't lock her up from us.

WESLEY. Keep her free.

MIKE. You're dead anyway, man.

SMOAK. Come back to how we were.

TAGGIS. I luff huh.

ALL. Awwwww!

CHET. You're such a faggot, Taggis.

> (*A hug to* TAGGIS *from* CHET.
> *Shots of Jim Beam distributed.*
> TAGGIS *finds himself a 'drink,' which is a block of wood.*)

MIKE. A toast: Here's to the land we love and the love we land.

LARS. We the people, yo—

> (*They drink.*
> TAGGIS *knocks himself out with the block of wood.*
> *They crash their shot glasses down into the hole.*
> TAGGIS lays unconscious on the screens.
> LARS *distributes more beers.*
> CHET *throws bills onto* TAGGIS.)

WESLEY. So what are we gettin', Chet?

TAGGIS. You know, Wesley...

CHET. Five Benjis from you Wesley.

MIKE. Yo, I thought we were gettin' strippers.

> (Onstage Cam.)

SMOAK. He got the French rug over the German double penetration.

CHET. There's a choreography to the threesie I didn't think we'd be into. Trust me on the Frenchie. She's—

LARS. It's like sticking your dick into a volcano without ever touchin' her.

MIKE. What? Is she like syphilis?

WESLEY. The party that keeps on giving.

SMOAK. Not past this night, you know what I'm sayin'?

TAGGIS. Thanks, you guys...I'm feee-lin da love ta see...ya all later...

ALL. We love you too, man.

> (*Puppy pile.*)

LARS. So what else we gettin' Chet?

CHET. C'mon, Mike, we need 3 more Benjis from you.

TAGGIS. Hey Guys—

MIKE. You didn't get my message? About the special performance?

CHET. What special performance?

7.

LARS. Mike means Special K.

TAGGIS. You know, guys…

WESLEY. (*Stops.*) Whoa, wait— you got Special K?

MIKE. He'll meet us at Barge.

ALL. (*Low-toned.*) Baaarrge.

WESLEY. You're gonna fag up Taggis?

SMOAK. Well, no—

CHET. —not technically…

LARS. …cuz Special K used to be a woman.

MIKE. He can Groom the Groom for us in public.

WESLEY. Deluxe.

TAGGIS. Guh— Guh— Guh

MIKE. Special K doing Taggis for free, just to make sure.

SMOAK. How many others you got?

TAGGIS. Guh-hise…

CHET. We got the French stripper first…

MIKE. She comes with cake!

CHET. …and we got Special K for later.

WESLEY. What about action for us?

TAGGIS. Guise…

LARS. Best man my ass.

WESLEY, SMOAK & LARS. We paid!

TAGGIS. I'm not sticking myself in her. Final answer.

LARS. Jesus Christ, Taggis! Is the right wing up and down your dick or what?

WESLEY. One last romp, Tag.

MIKE. You nee huh now mo than evah!

TAGGIS. No. I—

SMOAK. Marriage, Taggis—

>   (TAGGIS *is losing to gravity, but still does not fall.*
>   SMOAK *takes the Onstage Cam…*
>   TAGGIS, close up.)

SMOAK. Marriage is a separate thing from tonight. See tonight, Taggis, tonight has got to be *different* from any night you've *ever* had on this planet. It's when your highest desire gets lived, for real real. It's got to be so emblazoned in your cock's mind, that those grey sick silent days to come will never forget what it is to be rock hard

CHET. YEAH TAGGIS!

MIKE. HARD, TAGGIS!

LARS. Rock hard!

> (*They surround-sound him.*)

ALL. Rock hard! Rock hard! Rock hard! Rock hard! Rock hard!

> (*They throw their empty beer bottles to the ages, then suddenly bail, leaving* TAGGIS *solo with the Onstage Cam.*)

8.

TAGGIS. (*As if going under.*) What's happenin' what's happenin' what's happenin'? What's happenin' what's happenin' what's happenin'?

TAGGIS. (*He goes up close into the Onstage Cam.*)If I've way...did foh huh foh aaaaall dis time, I don wan na na na clooooooud... with, I mean, you. Know... I've waited—

> (*Screens freeze on extreme closeup of* TAGGIS's *face.*
> BETSY's *Hoop image will slowly transpose onto his frozen face.*
> The BATCH'ORS *reappear onstage from the hole.*)

CHET. What?

LARS. What, Taggy?

MIKE. (*Rubber-faced.*) Buluh Buluh Buluh

SMOAK. YEAH!

WESLEY. Help is on the way, Tag.

> (WESLEY *has bags of Pink.*)

WESLEY. The Pink won't sink.

SMOAK. Motherfucker Wesley, you been holding out on us.

WESLEY. Yes I have.

> (WESLEY *distributes the Pink.*)

LARS. Uh Oh! Uh Oh! Here comes the party line!

> (*The chew-chew train forms and they chew on the Pink.*
> *They emit animal sounds.*)

TAGGIS. (*Really wrecked, wavering.*) You guys...you.... Guys...take the hoo... hookers.

MIKE. I say Whah, I say whah...I say whah are you—

> (MIKE *collapses.*)

CHET. There's only one, technically.

TAGGIS. Share...

LARS. What are we, fucking communists? Fucking communists are the ones who (*Collapses into the underneath.*)

WESLEY. Meow-Tse Tung!

TAGGIS. ...you guys share her,...

CHET. So pussy-whipped, Taggis.

TAGGIS. ...in my honor...

> (MIKE *gets back up, still bottle in hand, finishes his sentence.*)

MIKE. (*Finishes.*)—I say, whah are you tah kin' 'bout, Taggis?

> (*They surround him and chant.*)

ALL. Puuuuussssssssss-ssssy, Puuuuuusssss-sssy, Puuuusssssssss-ssssy...

> (*Unto a single cell, embracing the* TAGGIS *nucleus.*
>
> The Screens show a spin of faces around the
> cell from TAGGIS's perspective.)

SMOAK. O wait!

CHET & TAGGIS. What?

SMOAK. I think I hear her.

> (*They all waver, as if underneath rules.*)

TAGGIS. How? Whah?

SMOAK. You don't hear the French accordion?

TAGGIS. What?

WESLEY. You guys are hiiiiiiigh...

CHET. (*"Hears."*) Oh yeah. That's her.

> (CHET *and* SMOAK *hum a cute little French tune.*
> TAGGIS *is super wobbly.*)

TAGGIS. Do you hear it, Mike?
Do you hear it Wesley?

> (*They strip* TAGGIS.
> *He sings* "I'm a Little Teapot.")

8. Marie A. Antoinette

Lo and behold, French music plays. MARIE A. ANTOINETTE, *avec sa tete, emerges from the hole.*
She is a kind of perfection, delivered from the clouds.
They all cock their rifles.

MARIE A. My card.

> (She presents a business card: A drawn eye.
> *She tosses bills at the party.*
> *All but* MARIE A. ANTOINETTE *sit. She asks permission from the circle of voyeurs.*)

MARIE A. May I?

> (*They give resounding permission.*
> CHET *holds the Onstage Cam.*
> *She sits in a chair with a grand straddle.*
> WESLEY *and* SMOAK *remove her huge Lucite shoes and suck on its heels.*)

MARIE A. May I?

> (*She licks* TAGGIS's *forehead and sticks a bill there.*
> TAGGIS *collapses.*)

MARIE A. May I?

> (*She sits and throws more bills at them.*
> *The party peels off a layer of their own clothes.*)

MARIE A. May I?

> (*She relishes 'the rug' on the floor and swings her legs are over her head.*)

MARIE A. May I?

> (*They peel off more.*
> *They slip* TAGGIS *under her.*)

MARIE A. May I?

> (*She coquettishly relishes* TAGGIS *like a woolly rug, full bodied, like a pig in mud. Effervescent delight.*
> *Have they peeled down to another gender?*
> *She rubs* TAGGIS's *cheeks with her feet.*)

MARIE A. My, what a lovely rug.

> (*She walks to the hole.*
> *She clutches fistfuls of bills.*
> *She drops into the underground; the bills flutter.*)

9. Privates

ANNOUNCER. (*Voice over.*) BACHELOR/ETTE PARTY: A STRIP-TEASE WHERE YOU WILL NEVER BE MORE NAKED! (*Ding!*)

> (*POP!*
> *The cork.*)

MARY BETTE. Yeah, girls!

> (*BIG BOOTY.*)

ALL. AHHHHHW Yeah Big Booty AHHHHW Yeah
Big Booty Big Booty Big Booty
Big booty #1
#1, #2
#2, #3
#3, #4
#5, #

AHHHHW YEAH!
> (*Dance.* BETTY LEE *enters from the hole.*)

ALL. Hey Betty Lee! Hold your balls…hold your balls, hold your balls! Betty Lee! Hold your balls!

BETTY LEE. Hey whassup, Bitches! I had to dispense some wisdom in the bathroom.

BETSY. Yeah? Dispense this!
> (BETSY's *supertoasted: she did agree, after all, to have her bachelorette party: RIGHT NOW! Peals of laughter into shrieking.*)

MARY BETTE. OK OK OK OK OK. I NEVER—

BETSY. Wait wait wait wait wait.

BETTY LEE. We're toasting to the bride!

MARY BETTE. It's my turn for I NEVER—

BETSY. Wait wait wait wait wait.

MATTY. We have to pin this on you
> (*Next four lines together.*)

MAYA. Let's blow bubbles!

BECKY STEEM. Pin it on me, pin it on me!

MARY BETTE. I NEVER

BETSY. It's my FUCKING PARTY!

BETTY LEE. To Betsy Competitive—

BETSY. Shuddup, Betty Lee.

BETTY LEE. Whatever.

MARY BETTE. I NEVER slipped Todd Taggis a slim jim—

MAYA. I gave him half of my sandwich once.

BETSY. Shuddup.
> (*Next two lines together.*)

BECKY STEEM. Let's give Betsy—
MARY BETTE. Bitch

BETSY. Shuddup.
> (*Next two lines together.*)

BECKY STEEM. I'm just saying—
MARY BETTE. Bitch

BETSY. Shuddup.

MATTY. This corsage—

BETTY LEE. It's fucking ugly.

BETSY. Shuddup. So this small small man goes to a doctor…

MAYA. I NEVER heard this one—

MARY BETTE. I NEVER gave him Ianthe's dong gong.

BETSY. Shuddup. And he's looking for a larger, how do we say, *membership*. Doctor's all, 'we have a new treatment, but it's still experimental.'

BETTY LEE. Fuck experimental!

MARY BETTE. Does anyone smell violets?

BECKY STEEM. Would you let Betsy finish?

MARY BETTE. I distinctly smell violets.

BETSY. Thank you Becky Steem.

MAYA. My bottle is empty.

MARY BETTE. There are violets growing out of my chair.

(*Flowers covered the chariots, panthers lurked beneath.*)

MATTY. This party sucks

MAYA. My bottle is empty

BETTY LEE. You ain't it, Matty Jay

BECKY STEEM. There are no violets.

BETSY. You guys you guys you guys you guys you guys—

(*Ding!*)

(*They instantly shift directions, and thus parties.*)

10. Batch 'or

SMOAK. I never used a potato chip bag for a condom before...

(CHET *drinks.*)

MIKE. Chet you salty dawg!

CHET. Ruffles have ridges!

(*Yug.*)

MIKE. I never did it with the same girl in reststop bathrooms in three consecutive states before, Lars.

(LARS *drinks. He does a jig.*)

TAGGIS. I never saw Betsy naked before.

ALL. Social!

(*All the men but* TAGGIS *drink. Then abruptly pause...for real real, what* TAGGIS *said?*)

SMOAK. (*Testing* TAGGIS *and choosing his words.*) I never...chewed her...tender button before.

(*All the men but* TAGGIS *drink.*)

WESLEY. I NEVER—

(*Ding!* WESLEY *is* BETSY, *in an instant.*)

11. Batch'ette

BETSY. —had a human try this experimental treatment', says the doctor. The small small man's all 'I wanna be the first.' So he goes in, the next day, and has, get this, an *elephant trunk* replace his own membership...

(*A shrill of shrieks.*)

BETSY. And the man is happy as can be— getting pussy right and left.... Until he's out on a date one night, a candlelight number cuz the ladies really like that shit, until they become 'members': getting the elephant trunk reaching up to their 'H' and 'I' and 'J' spots.

(*Another shrill of shrieks.*)

BETTY LEE. My 'X' and 'Y' spots could use a lil tickle...

MARY BETTE. Is that like, up your butt?

BETSY. So this one he likes, real pretty, got those dolly brown eyes like his dad likes and tits so perky, they're like the Himalayas even when layin' down, you know what I mean?

MARY BETTE. Will this end?

BETSY. Shuddup. And so at salad, he's watchin' the game over her shoulder, but lookin' like he's listenin'... the trunk creeps up over the table and snatches a roll and he *gulups*, once. 'Are you OK?', she asks. Yeah Yeah, he says, watching the screen beyond her, damn, Eagles are down by six and with a minute and a half left to play on their own 30. They're having their appetizer...

MAYA. What'd they have?

BETSY. Whatever. It happens again. Trunk creeps up, snatches another roll. He *gulup*s, again. 'I saw that,' she says. 'what the hell is going on?' 'Nothing, nothing, nothing...'

(*Ding!*)

12. Batch

TAGGIS. Nah, nah, nah, guys, nah, nah, nah. Lesssss ssssstop!

CHET. I never cried with Betsy before...

(CHET *hands* TAGGIS *a bottle.* TAGGIS *drinks.*)

SMOAK. I never gave Betsy a Valentine before...

(*He drinks.*)

MIKE. I never asked Betsy to marry me before.

(TAGGIS *doesn't drink...cuz he's so fucking drunk.*)

MIKE. Aw, you did that Taggie...

(*He drinks. The men react. He stands up.*)

TAGGIS. Don' talk 'bout me, fronna me—

(He falls to his face and crawls on his back towards the hole.)

TAGGIS. Nah nah nah, I nevah - - evah- - - - evah - - - even - - - touched huh befoh—

LARS. Liar!

TAGGIS. Isssssss - -izzz - -gonnnnnnah nah nah - - - killlllll - - me

CHET. Ahhhhh, just DRINK!

ALL. *(To* TAGGIS.*)* DRINK, drink, drink, drink, drink…

> *(He passes out.*
> *Ding!)*

BECKY STEEM. …Drink, drink, drink up girls. Cuz it's a never ending story.

BETSY. Shuddup.

BETTY LEE. Jesus Christ.

> *(The veil's down.)*

MARY BETTE. Maya's out.

MATTY. She's fakin'.

BETTY LEE. Maya! Maya!

MARY BETTE & MATTY JAY. Leave her be, Betty Lee.

BETSY. FINALLY, at sweets, the trunk creeps up, aiming to snatch another roll, but this time, she grabs it with her hand. 'What's this?' He looks at her with a, with a *twinkle,* in his good eye

MATTY. He's a pirate?

BETSY. Yes, Matty Jay he's a pirate. So he nods 'yes,' 'yes,' 'yes,' to which her eyes get bigger and bigger—the thought of his huge huge membership— and she slowly releases and caresses at the same time.

One more roll in the basket. She looks and looks and asks, 'you think I could see that again?' She's wetter than Atlantis, the fish in her pussy partying it up like when god first invented the ocean, Eagles on the three with two seconds left to play. 'I'd love to, baby. But my ass can't take another roll.'

> *(Silence.)*

BETSY. C'mon, you guys! Laugh at my joke!

> *(Freeze on* BETSY's *punchline face.*
> *Pause.)*

MARY BETTE. You and Taggis really never touched before?

MATTY. *(Gazing upward, breathing aloud.)* We need to get around men, Betsy.

BETSY. Let's get around men then!

> *(POP! Club music blasts. We hiccup forward for just a moment into the club called BARGE [hosted at the CONNECTION this eve.] They dance for just a moment, whirling, to that Ukranian/House/Madonna riff.)*

13. Special K Batch

TAGGIS *is still passed out. The men sink into a collective swagger.*

ALL. Baaarge

SMOAK. Yeah, I don't wanna get a bj unless I can see it on video. And so Taggis can see, too.

(SPECIAL K *has arrived, magically… enters, entrances hermaphroditically.
He presents a business card to the onstage cam:* Again, a drawn
eye.)

SPECIAL K. He's getting married when?

SMOAK. Like in 9 hours.

MIKE. I never seen you this passed out Taggis. Taggis,

(MIKE *pulls lavender from* TAGGIS's *sleep.*)

WESLEY. You really do this for free?

SPECIAL K. O this is my specialty. Straightboys before they marry. One last chance, just to make sure. Although—

SMOAK. Although?

LARS. What?

SPECIAL K. It's deeper if they're awake.

SMOAK. Yeah, Taggis: missing the best part of his bachelor party.

(*They prepare* TAGGIS *by sliding him mid-stage.*

A netherworld: An infinity of SPECIAL K on
the screens. The infinity gets stretched,
like waves.

SPECIAL K *straddles* TAGGIS's *mouth, whips his mike out, and gives it
to* TAGGIS.

TAGGIS *is cast to speak.*)

TAGGIS. (*Speaking into* SPECIAL K*'s mike.*) I want to turtle up
into my own little nevermind
for a while.
I'll sleep
at the top
of my lungs
If you promise not to tell me tomorrow what I'm doing tomorrow.

(BATCH'ORS *exit:* SPECIAL K *a lil too special.*

Nothing.)

TAGGIS. (*Into mike.*) Are we there yet?
Are we there yet?
I wanna be a stranger.
I wanna be disposable.

I can't remember this until it is over.

I can't be viewed like the old me was unless…

I never touched her at all, but once, in a dream, she bent down and covered my nose with her mouth and I inhaled only the bouquet of her very insides. I stormed into the sheets and then I woke up.

> (TAGGIS *slithers down the hole, to pop back up.*
> TAGGIS, *a kind of gutted-fish, awakening*
> *into the belly of—*
> *of androgeny?*
> *Into an epilepsy that jars towards another realm.*
> An aquarium of movement, where gender is fluid.)

14. BAR(GE)

ANNOUNCER. (*Voice over.*) BATCH: A CELEBRATION WHERE YOU DREAM OF DOING WHAT YOU CAN ONLY *DREAM* OF DOING! (*Ding!*)

> (*Music blares that previously hiccupped Madonna riff.*
> BETSY *rises in veil and twizzler belt.*
> She looks like a goddess ascending.
> *Twizzlers hang everywhere off of* BETSY.)

BETSY. Come on! Eat the twizzlers off me.

Eat 'em off me! Eat 'em off me!

BETTY LEE. I love ya Betsy, god I do.

BETSY. I love you too! Betty Lee.

BETTY LEE. You're so lucky, Betsy, I mean I was always thinkin': if I didn't find one, you know, I could always grow old with Betsy.

BETSY. O we still can, Betty Lee.

BETTY LEE. I mean…All right honestly: why am I really here?

I'm nobody's best friend,

I'm nobody's confidante,

BETSY. O Betty Lee

BETTY LEE. I'm nobody's shoulder-to-cry-on.

I'm nobody's partner-in-crime…

I'm nobody

I'm not even really here

I'm not even really *me* right now.

It's not my job to be me now anyway…

Party party

Fuck fuck

Poopin', yeah!

ALL RIGHT!

She needs three guys to sign her ass!

(BECKY STEEM *joins in the party, with video camera.*)

BETSY. Becky Steem!

BETTY LEE. She needs three guys to sign her ass!

BETSY. O Betty Lee!

BECKY STEEM. She needs three guys to sign her ass!

BETTY LEE. 'Sign my ass!' say that.

BETSY. I ain't say-nad.

BECKY STEEM. Thee o y'alls to but your John Hancock on her ass!

BETTY LEE. Say that, Betsy. Say that! "Sign my ass! Sign my ass.'

BETSY. OK Sign my ass.

BETTY LEE. Louder, c'mon: SIGN MY ASS!

BETSY. Sign my ass!

(*Three hands come up from the hole and sign her ass:*
'X
Y
X.')

15. PUNCH PUNCH and PUNCH

PUNCH PUNCH *and* PUNCH *arrive to Barge through the hole.*
Italianate trio to entertain BETSY *and her* BATCH'ETTE *party.*
It's PUNCH *and* PUNCH *and* PUNCH, *featuring* PUNCH. *It's a*
*Pizza Family—*POP PUNCH *is joined by his sons* PUNCH I *and*
PUNCH II.
POP PUNCH *leads with gold penis squirt gun.*

POP PUNCH. HELLLO! I ama Punch. I think-a there's-a Judy-a to be in
da house to-nighta.

BETSY. No thank you.

(*All push* BETSY. POP PUNCH *thrusts his gold wiener in her face.*
BECKY STEEM *shoots with Onstage Cam.*
He places his business card on the tip of his member: It is the same
drawn eye as the other business cards.)

POP PUNCH. Look at me when I'm pointing to you. I'm delicious!

(BETSY *so....*)

POP PUNCH. I willa teach-a a bride howa to bea a wife-a. O sorry but
first, I musta take-a pee pee

(*Pees into hole....*)

Ah better, better.

(... *into the mouth of* PUNCH II, *and then* PUNCH I.)

PUNCH II. EH!

PUNCH I. EH!

POP PUNCH. EH! I ama Punch! This is my son:

PUNCH II. PUNCH!

POP PUNCH. And this is my other son:

PUNCH I. PUNCH!

POP PUNCH. And together we are:

ALL THREE. PUNCH, PUNCH, and-a PUNCH! (*CLAP!*) HEY!

(*The* PARTY *applauds.*)

PUNCH II. Eyyyye, who ordered a pizza?

BETTY LEE & BECKY STEEM. (*Pointing to* BETSY.) She did! She did!

PUNCH I. Ehhhh, we make our own cheese!

PUNCH II. Give me da piz-za!

PUNCH I. You were supposed-a to bring-a da piz-za—

PUNCH II. Eh, you were!

PUNCH I. Eh, you were!

(*They fight.* POP PUNCH *bonks them.*)

POP PUNCH. EH!

(*A pizza box appears.*)

PUNCH I. Eh! Just-a kidding!

(PUNCH II *shows the pizza, shaped as an erect penis.*)

POP PUNCH. Eat it! Go ahead eat it!

THE PARTY. Eat it Betsy.

BETSY. No thank you.

PUNCH I. Eat it.

POP PUNCH. Ey you like-a da pizza?

PUNCH I. I like-a da pizza!

POP PUNCH. Give him da pizza.

(PUNCH II *smashes the pizza on* PUNCH I'*s head.*)

I'm-a gonna show you some Cock Magic.

(POP PUNCH *pulls off his gold wiener.*)

Ta-dah! My Todd Taggis!

(*The* PARTY *applauds.*)

We don't need this anymore.

(*Throws gold wiener over his shoulder into the hole.* PUNCH I *screams understage.*)

PUNCH I. AHHHHHH!

(*He got the dick in the eye.*)

PUNCHES. EH! JUST KIDDING!

(*They do a couple of Adonis poses in a lil dance.*)

POP PUNCH. So you must be Judy, the wife.

PUNCH II. It's very dangerous being a wife.

PUNCH I. We must proceed with CAU-tion.

(*They move cautiously, and then* POP PUNCH *and* PUNCH I *strip* PUNCH II *with one swift rip.* PUNCH II *wears an apron with erect member.*)

PUNCH II. Hey!

(POP PUNCH *and* PUNCH I *open their jumpers and rock out with their cocks out.*)

POP PUNCH and PUNCH I. Hey!

POP PUNCH. OK. Bride-a to be.

BETSY. No thank you.

POP PUNCH. Get up!

BETSY. No thank you

POP PUNCH. So you-a want-a to be a wife-a? How do we learn how to be a wife.

(PUNCH I *pulls caution tape from* PUNCH II'*s crotch.*)

POP PUNCH. We learn by reading, don't we?

PUNCH I. (*Mispronouncing.*) Cow-tee-on…

POP PUNCH. He's gonna need some help because he can't really read.

PUNCH I. Cow-tee-on… Dang-GER

POP PUNCH. What is there to be afraid of inside a man's pants?

(POP PUNCH *pushes* BETSY *forward.*)

POP PUNCH. He doesn't know how to read. Read for him.

(PUNCH I *sulks off.* BETSY *is knelt down.*)

POP PUNCH. Read it, Bride to be.

BETSY. Caution Caution Danger Caution Caution Danger Caution…

(*A big dong appears.* BETSY *shrieks.*)

BETSY. O!

POP PUNCH. Lucky you, eh? You want to make your husband happy? You need to touch it.

BETSY. No no no.

BECKY STEEM. Touch it Betsy, go ahead.

BETSY. No no no

THE PARTY. Touch it!

BETSY. I'm about to…

(*She's meekish like the participants in a Japanese handjob class.*)

BETSY. O my god! That's…

POP PUNCH. You want to make your husband feel good-a, yes?

BETSY. Uh, yeah

PUNCH I. Now pull on it!

POP PUNCH. Give it a stroke!

THE PARTY. Pull on it, Betsy.

PUNCH I. Give it a pull, c'mon!

(*It pops off. House of Horrors awful.*)

BETSY. That's AWFUL!

POP PUNCH. It's terrible you-a broke-a your husband's cock! There must be more to learn! Learn more.

(*She continues to pull more tape.*)

BETSY. Caution. Caution…

```
(BETSY finds a real cock at the end of the
caution tape.
```

BETSY '*sees*' PUNCH II *as* TAGGIS. *She goes to touch his face, to see if it's real…*)

'TAGGIS.' Don't touch me.

(*…and it all breaks open.*)

16. COLLAPSE (*gotterdammerung*)

BETSY *collapses.*

```
We see BETSY's KO vision on the screens: the
ceiling, basically.
```

TAGGIS *and* BETSY *switch places from previous scenes.*

ALL. Uh-oh, uh-oh, here comes the party line…

ALL. RAAAAHHHHHHHHHHH!

CHET. Another toast to Taggis—Tits and all

ALL. Tits and ALL!

MIKE. Here, here Taggis

LARS. Tits and all, Taggy!

TAGGIS. (*By* BETSY.) I juss wan na say—

```
>>>
```

BETSY. (*By* TAGGIS.) We're not really doing this are we?

(MATTY JAY *spooks her, and* BETSY *[by* TAGGIS*] collapses.*)

MATTY. I don't trust those grills.

BETTY LEE. Or the skating rink.

MATTY. You all skate?

BECKY STEEM. The skating rink is not just for skating.

MARY BETTE. So versatile, you are, Betsy?

BETSY. (*By* TAGGIS.) It's not gonna be like any marriage anyone could ever have dreamed of.

ALL. Bleeeeeeeeet!

> (*Everyone collapses. 'BETSY' [by* TAGGIS] *victory dance.*)
>
> <<<
>
> (TAGGIS *[by* BETSY] *socks one, the* PARTY *collapses.*
> *The* PARTY *immediately gets back up.*)

LARS. Jolly good shot, Taggy!

WESLEY. (*By* TAGGIS.) Fucking ringer, that Taggis.

SMOAK. Hold it hold it hold it hold it—

> (TAGGIS *[by* BETSY] *socks another one, the* PARTY *collapses,*
> *And gets back up.*)

TAGGIS. (*By* BETSY.) I - - - - - - m - - - - - thuhhhh - - - - - - - - -champion - - - - - bossing

> (*All but* BETSY *and* TAGGIS *exit to become* SAY-NADS.
> BETSY *and* TAGGIS *tailor piece. They dress each other with their spirits,*
> *experiencing each other's realms, without touching.*
> *Claudine Longet's "The Look of Love," again, is saying so much more than*
> *just words could ever say. We reboot to the first image, but this time* TAGGIS
> *circles* BETSY *live instead of from the screens.*)

17. betsy and taggis

TAGGIS. are we there yet?

BETSY. too soon.

TAGGIS. you're getting closer—

BETSY. the conclusion?

TAGGIS. to keep to ourselves, if you will

BETSY. I will

> (*Pause.*)

TAGGIS. until

BETSY. until

TAGGIS. two hearts are saved—

BETSY. both of ours

TAGGIS. yes, both of each of ours.

BETSY. Yes Taggis

TAGGIS. Yes Betsy.

(They are extremely magnetized to each other, [with a feeling they may break their vow], their attracting forces about to touch when....)

18. say-nads unto ssextapuss

A SAY-NAD *(Satyr/Maenad) peers up from the hole in bright goat/boxing regalia. And another* SAYNAD. *And another. These creatures jump up and down in the hole, as if their bodies are stimulating and penetrating the hole. They bleeeeeeeet.*

They take stage and approach a somewhat startled BETSY *and* TAGGIS.

They SAYNAD *huddle and speak into a microphone.*

MYCNAD. They look sick.

GONAD. She's bad sick.

ATTICNAD. They've got no eyes.

MONAD. They need the Ssextapuss.

*(*SAYNADS *do some unison dancing. They freeze.*

Two SAYNADS *point* TAGGIS *into a corner and two point* BETSY *into another.*

All parties are getting excited and wet.)

19. nymph

BETSY *is lubed and in the mood.*

She dances and dances and lifts her shirt, a giving to the saynad spirit.

The SAYNADS *are aroused.*

TAGGIS *takes her veil and slides it over her body.*

BETSY *continues to drive towards the hole, lays at its rim and fingers into the darkness. Her mid-finger potently vibrates.*

Onstage Cam, close: NYMPH edging onto the hole, laying her arm across the hole, examining the potency of fingers.

Three loud knocks come from the under the stage.

Three of the SAY-NADS *disappear down under.*

GONAD, *with microphone, remains, seen from the hole.*

GONAD, BETSY *and* TAGGIS *alternate.*

GBT. Went, go, gone

GBT. Gone, going, left

GBT. Left, goes, goad.

GBT. Go, mo, may

GBT. Mo may go

GONAD. Mo

BETSY. may

TAGGIS. go mo

GONAD. Mo may go

TAGGIS. Mo may go mo

GONAD. Mo may go

TAGGIS. Mo may go… mo

> (*They've unlocked the tonal key.*
> GONAD *waves them to come down understage.*
> BETSY *and* TAGGIS *follow* GONAD *down,* TAGGIS *taking the Onstage Cam with them.*
> BETSY and TAGGIS land in the MYCLOPS Cave.
> ATTICNAD, MYCNAD *and* MONAD *watch the screens from the hole until three more knocks from under beckon them down.*)

20. MYCLOPS

Here we see MYCLOPS' *cave. She is a blind clairvoyant with an eye on her left breast. It is the same eye that was drawn on the business cards of Marie A. Antoinette, of Special K, of Punch, Punch, and Punch. She is elegant and otherworldly.*

She lowers her head.

A constant sound of muffled speaking.

She lifts her head.

MYCLOPS. That someone upstairs
all night, all day
with the set on
does dully stare
at that grand ray
Does it sound?

> (*She lowers her head.*
> *Silence.*)

Irradiated—
this deity must be
an egg glowing,
incubated
never to hatch
So much
for the off button

I am Myclops. This, is my cave. It holds a lot. I am Myclops. Call me Mike.

TAGGIS. Mike.

MYCLOPS. Betsy

BETSY. Mike

> (*We pan over to see the wedding congregation witnessing this meeting.* They exit from underneath *onto stage, matching the screens' images with the live.*
> MYCLOPS takes TAGGIS and BETSY through her cave—we enter through her MYCLOPS eye. Her cave resembles the long halls and impossibly labyrinthine corridors of the Connection.
> *The stage regains presence.*
> *The* PARTY *is now the* CONGREGATION.
> *The stage is rebooted.*)

21. translucid *

The PARTY *watches* BETSY *and* TAGGIS *walk down the endless aisle, and turn in toward their inner selves.*

MARY. I wonder if my mom had a bachelorette party? Did they exist then? What was my Dad *thinking* before their wedding?
My mom. My mom has faith. I love my mom. I should call my mom.
I saw a J.C. Penney's commercial last night with kids in it and it made me cry. Does that mean I want kids?
I should buy a video camera.

MATT. Damn, I just wanna touch him. I just, I don't know, I just wanna put my face against his face, his stubble.
I just want to cry with that motherfucker, have a hug, like a twenty-minute hug.
Do I, do I want to kiss him? I don't know—I always, do I wanna kiss him?
Do I, do I want to fuck that motherfucker?
God, I love that motherfucker. I love him. He's gonna make a good dad.

MCKENNA. How many times have I wanted to say "you're kidding me!"
How many times have I thought "well, it's your life"
But really…
Run!
Not her and you
Not…her and him. Not him and you.
Not that I would ever say this but

---

* Self-scribed by performers.

This has got to stop. This is insane. This must not happen. Not this.

LEE. They're like 31, right? They were like, like 28 when they met, then you have to allow for the living-together time, which, like, of course they didn't do at all, I mean c'mon!

And the planning and coordinating should take at a minimum like 3 months. Which means I would have to meet someone before Thanksgiving so we could "meet the parents" around Christmas, which makes us 31 for the proposal, say, that August, and if we have the Wedding in November 2008, we'll only be 7 months behind.

Technically I could live with that. Totally.

JEB. I am losing it a little bit here. Seriously. Why am I so nervous? What is *wrong* with me?

There's 2 of everyone.

2 Taggis.

2 Betsy,

2 him.

2 her.

And 2 me.

2 him, 2 her.

2 him, 2 her…and 2 me.

We're dangling. Turning to vapor. Becoming…just…air.

Holy shit… I'm air.

AARON. All these people around me…they're my favorites.

Good. Thoughtful. Crazy. Neurotic…bitter…stupid. All of them.

I've let myself get loved by them no matter what.

Decades.

I'm really thirsty.

22. At the end of the aisle, three from the Saynads

BETSY *and* TAGGIS *are underground in a* SAYNAD *passage.*

MONAD *shoots pool.*

MONAD. Truth…arrives…to perfect.

* * *

GONAD. ("A LONG DRESS." *At the Shower Bar.*)

What is the current that makes machinery, that makes it crackle, what is the current that presents a long line and a necessary waist. What is this current.

What is the wind, what is it.

Where is the serene length, it is the
dark place is not a dark place, only a
red are black, only a yellow and green
a pink is scarlet, a bow is every color. A line
distinguishes it. A line just distinguishes it.
>   (*They move away and pass a urinal.*)
***

ATTICNAD. ("RED ROSES." *In the john.*) A cool red
rose and a pink cut pink, a collapse and a sold
hole, a little less hot.

> (*Individual movement evolves into a Unison Dance of the Party* CONGRE-
> GATION.
>
> *The movement slows as the* MYCLOPS *wedding nears, unto stillness.*)

MYCLOPS: Your greater perfection
will love and
will service
the whole
of creation.

> (MYCLOPS *joins their hands.*
> BETSY *and* TAGGIS *touch for the very first
> time.*
> *The* CONGREGATION *gently applauds.*
> *They are married by* MYCLOPS.
> TAGGIS *and* BETSY *ride away in a taxi.*
> *We hear* BETSY's *and* TAGGIS's *voice as we pan
> back to a screen to see the wedding
> congregation on stage.*)

BETSY. "...Are you jealous of the ocean's generos-
ity?
Why would you refuse to give this joy to anyone?
TAGGIS. Fish don't hold the sacred liquid in
cups!
They swim the huge fluid freedom."

> (*The congregation is posed, matching:*
> *The congregation on stage.*)

LARS. O wait!

> (*He shuts off the Onstage Cam.*
> *The screens go blank.*
> *Lights come up bright.*)

AMENDMENT

The CONGREGATION.

CHET.

LARS.

MATTY JAY.

WESLEY.

MARY BETTE.

MAYA.

LARS. Well?

MAYA. That's done.

MARY BETTE & WESLEY. For real real.

MATTY JAY. So what, what now?

CHET. Reception!

> *(They all rock out into an instant party, confetti blows out of the hole, cannons shoot streamers: POW!*
> *The Party continues, on and on.)*

End of Play

dark play

or

stories for boys

by Carlos Murillo

129

BIOGRAPHY

Carlos Murillo's *dark play or stories for boys* received its world premiere at the 31st Annual Humana Festival of New American Plays at Actors Theatre of Louisville. Other plays include: *Unfinished American Highwayscape #9 & 32, Mimesophobia, A Human Interest Story, Offspring of the Cold War, Schadenfreude, Near Death Experiences With Leni Riefenstahl, Never Whistle While You're Pissing* and *Subterraneans*. They have been produced in NY (SPF, En Garde Arts, Soho Rep, The Hangar), LA (Theatre @ Boston Court, Circle X, Son of Semele), Chicago (Walkabout Theatre, DePaul University), Atlanta (Actors Express), Minneapolis (Red Eye), Seattle (The Group) and Austin (dirigo group). They have been developed at The Public, NY Theatre Workshop, The Goodman, South Coast Rep, Portland Center Stage, Madison Rep, the Sundance Institute, The Playwrights' Center, Bay Area Playwrights Festival, A.S.K., Annex Theatre, UC Santa Barbara and others. His work has been published by *TheatreForum,* Heinemann and Smith & Kraus. He has received grants from the Rockefeller Foundation, the Minnesota State Arts Board, the Jerome Foundation and is a two-time recipient of the National Latino Playwriting Award. Carlos teaches at The Theatre School of DePaul University in Chicago and is a member of New Dramatists.

ACKNOWLEDGMENTS

dark play or stories for boys premiered at the Humana Festival of New American Plays in March 2007. It was directed by Michael John Garcés with the following cast and staff:

NICK	Matthew Stadelmann
MOLLY/RACHEL	Liz Morton
ADAM	Will Rogers
MALE NETIZEN	Lou Sumrall
FEMALE NETIZEN	Jennifer Mendenhall

Scenic Designer	Michael B. Raiford
Costume Designer	Lorraine Venberg
Lighting Designer	Brian J. Lilienthal
Sound Designer	Matt Callahan
Video Designer	Jason Czaja
Properties Designer	Mark Walston
Fight Director	Drew Fracher
Stage Manager	Megan Schwarz
Dramaturg	Mary Resing
Assistant Dramaturg	Diana Grisanti
Casting	Judy Bowman Casting
Directing Assistant	Tina Sanchez

dark play or stories for boys was written during a residency at the 2005 University of California Santa Barbara Summer Theatre Lab, Naomi Iizuka, Artistic Director. The playwright wishes to acknowledge the students in the lab who were instrumental in the writing of this play, as well as Lisa Portes, the director of the workshop.

The play received a workshop production at The Theatre School of DePaul University in January 2006, directed by the author.

The play was presented in a staged reading as part of the 2006 Latino Theatre Festival at the Goodman Theatre in Chicago, directed by the author.

CAST OF CHARACTERS

NICK

MOLLY/RACHEL

ADAM

MALE NETIZEN, also plays CHANGE HUSTLER, JOCK, SOCCERDUDE2891, THAIBABESLONELYINUSOFA@YAHOO.COM, DONTTREADONME76, TONY

FEMALE NETIZEN, also plays SARAH, MS. SPIEGEL, MOTHER, OLIVIA

TIME

Now.

PLACE

A college dorm room.
An affluent town along the Southern California coast.
Cyberspace.

A NOTE ON PUNCTUATION

A double slash (//) indicates the point where a subsequent speech overlaps.

Matthew Stadelmann and Liz Morton
in *dark play or stories for boys*

31st Annual Humana Festival of New American Plays
Actors Theatre of Louisville, 2007
Photo by Harlan Taylor

dark play or stories for boys

1

NICK. I make shit up.

I make shit up all the time
partly cause I like making shit up
partly cause I'm good at it
and partly cause
well
I *can*.
Which is not to say that I'm oblivious to the consequences
Christ, do I know there are consequences.
You find yourself in sticky situations, painted into corners
And it takes the dexterity of a sharp thinking Comic book hero to
Unstick yourself, tiptoe across the wet paint
Hoping you don't leave a trail of painted toe prints,
Or if you do,
that they're faint enough so no one will notice.

I'm thinking about this right now
Cause
Well
I find myself in one of those sticky situations
Situation I'll have to muster up the deepest wells of my superhero dexterity
To get out of

Or not.

See: there's a girl lying next to me
in my bed,
In the dark,
Here in my dorm room.
She's naked. We've just had sex.
I guess you can call her my girlfriend
Cause yes,
She's naked
She's lying next to me
And we've just had sex?

This is a new thing for me, this girl
so you'll understand my hesitation—
First time, you know, doing the ol'
in out in out

133

and stuff.

Yeah, we've been through those cagey first conversations
where you talk all over each others sentences
But we haven't crossed that threshold,
where suddenly it's like
This one might be around for a spell, she's shared such and such
I've shared such and such
We're not talking over each other's sentences anymore

All the stuff that adds up to
Intimacy.

Nope. We haven't gotten there yet.
Nope. We're in the middle of the post-first-time-humping awkward silence.
And let me emphasize that this post-first-time silence is incredibly meaning-
ful—
The whole future of the relationship hovers over this silence
Like a promise
Like a threat.

We could start talking and find out that we do in fact have all the things we
imagined we had in common
MOLLY. My dad's a total dick.

NICK. Yours too?

MOLLY. Oh, you don't know dick until you've met my dad.

NICK. Or she could put out her cigarette,
grab her panties off the floor,
Slip on her jeans and t-shirt and say

MOLLY. Yeah, that was nice. Um.
Give me a call some time— I mean I'm really busy the next month or so?
but yeah.
See ya.

NICK. Or she could finish up her cigarette
And fall asleep

MOLLY. (*Yawn.*)

NICK. But she doesn't do any of those things. No.
What she does do—
She extends her index finger,
Presses the tip of it against my Adam's Apple,
Drags it slowly down my neck
Over my ribs
Over my left nipple
And down down down
In the direction of my crotch.

When at a loss for words, why not start bumping uglies again, right?

And so her index finger is slowly making its way down towards my
Pubis,
All suggestive,
when she comes to an abrupt stop.
Just above the belly button,
Where she notices my skin
Is no longer the smooth,
Post-adolescent torso,
Where the tip of her finger finds a speed bump.
A pink strip of raised skin a few inches above my belly button
A quarter inch thick
About three-and-a-half inches long.
Yes, her finger stops at this sudden change in the geography of my skin.
Tentatively, she traces a line along the length of it.
Then, even more hesitant, she explores the rest of my abdomen
She feels other pink speed bumps, of different sizes and angles.
Some three inches
Some an inch
Some just thin wisps.

MOLLY. What are these?

NICK. And that's when time stops
And I feel the familiar sensation—
Sweat glands juicing up,
A hardening between my legs
That low-grade migraine
When I'm like an atom in a particle accelerator
And the world around me slows like it's moving through peanut butter.

MOLLY. Come on Nick, what are these?

Nick?

Nick?

NICK. Do I tell her?
Or do I let my comic book dexterity get me out of this one.
In other words,
do I tell her the truth
Or do I do what I do so well:
Make some shit up.

2

NICK. The question the choice the question the choice the question the
choice

MOLLY. What are these?

NICK. What are these?

MOLLY. Nick, can you hear me? What are these?

NICK. Do I tell the truth?

MOLLY. Nick

NICK. Or do I make shit up.

MOLLY. Nii-iick

NICK. The low-grade migraine, sweat glands juicing up, a hardening between my legs

MOLLY. Earth to Nick. Do you copy?

NICK. Me speeding up

MOLLY. What are these

NICK. The air taking on the consistency of peanut butter

MOLLY. NICK!

NICK. The question the choice the question the choice
Launches me backward in time.
To when I was fourteen
Period in my life where I was
living according to a theory I call
The Universal Theory of the Gullibility Threshold—
Or U.T.G.T., or even better, G.T. for short.
The theory organizes the chaos of twenty-first century life into a simple, managable model:
Everyone has a gullibility threshold,
Everyone at some point will come to recognize
That the wheelbarrow of caca they're being fed
Is in fact a wheelbarrow of caca. Nothing more. Nothing less.
The G.T. works on a scale of 1 to 10.
At the bottom of the scale, you have your ones.
The ones don't even bother taking a swallow of the caca,
they know it's caca
They can smell it a hundred miles away.
Their healthy skepticism becomes a cancer:
They end up paranoid conspiracy nut shut-ins
Thinking everything is caca.
"The world is round."

MALE NETIZEN. No it's not. You're fucking with me.

NICK. The sky is blue.

MALE NETIZEN. That's just an illusion man.

NICK. Now most people fall in the middle of the scale—
The fours, fives and sixes.
They'll give the wheelbarrow of caca the benefit of the doubt,

But then they'll get wise.

But the top of the scale you have your tens.
The suckers who'll gorge themselves on the caca
Repeat over and over,
"Yum, Yum, tastes just like chicken
can I have seconds, can I have thirds."
And when the wheelbarrow is empty,
They'll eat their own caca 'cause they're addicted.
The tens are those girls that collect unicorns
and draw rainbows on their biology class notebooks.
They're the ones who end the day with their wallets empty
Cause they believe every sob story they're told by every homeless person they meet on the street.

CHANGE HUSTLER. Hey, you got a twenty? I'm not like this, I don't do this, *ever*. It's just my husband? He just got back from Iraq? and he's like all messed up in the head? He's at the VA hospital up in Sacramento. And he spent his last disability check on crack? I don't have any money to get on the bus to Bakersfield? to pick up our kids? Who are staying with their grandmother who's deaf and on dialysis and can't drive cause the repo man got her car? And she can't keep them for another night cause her boyfriend is crazy and doesn't want the kids around the house no more so I got to go get them then go get my husband so we can go find a place to live? If you give me your phone number? I'll call you so I can pay you back. Can you help me out?

NICK. Yes, the tens are rare. But they do exist.
Adam fell into that category.

ADAM. I'm not gullible.

NICK. Adam was a perfect 10.

ADAM. I am not gullible.

NICK. A perfect 10. Or so he seemed.
Which was strange...
How do you account for a perfectly average sixteen year old
From southern California
Having a G.T. of 10?
You could write him off and say he was just stupid

ADAM. I'm not stupid.

NICK. But that would've been unscientific.
To get to the bottom of the mystery of Adam's existence
You gotta start with the question:
How did you get to be so gullible?
Did no one ever kick the scoop off your ice cream cone for no reason?
Was your backyard a Garden of Eden under the ever-present California sun?

Did your parents actually stay married?
Did your mother jab her nipple in your mouth any time you so much as
whimpered?
Did your parents decimate nature with an overabundance of nurture?
ADAM. My parents? I dunno.
They're all right I guess. I mean they're not like
weird or anything.
They kinda keep to themselves. I don't
Hate them.
They're just…
Kind of there.
Dad with his book.
Mom with her puttering around.
Me in my room doing
Homework or
Surfing the net.
It's like
We each have our own little areas of the house
And like
the dining room's the one place
Where we
You know,
eat.
And I guess that's what we do when we're together. Eat.
And then when we're done eating
We like
go back to our own little areas until it's time to go to bed.
Every day it's
Pretty much the same.
NICK. So no, the Garden-of-Eden-Nipple-On-Demand model couldn't
explain Adam.
And I started thinking maybe it was something more fundamental.
ADAM. I'm not gullible.
I'm not stupid.
NICK. Maybe
In the face of knowing that Mom, Dad,
Santa Claus,
The Tooth Fairy, The Easter Bunny, The Great Pumpkin,
And God are all Dead,
You still have to believe in something.
Don't you?
ADAM. I don't know.
I guess I believe in God.

I mean,
I don't go to church or anything—
We used to but
then we moved to California and we just
you know
Stopped.
And it's like, "Yeah, maybe there is something out there."
But is it like some bearded guy with white hair up in the sky?

I have this cousin? up in Oregon?
And she's like
One of those total religious freakoids.
One day we were on the beach at sunset?
And out of the blue she said:

SARAH. What do you see Adam?

ADAM. Uhh,
Water?

SARAH. Water, yes. What else?

ADAM. Waves?

SARAH. Water, waves, yes. But what *else*?

ADAM. The sky? Some clouds? Seagulls?
Sand?
A bunch of junk on the sand?

SARAH. Yes, Adam. Yes, I see all those things too. But you know what else
I see?
When you put them all together—
the water, the waves, the sky, the junk on the beach,
the little kid over there smiling at the waves with her mother—
you know what I see?

ADAM. No.

SARAH. I see God.

ADAM. Oh.

SARAH. You can see him too, Adam. If only you'd let him in your heart.

ADAM. I was like,
"Whatever."

NICK. So, Adam, like pretty much the rest of us
was a belief-starved kid hopscotching across the 500 channels of satellite TV
and wandering the infinite portals of the worldwide web
scavenging for that morsel of diversion that would sustain you
until you found the next one.
So that couldn't explain Adam's stratospheric G.T.
otherwise

we'd all be fish hanging stupidly from hooks

ADAM. I'm not stupid

NICK. But he wasn't totally belief-starved—
I recognized this reading the first six words Adam's online profile

ADAM. "I want to fall in love"

NICK. I read that I was like, "Whoa." Who uses that word?
Adam's like the first person I ever met my age who used that word "love"
without rolling his eyes
or making it sound like the punch line of a really stupid joke

ADAM. I want to fall in love with a girl
15-18. Would like her to have green eyes, dirty blonde hair,
she should be like 5'4", 5'6" tops,
have a good body (no fat girls, please, no offense)
she should be smart and likes to chill out on the beach.
I'm 16. Kinda tall. I used to play soccer, but trying to expand my horizons.
Email me at *JustWant2ChillWithU@aol.com*

NICK. Now when I read that I was like:
"Duh, who doesn't want a girl like that." I can imagine all the 15–18-year-old dirty blonde, green-eyed girls in the world reading that, breathing a sigh of relief saying,

MALE NETIZEN. "Finally. Finally there's someone out there who wants me!"

NICK. "I want to fall in love…"
Huh. "*Love*"
Did the fact he believed such a thing existed
explain why Adam's G.T. was way off the scale?
I mean, he wasn't just that rare 10,
He was like that amp in *Spinal Tap*—
His G.T. went up to 11.

Intrigued, I set out to find out.

OLIVIA. Now when you do it,
I need you to promise me that you'll tell him
That you love him.

3

NICK. The question the choice the question the choice the question the choice

MOLLY. What are these?

NICK. What are these?

MOLLY. Nick, can you hear me? What are these?

NICK. Do I tell the truth?

MOLLY. Nick

NICK. Or do I make shit up.

MOLLY. Nii-iick

NICK. The low-grade migraine, sweat glands juicing up, a hardening between my legs

MOLLY. Earth to Nick. Do you copy?

NICK. Me speeding up

MOLLY. What are these

NICK. The air taking on the consistency of peanut butter

MOLLY. NICK!

NICK. The question the choice the question the choice
Launches me backward in time.
Three and a half weeks before I read those
Six
Magic
Totally baffling words.

ADAM. I want to fall in love

NICK. Back to a time when I
took this Theatre Arts elective
Cause I thought it would be a total blow off,
Antidote to the accelerated English, Science, History and Math classes I was taking.
Teacher was this lady, Ms. Spiegel.
Who must have been like 40 or 50
And who was a
total
dyke.

MS. SPIEGEL. The best theatre is theatre that challenges the audience.
That provokes.
That's *dangerous.*

NICK. That's what she used to say, she liked that word

MS. SPIEGEL. *Dangerous.*
The best theatre holds a mirror up to the audience
And invites them—
No,
Demands them to look at the reflection,
No matter how unflattering,
No matter how *ugly* it is.

The best theatre takes the audience on a journey into the darkest,
Most *dangerous,*

Regions of the human soul.
And at the end of the journey,
The audience,
Having faced that *darkness,*
That
Danger,
Can recognize
The darkness and danger in their own souls,
And actively take steps to
Change
It.

NICK. Which I guess was all well and good,
Though,
I couldn't reconcile all this

MS. SPIEGEL. *darkness*

NICK. and

MS. SPIEGEL. *danger*

NICK. She was talking about with the fact that we spent the entire semester
Playing these stupid kid's games. Tag. Duck Duck Goose.
Finally one day in class,
After she practically broke down in tears
Telling us how *important*
It was to recognize the

MS. SPIEGEL. *Darkness*

NICK. And

MS. SPIEGEL. *danger*

NICK. in the human soul,
And that portraying that on the stage was one of nature's highest callings,
I raised my hand:

MS. SPIEGEL. Yes, Nick.

NICK. Um. Ms. Spiegel? I think I understand what you mean
With all this darkness and danger stuff
But
What I'm having trouble with
Is what does any of that have to do with playing
"Pussy Wants A Corner"?

There were all sorts of repressed giggles,
And a little bit of awe, I might say—
Other kids were used to not noticing me,
Flying as far under the radar as I did in school.

It took a moment to gather herself,

And improvise an answer to my question.

MS. SPIEGEL. Well...

Games are

Games are the essence of theatre.

When you play a game
You *allow* yourself to
let go.
You *allow* yourself to
believe.

Acting in a play is kind of like
Well,
Kind of like playing in a game.
Only instead of pretending you're a pussy cat,
You're pretending to be
Hamlet.
Instead of trying to get your "corner" in the circle,
You're trying to decide whether or not to kill your stepfather.

NICK. Oh.

And then she got on a roll.

She started talking about how there are games that are really *dangerous* for the players. That—

MS. SPIEGEL. When I was in grad school?— like a million years ago ha ha
Anyway,
We had this one professor—
A really intense guy who did all sorts of wild theatre in NY back in the 60s—
He would make us play games, but the dangerous kind.
He called these kinds of games "Dark Play"—
Does anyone know what "Dark Play" is?
Does anyone want to take a stab?

NICK. Silence.

MS. SPIEGEL. Dark play is a kind of game
Where certain players know the rules,
And other players don't.
In other words— some of the players
Are fully aware that they are participating in a game,
While others are completely in the dark.

Has anyone engaged in this kind of play?

NICK. I raised my hand to "take a stab," as it were.

MS. SPIEGEL. Yes, Nick.

NICK. Is that like
When you go on the internet,

And you go into a chat room and pretend you're someone else?

MS. SPIEGEL. Maybe. Could you unpack that for me?
I'm totally 19th Century when it comes to technology—
I still have a hard time getting my toaster to work.

NICK. Well… say you're some girl
And you're kind of ugly

MS. SPIEGEL. We should avoid making those kinds of judgments

NICK. I'm just saying, so I'm sure I understand:
Say you're some girl and
You look a certain way that no one wants to "get with you."
And you go on line,
And you meet a guy and he says,

MALE NETIZEN. What do u look like?

NICK. You could tell him the truth,

MALE NETIZEN. I'm overweight, I have bad acne,
I have facial hair
I don't dress cool at all.

NICK. Which would get you nowhere.
Or you could be like

MALE NETIZEN. I'm 5'7", I've got dirty blonde hair, green eyes
I wear short miniskirts. I'm totally hot.

NICK. Which would get the guy interested, right?

MS. SPIEGEL. Depends on the guy, but I think I see where you're going.

NICK. Anyway, so the guy's like

MALE NETIZEN. You sound hot
I wanna get to "know" you.

NICK. And he could be some fat pimply gay kid
Who's just bored and wants to see where the whole thing's gonna go, right?
And then they end up cybering

MS. SPIEGEL. Pardon? Cybering? Could you define that for me?

NICK. That's when one of the jocks in the class chimed in—

JOCK. That's when you get all nasty with some chick online.

MS. SPIEGEL. Oh…
I didn't know people did that.

NICK. Anyway,
Ms. Spiegel,
Is that what you mean by this
"Dark Play"?

MS. SPIEGEL. I suppose.
I'll have to think about that more

And get back to you.

NICK. She never did get back to me.

But I figured I was right,
And I sort of got the point she was trying to make about games,
And how theatre was supposed to be like a game,
Only more

MS. SPIEGEL. *Dangerous*

NICK. But I'd been to the school plays.
They were about as "dangerous" as "Pussy Wants a Corner"—
But this "dark play" thing— that was pretty cool.
And if they did a school play that was like the Internet?
With all the "dark play" happening there…?
I'd check it out.

But until they did that play
I'd get my dose of *dangerous*
and *dark* play
In the one place in the world where a kid my age
And well
Of my *demeanor*
Could escape the cruel and unusual punishments assigned you by your
"peers":
The World Wide Web.
Where you could be anything.
You could enact revenge on all the shits that made your world
A miserable place to inhabit.
At first it was mostly small potatoes stuff.
You'd pose as some girl,
Lure some dickhead soccer player into a private chat,
And you'd be all slutty
Say things like

FEMALE NETIZEN. "I wanna suck it. Put your mammoth cock in my mouth."

NICK. And you'd get the guy to say all sorts of stupid shit like

SOCCERDUDE2891. Lick it.
Lick it, bitch.
Lick it like an ice cream cone.

NICK. And you knew as you were spinning out the fantasy,
That some schmuck out in,
I don't know,
Yorba Linda,
Was upstairs in his room,
Pants rolled down to his ankles

One hand hunt and pecking on the computer keyboard
The other hand MIA deep in the jungle of his tightie whities.

And just as he was getting to the point of no return,
You'd pull the Lucy van Pelt to his Charlie Brown
Pulling the football away just as he was about to kick it:

FEMALE NETIZEN. "Oh, my cock is so hard for you! I'm gonna blow!!!!"

NICK. Then there'd be this silence.

And sometimes they'd split without typing in another word

SOCCERDUDE2891. *SoccerDude2891* has left the chat room.

NICK. Other times they'd get all threatening say shit like

SOCCERDUDE2891. "Motherfucker, I'll find out where you live and cut your fuckin faggot dick off!"

NICK. That was fun for about two and a half minutes.
Once you exhausted all the possibilities, and there were quite a few,
It was the same old same old.
Which got me thinking about what Ms. Spiegel said about going
Deeper
Darker
more

MS. SPIEGEL. *Dangerous*

NICK. digging into the murky recesses of human nature,
See what people were really made of.
That's when the fake ads started.

THAIBABESLONELYINUSOFA@YAHOO.COM. I am Kim. I am exchange student from Thailand. I am 17 years old. My sister Kim is also exchange student. We both are in Catholic High School here in California, United States. We are both lonely, as we are only starting to learn English and our hosts are not very fun. We are looking for mature American man to show us the "American way of life". He must have car, and maybe friend who can join us on American adventure. My sister and me are looking for new experience. We want to meet someone who, as you Americans say, will "Rock our world." Respond with picture of yourself to ThaiBabesLonely-inUSofA@yahoo.com.

NICK. I posted that
Thinking
No one is going to respond to this—
But the next day
There were like
Eight.
Hundred.
Emails.

In my Inbox.
It's like all the
Creepoids crawled out of their rocks, found that one,
Wrote back and sent pictures to prove their hideous existence.
One picture really freaked me out.
Some dude standing in front of a mirror
Shirtless,
Vienna Sausage prick sticking out of his scummy boxers,
Fat belly drooping down,
Old lady tits,
Ratty goatee
Shoulder length greasy hair.
He was holding his digital camera up and behind his head.
The harsh light of the flash made his skin even pastier…
And his eyes…

I can't even describe what his eyes looked like.
Creeped me out.
At the same time
It triggered this

Feeling
In me.

But the fake ads too lost their charm for me.
Once you put one up the rest were the same.
Same disgusting, depraved people
Sending their disgusting, depraved responses
With accompanying disgusting and depraved pictures.
Confirmation that the world was populated by disgusting, depraved people
Who for some reason believed their beer guts and old lady tits
Would attract a pair of nubile, underage, sex-hungry Asian chicks.

At that point I was ready to pack the whole thing in—
That is
Until I stumbled on Adam's profile
And those six words

ADAM. I want to fall in love…

NICK. Those words were so

Naked

Love.
What the fuck is that?

ADAM. I want to fall in love with a girl…
15-18. Would like her to have green eyes, dirty blonde hair,
she should be like 5'4", 5'6" tops,
have a good body (no fat girls, please, no offense)

she should be smart and likes to chill out on the beach.
I'm 16. Kinda tall. I used to play soccer, but trying to expand my horizons.
Email me at // *JustWant2ChillWithU@aol.com*

NICK. *JustWant2ChillWithU@aol.com*
Now:
I couldn't just write him and say,
"Hey, I'm Nick,
I'm like
Fourteen
And I'm pretty confused about most things
so
What's up with this "love" shit?"

I might get him on the "Smart" part,
But
You would never mistake me for a cute
Five foot, six inch
Dirty blonde
Green-eyed
Girl

ADAM. "Who likes to chill"

NICK. No, nature did not endow me with such generous gifts.
But nature,
With all its insurmountable obstacles,
Doesn't really exist anymore, does it?

Not when you have 512 megabytes of RAM,
650 megahertz of microprocessing power
And a high-speed Internet connection…
No,
armed with that, there is no natural boundary that once crossed over
can't be crossed back again.

So in spite of the physical shortcomings nature cursed me with,
In the nature-free world I could become this girl of his dreams
I could invent Rachel.

The tricky thing about inventing Rachel was
Unlike the horny Thai exchange student,
Rachel had to be
Well
Plausible—
Which you'd know is a tall order if you ever had to invent a human being
from scratch.
Especially one of the *female* species.

First and foremost

She had to fit the critera—

ADAM. What do u look like?

RACHEL. What do u think I look like?

ADAM. I dunno.

RACHEL. Wellll…
I have green eyes.

ADAM. Yeah?

RACHEL. Iiiiiiii
Have dirty blonde hair.

ADAM. Yeah?

RACHEL. Annnnnd
I'm about five foot five?

ADAM. Do u like to chill?

RACHEL. I loooove to chill.

NICK. Fitting the criteria was easy, cause Adam pretty much sketched her out for me
It was just a question of fleshing her out, so to speak.

She needed to be pretty,
but she couldn't be a total babe that was
Out of his league

ADAM. Describe what u look like.

RACHEL. Oh…
I'll try I guess…
I mean, I'm not good at talking about myself

ADAM. Try…

RACHEL. Well, okay.
People say I'm like a cross
Between Hillary Duff (but not so cutesy and annoying)
And Avril Lavigne (but not so faux edgy)
With a little bit of a Natalie Portman vibe

ADAM. Yeah, I can totally see that.
Cool.

NICK. She needed to be smart,
But not so smart that Adam would feel like an ox next to her

RACHEL. Let's see.
I got a B on my math midterm,

ADAM. Uh huh.

RACHEL. A B+ in English

ADAM. Huh.

RACHEL. I'm stuck somewhere between a B and a B+ in History

ADAM. Uh huh.

RACHEL. I totally aced French last semester

ADAM. Oh…

RACHEL. Chemistry totally sucks and right now my average is a C
But I think I can still pull off a B

ADAM. Cool.

NICK. I also wanted her to be quirky—
In the way that makes certain guys all smitten—
But not so quirky he'd think she was a freak.

RACHEL. I used to play practical jokes on my ex-boyfriend.
One time?
He was away on a band trip up in Sacramento?
I convinced his mom to let me and my friend Carrie into his room.
We filled his room up—
Waist high—
With foam packing peanuts.
You should have seen his face when he got back.
He opened his door and there was this tidal wave
Of packing peanuts.
He tried to get me back with a practical joke of his own
But…

I broke up with him cause
he didn't really have a good sense of humor.

NICK. Rachel also had to suggest to Adam the possibility of sex
Without coming off as a total ho

RACHEL. I read somewhere? That on average it lasts
Eleven minutes. Worldwide.

ADAM. No shit.

RACHEL. Think about it. Eleven minutes.
You might as well spend those eleven minutes
Writing the word "alone" over and over again on the wall.
But to answer your question: No
I don't have a boyfriend.
I mean I'd like to have one—
I'm really not into the whole hook up thing—
I mean I'm not against hooking up?
In principle?
It's just that
There's got to be something more.
You know?

NICK. In other words,
For Rachel to be

Plausible
She had to be
Well
Kind of
Average.

That first chat online
Was surprisingly easy
I figured out pretty quickly that
With every exchange,
Adam was inventing Rachel as much as I was.
She could say something totally generic like

RACHEL. Like, when is Ben Affleck NOT totally lame?

NICK. And that would lead Adam to construct a whole matrix of
assumptions about her
And what she thought about like
Iraq. Religion. The last election.
Which I guess is what people do, right?
You really don't know anything about anyone else
Just surfaces.
So you have to
Well
Make shit up
About what's going on underneath...

That first chat between Rachel and Adam
Time disappeared.
We'd started chatting around 7 at night.
It only seemed like maybe half an hour
But when I looked at the clock
It read
6:45 AM.
Eleven hours and forty-five minutes
Non-stop.
It kind of freaked me out,
But it also excited me,
That I could sustain Rachel for so long,

But I remembered I had a math quiz that day,
So Rachel wrote:

RACHEL. I don't want to get off
But
I've got a chemistry quiz tomorrow—well today.
I need to catch a few Z's. Gotta get that C to a B.

ADAM. Yeah. That's cool.

NICK. I wondered,
Do I just leave it at that?
Or
Do I keep the carrot dangling?

RACHEL. Will you be online tomorrow night?

ADAM. Yeah. Probably.

RACHEL. We shall meet again…

NICK. And with that…

RACHEL. RachelIsRoses has left the chatroom.

ADAM. We shall meet again.

NICK. And meet again they did.
They exchanged jokes.

RACHEL. So these horny gay pirates get shipwrecked on an island?
And it turns out that this island
Is home to a Catholic convent…

NICK. They exchanged intimacies.

ADAM. u ever feel like
like
u r the loneliest person on earth?

NICK. They exchanged pictures.

RACHEL. Did you get the picture I emailed you?

ADAM. Yup.

RACHEL. Annnd?

ADAM. u r totally cute.

RACHEL. Thanks.
Tho… Adam?
"cute" isn't exactly a
compliment
for a girl. I mean
Koala bears are cute.

ADAM. Sorry.
I mean
What do u want me 2 say?

RACHEL. A girl shouldn't have to tell a guy what she wants to hear.

ADAM. So, what? A guy has 2 be like
Psychic?

RACHEL. No.
Not psychic. Just

RACHEL & NICK. Imaginative.

ADAM. Ok. Ummm. How about this: u r perfect.

RACHEL. That's sweet, Adam. That's
So sweet.

But Adam.
I'm not perfect. I'm far from being perfect
I'm

ADAM. u r?

RACHEL. I'm just so afraid of disappointing you.

NICK. Yes, they laid down the groundwork
for the inevitable face to face that would prove
If their virtual world connection
Could survive the chaotic muck of the real world.

ADAM. I want 2 meet u

NICK. And if the connection did survive
Then they could
You know
Exchange bodily fluids.

ADAM. I want 2 meet u

RACHEL. I want to meet you too

ADAM. What's the problem then?

RACHEL. I can't tell you that. It's
Complicated.

NICK. Now the weird thing:
In spite of the impossibility of a real world face to face
Between Rachel and Adam,
Something in me
Craved for it as much as he did.

But I sensed Adam was on the verge of reaching his Gullibility Threshold.

ADAM. Sometimes
I get the feeling that

RACHEL. That what?

ADAM. Never mind.

RACHEL. If we're ever going to have a relationship, Adam
We need to be open with each other. I've been open with you.

ADAM. Yeah, until it's time 2 be like
Hey, why don't we meet?

RACHEL. I can't begin to tell you how much I want that.

ADAM. Then what's the problem?

RACHEL. I can't tell you that Adam.

ADAM. There u go again with all your
Mystery.

RACHEL. Be patient.
Please. Pretty please? For my sake?
Adam?

ADAM. It's just that
I've never met anyone like u.

RACHEL. I feel exactly the same.

ADAM. And I've never felt

RACHEL. Felt what, sweetie?

ADAM. U r gonna think its queer for me 2 say
But
I've never felt like this before about anyone.

RACHEL. Adam…
Oh, Adam. I don't think that's // queer.

NICK. Queer.

RACHEL. I think that's
That's the sweetest thing anyone's ever said to me.

ADAM. Rachel…
I think I luv you.

RACHEL. Adam. You don't know what that means to me.

ADAM. Why can't I meet you?
It's like
u r 2 good 2 be true.

RACHEL. I'm not good, Adam.
I'm bad.
Sometimes I think I'm the most awful person in the world.

ADAM. Why?

RACHEL. I can't tell you that.
Someday I hope that I can.
And face to face, not like this.
Someday I hope that I can kiss your beautiful mouth,
And cradle your beautiful head on my breast
And stroke your hair
And kiss your ears.

ADAM. I don't believe u.

RACHEL. Since things have to be this way
Let me love you the only way I can.
Will you let me do that?

ADAM. Maybe.

RACHEL. Turn on your webcam, Adam.

ADAM. I don't know if I want 2.

RACHEL. Please? Adam?

Please?

I want to love you.

I want to love you the only way I can love you right now.

Turn on your webcam.

ADAM. Fine.

I'm turning it on.

RACHEL. Show me how much you love me.

I want to see it Adam.

Show it to me.

Show it to me and show me how much you love me.

NICK. And there he was on screen.

Grainy, choppy.

Standing up from his chair.

Undoing the button and zipper of his jeans.

I urged him on.

RACHEL. I feel like you're here in my room with me.

You're so beautiful, Adam.

Show me how much you love me

Show me

Show me

Show me...

OLIVIA. Now when you do it,

I need you to promise me that you'll tell him

That you love him.

4

NICK. The question the choice the question the choice the question the choice

MOLLY. What are these?

NICK. What are these?

MOLLY. Nick, can you hear me? What are these?

NICK. Do I tell the truth?

MOLLY. Nick

NICK. Or do I make shit up.

MOLLY. Nii-iick

NICK. The low-grade migraine, sweat glands juicing up, a hardening between my legs

MOLLY. Earth to Nick. Do you copy?

NICK. Me speeding up

MOLLY. What are these

NICK. The air taking on the consistency of peanut butter

MOLLY. NICK!

NICK. The question the choice the question the choice

NICK. Those nightly sessions were

Whoa.

Rachel asked Adam to do things that

And he did them. I couldn't believe it.

Aside from the
Excitement of watching Adam,
The nightly sessions served their purpose:
To keep Adam hooked. To keep him from demanding
The face to face he wanted.
But it started to feel like a nightly tap dance to Squarepusher.
Just couldn't keep up.
So drastic measures were in order.

I had to insert myself as a character in the saga of Rachel and Adam.

MALE NETIZEN. *NickWillRockYou* has entered the chat room.

NICK. Of course I couldn't go online and seek him out—
No, Adam had to find me.
How I did this—
Well, I gotta say this was clever—

ADAM. No. I'm an only child. What about u?

RACHEL. I've got a brother, Nick.

ADAM. Older or younger?

RACHEL. Younger. He's 14.

ADAM. Is he cool?

RACHEL. I guess. I mean, he's my little brother so
How cool can he be?
I mean he's kind of a dweeb
Keeps to himself a lot at school
But he's like
The biggest brain I ever met.

And he can be pretty funny sometimes too.

ADAM. Cool.

RACHEL. Like his screen name?
You've got to swear to me that if you ever meet him
You won't tell him I told you this:
His screen name is

NickWillRockYou
I mean if you ever saw this kid?
Last thing you'd ever imagine him doing
Would be "rocking you".

ADAM. You should get him to change it to "DweebWillRockYou"
LOL

RACHEL. That's my little brother you're talking about, Adam.

ADAM. Sorry.

RACHEL. Yeah, he can be a total dweeb
But
In some ways?
And this is gonna sound weird
But
He's the only person in the world I have.

MALE NETIZEN. NickWillRockYou has entered the chat room.

NICK. I wish I could have seen Adam's reaction when that name popped up on his screen.

MALE NETIZEN. NickWillRockYou

NICK. I was pretty sure he'd interpret my arrival as
Some kind of divine synchronicity.
That's what people do when they think they're in love.
Don't they?

There were a few other people in the room in addition to Adam. I steered clear of him—
But made the point to provoke everyone else in the room
On the one hand to make sure my screen name was visible at all times
On the other to piss everyone off enough
With tirades of bullshit that I'd clear the room.

DONTTREADONME76. Dude, that's totaly fucked up. I hop Homland Sacuraty's monitiring this so they send your ass 2 Gwantanumo.

NICK. Did you actually read the 9/11 report, dickhead?
Probably not, cause seeing how badly you spell you must be an illiterate fuck.

DONTTREADONME76. u r

NICK. Well if you read it— and I have from cover to cover
You'd know there's holes in it you could fly 20 767s through.

DONTTREADONME76. You muthaf—

NICK. I'm telling you: The U.S. government orchestrated the whole thing.

DONTTREADONME76. Bullshit.

NICK. It's all over the web, dude,
You just gotta know where to look to get the facts.

DONTTREADONME76. u r

NICK. And fuck it
Those guys who hijacked the planes were totally right

DONTTREADONME76. u r a fucking dick!
Donttreadonme76 has left the chatroom.

NICK. It didn't take long to clear the room
Adam stuck out all the bullshit
cause he recognized my screen name

ADAM. *NickWillRockYou*
Hey.

NICK. Hey.

ADAM. All that stuff u were saying?
Do u mean it?

NICK. No. Of course not.

ADAM. Then why'd u say it.

NICK. I like seeing how far you can push people's reactions.

ADAM. That's weird.

NICK. There was silence.
Then Adam made the first move.

It was kind of funny
And at the same time kind of
Sad
Watching *him* try to play *me*.

ADAM. Yeah. I'm just hanging. Waiting for this girl—

NICK. After awhile of him getting nowhere
I decided to throw him a bone

ADAM. Wow. That's wild, see,
Cause this girl I'm waiting for?
She lives in that neighborhood too.

NICK. What's this girl's name?

ADAM. Rachel.

NICK. Rachel.
Not
Rachel
Suttcliffe
By any chance?

ADAM. No way…
Dude,
u know her?!?!?!

NICK. Know her?

Dude,
She's my sister.

ADAM. No. Fucking. Way.

NICK. Once that was out in the open
The questions just poured in

ADAM. Is she as cool in person as she is on line?

NICK. She's awesome.

ADAM. And is she as hot as she is in her picture?

NICK. Dude, you're asking me,
Her brother,
If I think my sister's hot.

That's gross man.

ADAM. You know what I mean.

NICK. Let me put it this way:
If she wasn't my sister
I'd like
Totally wanna do her.

ADAM. That's sick dude.

NICK. Then came the plea for help…

ADAM. She says she can't meet me
Cause
Well
She says

RACHEL. It's complicated.

NICK. Well,
Dude,
I'm sorry to say:
It is.

ADAM. Why?

NICK & RACHEL. I can't explain that to you right now.

ADAM. That's what she always says.

NICK. But hey— even with all the
Complications…?
I might be able to help you.

ADAM. Really?

NICK. Sure dude.
As they say
Your wish is my command.

OLIVIA. Now when you do it
I need you to promise me that you'll tell him

That you love him.

5

NICK. The question the choice the question the choice the question the choice

MOLLY. What are these?

NICK. What are these?

MOLLY. Nick, can you hear me? What are these?

NICK. Do I tell the truth?

MOLLY. Nick

NICK. Or do I make shit up.

MOLLY. Nii-iick

NICK. The low-grade migraine, sweat glands juicing up, a hardening between my legs

MOLLY. Earth to Nick. Do you copy?

NICK. Me speeding up

MOLLY. What are these

NICK. The air taking on the consistency of peanut butter

MOLLY. NICK!

NICK. The question the choice the question the choice
Adam became as addicted to me
As he was to Rachel.
I became his corrupt psychiatrist—
Instead of curing him of his fixation
I deepened it,
Until I could make my next move.

ADAM. Friday night?
And Rachel will be there.

NICK. I promise you.
Thing is though
It has to be a surprise.
She finds out I invited you
She'll go ballistic.

ADAM. Why?

NICK. Rachel has her reasons,
Which my friend,
Are sometimes a complete mystery to me.

ADAM. I'll think about it.

NICK. I didn't think about what I'd do
if I did manage to lure Adam to my house for the "sleep over"

I just figured I'd play it by ear. See:

That's the thing that separates pros from the amateurs in this kind of game.

Amateurs don't leave any room for uncertainty or

improvisation.

They try to lock in their strategy before they even start to play the game,

Not taking into account the infinite contingencies that might come into play,

Wishfully thinking that the course of the future is something within their

control.

But the pro,

On the other hand,

Knows that locking in too early

Is a recipe for disaster— See:

When you lock in, you cut off the possibility of restrategizing midgame,

Staying in the moment,

taking the unexpected wild left turn to keep your mark off balance—

And yeah, this method of playing is riskier—

Chances of making a fatal mistake are exponentially greater—

But then, that's why I'm a pro and everyone else are amateurs.

When he showed up that Friday night—

After he met my Mom (and that was really fucking awkward)

We went downstairs to my bat cave

ADAM. So where's Rachel, Nick?

NICK. I made my face go all serious, grave. I said:

"My

stepfather

has her."

ADAM. What do you mean he

"has her."

NICK. Long story.

ADAM. Is she gonna come back?

NICK. Hard to say.

When my

Stepfather

Has her,

There's no telling when she'll be back.

ADAM. Look. Maybe I should go…

NICK. No.

I mean…

If you want to

Go ahead

But like

My Mom'll ask all sorts of questions and…

And who knows?
You stick around, maybe Rachel will get back.

And there was this
weird silence
And I didn't know what to do—
I got him here,
To my house,
To my room,
Which is what I wanted—
I guess—
But I just stood there like a fucking retard

If I had a gun in that moment?
I would've stuck it in my mouth and pulled the trigger
But Adam saved me.

ADAM. Your mom's pretty cool.

NICK. No she's not.

ADAM. I think she's cool.

NICK. That's cause she was hitting on you.

ADAM. She was not.

NICK. You don't know my Mom.
You coming here is like
The first time she's been that close to a man in

ADAM. What about your stepdad?

NICK. My *stepdad's* got plenty of other places to dunk his you know what.

ADAM. And she was hitting on me?

NICK. Dude, what are you blind or something?

ADAM. Your mom is kinda hot.

NICK. Dude. That's my mom you're talking about.

ADAM. Sorry. I was just
Kidding.

Hey, where's Rachel's room?

NICK. Upstairs. Second floor.

ADAM. Can we like
You know

NICK. You wanna check out my sister's room?

ADAM. Well,
Yeah,
I mean

NICK. What are you a stalker?

ADAM. No,
I just thought
NICK. What do you think she'd do if she found out?
ADAM. Forget it, man
NICK. "Hey Sis, guess what, you know that guy you've been mooning about?
The one you met on the internet?"
ADAM. Forget it, Nick.
NICK. "Yeah, well he came over and you know what he wanted to do?"
ADAM. Nick.
NICK. "He wanted me to sneak him into your room."
ADAM. Shut up.
NICK. "So he could sniff around your panty drawer."
Hey.
Don't push.
ADAM. Just shut the fuck up, all right?
NICK. I was just kidding
ADAM. Look. This totally sucks. I'm gonna go.
NICK. NO
I mean

You can go if you want to
But.
I wanna show you something.
ADAM. What?
NICK. I took him over to a file cabinet in the basement storage area.
ADAM. This better be good.
NICK. I opened the bottom drawer
reached towards the back
pulled out a thin folder.
I sat next to Adam on the floor,
And looked him sharp in the eye.

What's my name?
ADAM. Uhhh… Nick?
NICK. What's my *full* name?
ADAM. This is stupid.
NICK. Come on, what's my full name?
ADAM. Your full name is Nick Suttcliffe.
NICK. Right. Nick Suttcliffe.
What does it say at the top here?

ADAM. "Birth Certificate."

NICK. And what does it say here?

ADAM. "Nick…"

Wait a minute.

NICK. Creepy, isn't it.

ADAM. That's not your last name.

NICK. That *is* my name.
Only no one—
Except my mom and me—
And now you—
Knows it.

ADAM. How do you know it isn't somebody else's?

NICK. How old am I Adam?

ADAM. Fourteen?

NICK. And what does it say here.

ADAM. Date of birth // November 9, 1989

NICK. November 9, 1989.

My birthday, Adam.

ADAM. Dude that's fucked up.

Wait.
Isn't that today?

NICK. Yep.

ADAM. Oh.

NICK. I'm fifteen today.

ADAM. Oh

NICK. I was fourteen yesterday.
But I'm fifteen today.

ADAM. Oh
Well
Happy uhh
birthday
dude

NICK. Thanks.

ADAM. Wait:
Did you ever ask your Mom about this?

NICK. No fucking way.

ADAM. But don't you wanna know?

NICK. Sure I wanna know.

I don't go a single night,
Where I don't toss and turn in my bed
Wondering
Who's my real Dad?

See:
Until I found this
My Mother?
That psycho upstairs?
Led me to believe that her "first" husband was my dad.

And when he shot himself

ADAM. He shot himself?

NICK. When I was eleven.
He disappeared one night.
Cops found him the next morning
In his car
In the parking lot of a Jewel Osco
Sucking on the wrong end of a rifle barrel.

ADAM. Holy shit.
Wait:
What's a Jewel Osco.

NICK. Supermarket chain.
Back in Chicago.
They don't have them here.

ADAM. Nick—that's
Whoa.

NICK. It wasn't until we were packing up the house there
That I found this.
Realized
My whole fucking life was a lie.
The dead guy in the parking lot—
The guy who I thought was my father—
He wasn't my father.
He was just

Some dead guy.

ADAM. Dude…
If that happened to me,
Man I'd go straight to my Mom
Shove this right in her face and be like
"What the fuck?!?!"

NICK. Oh I've been tempted.
But

I'm holding onto this little secret
In case I ever need to go nuclear on her

ADAM. Whoa.

NICK. A beautiful silence hung in the room.
A silence filled with awe. With mystery.

Adam looked

Beautiful

ADAM. What about Rachel? Who's her dad?

NICK. There she was again.

RACHEL.

Who is *Rachel's* dad?
That asshole
Was so obsessed by that little bitch
He couldn't recognize me in that moment.
Rachel
Was more REAL to him
Than ME.
Me: they very person who
INVENTED
Rachel
For Christ's sake.

I wish I could describe the rage inside of me in that moment
I wanted to tear his heart out, shove it down his throat.
I wanted to laugh in his face and say
"You fucking FOOL.
You FUCKING TWIT.
THERE IS NO RACHEL,
YOU PIECE OF SHIT.
I
AM RACHEL
YOU'RE SITTING RIGHT NEXT TO "HER".
DO YOU WANT TO FALL IN LOVE WITH ME NOW?
ARE YOU DYING TO MEET ME NOW?
ARE YOU DYING TO STICK YOUR COCK IN ME NOW?
YOU JERK OFF FOR HER EVERY NIGHT,
WILL YOU JERK OFF FOR ME NOW?
HUH?
HUH?

I could so destroy you…

But I take pride in my self-control.

ADAM. What about Rachel? Who's her dad?

NICK. Who's Rachel's Dad?
Well,
Knowing my Mom?
Your guess is as good as mine.

Hey: Here's an idea. Next time you talk to Rachel, why don't you ask her?

RACHEL. Why are you asking me about my stepdad?

ADAM. Just curious

RACHEL. I don't want to talk about him.

ADAM. Y Not?

RACHEL. Certain subjects are off-limits. Okay?

ADAM. Ok. Well what do u want 2 talk about.

RACHEL. I don't want to talk anymore.
I want to watch.

ADAM. Let me turn the webcam on.

NICK. After resisting the temptation to tear Adam's throat out,
I poured drinks.

ADAM. What's this?

NICK. Absolut Mandarin.

Here.

ADAM. What if your Mom finds out?

NICK. My Mom buys like three cases of this stuff a week.
There's never any orange juice in the house
So she gets her Vitamin C intake with this.
She's always too fucked up to notice if one goes missing.

To Mom! Cheers!

ADAM. Holy shit.

NICK. What?

ADAM. You downed that.

NICK. The longer you nurse it,
The longer it takes to get where you want to go.

Your turn.

ADAM. I don't know

NICK. Come on! A-dam! A-dam! A-dam! // Yeah!

ADAM. Fuck!

NICK. Gross isn't it. I don't know how my Mom drinks this stuff like water.

Here. Have another one.

ADAM. No, dude, I'm cool with one.

NICK. Don't be such a pussy

ADAM. Fine.

NICK. Drink it.

ADAM. Okay.

Fuck!

So what do you wanna do?

NICK. You.

ADAM. Whatever. Seriously—what do you wanna do?

NICK. You. Come on. Let me do you. I'll do you like you wanna do Rachel.

ADAM. Shut up, man
That's gross.

NICK. You're right. It's totally gross. Disgusting. Filthy. Makes me wanna throw up. Here.

ADAM. I don't want any more.

NICK. Fine. Means I'll have even more for myself.

ADAM. Alright. Pour me another one.

NICK. So what *is* new on the Rachel-the-cock-tease front?

Where are you going?

ADAM. I'm getting out of here, dude,
You're being a total dick.

NICK. Don't go…
Please. Please don't go.

ADAM. Don't call her a cock tease.

NICK. Look:
I'm sorry.

ADAM. You said you were gonna help me.

NICK. I know.
I'm sorry.

Another shot?

ADAM. Fine.

You think she really likes me?

NICK. Does Michael Jackson like doing it to little boys?

ADAM. Come on, I'm serious.

NICK. Yeah. She likes you.
The other day? She left her chemistry notebook on the kitchen table?
Front cover and back was covered.
With your name.
She drew little hearts.
"Rachel n Adam 4Ever"

You really like her?

ADAM. Dude, I've never…

Felt

This way.

NICK. You're totally whipped.

ADAM. I mean

She's so

Cool

Like

Her picture?

She's

But not like in that way that

You'd be like

"Dude, she's way out of my league."

You know what I mean?

NICK. She likes you.

ADAM. I feel

Totally weird

You know?

Like

I'm

Forget it.

NICK. Like what?

ADAM. It's gonna sound queer but…

I think I love her

Which is weird cause

NICK. Cause you haven't met her.

ADAM. Yeah.

NICK. You think you'll like her as much when you meet her?

ADAM. I think so.

I hope so.

You think she'll like me?

NICK. Dude,

She will not be disappointed.

ADAM. I've imagined it.

Meeting her

NICK. What do you imagine?

ADAM. It's stupid.

NICK. No.

ADAM. We're like

On the beach? Chilling?
And it's like six o'clock so the light's all
Orange?
And we're just walking

NICK. What's she wearing?

ADAM. She's wearing like a skirt. Tank top. Sandals so
You can see her toes
And her toenail polish
Is like
Chipped.
And we're just walking side by side
And she's laughing
And there's like
Water
And waves
And little kids playing on the beach
And we're like
In our own world

NICK. I'm gonna have another.

So you're walking on the beach

ADAM. Yeah,
Just talking
And the sun's coming down
So we like
We sit
Looking at the ocean
This shit's getting to my head, I need to lie down.

NICK. Me too.

Ocean… sky… seagulls…?

ADAM. Yeah, yeah.
And we're just sitting there
Quiet you know?
Like we're all wrapped up in some
Feeling
And then,
Without either of us knowing who made the first move
We're
Holding hands.

NICK. Like this?

ADAM. Yeah.

NICK. What does it feel like?

ADAM. It's like a surge of

Good.

NICK. I'd like to feel that.

ADAM. Then she touches my face.

And I touch hers.

And her hair.

And we're looking in each other's eyes

Those green eyes…

NICK. Yeah?

ADAM. And like when we started holding hands

Neither of us making the first move

We kiss.

NICK. Like this?

ADAM. I'm totally wasted.

NICK. Me too.

Don't stop.

(*They're all over each other.*)

OLIVIA. Now when you do it,

I need you to promise me that you'll tell him

That you love him.

6

NICK. The question the choice the question the choice the question the choice

MOLLY. What are these?

NICK. What are these?

MOLLY. Nick, can you hear me? What are these?

NICK. Do I tell the truth?

MOLLY. Nick

NICK. Or do I make shit up.

MOLLY. Nii-iick

NICK. The low-grade migraine, sweat glands juicing up, a hardening between my legs

MOLLY. Earth to Nick. Do you copy?

NICK. Me speeding up

MOLLY. What are these

NICK. The air taking on the consistency of peanut butter

MOLLY. NICK!

NICK. The question the choice the question the choice

I mentioned before
That what separates the pros from the amateurs
Is the capacity to improvise mid game.
Now, I'd be totally lying to you
If I told you that I planned what happened that night.
I guess I wanted it to happen,
But wanting something,
And that thing actually happening...

That night ended up a little one-sided—
Turned out I did most of the giving.
I remember feeling on the one hand like
Well
How
God
must feel.

At the same time
Having Adam in my mouth
Hearing him say,

ADAM. Rachel. Oh. Fuck. Rachel.

NICK. You can imagine how that felt.

Wished it was the barrel of a gun instead of Adam that was in my mouth.

When we were done,
Adam puked.
We passed out.

When I woke up,
he was already gone.

MOM. Nicky? Hon?

NICK. What.

MOM. Could you come in my room a sec?

NICK. What.

MOM. You slept late.

NICK. I got stuff to do, Mom.

MOM. You look—

NICK. Who's the lucky guy tonight?

MOM. Nick...

NICK. That's an awful lot of eye shadow you're wearing

MOM. Nick...

NICK. You just might convince him you're still 25

MOM. Ha. Ha. Sit down.

NICK. Can this wait?

MOM. It'll only take a minute.

NICK. Fine.

MOM. I liked your friend. Aaron, was it?

NICK. Adam. You liked him but you can't even remember his name.

MOM. I'm sorry Nicky,
I'm just…
Where did you two meet?

NICK. Around.

MOM. Just "around"?

NICK. What about "around" don't you understand?

MOM. Well…
Could you be more specific?

NICK. What's with the interrogation?

MOM. I'm not interr//ogating I'm

NICK. I mean what's next,
Are you gonna put a hood over my head? Attach electrodes to my nipples?
Take some souvenir photographs?

MOM. Nicky.

NICK. I mean what do you want me to say? Huh? I met him around. Why is
that so difficult to believe? You meet all sorts of people. In all sorts of places.
How am I supposed to remember shit // like that.

MOM. Language, Nicky.

NICK. Stuff
Like that?

MOM. Well, it's not exactly as if you have parades of friends walking
through that door.

NICK. Whatever.

MOM. Adam is the first friend you've brought to the house since we moved
here
I don't think it's unreasonable to ask a simple question // about where

NICK. Yeah, and I answered your question. Around.
Okay?
Now can I go?

MOM. What's happening to you?

NICK. Jesus

MOM. You didn't used to be this way. You used to talk to me.
Go ahead, Nick. Leave.
But before you leave let me make something clear:

Until you're willing to tell me where you met that boy

NICK. Oh, he's "that boy" now, // I see how it is

MOM. *Until* you're willing to tell me where you met that boy,
You are not allowed to bring him into this house // again.

NICK. But I thought you liked // him, Mom

MOM. You are not allowed to see him under *any* circumstances.
Have I made myself clear.

NICK. Clear
as
mud,
Mom.

MOM. Who are you?

NICK. And you don't have to worry about him coming over anymore.
Not after the way you acted.

MOM. Excuse me?

NICK. I know you're a lonely old hag
But did you have to hit on him?

MOM. WHAT.
DID.
YOU.
SAY?

NICK. I know you like them young,
But that was a little ridiculous.

MOM. Oh God. Oh my God.
Oh sweetie sweetie sweetie sweetie I didn't mean that

NICK. You hit me

MOM. Baby, I'm sorry I'm sorry

NICK. Why did you hit me?

MOM. Sweetie
Don't cry…
Please
Don't cry…

You're okay. We're okay. Shhhh. It's okay.

You used to be like a little cat.
I'd go from one room to the next
And I wouldn't notice
That you had followed me.
You were so quiet.
Content to be just close by.
I used to call you Kitty.

But when you got bigger
You hated me calling you that.
Then you were Nicky.
Don't stop being Nicky…
Please honey,
You'll always be my Nicky.

7

NICK. The question the choice the question the choice the question the choice

MOLLY. What are these?

NICK. What are these?

MOLLY. Nick, can you hear me? What are these?

NICK. Do I tell the truth?

MOLLY. Nick

NICK. Or do I make shit up.

MOLLY. Nii-iick

NICK. The low-grade migraine, sweat glands juicing up, a hardening between my legs

MOLLY. Earth to Nick. Do you copy?

NICK. Me speeding up

MOLLY. What are these

NICK. The air taking on the consistency of peanut butter

MOLLY. NICK!

NICK. The question the choice the question the choice
Adam cut me off. I'd come into the chat room, be like
"Hey, what's up?"

ADAM. JustWant2ChillWithU has left the chat room.

NICK. I'd Instant Message him.

ADAM. *JustWant2ChillWithU* is now offline.

NICK. I sent him emails.

ADAM. Message to
JustWant2ChillWithU@aol.com has been returned to sender.

NICK. The silence felt like fifty kicks to the stomach.
I would have walked onto the 101 in the direction of oncoming traffic—
And I'm not kidding when I say I seriously considered this option—
Were it not for Rachel.

She was still alive for Adam—
Though barely.

He started getting harsh with her.
Mean.

He told her one day:

ADAM. I think u r a fucking cock tease.

NICK. Wasn't the same Adam
That wrote in his profile way back when

ADAM. I want to fall in love with a girl

NICK. "Love" was no longer part of his vocabulary

RACHEL. But I love you.
How can you say such a thing?

ADAM. "LOVE"

NICK. Adam had gone from saying the word and meaning it
To making it sound like the punch line of a mean joke.

ADAM. "LOOOOVVVEEE"

RACHEL. How can you be so cruel?

ADAM. Me? Cruel?
What about u?
"I *can't* meet you."
"It's *complicated*."

I'm a fucking idiot.
I never want 2 talk 2 u again.

RACHEL. Please. Don't say that, Adam. I love you.

ADAM. Prove it.

RACHEL. I will.

ADAM. How.

RACHEL. Turn on your webcam?

ADAM. Fuck no.

RACHEL. I'll show you how much I love you.

ADAM. Turn on your webcam.

RACHEL. You know my stepfather won't let me have one.

ADAM. I believe that. Whatever.

RACHEL. Please, don't go.
I'll do anything.

ADAM. Anything.

RACHEL. Yes.
Anything.

ADAM. I want to meet u.

r u there?

RACHEL. Okay.

Fine.

I'll meet you.

ADAM. U will?

RACHEL. Yes.

Friday.

4:30.

By the carousel on the pier.

ADAM. Friday.

R u sure?

RACHEL. I've never been more sure of anything in my life.

ADAM. Okay.

RACHEL. Will you do something for me?
I want to watch.

ADAM. I'll
I'll turn my webcam on.

NICK. Of course this was a date Rachel couldn't keep.
Could you imagine? Me standing on the pier
by the carousel,
squeezed into a miniskirt and tanktop
"Hi Adam, It's me, Rachel."

I've gotten the shit kicked out of me before
It's no fun.
I don't like pain—
Though I will admit—
And it's totally fucked, I know—
But there was a certain amount of pleasure
In imagining Adam inflict it.
Better that than total silence from him,
Right?

I guess that's what you call being lovesick.
It was in this state of utter uselessness
That it became clear:
If I needed to keep Adam I had to do the unthinkable.

FEMALE NETIZEN. *Capiche911* has entered the chat room.

TONY. *JustWant2ChillWithU*
You're Adam, right?

ADAM. Yeah.

TONY. Nice to meet you, Adam.

ADAM. Who r u?

TONY. Adam Moody, right?

ADAM. Who the fuck r u?

TONY. I'd watch your language if I were you, Adam.
We don't like it when people use the F word to me

ADAM. Oh yeah?

TONY. There was one kid—
God bless him—
Who said that word to me one too many times,
You know what happened to him?

ADAM. What?

TONY. Cops found him one night
Hanging from a tree.
You wanna know how he was hanging from that tree?

ADAM. Um…. A rope?

TONY. Railroad spikes.

That's right. Some sick fuck crucified him with railroad spikes.
To a tree.
Sick, don't you think.

ADAM. Yeah.

TONY. Even sicker
He was missing parts.

ADAM. Like what parts.

TONY. Use your imagination,.
Can you use your imagination,
Or do I need to help you out?
Adam. Moody. of 1211 Camino Del Sur.

ADAM. Who r u?

TONY. That's a good question, Adam.
But I think a better question is
WHO
The
FUCK
R
U
!

We got a little problem here, Adam.
It seems you've been wanting to stick your toothpick dick
In places
Where your toothpick dick don't belong.

ADAM. I don't know what u r talking about.

TONY. "I don't know what you're talking about."
That's funny, Adam Moody of 1211 Camino del Sur.

I'll put it to you even simpler:
Stay.
The Fuck.
Away.
From Rachel.

ADAM. You know Rachel?

TONY. Yeah.
I know Rachel.
And I know what you're trying to do to her.

ADAM. I'm not doing anything.

TONY. You filthy little piece of shit,
"I'm not doing anything"—
I'll come over there right now,
take that web cam of yours and shove it right up your ass, you little prick,
Don't think I don't know what you're up to
Don't think I don't know what you do in front of that camera every night
I've seen it and it's disgusting. You're fucking sick,
You know that? Doing that in front of a fifteen year old girl?
What's the matter with you?

ADAM. It wasn't my idea

TONY. You spineless piece of shit.
You know what I have a mind to do?
I have a mind to send someone over there right now
To slowly cut your balls off in front of that web cam of yours
I would love to watch that. I'll sit here drinkin my fuckin bottle of Yoohoo
watch you scream like a little bitch, "pleeeeeeaaaaaase don't cut my
baaaaaaalls off".

Scared now?

Consider this little conversation a warning:
Stay.
The Fuck.
Away.
From my stepdaughter.

ADAM. She's
Your stepdaughter...?

TONY. Really scared now, aren't you.

I'll say it again. And slowly this time, so you get the message, nice and clear:
Stay.

The Fuck.

Away.

From.

My.

Stepdaughter.

Cause man to man,
Adam Moody of 1211 Camino del Sur.
Only one of us can have her.
And that one of us
Is not you.
You dig?

FEMALE NETIZEN. Capiche911 has left the chat room.

RACHEL. He did what?

ADAM. He said he was gonna crucify me to a tree
Using railroad spikes

RACHEL. He's such a bastard

ADAM. He said something…

RACHEL. What did he say?

ADAM. He said

TONY. Only one of us can have her.
And that one of us
Is Not You.

RACHEL. I'm so ashamed.
This is awful.

ADAM. What did he mean?

RACHEL. I'll tell you everything when I see you Friday

ADAM. I don't know if Friday's such a good idea

RACHEL. Fuck him.
I'm meeting you.
I'm tired of being his slave.
He can go fuck himself.

ADAM. Rachel, be careful

RACHEL. I'm tired of being careful.

I'll see you Friday.

Where we said we'd meet.

OLIVIA. Now when you do it,
I need you to promise me that you'll tell him
That you love him.

8

NICK. The question the choice the question the choice the question the choice

MOLLY. What are these?

NICK. What are these?

MOLLY. Nick, can you hear me? What are these?

NICK. Do I tell the truth?

MOLLY. Nick

NICK. Or do I make shit up.

MOLLY. Nii-iick

NICK. The low-grade migraine, sweat glands juicing up, a hardening between my legs

MOLLY. Earth to Nick. Do you copy?

NICK. Me speeding up

MOLLY. What are these

NICK. The air taking on the consistency of peanut butter

MOLLY. NICK!

NICK. The question the choice the question the choice

NICK. I waited on the pier,
Out of sight from the carousel,
So Adam wouldn't see me.
When he showed
He was so…

He'd dressed for the occasion.
He had a bouquet of roses in his hand.

I watched him for a bit

Everything moved so fast
Except for him
Except for me.
We moved like we lived in a world made of peanut butter.

ADAM. WHAT
The FUCK
Are YOU
Doing here?

NICK. Adam,
Please,
Hear me out.

ADAM. You sick little faggot,

I should kick your ass
NICK. Please, Adam.
I swear
I never would've come here
If it wasn't
Important.
ADAM. Two seconds.
NICK. Rachel's missing.
ADAM. Bullshit.
NICK. I swear to you on my life.
Our stepdad
He took her
ADAM. What do you mean he took her?
NICK. He found out that she had a date to meet you
He went ballistic.
Beat the shit out of my Mom,
Smashed up Rachel's room,
her computer
She ran into my room
Scared,
Crying,
Adam,
She was crying,
She told me she was meeting you
She begged me to come and tell you what happened
Then my stepdad came into the room,
Pulled her by the hair and dragged her out of the house
ADAM. I don't believe you.
What the fuck are you doing?
NICK. Look.
Does this look like I'm lying?
ADAM. Holy shit— what the fuck is that?
NICK. He put his cigar out on my shoulder.
ADAM. I'm
I'm sorry.
NICK. Yeah, well fuck you!
ADAM. Don't cry man,
I'm sorry—
NICK. I don't know where he took her

I'm so fucking scared, Adam

ADAM. Come on,
I'll take you back to your house.

NICK. NO!
I can't go there.
I'll sleep on the beach
Anything.
But not there.

ADAM. Come on.
I'll take you over to my house.

NICK. As we left the pier
Adam took the flowers he'd gotten for Rachel
And dumped them in a trash can.

Adam didn't have any Absolut Mandarin in his house.
We didn't need it.
I cried the whole time
I was so raw.
This time though
When I had him in my mouth
He didn't say

ADAM. Rachel, Fuck, Rachel

NICK. He said my name.

I fell asleep on his bed.
I don't know what time it was
But the words

MALE NETIZEN. You've got mail.

NICK. Coming from his computer
Woke me
Eyes half opened I watched his back
And the light from the computer monitor
outlining the muscles of his arms.

His shoulders started to shake…
His breathing…
Like he was hyperventilating.

TONY. You little fuck.
I told you to stay away from her,
Adam Moody of 1211 Camino del Sur.
But since you didn't listen.
Take a good long hard look at this picture.
You did this.

NICK. The photo…

Whoa.

Body of a girl,
About 5'6"
at the side of the freeway.
Thighs all bruised.
Clothes torn.

A few feet away from her body,
Her head.
She could've had dirty blonde hair,
But you couldn't tell cause it was all matted in blood.

She didn't have much of a face left.

I got the picture off this web site where you can download crime scene photos.

Sick shit.

Adam ran to the bathroom.
Locked the door.
I could hear him puking his guts out.

I knocked.

ADAM. Go away.

NICK. Adam
It's me
Nick

ADAM. Go away.
Please.

Go away.

NICK. So I left.

OLIVIA. Now when you do it
I need you to promise me that you'll tell him
That you love him.

9

NICK. After leaving his house
I stayed out all night.

I'd reached my own gullibility threshold,
And it broke my heart to realize
That I was a 10.
I believed everything,

I wondered
What Ms. Spiegel,

My Theatre Arts teacher,
Would've thought about my Dark Play?

MS. SPIEGEL. The best theatre takes the audience on a journey into the darkest,
Most *dangerous*,
Regions of the human soul.

NICK. Was my Dark Play dark enough?
Dangerous enough?

MS. SPIEGEL. At the end of the journey
The audience,
Having faced that
Darkness,
That
Danger,
Can recognize the darkness and danger lurking in their own souls,

NICK. I sure as hell recognized the darkness and danger lurking in my soul

MS. SPIEGEL. And actively take steps to
Change
It.

NICK. I couldn't do shit to change it.
There was only one thing left for me to do:

TONY. heinousbusterSVU has entered the chat room.

OLIVIA. Adam? Adam Moody?

ADAM. Who r u?

OLIVIA. My name is Olivia Stabler.
I work with the Special Victims Unit of the New York City Police Department.

ADAM. Riiight.

OLIVIA. In the criminal justice system, sexually based offences are considered especially heinous. In New York City, the dedicated detectives who investigate these vicious felonies are members of an elite squad known as the Special Victims Unit.

ADAM. What
ever.

OLIVIA. I'm a member of this elite squad. I've been asked to come here to southern California to help investigate a string of especially heinous brutal sex murders that have taken place in the area too complex and heinous for local law enforcement. Given our expertise in solving heinous cases I'm here to nail the heinous bastards that have been committing these heinous crimes.

ADAM. What do u want with me?

OLIVIA. Adam, Sweetie. I need to ask you a favor.

I don't really care how you write when you're chatting with people your own age.
But when you chat with me,
chat like an adult.

ADAM. What are u trying 2 say?

OLIVIA. I detest teen talk.
"U" and "R" are letters. If you mean "you are"— spell it out
Y-O-U-A-R-E. Same with "2". That's a number, not a preposition.

ADAM. Oh.

OLIVIA. How old are you Adam?

ADAM. Sixteen. Going on seventeen.

OLIVIA. You're almost a man.

ADAM. I guess.

OLIVIA. You guess.

Adam: Either you are almost a man or you aren't. Which is it?

ADAM. I'm almost a man.

OLIVIA. Good. So write like one.

You knew Rachel Sutcliffe.

Adam?

I'm asking you a simple yes/no question: did you know Rachel Sutcliffe.

ADAM. No.

OLIVIA. I see. What about her brother? Nick? Nick Sutcliffe?

ADAM. I don't know anyone named Nick.

OLIVIA. Okay.

I understand your need to deny that you know him.
To deny that you knew her.
To deny all the things you've done that...

Well,
things
that if I were in your shoes
I might deny too.

ADAM. Fuck off.

OLIVIA. Language, Adam.
How do you think that poor, decapitated girl would feel
If she knew you denied knowing her?
How will you live with yourself knowing you did that?

I ask you again:
Did you know Rachel Sutcliffe.

ADAM. Yes.

OLIVIA. How well did you know Rachel?

ADAM. I

Don't want you to think I'm like…

A freak or anything for saying it but—

OLIVIA. Adam:

What did I say to you before about teen language?

ADAM. That you don't like it.

OLIVIA. That's right. And what was wrong with that sentence.

ADAM. Which sentence?

OLIVIA. Scroll up. The one that reads: "Don't think I'm *like*… a freak for saying this"

Adam: You can't be "like" anything. You either are or you aren't a freak.

ADAM. Right.

OLIVIA. So what is it you want to tell me about Rachel

That makes you afraid I'll look at you as a freak?

ADAM. I

I loved her.

OLIVIA. That's what I thought.

And that's why I've sought you out.

We need your help.

NICK. At that point

To explain why she needed Adam's help,

Olivia rolled in a Titanic-sized wheelbarrow of caca

I can't remember exactly what I had Olivia tell Adam

Some bullshit

About our stepfather and some

criminal conspiracy

surrounding Rachel's murder.

That involved

illegal drug trafficking

"Coyotes" smuggling illegal aliens across the U.S.-Mexico border

child pornography

snuff movies

Internet identity theft…

OLIVIA. Al Qaeda // sleeper cells

NICK. Right: al Qaeda sleeper cells

The details aren't what's important,

What's important is that

Olivia tried to convince Adam

If he "followed the money"—

She actually *said* that—

OLIVIA. Follow the money

NICK. the trail would lead to Nick.

OLIVIA. Right now as we sit here chit-chatting, they're out there
Perpetrating their rape of southern California.
Adam: The Syndicate has used Nick
To procure victims for them on the world wide web.
Teenagers like you. Underage. Sometimes even younger.

You drink milk, don't you?

ADAM. Um. Yeah?

OLIVIA. You've seen the faces of those kids staring at you from the cartons?
What do you think happened to them?
Nick had every intention of turning you
From a normal, well-adjusted, middle class young man
Into one of those faces staring you down while you eat your Cap'n Crunch.

ADAM. I don't believe you.

OLIVIA. You are one lucky teenager. That could have been your head
Lying in a ditch at the side of the freeway.

ADAM. I'm not gullible.
I'm not stupid.

OLIVIA. That could have been you, had it not been for Rachel getting in the way.

ADAM. I am NOT gullible.
I am NOT stupid.

OLIVIA. Of course you aren't, Adam.
So it should be clear to you:
Nick sold Rachel out.
How do you think her stepfather knew she was planning to meet you?

Adam?

Don't get me wrong:
Nick was a victim here too—
But Nick stopped being a victim on the day he had his sister murdered.
Depravity begets depravity.
And now Nick is beyond depraved.
He's become an inhuman monster.

He must be put down.

We need you to eliminate him.

ADAM. Wait
Are you saying…

You want me to kill him?

OLIVIA. "Kill" is such an ugly word, Adam.

Criminals kill.

Law enforcement solves crimes.

ADAM. Okay…

Hypothetically…

OLIVIA. That's a good word, Adam. I'm impressed.

ADAM. Hypothetically…

If all this

Were real

And hypothetically…

If I went along with what you're asking…

What do I do?

OLIVIA. Make contact with him.

Have him meet you in a public place.

The mall.

When he shows, tell him you have to run an errand for your mother.

Take him to Williams Sonoma on the second level.

Buy a knife

(we'll reimburse you, don't worry).

ADAM. What kind of knife.

OLIVIA. A big knife.

ADAM. Like a butcher knife.

OLIVIA. Exactly.

Take him to where they keep the dumpsters behind the Sears.

Get him up against the wall.

Start stabbing him.

Hypothetically.

ADAM. God.

OLIVIA. I know it's a heavy burden.

But think of the burden Nick will be to all of us if he's allowed to live.

Think of the favor you'll be doing Southern California.

ADAM. What about me? What do I get out of it?

OLIVIA. The rewards for you, Adam, will be great.

ADAM. What kind of rewards?

OLIVIA. Use your // imagination

TONY. Use your // imagination

RACHEL. Use your // imagination

NICK. Use your imagination.

OLIVIA. And with all that he's put you through, Adam

Isn't there a part of you
That *wants* to kill him?

Will you do it?

ADAM. Yes.

OLIVIA. Good.

One more thing:
Now when you do it
I need you to promise me that you'll tell him
That you love him.

ADAM. What?

OLIVIA & NICK. You do love him, don't you.

NICK. Don't you?

10

NICK. Adam looked

Different

When we met in the food court of the mall.

He looked

Older.

Like a

Well

Like a man.

It was hard to look him in the eye.

ADAM. Hey.

NICK. Hey.

ADAM. Everything okay?

NICK. Yeah.

You?

ADAM. I'm fine.

Listen. I have to run an errand for my mother.
I need to find the Williams Sonoma.

NICK. We walked in silence.

He did everything Olivia instructed him to do
With calm
With grace
With

Dignity.

ADAM. Let's get out of here. Go find some place more quiet to
To talk.

NICK. We left the mall.
Walked back to the area behind Sears where they keep the dumpsters.
I was calm.

ADAM. I have something for you.

NICK. I didn't feel the first thrust.

ADAM. I love you

NICK. I didn't feel the second or third

ADAM. I love you
I love you

NICK. The fourth felt like a pinprick to a fingertip.

ADAM. I love you

NICK. Five,
Six,
Seven
Times

ADAM. I love you
I love you
I love you
I

NICK. I remember lying on the pavement
Feeling a smile spread across my face
The silhouette of Adam against the blue southern California sky
hovering above me for a second before he ran...

That's when I felt it
A wave
A hurricane
An earthquake
Mt. St. Helen's blowing her top.
A cloudburst and
A shower of wine
A swirl of color
Disappearing outlines
The sky splitting open,
Swallowing me
The earth cracking open
Levitating me
A gazillion tiny lightbulbs
Twinkling through the pores of my skin

The Virgin Mary and Mary Magdalene
Caressing,
Kissing
licking
my flesh
a skyscraper collapsing
a mother giving birth
No ME
I love you
No ME
I love you
Fire
Water

Light
Air
White.
I love you.

If this is what death is like.
I want to die every day.

But I lived.

11

MOLLY. What are these?

Nick, can you hear me? What are these?
Nick
Nii-iick

Earth to Nick. Do you copy?

What are these
NICK!

NICK. Do I tell her the truth?
Or do I make shit up.

She was about to get out of bed and leave
When I said,
"Okay okay okay. I'll tell you. I'll tell you everything."

And I told her.
Everything.

She didn't say anything for awhile.
She just smoked her cigarette in silence.
It was starting to get light outside.

Finally, she put out her cigarette and said:

MOLLY. Nick, you are totally full of shit. Why do you always have to make shit up?

NICK. And she went to sleep.

I go to college now
I work nights at the campus library.
I still live in the dorms,
But I'm hoping to save enough money this quarter
And over the summer
So I can get my own place this fall.

I guess you can say I have a girlfriend.
That's her lying naked on the bed.
Things are pretty much normal now. I guess.
I mean
There's still a lot of stuff I need to figure out
but
I'm pretty much indistinguishable from any other college kid.

I'm still undecided about my major.

End of Play

MR. AND MRS.
by Julie Marie Myatt

BIOGRAPHY

Julie Marie Myatt's play *My Wandering Boy* premiered at South Coast Repertory in April, 2007 and was featured in the 2007 Summer Play Festival in New York City. Her play *Boats on a River* premiered at the Guthrie Theater in May, 2007. *Welcome Home, Jenny Sutter* will premiere at Oregon Shakespeare Festival in early 2008, and will later tour to the Kennedy Center. *The Sex Habits of American Women* was produced by the Guthrie Theater, Signature Theatre in Arlington, VA, and Synchronicity Performance Group, and premiered at the Magic Theatre in San Francisco. Her work has been developed and/or seen at Actors Theatre of Louisville, Seattle Rep, LAByrinth Theater Company, and A.S.K Theater Projects, among others. She received a Walt Disney Studios Screenwriting Fellowship, a Jerome Fellowship at the Playwrights' Center, and a McKnight Advancement Grant. She is a member of New Dramatists. Her other plays include *August is a thin girl, Alice in the Badlands* and *49 Days to the Sun.*

ACKNOWLEDGMENTS

Mr. and Mrs. premiered at the Humana Festival of New American Plays in March 2007. It was directed by Jessica Burgess with the following cast and staff:

DEBRA ....Maurine Evans
STEVEN ....Mark Stringham

Scenic Designer ....Paul Owen
Costume Designer.................................... Susan Neason
Lighting Designer.................................... Paul Werner
Sound Designer ....Benjamin Marcum
Properties Designer ....Doc Manning
Fight Director..Lee Look
Stage Managers ....Michael D. Domue, Debra Anne Gasper
Production Assistant.............................. Melissa Miller
Dramaturg.............................. Joanna K. Donehower
Assistant Dramaturg.............................. Diana Grisanti

CAST OF CHARACTERS

DEBRA
STEVEN

Maurine Evans and Mark Stringham
in *Mr. and Mrs.*

31st Annual Humana Festival of New American Plays
Actors Theatre of Louisville, 2007
Photo by Harlan Taylor

MR. AND MRS.

MALE VOICE. (*Offstage.*) Ladies and gentlemen, I proudly present you, Mr. and Mrs.—

(*Crowd claps and cheers offstage.*)

(*A band plays, "At Last," offstage.*)

(DEBRA *and* STEVEN *enter holding hands and begin to dance. She is at least a foot taller than him. They both have had more than a few wedding toasts/drinks. They smile and a FLASHBULB goes off to capture the smile.*)

(*Flashbulbs will continue to go off throughout the play, and they will stop to smile just at the right moment for the picture, and continue dancing until the end.*)

DEBRA. I need to tell you something, Steven—oh, you've got something in your teeth, sweetheart. Right there. To the left. Yeah. There, you got it. I think it was a poppy seed from that hideous dressing. I was a little disappointed by the salad. I couldn't taste one bit of lemon. Could you?

STEVEN. I don't know.

DEBRA. It was all lettuce, seeds and oil. Please. No one ate it.

STEVEN. I did.

(*SMILE/FLASH.*)

DEBRA. Boy, your mother sure can put them away, huh?

STEVEN. Yeah.

DEBRA. No wonder she insisted on the open bar. My father really wasn't happy about that, you know. He doesn't drink.

STEVEN. Or smile.

DEBRA. This was a great expense for him. This wedding. It was all extremely extravagant for him.

STEVEN. Napkins are extravagant?

DEBRA. They don't grow on trees.

(*SMILE/FLASH.*)

I thought the ceremony was nice, didn't you?

STEVEN. Uh huh.

DEBRA. Your vows were lovely. Thank you.

STEVEN. You're welcome. So were yours.

DEBRA. Really? I wanted to surprise you—

(*SMILE/FLASH.*)

STEVEN. Though I think it's pronounced "eternity," not "entirety."

DEBRA. Really?

STEVEN. Yes.

DEBRA. Are you sure?

STEVEN. Positive.

    (SMILE/FLASH.)

DEBRA. Steven, I need to tell you—

    (SMILE/FLASH.)

Of course this is very difficult for me, but I can't go another minute without being completely honest with you—

    (SMILE/POSE/FLASH.)

This day has been so emotional and meaningful—

    (SMILE/FLASH.)

And you look so nice in your tux.

STEVEN. Thank you.

    (SMILE/FLASH.)

DEBRA. I married you for your money.

    (SMILE/FLASH.)

Steven?

STEVEN. Yes.

DEBRA. Did you hear me?

STEVEN. You married me for my money.

DEBRA. Well, what do you think, sweetheart? Are you devastated?

    (SMILE/FLASH.)

STEVEN. I married you for your looks.

    (SMILE/FLASH.)

DEBRA. What?

STEVEN. What?

DEBRA. I thought you married me because you loved me.

STEVEN. Really?

DEBRA. Yes.

STEVEN. What gave you that impression?

DEBRA. The engagement ring, I suppose.

    (SMILE/FLASH.)

Do you love me?

STEVEN. Do you love me?

DEBRA. I don't hate you.

STEVEN. That's a relief.

DEBRA. But I just assumed. I guess I assumed—
(*SMILE/FLASH.*)
I thought you were infatuated with me.
STEVEN. Infatuated?
DEBRA. Yes.
STEVEN. That's an awfully strong word.
DEBRA. What word would you use?
STEVEN. I don't know—
DEBRA. Head over heels?
STEVEN. No.
DEBRA. Enamored?
(*SMILE/DIP/FLASH.*)
STEVEN. No.
DEBRA. Smitten?
STEVEN. The sex is terrific.
DEBRA. Thank you.
STEVEN. But beyond that—
(*SMILE/FLASH.*)
(*Silence.*)
DEBRA. Beyond that...?
STEVEN. What?
DEBRA. Beyond the sex?
(*Silence.*)
Am I that hard to describe? ...Is it because I'm mysterious? Intimidating—
STEVEN. You're a little dull.
DEBRA. Dull?
(*SMILE/FLASH.*)
STEVEN. You're a little limited in the things you like to talk about.
DEBRA. I beg your pardon. I like to talk about a lot of things.
STEVEN. Like what?
DEBRA. The world.
STEVEN. What about it?
DEBRA. I have a lot of interests. And I am passionate about issues, Steven. Issues are very important to me.
STEVEN. Dieting is not an issue.
(*SMILE/FLASH.*)
DEBRA. Many people struggle with dietary issues, Steven. Food is a major issue. Major.

(SMILE/FLASH.)

STEVEN. Sudan is a major issue, Debra. George W. Bush driving this country into the ground and leaving it bankrupt for future generations, is a major issue. Solving world hunger is a major issue. You starving yourself, is a hobby.

DEBRA. It is not.

STEVEN. It is the speck of dust on the lice that rides the flea who rides the dog who sniffs the bone to find some purpose in life. Or a fire hydrant. Which ever comes first.

(SMILE/FLASH.)

DEBRA. You don't seem to mind f-u-c-k-ing this starved body.

(SMILE/FLASH.)

STEVEN. I didn't say I didn't like it.

DEBRA. Good—

STEVEN. I didn't say I didn't like doing ridiculously dirty, lewd things to it.

DEBRA. OK—

STEVEN. Or seeing it do amazingly athletic and illegal things to me—

DEBRA. Thank you—

STEVEN. I just don't want to hear you jabber on about it like it's Watergate or Perestroika.

(SMILE/FLASH.)

DEBRA. You think I like listening to the things you jabber on about?

STEVEN. Do you understand them?

DEBRA. Steven.

STEVEN. What?

DEBRA. You're really not as smart as you think you are.

STEVEN. Do you know what I do for a living, Debra?

DEBRA. For heaven's sake.

STEVEN. What?

DEBRA. You're a lawyer.

STEVEN. What kind?

DEBRA. Expensive.

STEVEN. What kind?

DEBRA. Does it matter?

(SMILE/FLASH.)

STEVEN. I'm a litigator.

DEBRA. OK.

STEVEN. Do you know what I do?

DEBRA. Litigate, I would imagine.

STEVEN. What does that mean?

DEBRA. Jesus, Steven. What is this, the third degree on our wedding day?

STEVEN. You brought it up.

DEBRA. This day is supposed to be special.

     (SMILE/FLASH.)

I have waited 31 years for this day, Steven. 31 years. I won't have you ruin it with insults.

STEVEN. They aren't insults.

DEBRA. What do you call them?

STEVEN. Facts.

DEBRA. Same thing.

     (SMILE/FLASH.)

I mean, look at me. Did you even notice my dress?

STEVEN. Your father is pouring that shit back into the bottles. Classic.

DEBRA. And my hair? Did you notice I have it up?

STEVEN. What are those things stuck in it?

DEBRA. Flowers.

STEVEN. Oh.

DEBRA. And my make-up?

STEVEN. A little thick, but you know, fine.

     (SMILE/FLASH.)

DEBRA. You married me for my looks, and yet you haven't ever *really* looked at me.

STEVEN. I'm only human, Debra.

DEBRA. Look at me.

STEVEN. I'm looking.

DEBRA. Look into my eyes.

STEVEN. I'm trying.

     (She stoops down so he can see better.)

DEBRA. Look into my eyes, Steven.

STEVEN. I'm a lawyer, not an optometrist.

DEBRA. Look into my eyes. What do you see?

     (SMILE/FLASH.)

STEVEN. Well.

DEBRA. Well, what? What do you see, honey?

STEVEN. Huh.

DEBRA. Is it love?

STEVEN. Not exactly.

DEBRA. You see forever?

STEVEN. I'm not sure.

DEBRA. What do you see?

STEVEN. I see two slightly vacant, but oddly sly desperate furry and searing angry endless old poodle/burnt plastic-scented dank black holes. Almost akin to an abyss. With something that seems like just a hint of Crystal Light or Dexatrim peeking through.

DEBRA. Oh, Steven. You know what that is?

STEVEN. Cheap champagne?

DEBRA. Your future, sweetheart. Entirety.

(*SMILE/FROWN/FLASH.*)

End of Play

I AM NOT BATMAN.
by Marco Ramirez

BIOGRAPHY

Marco Ramirez is a graduate of New York University's Tisch School of the Arts. His plays have been produced at City Theatre's Summer Shorts, the New York International Fringe Festival (FringeNYC), and the Humana Festival of New American Plays. He is the two-time winner of the Latino Playwriting Award at the Kennedy Center's American College Theatre Festival, and recently received a commission to write a full-length play for the Kennedy Center's Educational Theatre Program. He is currently working on two full-length plays: one is about a giant, the other is about a werewolf.

ACKNOWLEDGMENTS

I am not Batman. received the 2007 Heideman award from the Actors Theatre of Louisville. It premiered at the Humana Festival of New American Plays in March 2007. It was directed by Ian Frank with the following cast and staff:

A BOY .... Phil Pickens
A DRUMMER .... Zdenko Slobodnik

Scenic Designer .... Paul Owen
Costume Designer... Susan Neason
Lighting Designer... Paul Werner
Sound Designer .... Benjamin Marcum
Properties Designer .... Doc Manning
Fight Director.. Lee Look
Stage Managers .... Michael D. Domue, Debra Anne Gasper
Production Assistant.. Melissa Miller
Dramaturg .... Joanna K. Donehower
Assistant Dramaturg.. Diana Grisanti

CAST OF CHARACTERS

A BOY
A DRUMMER

Zdenko Slobodnik and Phil Pickens
in *I am not Batman.*

31st Annual Humana Festival of New American Plays
Actors Theatre of Louisville, 2007
Photo by Harlan Taylor

I AM NOT BATMAN.

Sudden drumming, then quiet. Lights up on a BOY, *maybe 7, maybe 27, wearing a hooded sweatshirt. He looks out directly before him, breathing nervously. A* DRUMMER *sits behind a drum set placed in the middle of the stage, in some kind of silhouette. The* BOY *is excited, but never gets ahead of himself.*

BOY. It's the middle of the night and the sky is glowing like mad radioactive red. And if you squint you could maybe see the moon through a thick layer of cigarette smoke and airplane exhaust that covers the whole city, like a mosquito net that won't let the angels in.

(LIGHT SNARE DRUMMING.)

And if you look up high enough you could see me. Standing on the edge of a eighty-seven story building,—

(Thick steam shoots out of some pipes behind him—)

—And up there, a place for gargoyles and broken clock towers that have stayed still and dead for maybe like a hundred years—up there is *me*.

(DRUMS.)

And I'm freakin' *Batman*.

(CYMBAL.)

And I gots Bat-mobiles and Bat-a-rangs and freakin' Bat-caves like for real, and all it takes is a broom closet or a back room or a fire escape, and Danny's hand-me-down jeans are gone.

(BOOM.)

And my navy blue polo shirt?—

(—BOOM—)

—The-one-that-looks-kinda-good-on-me-but-has-that-hole-on-it-near-the-butt-from-when-it-got-snagged-on-the-chain-link-fence-behind-Arturo's-but-it-isn't-even-a-big-deal-'cause-I-tuck-that-part-in-and-it's-like-all-good?—

(—BOOM—)

—*that* blue polo shirt?—

(—BOOM—)

—It's gone too. And I get like, like transformation-al.

(BOOM. SNARE.)

And nobody pulls out a belt and whips Batman for talking back—

208

(—*SNARE*—)

—Or for *not* talking back,—

(—*SNARE, CRASH*—)

And nobody calls Batman simple—

(—*SNARE*—)

—Or stupid—

(—*SNARE*—)

—Or skinny—

(—*CYMBAL*—)

—And *nobody* fires Batman's brother from the Eastern Taxi Company 'cause they was making cutbacks, neither, 'cause they got nothing but respect, and not like *afraid*-respect. Just like *respect*-respect. 'Cause nobody's afraid of you.

'Cause Batman doesn't mean nobody no harm.

(*BOOM.*)

Ever.

(*SNARE, SNARE.*)

'Cause all Batman really wants to do is save people and maybe pay Abuela's bills one day and die happy and maybe get like mad famous. For real.

...And kill the Joker.

(*DRUMS.*)

Tonight, like most nights, I'm all alone. And I'm watching... And I'm waiting...

Like a eagle. Or like a—no, yea, like a eagle.

(*The DRUMS start low but constant, almost tribal.*)

And my cape is flappin' in the wind ('cause it's freakin' long), and my pointy ears are on, and that mask that covers like half my face is on too, and I got like bulletproof stuff all in my chest so no one could hurt me and nobody— *nobody*—is gonna come between Batman,

(*CYMBAL.*)

and Justice.

(*The SLOW KICKS continue, now there are SHORT hits randomly placed on the drum set. They somehow resemble city noises.*)

From where I am I could hear everything.

(*The DRUMS build, then STOP.*)

Somewhere in the city there's a old lady picking Styrofoam leftovers up outta a trash can and she's putting a piece of sesame chicken someone spit out into her own mouth.

(*SNARE.*)

And somewhere there's a doctor with a whack haircut in a black lab coat trying to find a cure for the diseases that are gonna make us all extinct for real one day.

(*SNARE. SNARE.*)

And somewhere there's a man, a man in a janitor's uniform, stumbling home drunk and dizzy after spending half his paycheck on forty-ounce bottles of twist-off beer and the other half on a four hour visit to some lady's house on a street where the lights have all been shot out by people who'd rather do what they do, in *this* city, in the dark.

And half a block away from JanitorMan there's a group of good-for-nothings who don't know no better waiting to beat JanitorMan with rusted bicycle chains and imitation Louisville Sluggers, and if they don't find a cent on him—which they won't—they'll just pound at him till the muscles in their arms start burning, till there's no more teeth to crack out.

But they don't count on me.

(*The* BOY *becomes proud, stands up straight.*)

They don't count on no dark knight (with a stomach full of grocery store brand macaroni-and-cheese and cut up Vienna sausages),

'Cause they'd rather believe I don't exist,

(*CYMBAL. The DRUMS start to build slowly again. The steam comes out thicker and thicker.*)

And from eighty-seven stories up I could hear one of the good-for-nothings say "Gimmethecash" real fast (like that) just "Gimmethefuckingcash" and I see JanitorMan mumble something in drunk language and turn pale and from eighty-seven stories up I could hear his stomach trying to hurl its way out of his Dickies.

So I swoop down like mad fast and I'm like darkness. I'm like SWOOSH—

(*—A LIGHT DRUMROLL—*)

—And I throw a Bat-a-rang at the one naked lightbulb—

(*—Light CYMBAL—*)

—And they're all like "whoa-motherfucker-who-just-turned-out-the-lights?"—

(*Silence. The* BOY *breathes, re-enacting their fear, the largest and lowest CYMBAL builds slowly throughout this.*)

"What's that over there?"—

—"What?"—

—"Gimme whatchou got old man"—

—"Did anybody hear that?!"—

—"Hear what? There ain't nothing"—

—"No, really"—

—"There ain't. No. Bat."

(*The CYMBAL reaches its height.*)

But then—

(*—A KICK on the drums as the* BOY *suddenly springs into action—*)

—One out of three good-for-nothings gets it to the head!

And number Two swings blindly into the dark cape before him but before his fist hits anything I grab a trash can lid and—

(*—A CRASH on a CYMBAL—*)

—right in the gut, and number One comes back with a jump-kick but I know judo-karate too so I'm like—

(*—CRASH, happy from the response, he adds this part.*)

—Twice—

(*—CRASH—*)

—but before I can do any more damage suddenly we all hear a CLIC— CLIC—

(*—The* DRUMMER's *TOMS finish, BOOM. The steam stops.*)

And suddenly everything gets quiet.

(*The steam clears.*)

And the one good-for-nothing left standing grips a handgun and aims straight up, like he's holding Jesus hostage, like he's threatening maybe to blow a hole in the moon.

And the good-for-nothing who got it to the head who tried to jump-kick me and the other good-for-nothing who got it in the gut is both scrambling back away from the dark figure before him.

And the drunk man the JanitorMan is huddled in a corner, praying to Saint Anthony 'cause that's the only one he could remember.

(*HIT. HIT.*)

And there's me,

(*CYMBAL. HIT. HIT.*)

Eyes glowing white, cape blowing softly in the wind.

(*HIT. HIT.*)

Bulletproof chest heaving. My heart beating right through it in a Morse code for "fuck with me, just once, come on, just try."

(*HIT. HIT. HIT.*)

And the one good-for-nothing left standing, the one with the handgun, he laughs, he lowers his arm, and he points it at me and gives the moon a break, and he aims it right between my pointy ears, like goalposts and he's special teams.

(*The* BOY *stands, frozen, afraid.*)

And JanitorMan is still calling Saint Anthony but he ain't pickin' up,

(*Silence.*)

And for a second it seems like...*maybe I'm gonna lose.*

(*The* BOY *takes a breath. Sudden courage.*)

Naw.

(*—SNARE. The* BOY *mimes the fight.*)

SHOO—SHOO! FUACATA!—

(*—SNARE—*)

—"Don't kill me mannn!!"—

(*—CYMBAL—*)

—SNAP!—

(*—SNARE—*)

—Wrist CRACK—

(*—SNARE—*)

—Neck—

(*—SNARE—*)

—SLASH!—

(*—CYMBAL—*)

—Skin—meets—acid—

(*—SNARE—*)

—"AHH!!"—

(*—SNARE.*)

And he's on the floor. And I'm standing over him. And I got the gun in MY hands now. And I hate guns, I hate holding 'em cause I'm Batman, and—

ASTERICKS: Batman don't like guns 'cause his parents got iced by guns a long time ago—but for just a second, my eyes glow white, and I hold this thing, for I could speak to the good-for-nothing in a language he maybe understands,

> (*He aims the gun up at the sky.*)

...CLIC—CLIC...

> (*The BASS DRUM.*)

And the good-for-nothings become good-for-disappearing into whatever toxic-waste-chemical-sludge-shit-hole they crawled out of.

> (*A pause.*)

And it's just me and JanitorMan.

And I pick him up.

And I wipe sweat and cheap perfume off his forehead.

And he begs me not to hurt him and I grab him tight by his JanitorMan shirt collar and I pull him to my face, and he's taller than me, but the cape helps, so he listens when I look him straight in the eyes and I say two words to him:

"Go home."

And he does, checking behind his shoulder every ten feet.

And I SWOOSH from building to building on his way there, 'cause I know where he lives. And I watch his hands tremble as he pulls out his keychain and opens the door to his building.

And I'm back in bed before he even walks in through the front door.

> (*SNARE.*)

And I hear him turn on the faucet and pour himself a glass of warm tap water.

And he puts the glass back in the sink.

> (*SNARE.*)

And I hear his footsteps,

> (*BOOM. BOOM.*)

And they get slower as they get to my room.

> (*BOOM.*)

And he creaks my door open like mad slow.

> (*Silence.*)

And he takes a step in, which he never does.

> (*BOOM.*)

And he's staring off into nowhere, his face the color of sidewalks in summer, and I act like I'm just waking up, and I say,

"What's up, Pop?"

And JanitorMan says nothing to me.

But I see, in the dark, I see his arms go limp and his head turns back, like towards me, and he lifts it for I could see his face,

For I could see his eyes,

And his cheeks is dripping but not with sweat.

And he just stands there, breathing, like he remembers my eyes glowing white.

Like he remembers my bulletproof chest.

Like he remembers he's my pop.

(*Silence.*)

And for a long time I don't say nothing.

(*SILENCE.*)

And he turns around, hand on the doorknob, and he ain't looking my way but I hear him mumble two words to me.

(*A pause.*)

"I'm sorry."

(*A pause, the* BOY *is suddenly strong again.*)

And I lean over and open my window just a crack.

…If you look up high enough you could see me.

(*A couple SLOW KICKS, and some more, quiet, echoing SHORT hits.*)

And from where I am? …I could hear everything.

(*A slow blackout.*)

End of Play

THE AS IF BODY LOOP
by Ken Weitzman

BIOGRAPHY

Ken Weitzman's plays have been presented and developed at Atlantic Theater Company, Arena Stage, New York Stage and Film, Steppenwolf Theatre Company, Playwrights Horizons, The Mark Taper Forum, Williamstown Theatre Festival, Florida Stage, Bay Area Playwrights Festival and New York's Summer Play Festival. He has received commissions from Arena Stage, the Alliance Theatre, Actors Theatre of Louisville, and South Coast Repertory. Prizes include the 2003 L. Arnold Weissberger Award for his play *Arrangements*. Mr. Weitzman received his M.F.A. from University of California, San Diego and has taught playwriting at University of California, San Diego; Emory University; La Jolla Playhouse; The Old Globe; Playwrights Project; and Young Playwrights, Inc. Previously, Mr. Weitzman wrote and produced sports documentaries and narratives for television.

ACKNOWLEDGMENTS

The As If Body Loop premiered at the Humana Festival of New American Plays in March 2007. It was directed by Susan V. Booth with the following cast and staff:

AARON	Marc Grapey
SARAH	Kristen Fiorella
GLENN	Josh Lefkowitz
ATTIC LADY	Jana Robbins
MARTIN	Keith Randolph Smith
Scenic Designer	Paul Owen
Costume Designer	Christal Weatherly
Lighting Designer	Deb Sullivan
Sound Designer	Benjamin Marcum
Properties Designer	Doc Manning
Fight Director	Lee Look
Production Stage Manager	Paul Mills Holmes
Assistant Stage Manager	Michael D. Domue
Dramaturg	Julie Felise Dubiner
Assistant Dramaturg	Cara Pacifico
New York Casting	Cindi Rush Casting
Chicago Casting	Adam Belcuore
Directing Assistant	Kathi E. B. Ellis

Originally commissioned by Arena Stage, Washington, D.C. (Molly Smith, Artistic Director, Stephen Richard, Executive Director.)

The As If Body Loop was also read and developed at the UCSD Baldwin New Play Festival, New York Stage and Film, Steppenwolf Theatre Company, Black Dahlia Theatre and Playwrights Horizons.

CAST OF CHARACTERS

The siblings:
Aaron: the oldest. 35 or so.
Sarah: the middle. 32 or so.
Glenn: the youngest. 24 or so.
Attic Lady: their mother. Mid 50s.

And:
Martin: 40s.

TIME

On and around Christmas, 2002

PLACE

Philadelphia, Queens, and Manhattan

The set should be spare. No attempt at realism.
All spaces must easily flow into one another, as each scene should. Two rolling chairs will become a car or a train. They re-configure themselves around the set. Nothing should stop the speed and flow of the play.

A NOTE ON PERFORMANCE STYLE

Characters should be invested, not made fun of. The play works best if a hyper urgency, an urgent pitch drives all intentions. Big stakes for even seemingly small things (which is where much of the comedy comes in).

A NOTE ON PUNCTUATION

...at the end of a sentence means the character does not finish his/her sentence. Not because of being interrupted but because he/she is unable or chooses not to say the words. Or that the rest is implied.

— means he/she is cut off by the other character.

/ indicates where dialogue overlaps.

Keith Randolph Smith and Marc Grapey
in *The As If Body Loop*

31st Annual Humana Festival of New American Plays
Actors Theatre of Louisville, 2007
Photo by Harlan Taylor

THE AS IF BODY LOOP

Act 1

AARON'*s office at NFL Films. Equipment for video editing. A computer console and TV monitor.* *Football paraphernalia around it, as well as a ridiculous number of bottles of Tums, Pepto Bismol, Maalox, Beano, Immodium—all at least half empty. On the floor, several boxes are strewn about, clothes and toiletries stuffed sloppily inside them. One larger box has a pillow and blanket.*

At rise, AARON *stands or, rather, tries to remain standing as he grips a high-back desk chair with one hand and his stomach with the other. Pain. He grits his teeth and fights to mount his big comeback speech—it is part mantra, part poetry. Each word or phrase is like a hard-fought rung on a ladder he climbs to lift himself back up.*

AARON. Okay. Okay. Okay.

Uh, uh, Emmitt Smith. Emmit Smith.

1994.

Season

finale

against

the Giants.

Separates

his shoulder.

First half.

Comes back

to play

the fourth quarter.

Ends with 168

rushing yards,

Cowboys victory.

 (*A bit better.*)

Donovan McNabb. Donovan McNabb.

Week 11.

On a broken ankle,

throws

Four

touchdown

passes.

Four.

 (*The clincher, pumped up.*)

219

Ronnie Lott. (*Savors it.*) *Ronnie Lott.*
1985.
Catches his pinky finger
in a player's facemask.
Doctors recommend
surgery
to repair it.
Instead
Lott
has them
amputate
the darn thing
above the knuckle.
Doesn't. Miss. A. Down.
>   (*Revived, inspired, his mission statement.*)
I love Football!
Football is America.
The frontier mentality.
Pull yourself up by your own bootstraps.

>   (*On this,* AARON *straightens. Gingerly, he lets go of the chair and of his stomach. Relief. He stands there a beat, pleased. Then his face changes. Abruptly, he runs off to the bathroom. While he's gone,* SARAH *emerges from the dark. She stands on the periphery, watching. She is raw, panic churning inside her.* AARON *returns. He doesn't see* SARAH. AARON *picks up his remote and faces the monitor. A big breath.*)

AARON. Okay Aaron, get back in the game now. Back in the game.
Can't let the team down because of two little trips to the john.

SARAH. Five.

AARON. (*Startled.*) Jesus Christ!

SARAH. No, Sarah your sister.

AARON. You scared the crap out of me.

SARAH. Literally. Sorry, bad joke. I've been doing that. It's…it's not good.
Hi.

>   (*She rushes to* AARON *and hugs him, holding on for dear life.*)

AARON. (*A creeping feeling of worry.*) Sarah, what are you doing here?

SARAH. I came for a visit. New York to Philly. Only two hours.

AARON. Don't you have work?

SARAH. I do. Yes. Yes I do. Is it cold in here? I'm cold. Are you cold?

AARON. No.

SARAH. I've been really cold lately.

>   (*She burrows back in to* AARON.)

AARON. Sarah, what are you doing here?

SARAH. I love what you've done with the place. Box motif.

AARON. (*Covering unconvincingly.*) I've been working a lot.
Deadlines.
So I spent a few nights here in the office.
Karen's…fine with it.
(*A beat, then upbeat to change the topic.*)
Hey, check out the monitor. I'm doing a piece on the Packers. For ESPN.
You love the Packers.

SARAH. I like that thing they do. After the touchdown, when the player jumps up towards the stands and the fans all hold him up.

AARON. The Lambeau Leap.
(*AARON hits a key to bring up an image.*)
There it is.

SARAH. (*She studies the image.*) Funny. Lately I feel the reverse of that. Like a whole stadium has jumped on me, and it's just me holding them all up.
(*Abruptly singing/shouting.*) DECK THE HALLS WITH BOUGHS OF HOLLY, FA-LA-LA-LA-LA, LA-LA-LA-LA.
(*Tries to cover.*)
Almost Christmas.

AARON. About a month.

SARAH. (*Dread.*) About a month to Christmas.

AARON. Naughty Jews that we are, celebrating it.

SARAH. Well, we're really just Jew-*ish*.
Told you. Bad jokes.
(*Abruptly.*)
You'll be back in New York?

AARON. That's a good one.

SARAH. Oh.
(*Confused.*)
Are we…we're not going then?

AARON. Going where?

SARAH. To the apartment.

AARON. Whose?

SARAH. You know. Dad's.

AARON. Wow, the jokes get worse and worse.

SARAH. Did I make a joke?
(*Panicked when AARON doesn't answer.*)
Did I?

AARON. Considering he's been dead for fifteen years?
(*SARAH sits, disoriented.*)

AARON. Sarah?

SARAH. Sorry, I…sorry. I've…I've been a little forgetful lately. More than a little I guess.

I've had to increase my patient load, for funding purposes, to justify my grant. And it, well, it hasn't made me a very good social worker lately. That's an understatement actually.

I've been forgetting the details. Of my patients. Their most basic biographical details. I take home my notes, the intake forms, but the information, I can't…pull it up.

"Must not be that important then." Right? That's what people say when you can't recall something. A patient said it when—I went blank during a session. "Must not be that important to you then." But he was wrong. It's really the opposite. The things that are *most* important, those are what we FROSTY THE SNOWMAN, WAS A JOLLY HAPPY SOUL. WITH A CORNCOB PIPE AND A…

(She stops, seeing AARON's look.)

This is the other thing that's been happening. In the middle of a session, sometimes the middle of a sentence, I break out into song, a Christmas song to be exact. Are you really telling me you're not cold, it's freezing in here!

(AARON grabs his NY Jets ski hat and scarf, and puts them on SARAH.)

AARON. Sarah, it's time that you quit that job.

SARAH. What? No.

AARON. It's a burnout profession, and you are obviously burnt out.

SARAH. I only got the grant last January.

AARON. Time enough.

SARAH. I can't quit.

AARON. Sarah—

SARAH. Do you remember your Hebrew alphabet?

AARON. My what?

SARAH. *(Rises.)* Your Hebrew alphabet.

AARON. I never learned my Hebrew Alphabet. Your big brother vandalized the rabbi's pulpit instead, got expelled from Hebrew School. Remember?

SARAH. Well anyway, there are these two letters. Lamed and Vuv. Lamed is 30, numerologically, and Vuv is 6. Together they're 36. That's what the Lamed Vuv are. The 36. Have you heard of them?

AARON. Israeli rock band.

SARAH. Hebrew Legend. I recently read about it. It says that, at any given time, there are 36 people on Earth, chosen at birth, by God, to carry all the pain of the world.

AARON. Sarah—

SARAH. I know, I know what you're thinking. I had the same thought. 36? That seems hardly enough. I mean back in biblical times, maybe. How many people were around then? Fifty? But now, I mean baby boomers, billions in China, surely we need more than just—

AARON. Sarah, stop. Please.

It was a noble deed to get that grant and give free treatment to people who, who obviously needed it after—everything that happened. But it is December 2002 now.

SARAH. Exactly. December. Christmas. The most depressing time of the year. For instance, my one patient, what's his name, he...he...

    (*The thought is gone.*)

Maybe if I share the grant, get another social worker to help with my patient load.

AARON. You're barely making a living now.

SARAH. I can't quit, I'm—

AARON. No, you are not!

    (*Laying down the law.*)

You are not responsible. You are responsible for yourself. And your patients are responsible for themselves. That's how people get better. The only way people get better. They help themselves.

    (*A beat. Suddenly about to faint, SARAH reaches to find the chair. She falls into it.*)

Sarah?!

SARAH. Aaron...

I think...

maybe...

I'm...sick.

AARON. (*Deadly serious.*) You...you are not sick. Do not say that word. Put it out of your mind.

    (SARAH *says nothing.*)

You are not sick. Say it Sarah.

SARAH. (*Far away.*) I am not sick.

AARON. That's right. You're not. You are too strong now, too strong for that, that nonsense.

    (SARAH *doesn't respond.* AARON *rushes to the phone.*)

You know what. I'm calling the clinic. Right now. Tell them you quit. Effective...

    (*His stomach seizes.*)

...effective in five minutes when I get back from the bathroom.

    (AARON *runs off. Pause.* SARAH *stares off, lost.*)

SARAH. (*Trance-like, eerie.*)

I'm dreaming

of a white
Christmas…

> (SARAH *rises, and drifts away. Light change.* AARON *returns from the bathroom.*)

AARON. Sarah? Sarah?

> (*A cold wind whistles through.* AARON *moves and looks off to see if he can spot* SARAH. *Nothing.*)

Crap.

> (AARON *goes to the phone and quickly dials. He stops himself, mid-dial, and hangs up.*)

No. We are not going to do this Sarah. We do not do this anymore. You're strong, you can take care of yourself.

> (*Having talked himself down,* AARON *starts to go back to his desk when the phone rings. He checks the caller ID.*)

What in the world is going on here?

> (*He picks up.*)

Hello Glenn.

Been a long time.

> (*A light comes up on* GLENN, *phone to his ear. He tries to speak but he can't.* AARON, *and what he must tell him, makes* GLENN *too nervous. A beat.* AARON *speaks calmly, perhaps overly so which betrays the impatience that runs beneath it.*)

Start with hi.

GLENN. Hi. Aaron.

AARON. Hi Glenn.

GLENN. Uh…how's your stomach?

AARON. My stomach is fine Glenn.

GLENN. I only ask because, well, we thought…maybe you felt it.

AARON. Felt what Glenn?

GLENN. The disturbance. A major one Aaron. It's—macrocosmic.

AARON. Macrocosmic. Really? Do tell. Go ahead.

GLENN. It's, well it's like…it's kind of hard to explain exactly. (*Quickly.*) Can you come out to the house?

AARON. The loony bin? No. Never.

GLENN. But—

AARON. Thanks for calling Glenn, talk to you—

GLENN. (*Quickly.*) Sarah's here.

AARON. Where?

GLENN. (*Tentative.*) At the house.

You're mad, I knew you'd be mad.

AARON. I'm not mad. I would be mad if I thought Sarah was actually there. But she's not.

GLENN. She is.

AARON. She was just here Glenn.

GLENN. Where?

AARON. In my office.

GLENN. In Philadelphia?

AARON. (*Sitting at his desk.*) Very good Glenn. That's where my office is. Philadelphia. Which is how I know Sarah isn't back in New York right now.

GLENN. She is.

(AARON *sits at his monitor and resumes editing while he talks.*)

AARON. Look Glenn, I know you have a different concept of time—and space—and matter, but—

(AARON *stops suddenly.*)

That's not the Packers. What happened to the...

(*He peers closely at his computer.*)

That, that can't be right.

GLENN. Aaron?

AARON. My computer, it says...today's the 18th?

GLENN. That depends on which Calendar you use. If you use lunar or astrological it's not. Or Hebrew. But by the Gregorian calendar, yes, December 18th. One week to Christmas.

AARON. (*Thrown.*) How could I...all I did was go to bathroom. It was *three weeks ago?*

GLENN. What was?

AARON. That Sarah was here in my...

(AARON *rises, suddenly alarmed.*)

Glenn. Glenn, please tell me Sarah's not really at the loony bin. Please tell me that.

(GLENN *says nothing.*)

Put her on the phone. I want to talk to her. Now Glenn!

GLENN. I can't. I mean she can't. Talk. I mean, she can talk, sort of.

AARON. English please.

GLENN. (*Profoundly.*) Turn your attention inward.

AARON. Oh no. No. That's Attic Lady talk. Tell me she hasn't—

GLENN. Inward Aaron.

Turn your attention inward

and you'll feel it.

You're needed.

(GLENN *quickly hangs up. Lights down on him.*)

AARON. Glenn? Glenn?

> (AARON *raises the receiver to slam it down, but stops. He controls himself.*
> *Then, his stomach. The pain forces him into his chair. A cold wind whips*
> *through. Then a distant rumble, like a train, getting louder as it approaches.*
> AARON*'s office begins to shake.*)

What the...

> (*The lights flicker out. Only a single bright beam of light barrels through the*
> *darkness. A horn blast, deafening as it passes. Then...quiet.*)

Jesus Christ.

> (*In the dark, an upbeat Christmas song plays. Perhaps "Jingle Bell Rock."*
> *When the lights come back up,* GLENN *is sitting in a chair next to*
> AARON*'s. They're in a car.* GLENN*'s driving.* AARON *looks ashen.*
> *Pause.*)

GLENN. Rough ride?

> (*A beat.*)

I'm a little surprised. I figured you'd drive. You hate the train.

AARON. The subway. I hate the subway. This was Amtrak and the LIRR.
Above ground.

> (*A beat.*)

GLENN. Did you feel it? You look like you felt it.

> (AARON *turns to* GLENN.)

The earthquake.

About an hour ago.

The train shook, didn't it?

> (AARON *punches* GLENN *hard in the arm.*)

Ow!!

AARON. Do not mess with me. I'm not in the mood.

GLENN. I'm not messing with you.

AARON. They're doing track work in Trenton. They told me when I got off
the train.

GLENN. Ok.

AARON. You were driving to pick me up and you heard about it on the
radio. So you make up the earthquake thing to mess with me. Right? Right?

GLENN. No.

> (AARON *punches* GLENN *again.*)

Ow! Stop that! What are you, Dad?

> (*A beat.*)

AARON. Sorry.

GLENN. It's ok.

> (*A beat.*)

AARON. Your face looks okay. The rash. I don't see anything.

GLENN. It's gotten a lot better.

AARON. Good. I'm glad.

GLENN. Thank you.

(*A beat.*)

AARON. So what's the evil Attic Lady done this time?

GLENN. Do you have to call her that?

AARON. She lives in the attic. She's evil. What should I call her?

GLENN. Mom.

Or Roberta.

I call her professor.

AARON. Glenn.

GLENN. What else do you call someone who guides your studies?

AARON. Sitting up in the attic with mom, and listening as she talks crazy are not your studies.

GLENN. We read and discuss a wide range of texts.

AARON. I guess that means you haven't gone back to school.

GLENN. I'm in school.

AARON. The University of the Attic Lady? Attic Lady State? The Attic Lady School for Loopy Ideas and New-Age Idiocy?

GLENN. Do you call physics idiocy?

AARON. Physics?

GLENN. New Physics.

AARON. Oh, *New* Physics.

GLENN. Yes. Like Quantum Holograph Theory.

AARON. Uh-huh. And what's that? Describe it. Go ahead.

GLENN. It's like, it deals with, you know—sound—and waves—and energy, how it's, how we're all…it's kind of like The Force.

AARON. And there it is! *Star Wars.*

GLENN. I have a hard time explaining the science. To a layperson.
But it has powerful healing implications, I'll tell you that. And Mom says I'm almost ready to start using it.

AARON. (*Turns sharply to* GLENN.) Not on Sarah you're not.

GLENN. Just for some initial analysis.

AARON. She's our sister. Not some experiment for you and the New Age Mengele up there.

GLENN. We have to help her.

(*They've arrived.* AARON *gets right out of the car.*)

Aaron wait.

There's something you should know about what Sarah has, I mean what she *is*, before you—

>(AARON *turns and walks away. He enters the house. Lights come up on* SARAH, *on a couch. She is dressed for the Tundra. She wears a big billowy winter coat, ski pants, oversized mittens, and the NY Jets ski hat and scarf that* AARON *gave her. She stares out, in a trance, motionless.* AARON *stops in his tracks when he sees her. Pause.* GLENN *enters. He watches.*)

AARON. Sarah? Sarah I'm here to take you home.

>(SARAH *says nothing. A beat.* AARON *goes to her.*)

(*Softly.*) Sarah, it's me. Come on, let's get out of here.

>(*She doesn't stir.*)

Here, let me help you.

>(AARON *takes* SARAH*'s arm to help her off the couch.* SARAH *freaks.*)

SARAH. THIS IS MY LIST!! MY LIST!!

>(AARON *steps back.*)

(*To herself.*) Forty-three, forty-three, forty-three, forty-three, forty-three—

>(*Blurting suddenly.*)

—dashing through the snow, in a one-horse open sleigh, over the fields we go, laughing all the way, ha, ha, ha.

>(*A beat, then* AARON *turns and charges right past* GLENN *and off. Lights up on* ROBERTA *in the attic. She sits, reading. She lowers her book when she hears the sound of* AARON *coming. She takes a deep breath, bracing herself. She forces a hopeful smile onto her face—nervous.* AARON *runs in, out of breath and very upset.*)

AARON. What did you do to her? What did you do?!

ROBERTA. Sweetheart, it's so good to see—

AARON. She's shivering, spewing gibberish…

ROBERTA. It's very upsetting to see her like this, I know.

AARON. I got her out of here, I got her out. She was on her own, and doing fine.

ROBERTA. She wasn't doing fine.

AARON. Undo it. Whatever you did, undo it. Now.

ROBERTA. Sweetheart, please calm down. We will do whatever she needs to—

AARON. She doesn't need anything. From anybody. Especially you.

ROBERTA. I wish to God that was true. But as you can see, it obviously isn't.

>(*A beat.* ROBERTA *looks heavy-heartedly at* AARON. *She sighs dramatically.*)

AARON. Don't.

ROBERTA. You've lost weight.

AARON. I work a lot.

ROBERTA. Your stomach, it must be—

AARON. No. No. Don't do that. You will not do that.

ROBERTA. I'm your mother, I'm concerned—

AARON. Don't. Don't be concerned.

ROBERTA. I could just place my hand on your stomach, and I'd—

AARON. No! You...you stay right where you are.
Now tell me what you did to my sister.

ROBERTA. I didn't do—

AARON. Fine. Then tell me what she has. What you think she has.

ROBERTA. It's not what she has, it's what she is.

AARON. Then what is she?

ROBERTA. One of the 36.

AARON. (*Realizing.*) Of course. Of course that was you who told her that. I should have known.

ROBERTA. I didn't tell her, Mr. Know-It-All, she told me.

AARON. You lie.

ROBERTA. I suggest you put your rancor aside for a moment, and let me tell you what I know, so we can figure out a way to help your sister. Because I am worried. I am *very* worried about her. Very. Do you understand?

(AARON *says nothing.*)

(*Struggling to keep her composure but forging ahead.*) Sarah mentioned this idea of the 36, the Lamed Vuv, as she obviously did to you too. I hadn't heard of it, so I did some reading.

(*She gives* AARON *the book she's been holding.*)

Please...will you read it...I can't...not without...

(*She stops, not wanting to cry.* AARON *takes the book. He reads.*)

AARON. "The Lamed Vuv are the hearts of the world multiplied. And into them, as into one receptacle, pour all our griefs.
By taking the world's suffering upon themselves, they allow it to continue."
Christ.

ROBERTA. One more.

AARON. "If just one Lamed Vuvnick is lacking, the suffering of mankind would poison even the souls of the newborn, and humanity would suffocate with a single cry."

(ROBERTA *covers her mouth, deeply upset.* AARON *is silent. Enraged.*)

ROBERTA. I think you see now what we're up against.
And why you're needed.

(AARON *says nothing.*)

Thank goodness. Thank goodness you've come back to us.

(AARON *throws the book to the floor and storms off. Lights down on the attic, up on the downstairs.* GLENN *meets* AARON *as he enters.*)

GLENN. So?

AARON. I hate her. (*Directed to the attic.*) I hate her, I hate her, I hate her!

(AARON *grabs his stomach.*)

SARAH. Jingle bells, jingle bells, jingle all the way, (*Whispered.*) oh what fun it is to ride...

(AARON *pulls* GLENN *aside.*)

AARON. We gotta get Sarah out of here. You and me. We bust her out, take her back to her apartment, she quits that job—

GLENN. She can't. She has to get better and go back to work. Resume her duties. Didn't Mom explain? "If just one The 36 is lacking—"

AARON. "—The world comes to an end, humanity suffocates with a single cry."

GLENN. Yes.

AARON. You know, most Jewish mothers pressure their children to be doctors or lawyers. Ours...

GLENN. It's happening already.

AARON. What is?

GLENN. You'll hit me if I say.

AARON. I won't hit you.

GLENN. Promise?

AARON. Glenn.

GLENN. The first day she didn't show up to work. That's when they started.

AARON. (*Impatient.*) When what started?

GLENN. ...the earthquakes.

(AARON *hits* GLENN.)

Hey, you said—

AARON. She's a social worker you moron, not a Lamed Vuvnick.

GLENN. Then how do you explain—

AARON. Her resistance is down, she caught...the flu.

GLENN. The flu?

AARON. A fever. Chills. Did you two geniuses even take her temperature?

GLENN. Yes.

AARON. And?

GLENN. It wasn't high.

AARON. What was it?

GLENN. Low.

AARON. Like what? Ninety-seven? Ninety-six?

GLENN. Fifty-three.

SARAH. Frosty the snowman was a jolly happy soul...

GLENN. Then we took it again. And it was down to forty-eight. We're pretty afraid of what will happen if it dips below thirty-two.

(*A beat.*)

AARON. The thermometer, it was—

GLENN. Broken? That's what we thought. So Mom bought new ones. Five of them. Four of them said the same thing.

AARON. And the fifth?

GLENN. It's in the package. Mom told me to leave it that way, with the receipt. She assumed you'd want to check it yourself.

(GLENN *goes to the couch and pulls the packaged thermometer out. He gives it to* AARON.)

I read that when a Lamed Vuvnick rises to Heaven, he (or she) is so frozen that God must warm her for a thousand years between his fingers before her soul can open itself up to paradise.

(GLENN *exits.* AARON *turns and goes to* SARAH. *He pulls a blanket from under the couch and wraps it around her. He sits, thermometer package in hand.*)

AARON. Talk like that...it's enough to make anyone feel cold.

SARAH. Forty-three, forty-three, forty-three...

(AARON *opens the package and takes the thermometer out. He looks at the instructions.*)

AARON. You have to wait until it beeps to get an accurate read. Well, clearly the two numbskulls didn't do that.

(AARON *hesitates a beat, nervous despite himself, then...*)

Ok sis. Ok. Here we go.

(AARON *gently opens* SARAH*'s mouth, places the thermometer in. He puts his arm around her. She leans into him as they wait. A beat or two.*)

Starve a fever, feed a cold. Or is it feed a fever, starve a cold. I could never keep that straight.

(*Small beat.*)

Feeding it is definitely more fun. Remember the chocolate cake days?

What was Roberta's theory then? Epstein-Barr I think. You had the Epstein-Barr Virus. Which no one knew how to treat, of course. So I came up with the chocolate cake cure. I figured if you're going to feed a fever, why not do it with Duncan Hines.

Better than the cures Roberta inflicted on you.

(AARON *waits, listening for the beep of thermometer. Not yet.*)

I made you a cake a week for like four months. Gotta love Home Ec. class. The one useful thing about Junior High. I'd make a cake, wrap it up, put it in my backpack, sneak it in to you after school. Was a lot of cake for a 10-year-old to eat.

(AARON *waits for the beep again. Not yet.*)

It was working really well, too. Until Attic Lady found out. And gave you that book. As a *gift* she says. About the kid who breaks out in brown spots because he eats so much chocolate. *Chocolate Fever.* It scared the hell out of you and alas, all the cake eating came to an end.

And you got worse again.

Just like she wanted.

(*The beep of the thermometer. It's ready.* AARON *takes it out. He rises. Bracing himself.*)

Ok. Alright. Here we go.

(AARON *looks down and reads the thermometer. He throws it violently across the room.*)

Here's how I know your temperature isn't really forty-two. You'd be dead! You're not dead. So your temperature isn't really forty-two. *How does she do it?* I hate this place! I hate it!

(*Instantly the whipping wind, then the rumbling. As before.*)

Oh Crap.

(*The rumbling gets louder, the train horn sounds, the room shakes. Lights go out as the single bright beam of light barrels through.*)

SARAH. (*Fast, frantic.*) Good King Wenceslas looked out on the feast of Stephen. When the snow lay round about / deep and crisp and even. Brightly shown the moon that night, though the frost was cruel…

AARON. Shhh. Shh. It's ok. Shhh.

SARAH. (*Calmer, trailing off.*) When a poor man came in sight, gathering winter fuel.

(SARAH *stops. The lights come back up, with* AARON *holding her.*)

AARON. There we go. That's better. Just try to rest now. I'm going to be right here with you. All night. I'm not going anywhere.

(SARAH *rests her head on* AARON*'s shoulder.*)

That's the way. Shhh.

(*A beat, then…*)

SARAH. (*Softly, slowly, piecing it together.*) Forty-three, forty-three, forty-three…female.

Forty-three, female…divorced.

Forty-three, female, divorced, Legal Secretary, referred by, referred by…

Red Cross

(*The lights fade slowly.* SARAH *continues to whisper to herself as she drifts off.*)

Fifty-eight, male, married, African-American, mortgage broker, referred by Project Liberty.

AARON. Shhh.

SARAH. Twenty-nine, female, married, Ecuadorian, waitress, referred by September Space.

> (*Lights are down now. In the darkness,* SARAH *continues to whisper.*)

This is my list.

My list.

> (*When the lights come back up, it is morning.* SARAH *is asleep, but* AARON *is wide awake, staring straight out, not having slept all night. Pause.*)
>
> (AARON *carefully extricates himself. He pulls the covers up over* SARAH.)

AARON. Don't you worry. Your hear me? Big brother's going to fix this. I promise. (*Looking up to the attic.*) No matter how I have to do it.

> (*He exits. Light change. Later.* GLENN *and* ROBERTA *are seated in the attic.* AARON *stands before them, a dry-erase board on an easel next to him, ready to rally the team. They are mid-brainstorming session.* AARON *refers to* ROBERTA'*s book.* ROBERTA *watches him raptly, which* GLENN *takes jealous note of.*)

AARON. (*Referring to the book.*) Okay, according to the books, it's the job of the Lamed Vuvnick to receive the pain of the world into her heart, and then deliver it up to God.

GLENN. (*To* ROBERTA.) Or Goddess.

AARON. To place it at his / feet so that the world may continue.

GLENN. Or her.

> (AARON *goes to the dry-erase board and, like an impassioned football coach (John Madden preferably), diagrams his ideas with x's and o's, drawings of the heart, and whatever else is necessary.*)

AARON. Ok. Here's what I think.

Sarah's overloaded. The pain she's receiving, to her heart, it's too much, the flow is too heavy.

GLENN. Or too cold. I mean her temperature and all.

AARON. When a Lamed Vuvnick rises to Heaven, God has to warm her for a thousand years between his fingers.

GLENN. (*To* ROBERTA.) I'm the one who…I told him that.

AARON. I know you did. I was quoting you.

GLENN. Then you have to attribute it. Or she'll think that it's yours.

ROBERTA. Sweetheart, let your brother finish.

AARON. Thank you. Here's what we need to do. We need to lessen the flow of pain to her heart. Or divert it.

GLENN. So what are you proposing? By-pass surgery?

> (*To* ROBERTA.)

Kidding. I'm kidding. Obviously.

AARON. That's exactly what I'm proposing. Last night, Sarah kept repeating her rolls, her patient rolls. Over and over. All night.

It's their pain that flows within her, so that's where we start. She's taken on lots of new patients recently, which is obviously what's put her over the edge. So we find them, any of them, one of them, then find some way to help them, to ease their pain, so Sarah has to carry less of it.

Maybe if the load in her heart is lightened, even just a little, she'll be able to lift it again, lift the pain up to God, / empty her heart, and resume her job as one of the Lamed Vuv.

GLENN. Or Goddess.

(AARON *puts the pen down and steps away from the board.*)

AARON. (*To* ROBERTA.) That's my proposal. What do you think?

(*After a beat.*)

Roberta?

(ROBERTA *takes a deep breath, emotional.*)

ROBERTA. I think…I think your sister, and all of us, are extremely lucky to have you here.

(GLENN *immediately leaps up.*)

GLENN. I have an idea!

I'll call the clinic. Get the names of her newer patients.

AARON. There are confidentiality rules. They won't give us names.

GLENN. So what's your idea? Beat somebody up until they tell us? This isn't the NFL you know.

AARON. September Space.

GLENN. What's that?

AARON. It's one of the places that refers patients to Sarah. There were a few she mentioned but I called this place and it has lots of programs, group programs, that people can just drop in on. So that's what we're going to do.

GLENN. We?

AARON. You and me. We'll look for any of Sarah's patients that still go to this place, use its programs. Then, when we find someone, you'll, you know, do your thing.

GLENN. I will?

AARON. You're the healer in training, right?

(GLENN *and* ROBERTA *exchange a look.*)

What?

ROBERTA. Glenn won't be joining you.

AARON. Why not?

GLENN. My rash.

It gets bad when I'm on the outside.
When I'm around other people, and their—frequencies.

AARON. Their what?

ROBERTA. The energy that emanates from them, in waves and frequencies. Glenn has a profound sensitivity to it.

GLENN. For me, going out is like stepping into the middle of a giant marching band playing this horrible dissonant music. And that makes me, you know...(*Whispers.*) break out.

AARON. You were fine picking me up from the station.

GLENN. I didn't leave the car. Which is really an extension of home.

AARON. I thought you'd be eager to help out.

ROBERTA. Glenn's abilities shine brightest here in the house.

GLENN. (*Proud.*) "I am the light between the full moon and the cat's eye."

AARON. ???

GLENN. That's my animus. My spirit phrase. The phrase I utter before doing an energy healing, or will, when I'm ready to do one. Mom and I came to it together. The cat, an indoor animal.

ROBERTA. Perceptive, instinctual.

GLENN. And the moon, it's far away. So I work best from a distance.

ROBERTA. And the light between them, the special energy that our Glenn possesses...

GLENN. It's both of this earth and beyond it.

(*A beat.* AARON *is stunned beyond even making fun of it.*)

AARON. Okay then.
Guess I'll be going this one alone.

ROBERTA. (*To* AARON.) Yes. Yes, good idea. Perfect. You do it alone. That would be best. You alone. I have complete and utter faith in you.

(ROBERTA *quickly gets the matches* (*before* AARON *can change his mind*) *and presents them* AARON.)

GLENN. (*Crushed.*)You're giving *him* the matches?

(ROBERTA *pulls out a small canvas satchel. She undoes the tie.*)
She's giving *you* the matches?

AARON. I'm the one saving the world. Alone.

(ROBERTA *presents the open satchel to* AARON *for the ritual.* GLENN *watches, fuming.*)

ROBERTA. Let us purify the room.

(AARON *reaches in and removes a sprig of sage. He gives it to* ROBERTA *who separates the sprig into two pieces. She holds them out for* AARON *to light.* AARON *strikes a match. He lights one sprig then the other.* ROBERTA *holds the burning sage. She hands* AARON *one of the sprigs and keeps the other. They each wave the smoke of the burning sage in the air. They walk around the room this way. When they're done,* AARON *returns his sage to* ROBERTA. *They look at each other.* ROBERTA *moves closer.*)

ROBERTA. (*Whispered, meaningfully.*) You are the chosen one.

(AARON *moves around* ROBERTA *and starts off.*)

AARON. (*To* GLENN.) Let's go, you're going to drive me there. In your "extension of home."

(GLENN *gets up.* ROBERTA *quickly interjects.*)

ROBERTA. Glenn wait!

(*Improvising.*)

Wouldn't you like to place the sage?

GLENN. (*Sullen.*) I guess. If you want me to.

AARON. Don't be long.

(AARON *exits.* GLENN *mopes over to* ROBERTA.)

GLENN. I guess…I guess we could put them on the book.

ROBERTA. Yes. Yes. What an excellent idea.

(GLENN *retrieves the book. He holds it as* ROBERTA *rests the sage on top of it.*)

Sweetheart, don't be glum. Your time will come.

GLENN. Do you really think so?

ROBERTA. I know it.

(GLENN *smiles, hopeful.*)

But remember, it's important not to rush it. Not to be rash.

(*She lets the double entendre land, then…*)

So don't let Aaron push you into doing anything that you shouldn't.

GLENN. I'm just driving him.

ROBERTA. Which will be stressful enough as it is. Going into Manhattan, even parking outside this September Space—with your sensitivity…well, you know what stressful energy like that can do.

(ROBERTA *steps closer.*)

I want these cheeks to stay as clear and beautiful as they are right now.

(ROBERTA *runs a single finger ever so lightly down* GLENN*'s left cheek. She lets it linger there a moment. When* ROBERTA *exits,* GLENN *remains a beat, his hand on his cheek, unsure. He crosses to the car and takes his seat next to* AARON. GLENN *drives. A beat.*)

GLENN. (*Under his breath, mocking.*) That's exactly what I'm proposing.

(*A beat.*)

They won't give us names. There are confidentiality rules.

(*A beat.*)

Let's go, I need a ride in your extension of home.

(AARON *peers out.*)

AARON. This is it.

(GLENN *stops. They sit there in silence.*)

Something you want to say Glenn?

GLENN. (*Exploding out of him.*) Me. I'm her student. Not you. I read every-thing she assigns, I study hard.

AARON. Uh-huh.

GLENN. But she asks *you* to light the sage. *You* get to purify the room.

AARON. So what?

GLENN. So that's what I do! I purify the room. That's my job. Except when you're around. Aaron the hero, Aaron the savior. He gets to light the sage. While Glenn the accident, Glenn the mistake gets to be the car service.

AARON. You weren't a mistake.

GLENN. I'm eleven years younger then you. So, obviously.
I can't believe you got to light the sage! I bet you don't even believe what you said in there. You were just sucking up.

AARON. Sucking up?

GLENN. That's how it looked to me. I mean, why else would you—

AARON. Because I love my sister, that's why else. And because despite my best efforts to keep Sarah away from her, the Evil Attic Lady has got her again. And got her good. And once that happens then...then there's no other way. This is how it has to work.

GLENN. How what has to—

AARON. "Healing" Sarah. When she's under Attic Lady's spell. Like she's hypnotized. When that happens, the only way to snap her out of it is to come up with a remedy. One that matches the illness Attic Lady convinced her she has.

GLENN. But it was Sarah, she told Mom about the Lamed Vuv. Not the other way around.

AARON. How do you know that? Because Attic Lady *told* you? Come on Glenn, think. Think about the history. Sarah gets a cold, but Attic Lady says no, it's not a cold. It's something else. Some illness she's been reading about. That, coincidentally, no one knows how to cure—Epstein-Barr, chronic fatigue, migraines, panic attacks. And Sarah suddenly takes on those symp-toms.

(*Lights up on the house as* ROBERTA *enters downstairs. She observes* SARAH *for a beat, then musters the courage to go to her.* SARAH *stares out, trance-like, as* ROBERTA *slowly sits next to her on the couch. Carefully* ROBERTA *takes the blanket out from around* SARAH. SARAH *shivers.*)

SARAH. (*Shaking.*) Chestnuts roasting on an open fire...

(*Next* ROBERTA *gently unzips* SARAH's *jacket and opens it. Then she exits.*)

Jack Frost nipping at your nose.

(*After a beat,* ROBERTA *re-enters, with a bag. She sits down next to the shivering* SARAH. *She opens the bag and reaches in. She pulls out a hot water bottle. Then another. She places them inside* SARAH*'s jacket, then carefully zips it back up, and puts the blanket back around her.*)

AARON. At least Roberta let me come up with the remedy for this one. Instead of her.

GLENN. Why did she?

AARON. She loves to involve me. Always has. Gives her a special glee. To catch me in her web.

GLENN. Maybe she's just wants your help. Another healer—

AARON. *Healer*, right. Her children's special gift.

GLENN. You're the only one who hasn't embraced it.

AARON. It's a rationalization, Glenn. To avoid taking the blame for making us all sick she casts us as these super sensitive healers with these super sensitive physical instruments. That way it's not her fault that we're sick, it's not her doing.

(*A beat.*)

GLENN. There was another one last night. Of those things I can't mention because you'll hit me if I do. It wasn't in the paper this morning. Or on TV. But the whole house shook. I felt it. And so did you. Right?

(AARON *says nothing, then grudgingly, nods.*)

Super sensitive instruments.

(*A beat.*)

AARON. Look, things are happening that I can't explain. A lot of them. I admit that. Okay? So if I need to believe Sarah is one of the Lamed Vuv and that the world hinges on her, then that's what I'll do. Because Sarah…Sarah *is* the world to me. Okay?

So now please, please, let's just both shut up, go in there, and do what we're here to do.

GLENN. I told you, I'm not—

AARON. You're coming with me Glenn. I need you to.

GLENN. Aaron—

AARON. I'm not asking, I'm telling you.

GLENN. You're pushing me. Please don't push me.

AARON. (*Mocking.*) *Please don't push me.* What are you, a schoolgirl?

GLENN. It's important that I don't rush into anything.

AARON. Girlie man. Milksop.

GLENN. Stop it.

AARON. Fraidy-cat.

GLENN. Bully.

AARON. Sissy.

GLENN. Neanderthal.

AARON. Invertebrate.

GLENN. You're no savior, you're no hero!

AARON. Pantywaist!

GLENN. You're no Luke Skywalker!

AARON. (*Mocking.*) Hi, I'm Glenn, I want to be this great healer guy. The only problem is I never leave the house!

GLENN. I'll heal by proxy. Which is totally possible with energy work!

AARON. Right.

GLENN. It is. It totally is. You don't know. You don't know anything!

AARON. What don't I know? Tell me.

GLENN. Like—that it's recently been discovered that all molecules in the body act as semi-conductors. Which enables high-energy electrons to travel through our system at a much faster rate than is possible through neurons. Bet you didn't know that.

AARON. Nope.

GLENN. Didn't think so. You see our bodies are really one big electronic communication network. Full of electrical signals, phasing, pulsating, vibrating. Each person is like their very own broadcasting station. Sending and receiving these signals. Which means someone, someone like me, who's sensitive to these signals, could pick them up, tune them in, adjust them, even from a great distance away. So you're wrong. Wrong, wrong, wrong. Proxy healing—totally possible.

(*A beat. AARON smiles.*)

What? What are you smiling about.

AARON. Piss you off a little and you perk right up.

GLENN. You're such a jerk.

AARON. Come on, that was perfect. What you just said. Do that for your presentation and we're gold.

GLENN. (*Panicked.*) My presentation?

AARON. In there. In September Space. When I called. They told me about these informal evenings where health practitioners can volunteer. *Alternative* health practitioners. You make a presentation about the kind of work you do then whoever's interested, signs up. What do you say? Come on, it's right up your alley.

GLENN. Why didn't you mention this earlier when—

AARON. I didn't want Attic Lady to know. She'd find some way to sabotage it. It's what she does.

GLENN. Why do you always blame her for everything—

AARON. If the shoe fits—

GLENN. —when Dad's the one who smacked you around.

(*Quiet.*)

This was a mistake. I should have just have just given you the keys to my car

AARON. Wouldn't matter. I can't drive.

GLENN. What do you mean?

AARON. My stomach's too bad. Couple of months ago it seized up on me on my way to work. I veered out of my lane and hit the car next to me. So Karen drives me now. Or she did. Before I moved out.

GLENN. You and Karen broke up?

AARON. I look at it more like—I relieved her. From having to deal with me.

(*A beat.*)

GLENN. I'm sorry. I'll be happy to drive you wherever—

AARON. Nope. Not enough.

GLENN. Aaron, I—

AARON. Goddammit Glenn. You weren't the mistake you moron. *I* was!

(*A beat.*)

See what you learn when you get out of the house a bit.

GLENN. I don't understand.

AARON. Dad was studying to be an engineer when I was conceived. Then suddenly, a few months before I was born, he drops out and becomes a track worker for the MTA. Think that was the plan?

You, on the other hand, were the Attic Lady's last hope. To have a child untouched by him. She begged him for you. Told him he didn't need to do a thing. And when you were born, she moved up to the attic with you, where she spent most of her time anyway. And not too long after that, he moved out.

(*A beat, GLENN is stunned.*)

You see Glenn? Roberta's wrong. I'm not the hero, as you put it. And if that's the case...?

GLENN. (*A bright light comes on.*) Then maybe...I am.

AARON. Bingo.

(*Lights down on AARON and GLENN. Up on ROBERTA, staring out, holding SARAH's hand.*)

ROBERTA. Your brother's come up with a plan, so you don't have to worry. You should have seen him. He's...he's so gifted.

I've prayed for him to come back to us. So many times I've prayed. The chosen one.

I whispered that to him, before he left. He just stared at me. Scared I think. Of what he's capable of. He'd rather it was Glenn. He suggested as much. But I couldn't let that happen. I couldn't.

Not when I know. When I know that it must be Aaron that heals you.

And when he does, when he experiences what that feels like, he'll embrace his abilities, and he'll return to us. He'll return to the family.

(*A beat.*)

I just hope I didn't...I hope your younger brother isn't—*too* bad when he returns.

(*Lights down on* ROBERTA, *up on* AARON *and* GLENN *as they enter September Space.*)

(*They look around for a beat or two.* GLENN *is both nervous and excited.*)

GLENN. Here we are.

AARON. Yep.

GLENN. A lot of people.

AARON. You can handle it.

GLENN. I'm going to the bathroom. To practice in front of a mirror.

AARON. Good idea.

(GLENN *dashes off.* AARON *pulls out a pad and consults some notes he's taken.* MARTIN *enters with a cup of punch. He stands near* AARON.)

MARTIN. This is crap.

(*When* AARON *doesn't answer*)

I'm talking about the punch.

AARON. Oh.

MARTIN. (*Titanic shouting to no one in particular.*) IT TASTES LIKE CRAP! CRAP!

(*To* AARON.)

You want it?

AARON. Uh...no.

(MARTIN *remains.* AARON *looks at his pad then sneaks a look at* MARTIN.)

MARTIN. What's the problem?

AARON. You're not a forty-three year old female legal secretary.

MARTIN. Keen powers of perception you got there.

AARON. Fifty-eight year old African-American mortgage broker?

MARTIN. What is this place running a dating service now?

Ooh, here we go. Everyone's gathering. Time for "*the presentations.*"

(GLENN *enters in a hurry. He comes up to* AARON.)

GLENN. Look.

AARON. What?

GLENN. (*Turning his head.*) Look. My cheek?

(GLENN *moves closer, points to his left cheek, the exact spot where* ROBERTA *touched him.*)

AARON. I don't see anything.

GLENN. There's a tickle.

AARON. So?

GLENN. (*Significantly.*) So that's how it starts.

AARON. Glenn, you can do this. It's within your power. It just takes a little will.

(GLENN *nods tentatively.*)

Clap with me.

GLENN. What?

AARON. Come on.

(*They clap, hard, starting slowly then gaining momentum.*)

(*As the clapping peaks.*) That's it. That's it. Now go. Go. Be a hero.

GLENN. I'm going! I'm going! Here I go!

(GLENN *jumps up to take his place in front of the group.*)

(*Confident, with gusto.*) Hi everybody. I'm Glenn.

I'm an alternative health practitioner here to volunteer my service. Or services. Plural because there's more than one. Though at core it's "all one" isn't it?

(GLENN *looks out expecting to get a few laughs. He doesn't.*)

That's a Buddhist saying. Or idea. Precept. It's a precept really.

Any Buddhists in the house?

(GLENN *stares out at the silence, his confidence starts to wane. He scratches at his cheek.*)

I guess, I guess if there were any Buddhists here, they'd be more interested in the healing precepts of Buddhism then in what I'm talking about. Which I haven't told you about yet. But I will. I will.

MARTIN. (*To* AARON.) This guy's an idiot.

GLENN. Of course energy healing draws on several *precepts* of Buddhism and other Eastern religions or philosophies if you prefer to call them that. Like my joke from earlier, it's all one. Remember? Actually it wasn't a joke, I do mean it.

AARON. (*Prompting.*) Tell us what you're here for.

GLENN. (*Trying to talk aside to* AARON.) What I'm here for? We talked about this.

(*Back to the group.*) I'm here, I'm here to volunteer my service, services, plural.

AARON. What are your services?

GLENN. Right, right. Thank you sir who I've never seen before in my life. My services. My services employ energy work, like like we all have—energy you know. It's electrons and, and atoms, particles. The whole world it's… Has anyone here seen *Star Wars?*

AARON. *(To himself.)* Christ.

(GLENN scratches his face.)

GLENN. All of it—the spirit phrase, I am the light between the full moon and the cat's eye for instance—it's science. It's scientific.

MARTIN. This guy's going to get a rousing number of people signing up.

GLENN. I—I know this really well. I swear. I've studied, I…

(GLENN runs off.)

AARON. Glenn—

(He's gone. AARON turns back to the group. Silence.)

Crap.

Well I guess it'll have to be me.

(AARON jumps up into the spotlight and does the famous Rockne speech.)

All right men! This is what we're going to do!

"We're going inside of 'em, we're going outside of 'em—inside of 'em! outside of 'em! And when we get them on the run once, we're going to keep 'em on the run. And we're not going to pass unless their secondary comes up too close. But don't forget, men—we're gonna get 'em on the run, we're gonna go, go, go, go!—and we aren't going to stop until we go over that goal line! And don't forget, men—today is the day we're gonna win. They can't lick us—and that's how it goes… The first platoon of men—go in there and fight, fight, fight, fight, fight! What do you say, men!"

(AARON waits for a response.)

That's Knute Rockne! The great coach of Notre Dame football. The Fighting Irish.

MARTIN. This guy's crazier than the last one.

AARON. "Life is ten percent what happens to you and ninety percent how you respond to it." That's Lou Holtz, another Notre Dame coach. Who also said, "No one has ever drowned in sweat." I don't quite understand that one. There's another famous quote I don't get. It's from John Heisman who the Heisman Trophy is named after. He said, "Gentlemen, it is better to have died as a small boy than to fumble this football." That always seemed excessive to me.

(Back on track.)

Alright, who's with me?! Let's go go go go!

(AARON charges off, as if legions of men were going to follow him. MARTIN rises.)

MARTIN. *(Inspired.)* THE PUNCH SUCKS! NOBODY DRINK THE PUNCH!

(MARTIN *exits. Lights down on the clinic, up on* GLENN, *in the car, staring straight out. His face now has a few noticeable, red blotches on it. A beat, then* AARON *enters.*)

GLENN. Please...please don't say anything.

(AARON *doesn't. Instead he pulls out a Baby Jesus Beanie-Baby and places it on the seat next to* GLENN.)

AARON. Here. They gave these out to everyone.

(GLENN *stares straight out.*)

It's a Baby Jesus Beanie-Baby.

I think they're kind of cute.

If you don't want it—

GLENN. I study, I study really hard...

(GLENN *digs and scratches at his face.*)

AARON. Stop scratching, you'll make it worse.

GLENN. Let's just go. I want to go home.

AARON. No. We're going back in, see who signed up.

GLENN. You think anyone actually signed up after that, that debacle?

AARON. Probably not.

GLENN. So?

AARON. So, this was the plan. You executed it miserably I agree. But you have to get back in there. In case someone signed up for one of us.

GLENN. What do you mean, one of us?

AARON. You fled, so I had to do something. Try to increase our chances at least.

GLENN. You gave a presentation?

AARON. A Rockne speech. A little Lou Holtz peppered in. Went pretty well.

GLENN. No one is going to sign up.

AARON. Probably not.

GLENN. I mean, what would they be signing up for anyway? What would you do? Tackle them?

AARON. (*Pointed.*) I don't know. That's why I hoped *you* would do it!

GLENN. I should have never gone in there.

AARON. You're going back in.

GLENN. Look at me Aaron. Look at my face.

AARON. What if someone signs up? What if one of Sarah's patients signs up?

GLENN. I don't know.

AARON. Ronnie Lott amputated his finger so he could keep playing.

GLENN. Who's Ronnie Lott?

AARON. *Who's Ronnie Lott?!*

Forget it. Just come back in. You can bring Baby Jesus.

GLENN. You think this is funny!

AARON. No, I don't!

GLENN. Aaron please, I have to get home before I tear my whole face off!

(*A beat.*)

AARON. It's my fault. It is. If you were downstairs and Dad came to visit, the second we heard the door, whoosh, I shuttled you right up to the attic. Or Sarah did. Keep you as far away from him as possible. And later, when we went to visit him, regardless of how you'd whine, we'd never take you with us.

I used to be proud of that. But not anymore. Because as it turns out, you could have used a little bit of Dad. A little fight. A little old school get up off your ass and make something happen.

GLENN. I tried—

AARON. You tried. Well let's give you a medal then. For trying. Right? That's what it's like with you. Like you're competing in some sort of emotional Special Olympics. This event, ladies and gentlemen, is to see if our emotionally crippled contestant can make it a full five minutes out the world before he breaks into a rash and cries for Mommy. Oh, and I believe congratulations are in order as our competitor lasted for a full 3.5 minutes and that's enough to earn him the bronze. Of course the medal will have to be mailed to him. Because our emotional cripple can't step foot outside, into all that scary scary bad energy and dissonant sound waves. All of which belongs to the bullshit world he and his "professor" have created to justify his being an emotional cripple in the first place!

(AARON *exits. Pause.*)

GLENN. (*Calling off, knowing he's clearly gone.*) I'm not an emotional cripple! I'm just sensitive!

(GLENN *turns to the Baby Jesus Beanie-Baby.*)

Just like you were.

That's what they say. That you could feel all the imperfect frequencies in a person. And then, by laying hands on them, transmit a corrective. Removing dissonance, or spikes in their frequency. Like some sort of sound engineer. The *ultimate* sound engineer. That's what you were.

And what I wish I could be.

If I wasn't such an emotional cripple.

(GLENN *puts the Baby Jesus Beanie-Baby on his lap and drives off.*)

(AARON *re-enters. He holds a sheet of paper. He goes right to where the car was and notices its absence.* MARTIN *enters behind* AARON, *with two plastic cups.*)

MARTIN. Want some punch?

(AARON *turns.*)

AARON. Excuse me?

MARTIN. Punch. Want some.

AARON. No thank you.

(AARON *turns back, scanning for* GLENN *and the car.* MARTIN *moves next to* AARON *and stands with him.*)

MARTIN. What are you looking for?

AARON. My car.

MARTIN. What kind?

AARON. Puke green Honda Civic. Old.

MARTIN. Saw it drive off.

AARON. When?

MARTIN. Just now. Turned over there, onto the bridge entrance.

AARON. Goddammit Glenn!

MARTIN. (*Not mocking, just an opportunity for him to yell.*) GODDAMMIT GLENN!

(AARON *turns to* MARTIN.)

Punch?

AARON. What's your problem? Why do keep offering me punch? Aren't you…you're the guy in there that told me it sucked, right?

MARTIN. That was me.

AARON. Look buddy, if you're trying to agitate me, it's too late, I'm already agitated. And if it sucks so much, why are you drinking it?

MARTIN. I'm drinking it *because* it sucks. It pisses me off. And that's the only way to be. Pissed off. Say the punch was good, what then? Would we all stand around in there and feel warm and fuzzy and think the world was just a beautiful place and let's all have a big hug and drink some punch together. Well no thank you, not for me. The world is not a beautiful place so let's please stop all the goddamn hugging and drink some goddamn punch that lives up to its name and makes you goddamn want to *punch* somebody!

(*A beat.* AARON *sticks out his hand.*)

AARON. Aaron.

MARTIN. Martin. Pleased to meet you.

Liked your speech in there.

AARON. Well you're in the minority. Only one person signed up. And she thought the better of it and didn't show.

MARTIN. He.

AARON. He?

MARTIN. The person who signed up.

AARON. Her name was Judy.

MARTIN. It's a pseudonym. Punch...and...

AARON. You?

MARTIN. I was messing with you.

AARON. Funny.

MARTIN. Not really. That place makes me act stupid.

AARON. Don't worry about it.

(AARON *starts to leave.*)

MARTIN. Hey, where ya going?

AARON. Catch a cab.

MARTIN. I signed up for your services.

AARON. You were joking.

MARTIN. I wasn't. I just didn't feel like meeting you up in there. I've never signed up for one of these before. Then I heard your speech, which was bizarre, but you seemed good and angry so I thought you were someone I could be around who wouldn't make me want to stab him with a scissors. So I signed up.

So there you go. I'm all yours. Do with me what you will. Just no talk about how I'm feeling. I'm pissed off. That's how I feel and that's how I'll be feeling anytime you ask that question. Or any other question.

See, this is the attitude that helped drive Sarah batty.

AARON. (*Suddenly very hopeful.*) Sarah?

MARTIN. My therapist. Former therapist. Two months with me and she lost it. Started wearing a ski coat in session, breaking into Christmas songs. What are you smiling about you sadistic bastard, she was a nice girl.

AARON. Sorry I...the name. Sarah. It makes me feel—hopeful. Like all my crazy plans might just work out.

MARTIN. Well bully for you.

AARON. So...should we...uh, do you wanna...go get a beer or something?

MARTIN. Well I sure as hell don't want to stand here in the freezing cold all goddamn night.

(*Lights down on* AARON *and* MARTIN. *Up on* SARAH *and* ROBERTA. SARAH *sleeps, her head on* ROBERTA's *lap. She stirs. Pulling and kicking the blanket off.*)

ROBERTA. Sarah?
(*When the blanket is off,* SARAH *settles back down into* ROBERTA.
ROBERTA *puts her hand on* SARAH's *forehead.*)
Sweetheart, you're warmer.
(*Looking out, sensing it.*)
Something good is happening.

End of Act I

Act II

A couple of hours after the end of Act I. Sounds of a "Monday Night Football" game can be heard. Lights up on AARON *and* MARTIN *at a bar. They have beers and watch the game. A beat or two (or three or four) of awkwardness as* AARON *searches for how to break the ice.*

AARON. They're going to turn the ball over here.
You know how I know?

MARTIN. How?

AARON. Because I'm a Jets fan and I know them. They're ahead. They're the better team so this is a game they should win. If they score here they put the game away. Which means they won't score. They'll do something stupid instead. They always do.
(*No response from* MARTIN.)
You like football?

MARTIN. Huge guys full of rage because they're so doped up on steroids, all running around knocking the hell out of each other. What's not to like?

AARON. Exactly.
Oh come on! You don't have to prove me right every time!

MARTIN. YOU DON'T HAVE TO PROVE HIM RIGHT EVERY TIME!

AARON. What a time to fumble!

MARTIN. WHAT A TIME!
(*MARTIN slugs his beer.*)
I'm drinking alone here.

AARON. I can't. Stomach.

MARTIN. Jets make you that sick huh?
(*AARON smiles.*)
If it makes you feel any better, you can't blame the guy for fumbling. The speed at which these guys collide, and given how much they weigh, it's probably about 1500 pounds of force, about that of a midsized sedan traveling thirty miles per hour.
(*Turns to* AARON.)
I teach high school physics. Excuse me, *taught.*

AARON. What happened? You get fired?

MARTIN. HEY! Did we not agree on this? Do I need to make it any more clear? I. Hate. Probing. Questions. From concerned friends, concerned colleagues, concerned parents of concerned students, from reporters, case workers, social workers. You're an *alternative* health practitioner, right? So how about you find an alternative to asking me those type of questions.

(*They turn back and watch the game. Pause.*)

Two-minute warning. Think they can still screw it up?

AARON. Probably.

(*A beat.*)

MARTIN. I lost someone. Someone…important to me. She was taken I should say. So going into the classroom every day, teaching F=MA, force equals mass times acceleration, it…let's just say calculating the force of things colliding, which is what we did, cars or trains or airplanes, colliding into each other or into stationary objects, well, that wasn't so much fun for me anymore. And don't say you're sorry, that's the other damn thing I hate.

(*He gets up.*)

Thanks for the beer and the game. Better night than what I expected.

AARON. Wait.

MARTIN. If you've suddenly thought of something profound to say, please don't.

AARON. This…this is a big play. You can't walk out now. They stop them here it's over.

(MARTIN *considers, then sits back down. They watch the game.*)

Holy crap.

MARTIN. They did it.

AARON. Boo-yeah!

MARTIN. Boo-yeah!

AARON. Boo-yeah!

MARTIN. Boo-yeah!

(*They continue chanting "boo-yeah!" to each other as* MARTIN *exits and* AARON *crosses back to the house.* ROBERTA *strokes* SARAH*'s hair as she sleeps. She sees* AARON *come in, excited. They whisper.*)

ROBERTA. Tell me.

AARON. I found one of Sarah's patients. One of her newer ones.

(ROBERTA *extricates herself from* SARAH *and goes to* AARON.)

ROBERTA. I knew it.

AARON. I spent a few hours with him tonight. I think, I don't know, I think I gave him something a little bit different than what he's used to.

ROBERTA. I have no doubt.

AARON. How is she?

ROBERTA. Her temperature rose. Twelve degrees.

AARON. To what?

ROBERTA. Sixty.

Because of you. Because of what you did tonight.

AARON. Good. This is going to work then.

(ROBERTA *peers at* AARON.)

What?

ROBERTA. There's something else.

AARON. No.

ROBERTA. There is.

AARON. It's nothing.

(*A beat as* ROBERTA *reads him.*)

ROBERTA. I see. I see what it is.

You doubt yourself.

(ROBERTA *waits.* AARON *nods reluctantly.*)

My darling, you can do this. You can help this person.

AARON. He's…he's not exactly easy, this guy.

(ROBERTA *steps uncomfortably close to* AARON.)

ROBERTA. (*Pointed, instructing him.*) All your life, you've done things your own way. And so that's how you'll handle this.

Your way.

(ROBERTA *exits.* AARON *stands there a beat, thinking about what she said. Then he turns and goes to* SARAH. *He stands there watching her sleep. She doesn't stir.* AARON *takes a seat on the floor at the base of the couch.* SARAH *drapes an arm off the couch and over* AARON. *He takes her hand in his.*)

AARON. You do feel warmer.

SARAH. (*Whispered, in her sleep.*) Fifty-eight, male, married, African-American, mortgage broker, referred by Project Liberty.

AARON. Here we go.

SARAH. Thirty-seven, male, organic. Sour cream.

Organic heavy whipping cream.

Organic peaches,

Organic frozen cherries, frozen waffles…

This is my list.

(SARAH*'s quiet.*)

AARON. Well. That was different. Progress maybe.

(AARON *leans back against the couch, holds* SARAH*'s hand, and settles in for the night. He closes his eyes. As he does, the deafening horn blast and bright*

light barrels through. Blackout. When the lights come up, it is morning. The at-
tic. GLENN sits facing upstage, cross-legged, studying a text book. His head is
obscured by the hooded sweatshirt he wears. AARON enters, with some trepi-
dation, unsure of the state he'll find GLENN in. AARON stands at the
entrance, holding a NY Jets football helmet, looking at GLENN a beat.)

AARON. Where's Roberta?

GLENN. Out.

AARON. Why is your head so big?

(GLENN turns around. He wears a rubber Yoda mask.)

Ah! What the hell is that?

GLENN. It's Yoda. Obviously.

(Sarcastic.)

What's that?

AARON. My old football helmet.

(GLENN returns to his reading.)

Hey, you owe me forty bucks. I had to take a cab last night.

GLENN. You could have taken the train.

AARON. It's pretty annoying to talk to you with that on.

GLENN. So don't talk to me.

AARON. Is it that bad?

GLENN. Talking to you? Yes.

AARON. The rash.

(GLENN pulls the mask off and turns his head. His face is covered with red
splotches, raw from scratching. He puts the mask back on. A beat.)

I didn't...I mean I forgot how bad it...gets.

(A beat.)

So, good news. I found one. A patient of Sarah's.

GLENN. Mom told me.

AARON. I'm going back to The Space to fill out the report on our "meeting." I'll snoop around, see what info I can get about him.

(GLENN doesn't say anything.)

Is Roberta coming back soon? Because Sarah's still sleeping.

GLENN. I'll listen for Sarah.

AARON. If you're up here—

(GLENN takes out a baby monitor.)

GLENN. We used it to listen for her. Before *you* came.

(A beat.)

AARON. Glenn...is there anything...I can get for you? While I'm out?
Something topical to—

(GLENN *waves him away*. AARON *remains a moment, unsure how to help. He turns and exits. When he's gone,* GLENN *continues to read. Then he carefully closes the book and hurls it across the room. Light change. Later. In a different playing area,* MARTIN *enters, angry. Followed by* AARON.)

MARTIN. You're not supposed to contact me. That's against the rules.

AARON. I don't give a crap.

MARTIN. How'd you get my number?

AARON. They had me in, to ask how it went with you. I stole a contact list.

MARTIN. I go once a week. Job clinic in the afternoon, the presentations in the evening. I have to prove I'm seeking help. My benefits are tied to it.

AARON. A second day won't blow that. I asked.

MARTIN. Sweety, I had nice time with you at the football game and it's a lovely day in the park, but I'm just not ready to get pinned and go steady.

AARON. Yet here you are.

MARTIN. I have too much time on my hands.

AARON. We'll fix that. Screw the alternative crap, I offer something practical; I'm going to help you get a job.

MARTIN. I get that at The Space. They get listings, they send me out on interviews.

AARON. But you don't do so well at the interviews apparently.

MARTIN. They ask questions, a lot of them.

AARON. I'll help you do better.

MARTIN. With what, a rousing football speech? Go fight win!

AARON. You said you liked the speech.

MARTIN. I lied.

AARON. A mock interview.

MARTIN. I do that at The Space.

AARON. Not with this.

(AARON *exits and returns wearing his football helmet and pushing a single man blocking sled.*)

MARTIN. A blocking sled?

(AARON *steps on the platform, on the coach's side of the sled. He pulls out a whistle and blows it.*)

AARON. Three point stance. Right now.

MARTIN. You're out of your mind.

AARON. Get ready for the first question.

MARTIN. Piss off.

AARON. Here it comes:

(*Raises his helmet.*)

How would you like me to write a report to your case worker challenging your attendance at The Space and your genuine desire to progress, thus holding up your benefits until you can file an appeal and cut through a mile of red tape?

MARTIN. I wouldn't like that very much.

AARON. (*Pulls his helmet back on.*) Tell the sled.

MARTIN. I wouldn't—

AARON. While you're hitting it.

    (MARTIN *charges the sled and hits the pad, moving the sled, and* AARON, *a foot or two.*)

MARTIN. I wouldn't like that very much!

AARON. Good. Why not?

MARTIN. Because I need my benefits you moron. I'm jobless.

    (AARON *blows the whistle and throws a yellow penalty flag. Raises his helmet.*)

AARON. Penalty! Illegal use of the tongue. Repeat second down.
And it's not me you're talking to, it's a potential employer. I ask again, why not?

    (MARTIN *hits the sled and keeps pushing it throughout the below.*)

MARTIN. Because I have a sincere desire to get better, to move on with my crappy barren life in a hollow mockery of an attempt to be a productive worker bee for your stupid meaningless company.

    (AARON *blows the whistle.*)

AARON. Repeat second down!

MARTIN. Ahhh!

    (MARTIN *charges and hits the sled especially hard this time. He collapses, out of breath.*)

My benefits and the support I receive has helped me through a dark time so that I can be here and ask you to give me a chance to prove I can once again be a highly competent, motivated member of the work force.

    (AARON *steps off the sled and pulls his helmet off.*)

AARON. Touchdown.

    (*A beat.*)

MARTIN. So, what? I bring a blocking sled to my interviews? You know most guys bring a briefcase.

AARON. All you have to do is think about the whistle and the penalty flag and hit those questions like you hit this blocking sled. When's the next interview?

MARTIN. Tomorrow morning. Some scholastic textbook company.

AARON. I'll meet you here after. We'll toss the pigskin. You can tell me all the answers you wanted to give in the interview, but didn't. What do you say?

MARTIN. I say it's stupid and I'm pissed off you contacted me.

AARON. Pissed off, the only way to be.

(*A beat.*)

MARTIN. That speech. The psycho one. Give it to me.

AARON. (*Puts his helmet back on.*) We're going inside of 'em, we're going outside of 'em—inside of 'em! outside of 'em!—

MARTIN. Alright, alright. Skip to the end.

AARON. What do you say, men! Who's with me?! Let's go. Let's go go go go!

MARTIN. Ahh!

(MARTIN *charges the sled, driving it and* AARON *off stage. Lights down on the park.... Up on the attic as* GLENN *enters, still wearing his Yoda mask. In his hands is an old black medicine bag.* GLENN *sits down, cross-legged, and opens the bag. From it he pulls a tuning fork. Then another. He places them down then reaches back into the bag. He pulls out a dog collar, an empty bottle of whiskey, a threadbare mitten, and a coffee thermos. He lays the objects down in front of him and picks up his tuning forks. He raises them up in the air, pauses, then taps each of them down on the dog collar. He puts the tuning forks to his ears. Lights down. From off, we hear* AARON's *voice.*)

AARON. Roberta!

(*Lights up on the downstairs as* AARON *charges on.*)

Roberta!

(ROBERTA *enters.*)

ROBERTA. I'm right here, sweetheart. What is it? Is everything all right?

(AARON *nods, excitedly, out of breath.*)

AARON. I thought about what you said, about doing things my own way, and that's...that's what I did. And it worked. I think I'm really helping him.

ROBERTA. I am so proud of you.

AARON. Sarah? Did she...

ROBERTA. Another twelve degrees.

AARON. Is she...lucid?

ROBERTA. In and out.

(*Smiling.*)

Go see for yourself.

(AARON *remains, looking expectantly at* ROBERTA.)

Aaron?

(*When* AARON *hesitates.*)

What is it?

AARON. (*After a beat.*) Maybe you're right. About us. Having…special abilities.

> (AARON *smiles slightly, then turns and runs in to* SARAH. ROBERTA *stands there a beat, flooding with joy. She exits.* AARON *kneels next to the couch.* SARAH *watches him. It exhausts her to talk, which she does laboriously. She's seems less in a trance, but still goes in and out of lucidity.*)

SARAH. Is it Christmas today?

AARON. No. Not yet.

But I do have a present for you.

> (*From a paper bag,* AARON *pulls out a piece of store-bought chocolate cake and a plastic fork.*)

Thought you might like this.

> (*He presents it to* SARAH.)

SARAH. Cake.

> (SARAH *takes a tiny bite.*)

AARON. It's just great to see you so—

SARAH. (*A creeping panic.*) It's coming, though, isn't it?

AARON. What is?

SARAH. Christmas.

AARON. Yes. Day after tomorrow.

SARAH. (*Dread.*) So tomorrow's Christmas Eve?

AARON. That's right.

> (AARON *goes and sits down next to* SARAH. *He takes her hand which helps to mollify her.*)

Better?

> (SARAH *nods. Lights come up on* ROBERTA, *coat on, sitting in the car. She pulls the baby monitor from her coat. She turns it on and listens in on* AARON *and* SARAH.)

SARAH. You seem. Happy. That's…

AARON. Strange?

> (SARAH *nods. In the car,* ROBERTA *smiles.*)

SARAH. Makes me. Feel good. Warm.

AARON. Well, tomorrow I think you'll feel even warmer.

SARAH. (*Panicked again.*) Tomorrow? What's tomorrow? Oh God, do I have someone scheduled? Do I have to—

AARON. No, Sarah, me. I have someone scheduled.

It's someone you know, though.

> (*Carefully.*)

Martin?

> (SARAH *says nothing.*)

Do you remember—

SARAH. LEGGO MY EGGO!

AARON. Sorry, I'm sorry.

SARAH. LEGGO MY EGGO! LEGGO MY EGGO! LEGGO MY EGGO! LEGGO MY EGGO! LEGGO MY EGGO!

AARON. I shouldn't have mentioned him. I just thought if there was anything about him you remembered.

(SARAH*'s stopped by now.*)

Nevermind. You'll feel it. You'll feel the good, the good I've done, when it happens tomorrow.

(*In the car,* ROBERTA *nods. Proud.*)

SARAH. Tomorrow's Christmas?

AARON. Christmas Eve.

SARAH. Let's not go. Let's not see him this year. Please.

AARON. Sarah, Dad's dead. We're not going to see him.

(SARAH *is quiet.*)

Come on, let's get you some sleep.

(AARON *puts his arm around* SARAH *and she huddles into him. A beat.*)

SARAH. Keep talking to me. Please.

AARON. Sure. Anything in particular you'd like me to—

SARAH. Christmas.

AARON. Christmas. Naturally. Okay. Well…I can tell you that by Christmas Day, you're going to feel much better.

So much so that you and I will go outside and resume our dominance as the best brother-sister football pair in the neighborhood. We'll take on all comers.

I introduced Karen to that tradition. A few years ago. She's really gotten to like football. Believe it or not. So much so, it's how she'd talk about, you know, my impregnating her. She'd say stuff like, "Tonight, your little football players are going to sprint for my eggy endzone, like it's the opening kickoff of the Superbowl."

(*He chuckles.*)

Too bad my little football players never make it out of the locker room. I…I haven't been able to—play the game, for quite some time.

(*A beat.*)

I think I did the right thing. I do. Who knows when my stomach was going to allow me to…she really really wants a baby. So I thought it would be best if I made her—move on without me.

(SARAH *sings, panicked.*)

SARAH. Sire, the night is darker now, and the wind blows stronger.

AARON. Shh—

SARAH. Fails my heart, I know not how, I can go no longer.

AARON. Shh, it's okay.

SARAH. Frozen cherries, frozen waffles, frozen. Frozen, frozen, frozen, frozen.

(*AARON quickly pulls the blanket up around SARAH. He holds her tightly.*)

AARON. Shh.

(*SARAH settles. She closes her eyes. In the car, ROBERTA clicks off the baby monitor, stunned. Blackout. When the lights come up it is morning. A crisp, cold, chipper one. AARON gets up eagerly, ready to go. He whispers to the sleeping SARAH.*)

AARON. Today's the day.

(*SARAH grips onto AARON's arm just as he starts to move away.*)

SARAH. Leggo my Eggo.

(*AARON tries to pry SARAH's hand off his arm but she holds on tight. Trying to communicate.*)

Organic sour cream, organic heavy whipping cream, organic peaches, organic frozen cherries, frozen waffles...

(*AARON manages to pull SARAH's hand off.*)

This is my list.

(*AARON backs away, a little freaked out. He exits. Lights down on SARAH, up on the attic. GLENN sits cross-legged with the dog collar, whiskey bottle, threadbare mitten, and coffee thermos laid out before him. He alternates, tapping each of the objects, then raising the tuning forks to his ears. He does this with varied intensity, rhythm and speed. It should look like he's performing some sort of groovy and ethereal xylophone dance. AARON enters, holding his helmet and a football. He watches GLENN a moment. As they talk, GLENN continues to work.*)

AARON. Hey.

GLENN. Shh.

AARON. Whatcha doing?

GLENN. Practicing.

AARON. Ah. Going well?

GLENN. Hard to tell.

(*AARON watches GLENN another beat.*)

AARON. If you don't mind my asking...

GLENN. They're objects I've collected. Around the neighborhood. I use them to train with.

AARON. I see.

So somewhere in the neighborhood there's a wino with a dog, no caffeine, and one mitten feeling a little better today.

GLENN. I don't know who the objects belong to. So I don't know what effect I'm getting. I'm just practicing, okay?

AARON. Okay. I get it. I mean, good for you. You're doing your thing. (*A beat.*) Me too, by the way. I'm about to go do my thing. Little nervous about it actually. Excited too. (*AARON waits for GLENN to ask. He doesn't. He's consumed with his work.*) I'm meeting Martin. Sarah's patient. He had his big interview this morning. (*GLENN rises. He senses something. He goes to AARON, zeroing in on AARON's football helmet. He puts a tuning fork to it.*)

GLENN. (*Ominously.*) Don't bring this.

(*GLENN takes the helmet away from AARON. He then goes back to his other objects and sits. He decides to place AARON's helmet down in the middle of them. He begins to resume his work, but his focus is drawn to helmet. After a moment, he moves the other objects out of the way and concentrates solely on the helmet. AARON stands there a beat, a little spooked. He decides to leave the helmet with GLENN. AARON exits. Lights down on the attic.... Up on the downstairs as AARON gets his coat on. ROBERTA enters hastily.*)

ROBERTA. Don't go.

AARON. What is going on here?

ROBERTA. I didn't know, I didn't know how bad it was.

AARON. How bad what was?

ROBERTA. Your stomach.

AARON. My stomach's fine. Feeling a little better actually.

ROBERTA. No.

AARON. No?

ROBERTA. How can it be? When it's preventing you from having a child. (*AARON stops.*)

AARON. Now how would you know something like that.

ROBERTA. It came to me—in a dream.

AARON. Right.

(*AARON bundles up to go. ROBERTA moves to him. She reaches out to touch his stomach. AARON quickly dodges her.*) Woh. What are you doing?

ROBERTA. Sweetheart, I'm afraid. I'm afraid you're not up to this. Stay here, let me help you.

AARON. Really? That's really what you think I should do? Stay here?

ROBERTA. I have a bad feeling.

I don't want things to get worse for you.

AARON. And Sarah? What about her? What about the world?!

ROBERTA. We'll…we'll have to find another way.

AARON. Predictable. Things are going well. Sarah's getting better, we're almost done. So you try to prevent it. Prevent me from taking this final step, to heal Sarah and get her back on her feet. And at the same time keep me here. Two for the price of one.

ROBERTA. No, that's not—

AARON. Come on Roberta. Don't do this.

ROBERTA. I wanted it to be you. I so badly wanted it to be you. So I pushed you. To do this. I pushed you too hard.

(AARON *starts to go.* ROBERTA *steps in his way.*)

Aaron, please, your stomach. If you just let me examine—

(*Again* ROBERTA *reaches towards* AARON*'s stomach.*)

AARON. No. No way. Not this time.

(AARON *makes a nifty football move around* ROBERTA. *He fakes one way then spins around her and runs off, exiting [ideally to some type of NFL music]. Lights down on the house. Up on Central Park.* AARON *runs on, playfully tossing the ball to himself and running around, trying to keep warm. He makes a shadow move or two. He does the Heisman pose as* MARTIN *enters, dressed nicely.*)

AARON. Look at me. I won the Heisman.

(MARTIN *nods.*)

You're late. As your coach, I should make you run laps.

In your loafers.

(MARTIN *is silent.*)

Nevermind. We score here, you're off the hook. Go deep.

(*Playing quarterback,* AARON *drops back, and bounces on his feet, ready for* MARTIN *to run out for the pass.* MARTIN *doesn't. He remains unmoved. After a moment* AARON *drops his stance.*)

So, you seem a little reticent for someone who got to, at least, the third step in the interview process today.

Okay, okay. Full disclosure. I called The Space, told them you were late to meet me. That I was oh so worried about you. I insisted they call over to your interview and inquire. And they told me. The first interview went so well she brought you right up to her supervisor who brought you right up to his. So even if you didn't get the job—

MARTIN. I didn't.

AARON. You didn't?

MARTIN. No.

AARON. But it sounded...really?

MARTIN. Really.

AARON. What I was going to say was that even if you didn't get the job, you obviously did really well in the interview process. And that's, that's no small thing. Right? I mean, you never know, in the final analysis why one person gets the job and another doesn't.

MARTIN. I knocked everything off the guy's desk. Stormed out of his office.

AARON. Ah.

MARTIN. But you're right. I did well before that. That stupid flag thing of yours. It worked. I was tempted. I was. They gave me the same stupid questions, the "Are you sure you're sufficiently recovered to handle full-time employment?" I was pissed off, but that yellow flag. I thought about you saying, "Illegal use of the tongue." So damn stupid it made me smile.

AARON. That's great.

MARTIN. Yeah. Right up until the guy started in about my arrest.

AARON. Your arrest?

MARTIN. What, they didn't tell you I was a violent criminal? Don't worry, I wasn't convicted. I don't have a record. The thing was settled out of court. So I can truthfully answer no to the, "Were you ever convicted of a crime" thing. But this guy, he pressed the issue, asked me if I was ever arrested. Said, in the interest of the company it was fair to ask. Fair. That word coming from his smug mouth, it—did something to me. "Wanna hear about it?" I asked him. "It won't take long." I don't know, maybe I wanted to hit that sled, knock his question back into...

"There I am." I try to make the story dramatic for him. Give him his money's worth. *"There I am,* in the Super Market. Gristedes. Doing some shopping before school. My wife was at work already. Windows on the World. She's a pastry chef. Gets there at 5 a.m. To start baking. Anyway, I'm in the frozen food aisle, running late, it's five to 9, my first class is 9:30, when Annie calls. This I find annoying because I know she's calling to check on me. She doesn't trust me to do the shopping. Even though she gives me a very explicit list. According to her, I still always miss something crucial or buy the wrong brand of something. So, because I'm annoyed and because I'm running late, I decide to...screen her call. I know this will irritate her and that particular morning it gave me a feeling of vindictive satisfaction."

(*A beat.*)

"She didn't...she didn't leave a voicemail. When she called."

(*Small beat.*)

Now our friendly interviewer, he's a little uncomfortable, so I skip ahead, and spare him some of the more grisly details of the days immediately following.

"You see, after some time, I found myself alone in my apartment—*our* apartment—one day, staring into an empty refrigerator. And, I don't know, maybe the thought of ordering Chinese on Christmas day was too depressing, but I decided I would go shopping. A sign of health, a grief counselor might say. A sign of health. So, like the dependent child I was when it came to food, I brought Annie's list with me. The last note she wrote me. Our final correspondence. Romantic, yes?"

(Lights up on SARAH *on the couch.)*

SARAH. Organic sour cream, organic heavy whipping cream, organic peaches, organic frozen cherries, frozen waffles—

MARTIN. "Organic sour cream, organic heavy whipping cream, organic peaches, organic frozen cherries, frozen waffles—"

AARON. That's, that's your list?

MARTIN. Annie's. I know, frozen waffles are an odd item to be on a pastry chef's grocery list. Which brings us to the climax of this particular story. "*Frozen waffles.* I like them. The really nasty Eggo kind especially. Made Annie crazy to see me eat them for breakfast. But she put them on the list. For me. And so I kept eating them, every morning, even when I was sick of them. Because seeing her exasperated was so damn charming, and because I loved the fact that, despite that, she put it on the list every time."

"But now, there I am at the market, in the frozen food section and there are no Eggo Waffles in sight. They were out of them. And, well, that was unacceptable to me. Because Annie put it on the list. And that list had come to be very important to me."

"So I ask an employee to look in the back to see if any have come in that haven't made it to the shelf. But they don't want to do that. Restocking doesn't happen for another hour and a half. UNACCEPTABLE! I say in a voice that was perhaps a bit too loud. Perhaps a bit too belligerent. So the employee gets the manager, who apparently, at the Gristedes School of Management, did not major in customer relations. Because instead of just telling his employee to go back and get me a box of Eggo Frozen Waffles, he recommends another brand instead. And then in a sudden burst of jocular inspiration he advises me to, 'leggo those Eggos'."

"I was unable to provide the manager with the response I believe he was looking for. Unless, 'If you don't go back there and get me a box of Eggos I'm going to tear out your trachea,' was in fact the desired response. But judging by the fact that he called over his security guard and several other employees for backup…"

SARAH. GET AWAY FROM ME! THIS IS MY LIST! MY LIST!

MARTIN. "Anyway, long story made shorter, some mostly minor injuries occurred when I tried to storm the supply room."

(*Pause.*)

AARON. I'm not an alternative health practitioner. I lied. I lied my way into The Space. I'm not a healer. I have no experience dealing with anyone affected by anything like what you…I'm sorry.

(MARTIN *goes right to* AARON *and punches him hard in the stomach.* AARON *crumples to the ground.*)

MARTIN. See, that's what made me blow the interview. That response. "I'm sorry." "You've had to deal with so much more blah, blah, blah." It's why I hate questions so much. Because it presumes there's a you and there's a me, and that we are separate. It presumes one of us was affected and one of us was not. And that's unacceptable.

(MARTIN *starts to exit. Stops, not turning to* AARON.)

A colleague, before I left, he gave me this book. By a guy named Damasio. A neuroscientist, who says it's proven, that seeing someone suffer, is very much like suffering yourself. A nearly identical biological response happens in the body of the witness as happens in body of the actual sufferer. He calls it "The As If Body Loop."

So you see, you're wrong. You're every bit as affected as I am.

(MARTIN *exits. Then—the rumbling. Coming closer, getting louder. The single beam of light screams through. When it passes, it's dark. Night. Sinister. A hooded figure looms over* AARON, *who's still on the ground. The figure faces upstage, a hood over his head, unrecognizable.*)

AARON. Dad?

(*The figure bends down and lifts* AARON *up, over his shoulder, in a fireman's carry. He turns to go and we see that it's* GLENN, *wearing a snow suit and* AARON's *football helmet. He carries* AARON *off. Lights down on the park. Lights come back up on* SARAH *and* ROBERTA. ROBERTA *wears a parka and gloves as it's now the Arctic inside the house. Wind whipping, snow, frost, a terrible storm. Tremors. Lights flickering and flashing.* SARAH *is shivering, worse than ever. There is a thermometer in her mouth and* ROBERTA *is in the process of bundling her up with several more blankets. There is a desperate sense of urgency in the air.*)

GLENN. (*Offstage.*) Mom! I found him!

(ROBERTA *quickly goes to meet* GLENN *as he enters, carrying* AARON.)

GLENN. I found him.

He must have been lying there for hours.

(*Together they lay* AARON *on the floor.* AARON *is freezing and in pain.* GLENN *takes off the football helmet and goes to* SARAH.)

What is she down to?

ROBERTA. Thirty-nine.

GLENN. (*To* AARON) She took a bad turn this afternoon.

(*A tremor hits the room.*)

(**Note: the below should go rapid-fire, with great urgency, except where a pause or beat is indicated.*)

They're being reported now. The earthquakes. In places that have never had one before. In places that don't even have fault lines.

(GLENN *checks* SARAH's *thermometer.*)

Thirty-eight!

(*To* ROBERTA.) What are we going to do?

ROBERTA. We'll have try to heal her directly.

GLENN. Maybe if you do an energy healing. If you can speed up the molecules in her—

AARON. No. No one touches Sarah.

GLENN. We have to Aaron. We're running out of time.

AARON. We stick to the gameplan.

GLENN. How? Her patients aren't here. We would need one of the people whose pain she's carrying.

AARON. *I'm one of those people.*

GLENN. Are you saying…?

AARON. Do it to *me.*

GLENN. An energy healing?

ROBERTA. Finally.

My darling you will not regret this.

AARON. Not you. Glenn.

GLENN. Me?

AARON. Only way I'll do it.

ROBERTA. Sweetheart, Glenn is still a student.

AARON. Then it's time for the test.

ROBERTA. Me. I'm the one who has to help you. *Me. Me.*

AARON. No.

GLENN. Aaron, if Sarah's temperature dips below thirty-two…

ROBERTA. That would be very very bad.

GLENN. (*Checking the thermometer.*) Thirty-six!

AARON. Now or never Glenn. Because Roberta ain't sinking her hooks into me. I don't care what happens.

ROBERTA. After all this time you still doubt my intentions?

(*When* AARON *doesn't answer.*)

Fine!
(ROBERTA *turns to* GLENN.)
Do you have an object?
(GLENN *picks up* AARON's *football helmet.*)
GLENN. It's how I found him.
In Central Park. And that's a pretty big place.
(*The wind whips even more ferociously.*)
ROBERTA. Get your instruments. Hurry.
(GLENN *smiles. Like a gunslinger, he reaches into the pockets of his parka
and whips out his tuning forks.*)
GLENN. I like to be prepared.
(GLENN *sits Indian style, the football helmet in his lap.*)
Okay, Aaron. All I'm going to do is tap into its energy, so I can journey in-
side you, and describe to you what I see. Close your eyes and try to relax.
AARON. (*Shutting his eyes.*) Yeah, right.
(GLENN *takes a deep breath. Dramatically, he raises the tuning forks up in
ready position.*)
GLENN. I am the light between the full—oh, forget it. Here I go.
(*With a quick, sudden movement,* GLENN *strikes the helmet hard.*
AARON *recoils sharply.*)
AARON. Woh.
(GLENN *does it again.*)
Jesus!
(GLENN *holds the tuning forks up, gripping them steady in each hand.*)
(**Note: when* SARAH *pipes in, she does so unconsciously.*)
GLENN. I made it. I'm inside now.
AARON. *Jesus.*
GLENN. (*Inside the images, painting them.*) I see your intestines. Winding their
way through your abdomen, they're like, like a…
SARAH. Subway tunnel.
GLENN. The hollow echo, wind whipping. The sound of your stomach—
SARAH. Rumbling.
(GLENN *taps the helmet again.*)
GLENN. There. A door. A big steel door. An entrance maybe.
To your stomach.
I'm going to open it, and look inside.
(*A quick beat as he "looks".*)
Uhh…
AARON. What? What do you see?
GLENN. (*Baffled.*) I see…I see a urinal.

And this football helmet.
    (GLENN *recoils.*)
That's it. I'm out. That's all I could see.
    (GLENN *opens his eyes, turns to* AARON.)
Aaron. Can you account for any of these images?
    (AARON *can only laugh.*)
(*Defensive.*) What? Are they not familiar? You don't recognize any of the
images I received? Am I completely—
AARON. Take it easy. I recognize them. They're from the last fun-filled
Christmas I spent at Dad's.
GLENN. What happened?
    (**Note:* AARON*'s retelling should be sardonic, amused even. Telling a Dad
    story is not an event, it's business as usual. This is not a therapeutic, emotional
    revelation.*)
AARON. What happened? Dad happened.
I gave him a Christmas gift and he went ballistic.
GLENN. What was the gift?
AARON. One I thought might be bonding for a fourteen-year-old and his
father. A secret. I told him I lost my virginity. The night before, Christmas
Eve, 'round midnight.
GLENN. (*Jealous.*) You got laid at fourteen?
AARON. I thought he'd be kind of proud of that. I was wrong.
He went bonkers. Even for him. He made me put my football helmet on,
which he had just given me as a gift. Told me I was going to need it. Then he
dragged me out of the apartment.
GLENN. He kicked you out?
AARON. He took me on the subway. A little joyride, to some station in the
Bronx. Told me if I had a kid at my age, this is where I'd end up working.
Just like he did.
Then he took me into the bathroom,
slugged me in the stomach,
and said—
SARAH. "That's what it's like. Having a kid. Being a father. Like getting
slugged in the gut. Every step your kid takes, every thing he goes through,
every up and down…you feel it. Right in the gut. And it knocks the damn
wind out of you. Every goddamn day of your life.
So now you stay right here, and you think about that."
AARON. Sarah?
SARAH. (*Coming back to life.*) Then…then the padlock. He padlocked you in.
He padlocked you in and left.

AARON. (*Staring at* SARAH, *questioning.*) A janitor got me out in the morning. Hammered the lock off.

GLENN. Were you there Sarah?

AARON. (*While looking at* SARAH.) At Christmas, yes. But she didn't come with us. He made her stay in the apartment. Thankfully.

SARAH. I didn't. I followed you.

AARON. On the subway? You were twelve. It was the middle of the night.

SARAH. (*Her confession pouring out of her now.*) I got in the back. The last car. I sang Christmas songs to myself to keep from getting scared. And then I got off. I got off when you did. And I hid. And I watched. And I saw. And then I…I *fled.* I fled. I got on the next train and went home.

AARON. Sarah, there was nothing you—

SARAH. I witnessed, I always witness but it's never me! Sometime it should be me!

AARON. It was you!

(*Small beat.*)

Someone recently showed me. That nearly the same biological response happens in the body of the person who witnesses the suffering as the person who suffers.

So, I'm sorry to say little sister—it happened to you too.

ROBERTA. (*Devastated.*) And now to all of us.

(AARON *looks to* ROBERTA.)

I'm very sorry.

AARON. Why? It exonerates you. The memory of Dad's demented and, I must admit, very effective method of birth control, that's obviously why my symptoms flared up. They started the moment Karen and I began trying to have a baby.

So be happy. You're off the hook. That one anyway.

(*A beat.*)

ROBERTA. (*Very much inside herself.*) I remember…I remember saying to myself—a mother can't prevent her children from feeling pain. It's not possible. All she can do is to help soothe that pain, help heal it. But maybe…maybe that was a rationalization after all. As you've often accused. Maybe I just couldn't bear it, to be witness to it. And so I retreated. To the attic. To search. For ways to make it better, for ways to heal you. But…my initial retreat…I see…it was enough. Enough to jeopardize the family.

AARON. Yes. It was.

(*A beat.*)

But the truth of it is—we've all fled. Each in our way.

But no more.

(*He turns.*)

Sarah, you've got to go back to work.

SARAH. I can't.

AARON. You can now. We traced it. Christmas coming, your patients, Martin, what happened to him on Christmas, reminded you of what happened to me. Then you come to my office and see me and, and it all became too much. But now, now you've released it. You don't need to carry it anymore.

SARAH. *That's not how it works!* You think my patients come in, talk about the event or figure out how it dredges up something hidden from their past—then have a good cathartic cry and they're on the road to recovery? *No.* It takes *years.* For anyone. And my patients, with what they went through, and what all of us witnessed…this will still be churning around in ten years. In twenty. And it will rear its head again and again, at times and in ways that we can't possibly predict.

AARON. So go back. Keep doing your job.

SARAH. People are responsible for themselves. Isn't that what you said?

AARON. I was wrong and you know it.

SARAH. *I am not enough!*

(*A beat.*)

AARON. You're right.

GLENN. Aaron.

AARON. She's right.

(*To* SARAH.)

Look at her. Never lifted a weight in her life.

GLENN. *Aaron.*

AARON. Let's face it, she's no Atlas. I mean forget the world, she couldn't even lift one crazy Christmas and her big brother's tummy ache.

SARAH. I wish I could have, Aaron. I wish it more than anything.

AARON. I know. I know you do.
But you couldn't.
Right?

SARAH. Not by myself.

AARON. It's what you said at my office. That the Lamed Vuv can't be just 36 anymore. Maybe in biblical times, but not today. Today…

SARAH. …more are needed.

AARON. So maybe more have been chosen. Maybe you're not even the only one in this loonball family who's one of them.

GLENN. (*Excited by the prospect.*) You think I am?

AARON. Maybe so Glenn. Maybe so. Who knows, maybe anytime *anyone* gets ill, with a rash or stomach pain or any other thing that no one really knows what it is…maybe it's this. Maybe it means they're one of them.

(*Turning to* SARAH.)

So, you're right. You're not enough. You need help. And you're going to get it. From Glenn and...from me. Right Glenn?

(GLENN *raises a tuning fork in solidarity.*)

Alright then...here we go...

(AARON, *with difficulty, attempts to rise—similar to the way he did in his opening monologue.*)

We're all going to...get up...and...get out there...and do...what needs to be done.

(*As* AARON *manages to get to his feet.—*)

There.

(*Then his stomach grabs. He doubles over.*)

Crap.

ROBERTA. (*Moving to him, reaching for his stomach.*) Sweetheart, maybe I could still—

AARON. No. No touching.

ROBERTA. But your stomach, you're still—

AARON. In pain, yes. Yes I am.

But so was Ronnie Lott.

GLENN. Who?

AARON. *Ronnie Lott,* Glenn, *Ronnie pinky-finger Lott.*

Doctors recommended surgery to repair it. Instead Lott has them amputate the damn thing above the knuckle. Didn't miss a down.

And neither will we. Despite our illnesses or our injuries, we are going to get out there, and do our job. Because if we don't, if we shrink from it, our future is in trouble.

So we must not retreat.

(AARON *grabs his football.*)

The ball is in our hands so we must not drop it.

Like the man said, "It is better to have died as a small boy than to fumble this football."

GLENN. Who said that?

AARON. John Heisman.

(*Smiles.*)

And I finally understand what he meant by that.

God I love football!

What do you say gang? Who's with me? There's no time to waste. There's too much to lose. Who's with me?

Who's with me? Let's go. Let's go. Let's go go go go go!

(AARON *runs forward with the ball. He takes a few steps then stops, tucks the ball securely in one arm and throws a stiff arm with the other. As he hits the Heisman pose, all around him melts away.*)

(*Slowly, the sun comes out. A new day. Though still chilly. A crisp morning towards the end of January. In Central Park.* AARON *is alone, still in his pose, when* MARTIN *enters and sees him. A beat.*)

MARTIN. You win the Heisman again?

AARON. What?

(*He realizes he's still in the pose. He relaxes.*)

Oh. No. I—

MARTIN. Happy New Year.

AARON. To you too.

MARTIN. You look better than the last time I saw you.

AARON. Lying on the ground?

MARTIN. I'm not apologizing, if that's why you called me.

AARON. It's not.

MARTIN. Okay then.

You do look better. Or different or something.

AARON. Martin, I owe you an apology—

MARTIN. Why? Do I look that bad to you?

AARON. No, I just—

MARTIN. Because I think I'm looking pretty good. I think slugging you helped a bit.

The other stuff we did helped too. I've had a few really good interviews the last few weeks.

AARON. You didn't get a job did you?

MARTIN. Sounds like you'd be disappointed if I did. That some sort of therapy thing? Not wanting your patients to heal because then you're not needed.

AARON. I'm not a therapist.

MARTIN. True. And I'm not employed.

AARON. That's great! I mean it's great because I got you one. A job. That is, if you want it. It's pretty entry level.

MARTIN. You got me a job?

AARON. With the NFL. That's what I do, my real job. Football highlights.

MARTIN. Now that makes more sense.

AARON. The job would be as my assistant. Not to get coffee or anything like that. You'd watch football. Sit around with a bunch of guys recording clips into a database, screaming and yelling when there's a good hit. High-fiving, head butting.

MARTIN. An informal work atmosphere is it?

AARON. Leave your tie at home.

MARTIN. Sounds okay.

AARON. Really? You'll do it?

MARTIN. I don't know. Maybe.

AARON. You could start part-time at first.

MARTIN. It's a big transition.

AARON. Of course. You can take it as slowly as you want. Everything's arranged. Plus...there might be something I can do to make it go more smoothly. Your transition. Though you're going to think it's a little weird.

MARTIN. What?

AARON. My younger brother, he does something called—proxy healing. If someone gives him something of theirs, an article of clothing or an object that has meaning to them, he does this, this kind of energy healing, using the object. It sounds dippy I know but he's working with The Space now and he's gotten some good results.

MARTIN. Your brother huh?

AARON. Yeah. He's oddly good at what he does.

MARTIN. And I don't have to be there?

AARON. No.

MARTIN. Why not? Worth a shot.

(MARTIN *takes out his wallet and digs into it.*)

AARON. No, no, it's free, he wouldn't take—

MARTIN. Here. Give him this.

(MARTIN *hands* AARON *a worn slip of paper.* AARON *unfolds it and reads. He looks up at* MARTIN, *speechless.*)

I've got the list pretty well memorized by now.

(*A beat. Note: this must be the first time we see the actual list.*)

Well...maybe I'll see you at the office.

(AARON *looks up.*)

I'm open.

(AARON *throws him the ball.* MARTIN *catches it and continues off stage.*)
(*From offstage.*) Touchdown!

(AARON *stands alone. Slowly, he stares back down at the list. Daunted, overwhelmed. An awesome weight now in his hands. Blackout.*)

End of Play

THE UNSEEN
by Craig Wright

BIOGRAPHY

Craig Wright's plays include *Better Late* (co-authored with Larry Gelbart) at the Northlight Theater; *Lady* (Northlight Theatre); *Grace* (Woolly Mammoth theatre); *Recent Tragic Events* (Woolly Mammoth Theatre Company, Playwrights Horizons); *Melissa Arctic* (Folger Theatre); *Main Street* (Great American History Theatre); *Orange Flower Water* (Steppenwolf Theatre Company, The Edge Theatre, Jungle Theater); *Molly's Delicious* (Arden Theatre Company, Arizona Theatre Company); *The Pavilion*, dozens of productions around the country including an extended run at Rattlestick Playwrights Theatre, and a Drama Desk nomination for Outstanding New Play. Mr. Wright received an Emmy nomination for his *Six Feet Under* episode *Twilight* and served as writer and producer for *Lost* and *Brothers & Sisters*. He has received several awards for his writing, including the Helen Hayes Award for Outstanding New Play and fellowships from McKnight Foundation and National Endowment for the Arts. A graduate of United Theological Seminary, Mr. Wright lives in Los Angeles.

ACKNOWLEDGMENTS

The Unseen premiered at the Humana Festival of New American Plays in March 2007. It was directed by Marc Masterson with the following cast and staff:

WALLACE	Richard Bekins
VALDEZ	Gregor Paslawsky
SMEIJA	Richard Furlong
Scenic Designer	Michael B. Raiford
Costume Designer	Lorraine Venberg
Lighting Designer	Brian J. Lilienthal
Properties Designer	Doc Manning
Sound Designer	Matt Callahan
Stage Manager	Kathy Preher
Production Assistan	Sara Kmack
Dramaturg	Adrien-Alice Hansel
Assistant Dramaturg	Cara Pacifico
New York Casting	Cindi Rush Casting
Chicago Casting	Adam Belcuore
Directing Assistant	Ian Frank

CAST OF CHARACTERS
WALLACE, male, prisoner
VALDEZ, male, prisoner
SMASH (SMEIJA), male, guard

PLACE -
A prison. There are two cells on stage, with a third cell, in some manner, between them.

TIME
Scene One: Morning.
Scene Two: Morning, ten days later.

To Lorraine

"O, let my keel burst! Let me go to the sea!"
—Arthur Rimbaud, *The Drunken Boat*

Richard Bekins and Gregor Paslawsky
in *The Unseen*

31st Annual Humana Festival of New American Plays
Actors Theatre of Louisville, 2007
Photo by Harlan Taylor

THE UNSEEN

Scene 1

When lights rise, WALLACE *and* VALDEZ *are in their respective cells. Each cell is equipped with a cot, bucket, metal bowl with a lid, a spoon, and a hole in the floor. These men have been here a long time.*

WALLACE. (*Weary of this.*) I went to the ocean. (*After a beat.*) I went to the ocean.

(*Long pause.*)

VALDEZ. I win.

WALLACE. No. I was just taking a moment to gather my thoughts, Mister Valdez.

VALDEZ. Oh.

WALLACE. I'm still a little muddled. Forgive me.

VALDEZ. (*After a beat.*) They were hard on you?

WALLACE. (*After a beat.*) In a word?

VALDEZ. More than usual?

WALLACE. Exceedingly.

VALDEZ. What did they do?

WALLACE. Nothing novel. Nothing that would betray a mind at work. A lot of trips to the sink, of course. And then some making knots. Dogs. Shocks. And, of course, you know, the good long cry. At the end. For good measure. Twice. For the whole drooling gang.

VALDEZ. Rest a minute.

WALLACE. Thank you. Thank you for that gracious forbearance.

(*A loud buzzer goes off, followed by a brief pause, during which* WALLACE *carefully rearranges his bucket, bowl and spoon on the floor.*)

VALDEZ. Did you talk?

WALLACE. Of course I talked, Mister Valdez. I talked until my voice broke in pieces. I talked until my mind was raw and red from being scraped for words.

VALDEZ. What did you tell them?

WALLACE. Everything, just like always. I scoured my life, same as every night, searching the facts of my existence for what might be the secret substance they're seeking. The quicksilver or the tin. It did no good, of course. They don't believe me.

VALDEZ. They never believe me either. I've told them the truest things I know, the saddest, truest things, and they never believe me. My life outside, before they brought me here, was a lie by comparison.

WALLACE. Mine as well.

VALDEZ. All I've done, from the moment I got here, is tell the truth. They never believe me.

(*Pause.*)

WALLACE. Perhaps it's not a question of belief, anymore.

(*Brief pause.*)

VALDEZ. They've been harder on me too, lately. I don't know why.

WALLACE. I'm beginning to think there's a deterioration at work, Mister Valdez. In the system. The nature of which I am still

(*Buzzer sounds.*)

puzzling out.

VALDEZ. What kind of deterioration?

WALLACE. I'm not sure. It's exquisitely unclear. It seemed, at first, that they wanted information. Then it seemed they merely wanted submission.

VALDEZ. Sometimes they don't even *ask* me anything anymore, they just *do* it.

WALLACE. Exactly. That's my point. It's no longer clear why we're being held here, Mister Valdez, let alone systematically, how shall I put it—undone.

VALDEZ. It's maddening.

WALLACE. It's not ideal.

VALDEZ. I mean, what kind of place is it, Wallace, where they torture you and they don't even want to *know* anything?

WALLACE. I'm no longer sure. It seems there's some sort of paradoxical algorithm at work—an impossible material equation we're being pushed through, like meat through a chamber of slowly grinding gears. All of us. (*After a beat.*) If there was such a thing as an engine that ran on human agony, I'd say that's where we were. But as far as I know, no such thing exists.

(*Two loud buzzer blasts. WALLACE rearranges his "clock." Brief pause. VALDEZ seems to, all of a sudden, feel something in the air. He goes to the central-facing wall and listens.*)

VALDEZ. Wallace?

WALLACE. Yes, Mister Valdez?

VALDEZ. (*After a beat.*) I think…

WALLACE. What? (*After a beat.*) What, Mister Valdez?

VALDEZ. I think there's someone in between us.

WALLACE. There's no one in between us, Mister Valdez.

VALDEZ. It *feels* like there is, all of a sudden.

WALLACE. There's not. There never has been. There never is. There never will be.

VALDEZ. It feels like there is.

WALLACE. You've felt that way before. And we always turn out to be, in the final analysis, alone.

VALDEZ. I know, but—I can't explain it, Wallace, I feel very strongly all of a sudden that there IS someone in between us. Like they've put someone there, or someone's there...somehow... I feel it.

WALLACE. Above or below?

VALDEZ. Below.

WALLACE. (*Unconvinced.*) Very well then. Let's find out. Let's get this over with.

(WALLACE *goes to his central-facing wall and listens. Brief pause.*)

WALLACE. (*Calling out.*) Hello? Hello? (*After a beat.*) There's no one there.

VALDEZ. (*Exasperated.*) They might be asleep.

WALLACE. Mister Valdez...

VALDEZ. They might be, Wallace! When they brought me in, I slept for seven days!

WALLACE. Very well. Let's push to a grim conclusion. HELLO! HELLO! If you're in there, would you do us the kind favor of responding?

(WALLACE *pounds on the wall a few times. A loud buzzer blast.*)

WALLACE. There's no one in there, Mister Valdez. There's no one in between us, sleeping or otherwise.

(WALLACE *rearranges his "clock."*)

VALDEZ. I think there is, though. I feel a presence.

WALLACE. Well, if you feel a "presence," by all means, keep making a fool of yourself.

VALDEZ. (*After a beat.*) HELLO? MY NAME IS VALDEZ! AND THIS IS MY COMPATRIOT, MISTER WALLACE! WE'RE PRISONERS JUST LIKE YOU! ARE YOU IN THERE?

WALLACE. (*After a beat.*) See? There's no one in there.

VALDEZ. I think there is, though.

WALLACE. Well, Mister Valdez, how shall I put this? Time will tell. (*After a beat.*) If someone's in there, I'm sure he'll show himself. It is what beings do.

(*Seven odd beeps.* WALLACE *rearranges his "clock."*)

VALDEZ. It could be a woman, you know...

WALLACE. No it couldn't.

VALDEZ. But it feels like a woman. A little. To me.

WALLACE. Mister Valdez.

VALDEZ. Yes?

WALLACE. I have some news for you, from the tragic land of observable reality.

VALDEZ. What's that?

WALLACE. This is a prison for *men*.

VALDEZ. *(After a beat.)* I know it seems that way...

WALLACE. Have you ever seen a woman, Mister Valdez? In the entire time you've been here?

VALDEZ. No.

WALLACE. Well...

VALDEZ. But I've never seen anyone in the entire time I've been here—except for Smash and a few other guards. I've never even seen you.

WALLACE. Well all the guards are men.

VALDEZ. That we've met.

WALLACE. But the ones we've met tell us *something*.

VALDEZ. Or they tell us nothing at all!

> *(Buzzer blast. Then: two more.* WALLACE *rearranges his "clock."*
> VALDEZ *continues sensing the presence of the Unseen.)*

VALDEZ. Seriously, Wallace. Think about it. This prison could be full of women. Beautiful women.

WALLACE. Of course.

VALDEZ. It's true! There could be more beautiful women in this prison than we ever saw in the world, than we ever knew even existed. And we could be the only men here, prisoner-wise. We don't really know.

WALLACE. It seems to me highly unlikely that this prison, aside from us, is filled with beautiful women.

VALDEZ. But that doesn't mean that isn't how it is.

WALLACE. Nicely put.

VALDEZ. There could be women in this prison. And children. And animals.

WALLACE. Children and animals?

VALDEZ. Yes.

WALLACE. Imprisoned for what?

VALDEZ. Childlike animal crimes.

WALLACE. And treated like us?

VALDEZ. Or better. Or far worse. Who knows? It suddenly strikes me, Wallace, this prison could go on for miles. Cell after cell, for hundreds of miles...

WALLACE. I've never heard of a prison that extensive.

VALDEZ. That doesn't mean that isn't how it is. This prison could go on forever. It could be filled with women, children, animals...

WALLACE. What's your point, Mister Valdez?

VALDEZ. My point is, we don't really know! We don't know anything. We don't really know if someone's not in there or not. (*After a beat.*) Admit it, Wallace, we don't really know the structure of this place. Or the rules. We don't really have a sense of the grand design.

WALLACE. You might not, Mister Valdez, you might not. But I have to say, I think I have a little sense of "the grand design." I know a *few* things.

VALDEZ. Like what?

WALLACE. Well...for instance...

VALDEZ. Like what? What do you really KNOW?

(WALLACE *seems reluctant to divulge his information.*)

WALLACE. Well, I know there's this alternating pattern of cells...

VALDEZ. In this very small part of the prison.

WALLACE. I'm assuming we live in a representative sample.

VALDEZ. But maybe your assumption is wrong. Maybe they make each little part of the prison different, unimaginably different from the next.

WALLACE. Why would they do that?

VALDEZ. To trick us. Into thinking we understand. Into thinking if we could just get out of our cells, we'd know our way around.

WALLACE. Every part different...?

VALDEZ. Yes.

WALLACE. Unimaginably different from the next...?

VALDEZ. Yes.

(*Buzzer.* WALLACE *rearranges his "clock."*)

WALLACE. That doesn't seem like the most cost-efficient way to design a prison.

VALDEZ. Maybe they don't consider costs. Maybe they have considerable resources. Maybe their resources are infinite.

WALLACE. Unlikely.

VALDEZ. Unlikely, but not impossible.

WALLACE. I'm not even sure the construction of a patternless structure is plausible.

VALDEZ. But you can't be certain that it's not. That's how *I'd* make a prison, if *I* made one, and I had infinite resources. I'd make it very predictable, locally, and then I'd make it completely patternless throughout, so no one could ever find their way. The entire prison would be one patternless, infinite lock.

WALLACE. (*After a beat.*) Well, Mister Valdez, if you did make a prison like that...

VALDEZ. Yes?

WALLACE. I just have to warn you, rhetorically speaking...

VALDEZ. Yes?

WALLACE. I would make a key.

VALDEZ. But you wouldn't know the structure of my lock. You couldn't.

WALLACE. Then I would make what is known as a "skeleton key."

VALDEZ. Then I would make my lock be constantly changing.

WALLACE. Then I would make a key that thinks.

VALDEZ. Then I would make my lock be constantly reconfiguring itself at infinite speed.

WALLACE. My key would change just as quickly.

VALDEZ. Right, but even so, Wallace, you have to concede, my lock came first, so it would always be one step ahead of your key.

WALLACE. Then I would make the key that made the infinite lock to begin with!

VALDEZ. (*After a beat, fatefully.*) Well, that would do it, wouldn't it?

(*Buzzer.* VALDEZ *goes to the Unseen's wall and taps on it a few times.*)

VALDEZ. Hello? Hello?

WALLACE. How many times do I have to tell you, Mister Valdez, there's no one in there!

VALDEZ. I still feel like there IS. I can't help it. I feel like someone's in there. (*After a beat.*) It would be nice to hear news, wouldn't it? From the world...?

WALLACE. Possibly. It could also fill the heart with unsatisfiable hunger for the peach that can never be reached.

VALDEZ. I don't know. I think it would be nice to hear something out there had changed. Anything. Just to hear life had continued in our absence. There's hope in that.

WALLACE. Or melancholy.

VALDEZ. Or faith.

WALLACE. Or suffocating despair upon discovering one's absolutely unnecessary.

(*A series of buzzers.* WALLACE *rearranges his "clock" furiously.*)

VALDEZ. Even just some news about fashion would be nice.

WALLACE. (*After a beat.*) Fashion?

VALDEZ. Yes. That's how big changes in the world always start, Wallace. Fashion.

WALLACE. Who told you that?

VALDEZ. My mother. She told me every great change in the world starts with buttons. With the shape of the buttons, the substance of the buttons, the number of eyes. And it all spreads out from there. She said you could look through the eyes of a button and see the next world coming.

WALLACE. Truly?

VALDEZ. Yes.

WALLACE. This was her privately concocted socio-evolutionary theory of fashion?

VALDEZ. Yes.

WALLACE. What did your mother do?

VALDEZ. She was a seamstress.

WALLACE. Of course. (*After a beat.*) And I suppose your father the furrier had a similar system based on fur.

VALDEZ. My father was a janitor.

WALLACE. And you sister, the whore, had one on sex…

VALDEZ. I never had a sister.

WALLACE. Each person in your family was a private genius with a private language like a private tower stretching up into a private sky.

VALDEZ. But maybe she was right, Wallace, maybe it's true. We don't know it's not. (*After a beat.*) Our freedom could be starting today. Right now. And we'd only need one little button to know.

(*The flurry of buzzers ceases. Brief pause.*)

VALDEZ. (*Knocks.*) Hello. Hello.

WALLACE. Shall we continue?

VALDEZ. With what?

WALLACE. With the game.

VALDEZ. If you want to. Or you could rest.

WALLACE. No, let's play, Mister Valdez. Let's keep our minds sharp. A day is coming, very soon, when we'll be grateful an effort was made to keep the lighthouse manned. For us, and all the ships at sea.

VALDEZ. Okay. (*After a beat.*) It's your turn.

(*Brief pause.*)

WALLACE. I went to the ocean.

VALDEZ. (*Knocks.*) Hello.

WALLACE. Pay attention Mr. Valdez. I went to the ocean. And I brought an apple. And a beam of light. And a cat. And a delphinium in a brightly patterned vase. And an egg. And a flame in cupped hands feeding only on itself. And a grass skirt. And a hoop skirt. And an ice cream cone. And a juniper berry. And a king.

(VALDEZ *knocks.*)

Mr. Valdez! And lemon-scented tea. And a mattress. And a nest of vipers, twirling and copulating incessantly. And an orange. And a peevish dwarf with a key in a locket around his neck. And quicksand. And a relic plucked from the tomb of an ancient prophet. And a smile. And a tin whistle, speckled with lichens. And a unicycle. And vanilla beans. And a window. And—xenon.

VALDEZ. (*After a beat.*) Xenon?

WALLACE. Yes. I went to the ocean and I brought—xenon. Your turn.

VALDEZ. "Xenon" with an X?

WALLACE. Yes. (*After a beat.*) Go.

VALDEZ. Is that really a real word?

WALLACE. Yes, Mister Valdez, "xenon" is really a real word.

VALDEZ. I want to believe you.

WALLACE. I am eminently trustworthy.

VALDEZ. I know, you always say that, but...

WALLACE. Mister Valdez...

VALDEZ. Eleven years now we've been playing this game and you keep coming up with these X-words, never repeating...

WALLACE. There are more X-words than you think.

VALDEZ. What does it mean?

WALLACE. It is number 54 in Mendeleev's periodic table of the elements.

VALDEZ. (*After a beat, convinced.*) Oh.

WALLACE. Yes. Xenon. A building block of nature. A word in the sentence of creation. A colorless gas seated invisibly between iodine and cesium. Used for lighting, but also as a general anesthetic. Witness the soft blue glow.

(*A series of beeps. WALLACE rearranges his "clock." VALDEZ sits, suddenly melancholy.*)

WALLACE. Your turn, Mister Valdez. (*After a beat.*) Go. You went to the ocean. (*After a beat.*) Mister Valdez, it's your turn.

(*Brief pause.*)

VALDEZ. Okay. Let's see. I went to the ocean and I brought an apple. And a beam of light. And a cat. And a—delphinium in a vase.

(*A loud buzzer blast, followed by several more. WALLACE rearranges his "clock" continuously as the buzzers blast, gradually becoming excited by something he deduces from the moving pieces.*)

VALDEZ. And an egg. And a flame. And a grass skirt. And a hoop skirt. And an ice cream cone. And a juniper berry. And a king. And lemon tea. And a mattress. And a nest of vipers. And an orange.

WALLACE. Mister Valdez!

VALDEZ. And a—peevish dwarf—

WALLACE. Mister Valdez, stop!

VALDEZ. Wait, Wallace, I'm almost done, and quicksand—

WALLACE. Stop playing the game!

VALDEZ. But you just told me to play the game!

WALLACE. I know, but reality has processed like a queen down a map-lined hallway, and now you need to stop!

VALDEZ. Why?

(The intermittent buzzers continue.)

WALLACE. *(Still calculating.)* Because if I'm correct…which I'm fairly certain I am…

(The buzzers stop. WALLACE leaves his "clock" and goes to the door.)
(Intensely, quietly excited.)

This is the day.

VALDEZ. *(After a beat.)* What does that mean?

WALLACE. It means…

VALDEZ. *(After a beat.)* What? What, Wallace? What does it mean, "this is the day"?

(Brief pause. Buzzer. WALLACE rearranges his "clock.")

WALLACE. Mister Valdez…?

VALDEZ. Yes…?

WALLACE. I'm going to ask you a question I've never asked you before.

VALDEZ. Okay.

WALLACE. Please don't be offended.

VALDEZ. Okay.

WALLACE. No offense is meant.

VALDEZ. What's the question?

WALLACE. Can you be trusted?

VALDEZ. *(After a beat.)* That's the question?

WALLACE. Yes.

VALDEZ. I wasn't sure.

WALLACE. That's the question. Can you be trusted?

(Brief pause.)

VALDEZ. I *think* so.

WALLACE. You're not a spy?

VALDEZ. No.

WALLACE. Truly?

VALDEZ. Yes.

WALLACE. (*Momentarily confused.*) Yes, you are, or yes, you're truly not?

VALDEZ. Yes, I'm not!

WALLACE. Do you promise?

VALDEZ. Yes! I'm not a spy! Believe me, I've offered several times to be one.

WALLACE. You have?

VALDEZ. Yes! In the course of my trips to the sink and what have you? I offer every time. They don't want me for a spy.

WALLACE. Why?

VALDEZ. They think I'm untrustworthy.

(*Beat.*)

WALLACE. You know what, Mister Valdez? Forget I said anything. Forget I asked.

VALDEZ. If I was a spy, Wallace, would I have told you I'd offered to be one?

WALLACE. (*After a beat.*) I don't know, Mister Valdez! That's the thing about spies!

VALDEZ. Anyway, Wallace, you're my friend! I wouldn't spy on you. I couldn't. (*After a beat.*) It's impossible.

(*Brief pause. Buzzer.* WALLACE *rearranges his "clock."*)

WALLACE. Seemingly. You could be a spy and not know it.

VALDEZ. How?

(*A series of beeps sets off a rapid reconfiguration of the "clock."*)

WALLACE. You could be hypnotized or programmed or somehow surgically altered, Mister Valdez, and you could be taking everything in that I say and do without even realizing it, and you could be painstakingly, unconsciously recording it in a secret sector of your brain hidden even from you, Mister Valdez—even from you. And then, when they take you to the room for treatment, they could activate that secret sector of your brain with a signatory word, for instance, or an electrode, or a pulsing electromagnetic device of some sort, and thus make you talk and divulge the contents of that secret sector of your brain that is hidden even from you, Mister Valdez—even from you. And then, once they'd extracted the information, they could close the doors once more, and darken the long cerebral hallways leading to that secret sector of your brain hidden even from you, Mister Valdez, even from you—and then they'd sweetly send you back here to continue sponging up the messy information that's continuously dripping from my mouth. In this manner, you could be a spy and you would not even know it.

VALDEZ. I really don't think they've done any of those things.

(*The beeps stop, as does* WALLACE.)

WALLACE. But you wouldn't know if they had, Mister Valdez, that's the key. That's the crux. That's the nut. That's the thing. It's impossible, absolutely impossible, to know.

VALDEZ. Then I guess you shouldn't talk to me any more.

WALLACE. Right. Yes. That's right. I won't talk to you anymore. We'll never speak again. (*To himself.*) The epistemological problem dictates it must be so.

VALDEZ. What?

WALLACE. Goodbye!

(*Brief pause.*)

VALDEZ. They could have done all that secret stuff to you, too, you know!

WALLACE. Believe me, Mister Valdez, they haven't!

VALDEZ. Well, probably not, but if they had, you wouldn't know it either! It could be hidden from you, Wallace—even from you!

WALLACE. No, *I* would know, Mister Valdez, if they'd done things like that unto me!

VALDEZ. Oh, so you would know, but I wouldn't?

WALLACE. Yes, of course!

VALDEZ. Why?

WALLACE. Because I have a superior mind! (*After a beat.*) I have an analytical mind that is completely impervious to illusion.

VALDEZ. But they could make you think that, too! That could be the *real* illusion!

WALLACE. Mister Valdez, I said GOODBYE!

(*Long pause.* WALLACE *eyes his "clock" and his calculations.*)
(*At the end of his rope.*)

Why?

VALDEZ. Why what?

WALLACE. Why does everything—every concept, every action, every being—require a counterpart?

VALDEZ. It's the way things work.

WALLACE. But the way things work doesn't work. Every notion is destroyed by its converse, without which the notion itself is incomprehensible—every idea's a stiffening trap.

(*Brief pause.*)

VALDEZ. Tell me why "this is the day," Wallace. I promise I'm not a spy.

(*Brief pause while* WALLACE *gives up.*)

WALLACE. This is the day, Mister Valdez, about the temporal location of which I have been steadily gathering information, lo, these past ten years. This is the day around which, according to my calculations, a massive number of concentric conceptual calendars have long been circling. (*After a beat, quietly.*) This is the day we escape.

VALDEZ. (*Didn't hear that.*) What?

WALLACE. (*Still whispered.*) This is the day we escape.

VALDEZ. I can't hear you.

WALLACE. (*Loud and clear.*) THIS IS THE DAY WE ESCAPE!

VALDEZ. You shouldn't say that so loud.

WALLACE. THANK YOU FOR THE FRIENDLY ADVICE!

(*Brief pause.*)

VALDEZ. Why today?

WALLACE. Because today is the only day we *can* escape.

VALDEZ. Are you sure?

WALLACE. Yes, I've done the calculations. I'm positive. I'm crystalline. It's the only day it's possible.

VALDEZ. Why?

WALLACE. Because: according to my calculations, Mister Valdez, this is the day the hot air balloons are leaving from the red velvet ballroom in the center of the prison through the vast vertical airshaft lined with colored lights.

(*Long pause.* VALDEZ *lingers by the Unseen's wall, listening.*)

VALDEZ. Colored lights?

WALLACE. According to my calculations, yes.

VALDEZ. (*After a beat.*) Hot air balloons?

WALLACE. According to my calculations, yes. I know it sounds unlikely…

VALDEZ. It sounds slightly more than unlikely…

WALLACE. I know, but trust me, they have all these things in place today for the celebration.

VALDEZ. What celebration?

WALLACE. I'm not entirely sure. I just know it's been in the works for years now.

VALDEZ. How do you know?

WALLACE. I've reasoned it out. I've looked and listened and reasoned it out. And after years of careful observation, contrary to your earlier critique in which you posited an utterly absurd situation in which women and children and animals are pointlessly tortured in an infinitely extending hell, I have been able to accurately and coherently infer the *actual* superstructure of this place through fastidious and microscopic examination of a number of visible material realities.

VALDEZ. You have a microscope in there?

WALLACE. No, I mean, by paying attention to details. Visible details. Unlike you, Mister Valdez, I have no truck with the unseen.

(*Feeling caught,* VALDEZ *leaves the Unseen's wall.*)

VALDEZ. What kind of details are you talking about?

WALLACE. Well, the arrangement of the stones in our cells, for example. And the arrangement of the cells on our floor and the floors above and below. I've also been able to draw some conclusions from the seemingly chaotic but actually quite predictable pattern of sounds with which we're continually battered and rattled and brained. And, perhaps most importantly, from snatches of conversation I've caught during my thousands of trips to the sink.

VALDEZ. You feel like your mind is dependable then?

WALLACE. Completely.

VALDEZ. Really?

WALLACE. Yes.

VALDEZ. Because when they tie me down and put that rag in my mouth and put my head under that faucet, I tend to get confused.

WALLACE. I'm exactly the opposite. I feel those are moments of great clarity. It's the rest of my life that's confusing.

VALDEZ. Okay.

WALLACE. The point is, from all these details and sensations and impressions I have meticulously quilted together an absolutely uninterrupted fabric of conclusions, first and foremost of which is this: this prison, Mister Valdez, is structured like an immense, elaborate beehive.

VALDEZ. A beehive?

WALLACE. Yes. The world as we know it has a few basic structures in it, Mister Valdez—a few basic structures that evolution has generated by chance, but which have proven their power over time to perform certain tasks in the ongoing work of making and maintaining reality as it continues to wetly unfold like water, and then like flannel, and then like flesh, and then slowly but surely like crystals and iron as it concretizes into the visible material facts of physical history. Agreed? Provisionally?

VALDEZ. Sure.

WALLACE. The symmetrical structure of the snowflake, for instance, or the structure of the vertebrate spine, for instance, all men and women of reason agree these can be taken at this point as givens in this world—as can be the honeycombed structure of the beehive as nature's primary model for housing a multiplicitous population of discrete individuals in the smallest possible space. Witness the coliseum. Witness the skyscraper. Witness the ever-spreading structure of the modern megalopolis. We, as a species, are building ourselves, and have been since the beginning of time, a beehive.

VALDEZ. Wallace?

WALLACE. What, Mister Valdez?

VALDEZ. Is this what you think about when we're not talking?

WALLACE. No, this is what I think about while *you're* talking. Now, I'll explain the escape plan in all its intricate detail.

VALDEZ. Can I ask one question first?

WALLACE. Just wait, Mister Valdez, let me explain the plan, because time is of the essence, and it's quite complex—

VALDEZ. I'm sure it is, but—

WALLACE. It involves a number of jury-rigged devices we'll fashion on the go—

VALDEZ. Just tell me how we—

WALLACE. Communicators and lock-picks, disguises and simple explosives—

VALDEZ. How do we get—

WALLACE. And a series of branching possibilities that will require the two of us to be continually cross-correlating as we proceed to the center of the structure—

VALDEZ. *How do we get out of the cells?*

WALLACE. Excuse me?

VALDEZ. I know the plan is complicated, and I'm eager to hear all about it, I just want to know, how do we get out of the cells? To begin with?

WALLACE. How do we get out to *begin with…*?

VALDEZ. Yes. How do we get out to *begin with*?

(*Brief pause.*)

WALLACE. (*After a beat.*) Mister Smeija is going to *let* us out.

VALDEZ. (*After a beat.*) Smash is going to *let* us out?

WALLACE. Yes.

VALDEZ. Just like that?

WALLACE. Yes.

VALDEZ. You've talked with him about this?

WALLACE. No. If I had, I'd think the plan would be severely compromised.

VALDEZ. So you've never mentioned it to him?

WALLACE. No. Just like I've never mentioned it to you. I've been formulating it, and clarifying it, testing, reasoning, and waiting. But this—this is the day.

VALDEZ. And you honestly think Smash is just going to—let us out?

WALLACE. Yes. And then the plan will unfold from there. Like a thundering waterfall, if you'll just let me explain—

VALDEZ. Wallace...?

WALLACE. What?

VALDEZ. Forgive me for saying this.

WALLACE. What?

VALDEZ. I'm sure it's a wonderful plan.

WALLACE. It is!

VALDEZ. But Smash has spent the past eleven years beating us, drowning us...

WALLACE. I know where you're going, Mister Valdez...

VALDEZ. Just wait—shocking our privates, making us swallow until our throats are tangled in knots with pain—

WALLACE. Mister Valdez—

VALDEZ. Just wait—stretching us, cracking us, screaming at us, spitting on us, raping us, attacking us with dogs and masturbating us over and over again while crowds of laughing monsters ejaculate on our faces while we cry—

WALLACE. I know what you're thinking—

VALDEZ. WHY WOULD HE LET US OUT?

WALLACE. (*The simple truth.*) BECAUSE HE LIKES ME! Now would you let me explain the plan?

(*A different-sounding buzzer blasts.*)

Damn it! Just bear with me, Mister Valdez. Bear with me, and follow my lead.

(SMASH *enters, agitated, carrying two small metal bowls with lids. He hands one to* VALDEZ, *who hands over his used bowl.*)

VALDEZ. Thank you.

SMASH. Don't talk to me.

VALDEZ. Is there someone in between us?

SMASH. I said, don't talk to me!

(SMASH *moves swiftly on and roughly hands a bowl to* WALLACE, *who hands over his old bowl, as well.*)

WALLACE. Thank you, Mister Smeija. (*As* SMASH *heads away.*) Mister Smeija?

SMASH. (*Brooding.*) Don't start.

WALLACE. I was just—

SMASH. I mean it, seriously, don't, Wallace, this is not the day—

WALLACE. I was just going to—

SMASH. (*Exploding.*) I said don't talk to me, GOD, FUCKING FUCK, WOULD YOU FUCKING FUCK LISTEN!?

WALLACE. I apologize.

VALDEZ. I'm sorry.

SMASH. LISTEN WHEN OTHER PEOPLE TALK! FUCK!

WALLACE. (*After a beat.*) I'm listening, Mister Smeija. I apologize. I'm listening.

VALDEZ. Me too.

(SMASH *heads away.*)

WALLACE. You're having a difficult day?

(SMASH *stops and churns in place, tormented. Brief pause.*)

Mister Smeija? Are you still there? You're having a difficult day?

SMASH. (*After a beat, grimly.*) I am having the worst day of my shit-cunt LIFE.

VALDEZ. What happened?

SMASH. I can't talk about it.

VALDEZ. (*After a beat.*) Why not?

SMASH. Because. I'm not allowed. (*After a beat.*) I'm not allowed.

(SMASH *heads away again.*)

WALLACE. Mister Smeija.

SMASH. (*After a beat.*) What?

WALLACE. I hope you know that I would never reveal to anyone the fact that you spoke with me, if you did choose to speak with me.

VALDEZ. I wouldn't either.

(SMASH *stops.*)

WALLACE. We never have broken a confidence. We never will. We never would.

VALDEZ. Mum's the word.

WALLACE. Exactly. Your secrets are safe with us.

VALDEZ. Anyway, who would we tell besides you? And even then, you'd have to beat it out of us.

WALLACE. I don't think it's too much of a stretch, in fact, to say, Mister Smeija, that we consider you a very good friend, isn't that right, Mister Valdez?

VALDEZ. Best friend.

WALLACE. Exactly. And the thing about best friends is, they listen. (*After a beat.*) If you're facing a challenge right now, Mister Smeija, a pressure, that we could in any way relieve by being receptacles, as it were, for your anxiety, or your narrative, we would be more than happy to do so. We are, in every sense, here for you...

VALDEZ. ...and we love you just the way you are.

(SMASH *takes a beat and then, churning, goes back to* WALLACE's *cell.*)

SMASH. Okay. I'll tell you.

WALLACE. Tell me.

SMASH. You know what the thing is?

WALLACE. No, Mister Smeija, what is the thing?

SMASH. I'll tell you.

WALLACE. Tell me.

SMASH. You don't understand the position you put a person in!

WALLACE. Me...?

SMASH. You, him, the both of you! All you people think about is yourselves!

WALLACE. We've caused you distress.

SMASH. (*After a microbeat, as in "duh".*) Yeah!

VALDEZ. (*Sweet and meek.*) Sorry!

WALLACE. What have we done?

SMASH. Nothing! Or, I don't know, everything! You exist! You stand here all miserable every day with your hunger and your pain and your—*faces*—and you draw a person in! No one with a heart is safe around you people!

WALLACE. What happened, Mister Smeija?

SMASH. I toldja, I don't want to talk about it! It's too depressing!

(*A series of brief buzzer blasts.* WALLACE *rearranges his "clock," seeming more and more concerned.*)

SMASH. Every morning I wake up and I tell myself I'm not gonna get drawn in. I tell myself, today, I'm just gonna come to work and do my job. But then I get here and—I don't know what happens, I see your faces and I get drawn in! I was thinking last night, laying in bed, we should just take out all your fucking eyes. It would make everything simpler.

VALDEZ. Take out our eyes?

WALLACE. Why would you take out our eyes?

SMASH. So I wouldn't have to see what you were thinking all the time! So I wouldn't have to know you were always in, you know, pain!

WALLACE. It weighs heavily on you. The pain of others.

SMASH. It does, you know? No one else thinks so. But it does. So I spent a few minutes last night, you know, just thinking out loud in bed with my wife, trying to design a little machine that would, you know, remove people's eyes? Something simple we could maybe run people through when they first come in? I figured maybe I could design it, maybe show it to the people in charge, maybe make an impression, you know, get ahead?

VALDEZ. Don't take out my eyes.

SMASH. Don't worry, I'm not going to. Because then I realized, even if we took out your eyes...?

WALLACE. We'd still be able to talk.

SMASH. Right! You'd still be able to let people know what you were thinking all the time, only then just with words, but I'd still be stuck knowing. All the time, knowing. I HATE IT!

WALLACE. You're sensitive.

SMASH. I am! No one else thinks so, but I am! So, so, then I spent a few more minutes, you know, thinking out loud in bed with my wife, trying to design a little machine that would, you know, remove people's tongues? Something simple we could run people through when they first come in.

WALLACE. After they passed through the eye-removing apparatus.

SMASH. Yeah.

WALLACE. A gauntlet of sorts.

SMASH. Yeah.

WALLACE. A disassembler.

VALDEZ. Don't take out my tongue.

SMASH. Don't worry, I'm not gonna! Because after I got that figured out, I realized, even if we made it so you couldn't talk, you know, you'd still be able to cry and moan all the time, probably, so it still wouldn't be ideal.

WALLACE. Even the animal noise of the suffering is too much to bear.

SMASH. Yeah. It's awful. So, little by little I realized, no matter how many machines we pushed you through, no matter how much we ever removed to keep you from letting other people know you're in pain, I'd still really always know—because even if I could get you down to just, like, you know, a little four-square inch piece of meat with no eyes and no mouth, just the sight of a stick pin going into that little patch of skin would make me hurt a little, because I know what it feels like, right? You know? To be stuck with a pin? I just have to see it happen and I imagine it.

WALLACE. You're a prisoner of your own empathy.

SMASH. Basically, yeah! So I finally figured it out, the only way to keep from knowing you're in pain...

WALLACE. Is to kill us.

SMASH. Yeah, but they won't let me do that either, so I'm stuck!

WALLACE. You could, if you wanted, let us go.

SMASH. Yeah, like I'm gonna do THAT! I don't think so! (*After a beat.*) No, I just have to come here every day and torture you and see your pain and deal with it. That's just what it is. That's life.

WALLACE. You could let us go, Mister Smeija.

SMASH. No. That's not gonna happen. They'd kill me.

WALLACE. You wouldn't have to get us out of the prison, you could just open the doors and let us go. We'd take care of the rest. No one would know.

SMASH. No. No way. Maybe yesterday. But not today. Not after what happened today.

VALDEZ. What happened today?

SMASH. What happened today? I'll tell you. I got sat down this morning for you two. Sat down and shit on.

VALDEZ. Reprimanded?

SMASH. No, shit on! With hot, steaming, chunky human shit! Like I do to you!

VALDEZ. For what?

SMASH. What do you think? This! Fraternizing! Letting myself get drawn in! I won't be at my own birthday party tonight thanks to you two!

VALDEZ. Happy Birthday.

SMASH. Thank you! And I've been planning this party TEN YEARS! It's gonna have everything I ever wanted when I was a little kid and I couldn't have.

VALDEZ. Like what?

SMASH. Everything! Everything. Red velvet cake.

WALLACE. Red velvet cake?

SMASH. What, you think that's stupid?

WALLACE. No, not at all.

SMASH. It's good cake!

WALLACE. I'm sure it is.

SMASH. Hot air balloon rides.

WALLACE. Hot air balloon rides?

SMASH. What, you think that's stupid?

WALLACE. No. No, not at all.

SMASH. I always wanted to do that, you know? I always wanted to go up in a hot air balloon. But my parents could never afford it.

VALDEZ. What else?

SMASH. You know, everything. A bouncy house. A magician. And lots of colored lights in the trees.

WALLACE. Colored lights?

SMASH. Yeah, thousands of 'em! Ten years I've been saving up for this thing. It was gonna be a dream come true. But now, they've got me on a double to teach me a lesson, I won't see the sun today once, and I'll miss my own fucking birthday party, because you two can't stop crying and screaming when I hit you, and because I'm too nice a guy not to care!

(*A buzzer blasts.*)

FUCK! (*After a beat.*) FUCKING SHIT CUNT PISS FUCK! (*After a beat.*) I gotta go.

(SMASH *exits. Long pause.*)

VALDEZ. Wallace?

WALLACE. (*Exploding.*) Mister Valdez, I have just watched ten years of yearning, distilled through my needle-thin reason, reduced to nothing in an instant, like so many candles on a cake! Would you please grant me one moment's silence?

(*Long pause. Then: three taps on* VALDEZ's *wall are heard, coming from inside the Unseen Cell.* VALDEZ *notices.* WALLACE *does not.*)

VALDEZ. Wallace.

WALLACE. What, Mister Valdez?

VALDEZ. Did you hear that?

WALLACE. Did I hear what?

VALDEZ. That—sound? That tapping...?

WALLACE. No.

(VALDEZ *goes to the wall and listens. Long pause. Finally: three taps.*)

VALDEZ. Wallace...?

WALLACE. What?

VALDEZ. Did you hear *that?*

(*Three more taps.*)

DO you hear that?

WALLACE. Yes.

(*A long series of taps, followed by silence.*)

VALDEZ. See? (*After a beat.*) Someone's in there.

Scene 2

Ten days later. Night. VALDEZ *is excited;* WALLACE, *wasted and hopeless.*

VALDEZ. There's a vast network of tunnels.

WALLACE. In the prison?

VALDEZ. No, in the world, Wallace. In the outside world.

WALLACE. You mean subways and sewers...?

VALDEZ. No, I mean tunnels. Actual secret tunnels. Underneath the surface. And there always have been.

WALLACE. (*After a beat.*) That's ludicrous.

VALDEZ. Nevertheless—it's true.

    (*A buzzer sounds.*)

WALLACE. So, under the cities where business is conducted, there are networks of secret tunnels?

VALDEZ. Yes.

WALLACE. Under the parks where lovers wander, there are tunnels?

VALDEZ. Yes.

WALLACE. Under the fields where grain is grown?

VALDEZ. Everywhere, Wallace. They're everywhere.

    (*A series of beeps.*)

WALLACE. So why did I never see *any* sign of these tunnels, Mister Valdez, when I was, how shall I put it, extant?

VALDEZ. Because they're hidden.

WALLACE. (*After a beat.*) Of course.

VALDEZ. They're hidden just under the surface. Like arteries and veins.

WALLACE. But then there would have to be entrances, Mister Valdez, there would have to be holes in the fabric of the world where people could slip through, the way oxygen slips through the lungs and into the blood...

VALDEZ. And there are, Wallace.

WALLACE. Where?

VALDEZ. In the graveyards.

WALLACE. (*After a beat.*) Of course.

VALDEZ. There are false graves with headstones and names that—

WALLACE. "False graves?"

VALDEZ. Yes.

WALLACE. Mister Valdez.

VALDEZ. What?

WALLACE. This cosmology of yours sounds slightly less likely by the second.

VALDEZ. Nevertheless—it's true.

WALLACE. How do you know?

VALDEZ. I just do.

WALLACE. Did *you* ever see anything in the outside world, Mister Valdez, to support these claims, before you were brought here?

VALDEZ. No, but I wasn't looking. I was a dope.

WALLACE. Did you ever walk by even one open grave that went down to a network of tunnels? That didn't have a body in it, rotting, six feet down?

VALDEZ. No, but I didn't look into graves, I avoided them. I was a dope.

WALLACE. (*Overlapping, driving on.*) Don't you think, Mister Valdez, that if the world was riddled with secret tunnels, we'd *know*?

VALDEZ. No.

WALLACE. Why?

VALDEZ. Because! It's a hidden world, Wallace. Hidden for *many* good reasons.

WALLACE. Hidden *from* many good reasons, I'd say. Hidden from Reason itself.

VALDEZ. I felt the same way when she first explained it to me.

WALLACE. In his code of taps and scratches through the wall.

VALDEZ. Hers.

WALLACE. You did?

VALDEZ. I felt the same doubtful, critical way.

WALLACE. I highly, critically, doubt that, Mister Valdez.

VALDEZ. I'm not a fool, Wallace. I may not be a jeweler of language like you, I can't perpetually generate brand-new X-words like a geyser in the desert of silence, but I'm not an uncritical fool! My world is just as real as yours, my senses just as accurate...

(*A buzzer sounds.*)

I don't believe everything I hear!

WALLACE. But you do believe this—"person's"—"stories."

(*A buzzer sounds.*)

VALDEZ. Yes. And you should too, in the small amount of time you have left.

WALLACE. Why?

VALDEZ. Because you have to, Wallace. Because when Smash brings her back from the room today, everything's going to change and then it just might be too late

WALLACE. Mister Valdez!

VALDEZ. What?

WALLACE. Let me die.

VALDEZ. No.

WALLACE. Yes, please, Mister Valdez, let me die. Let me die and leave me in peace.

VALDEZ. No.

WALLACE. Please. I am close to the end of myself. So close. I can see it like a line in the distance, a stripe on the nearing horizon. It's taken me ten days refusing food to get here, Mister Valdez, to this flat, blasted, vibrating space. My head aches like an explosive. Every muscle in my body's on fire. My penis feels like a knife. I am keenly aware of my kidneys. My mind is a piss-sour puddle of slowly congealing disease, and all this could end if you'd let it. If you'd stop attracting my helpless attention with these stories, it could end. I could crawl to the edge and slip off.

VALDEZ. But I can't let you do that, Wallace.

WALLACE. Why not?

VALDEZ. Because. It wouldn't be right. You have to know to be free to choose.

(*Sound of a buzzer. Brief pause.*)

For ten thousand years, the resistance—

WALLACE. (*With the weak but renewed energy of wonder.*) Ten thousand years?

VALDEZ. That's what she says.

WALLACE. You're sure he said ten thousand, and not just—ten?

VALDEZ. Yes. And I swear to you, Wallace, it's a woman.

WALLACE. May I humbly remind you, Mister Valdez, the regime by which we are being so genially maintained has only been in power a few hundred years?

VALDEZ. I know that.

WALLACE. So why would there be a "resistance" nine-hundred and ninety-thousand some-odd years before the regime to be resisted had even arisen?

VALDEZ. (*After a beat.*) It's complicated.

WALLACE. "Complicated?" Mister Valdez, it's absolutely insane.

VALDEZ. You had your airshaft, Wallace, and your hot air balloons.

WALLACE. And I was completely mistaken!

VALDEZ. But I listened! The courtesy of an ear was extended! (*After a beat.*) Whether I'm ultimately right or not, and I am, you could listen.

(*Brief pause.*)

WALLACE. Very well. Go ahead. My ear is extended.

(*A buzzer sounds.*)

VALDEZ. Ten thousand years ago, a resistance formed.

WALLACE. (*After a beat.*) And they were resisting…? At that time…?

VALDEZ. A regime.

WALLACE. This same regime?

VALDEZ. Yes and no.

WALLACE. Yes and no?

VALDEZ. It was a regime much like this one, and it contained the potential for this one. And within it, like a pearl in an oyster, a resistance instantly formed.

WALLACE. He told you this?

VALDEZ. She.

WALLACE. IT used those exact words?

VALDEZ. Yes. At first, the resistance was small. But as the regime grew, the resistance grew, too, until it needed a secret structure, of equal size, to contain it. It started as a small project, just a few miles of tunnels.

WALLACE. And where did all this supposedly occur?

VALDEZ. Under a castle.

WALLACE. So this *is* a fairy tale. Good. I can die now.

VALDEZ. No.

WALLACE. A "castle"?

VALDEZ. There used to be castles in the world, Wallace, that's not the most unreasonable thing!

WALLACE. And whose castle supposedly sat atop this—fond dream?

VALDEZ. A king's.

WALLACE. An evil king, I assume.

VALDEZ. She never said the king was evil. She just said a resistance instantly formed. But, like the roots of a tree are as wide and deep beneath the ground as the tree is wide and high, so the network of tunnels grew. And as the regime splintered and spread across the land, the resistance splintered and spread beneath the land, like twin sisters, she said, twin civilizations, staring at each other in the mirror of the surface of the world.

WALLACE. So the regime by which we're being held is technically that same regime?

VALDEZ. Essentially. It's hard to explain.

WALLACE. It's easy to explain. It's hard to believe.

VALDEZ. The point is, *they knew about this prison.*

WALLACE. Who?

VALDEZ. *Everyone.* The rulers of the regime *and* the founders of the resistance. They both predicted, ten thousand years ago, that the struggle between the two of them would eventually result in the formation of *this* prison.

WALLACE. They both predicted that the regime would someday *build* this prison?

VALDEZ. No, Wallace, they predicted that the struggle between the regime and the resistance would *result* in the *formation* of this prison.

WALLACE. They built it together?

VALDEZ. No, it just happened. It's something that happened between them.

WALLACE. Like a child.

VALDEZ. Essentially.

WALLACE. We're being remorselessly tortured inside the body of an innocent child?

VALDEZ. In theory.

WALLACE. Fascinating.

VALDEZ. But see, *that's why there are no tunnels IN the prison. That's why there's no way out, see?*

(*Brief pause.*)

WALLACE. No, Mister Valdez, I don't see.

VALDEZ. There are no tunnels *in* the prison because the prison is *made* of *tunnels!*

WALLACE. So according to this logic we're in a resistance tunnel now?

VALDEZ. No.

WALLACE. (*After a beat.*) We're in a tunnel that was built by the regime?

VALDEZ. No. We're *in between* the regime and the resistance, Wallace, in a structure that grew on its own.

WALLACE. But which survives by their mutual consent?

VALDEZ. No. Neither one has a choice in the matter. But they do both allow it to continue.

WALLACE. (*Trying to understand, getting frustrated.*) They "allow" it but they "have no choice…?"

VALDEZ. Yes and no.

WALLACE. Mister Valdez!

VALDEZ. What?

WALLACE. Are there ANY completely conclusive dust specks floating through the hazy summer afternoon of this misbegotten living room?

VALDEZ. Just that we're here, in a place that's not one or the other!

WALLACE. But isn't it possible, Mister Valdez, that we're really just "in this place" and there is no "one or the other?"

VALDEZ. No, that's the only thing that's truly impossible! The regime and the resistance co-exist, Wallace, connected to each other *through this prison.* The only real difference between the regime and the resistance is that the regime *wants* the prison to last forever, but the members of the resistance believe a time is coming soon, very soon, maybe even today, when someone will arise and destroy it. They want that destruction to happen. And when it does happen, maybe even today, the flow of freedom from the tunnels of resistance into the ruined regime will be right through this prison itself. When she comes back, maybe even today, this whole place will flood with pure freedom. And it will be seen in that moment that the purpose of the prison's existence has been and has always been to be a passage for Being. A passage for Being from time-tortured ruin to hope.

WALLACE. (*After a beat.*) It said this?

VALDEZ. Yes. Word for word.

WALLACE. And that's who It is, it's this Conqueror?

VALDEZ. It's a woman, Wallace, it's a woman!

WALLACE. Is that who It says that It is, Mister Valdez? Is that who this uncertain, unseen, unconfirmed, utterly uncorrelatable Being has told you It is, in Its seeming code of taps and scratches over the past ten days since it arrived?

VALDEZ. Yes.

WALLACE. And you believe—

VALDEZ. (*Rushing to get it in.*) Her.

WALLACE. It.

VALDEZ. Yes.

WALLACE. Why?

VALDEZ. I just do.

WALLACE. I know you just do, but really. When you have no proof at all, Mister Valdez—when not a single thread that connects one idea to the next in this quilt bears any resemblance to the modes of connection one sees in the world as we know it—when even to listen all the way to the end requires a stretch of the imagination equivalent to an irreparable tear—why do you believe it?

(*Beat.*)

VALDEZ. I'll tell you. When she first started tapping, she tapped on the lower part of the wall, back by the foot of my cot. And I gradually figured out, after a few hours, she wasn't only using the same part of the wall to talk to me, Wallace, she was using the same stone. The exact same stone in the wall. So I used the same stone, too. On the other side.

WALLACE. And that's what convinced you? The persistent location?

VALDEZ. No. Over the course of the next few days, we sped up the process of talking by switching from a number code to a shape code. Instead of two taps and a scratch meaning "C," a spot on a circle meant "C." And the whole alphabet went in a circle with A and Z at the top, with four spots in the middle for YES, NO, STOP, and GO.

WALLACE. And that's what convinced you? The apparent use of a language you knew?

VALDEZ. No. (*After a beat.*) One morning, five days ago, I woke up and heard her tapping and scratching. So I crawled down to the foot of the cot. And when I did…when I looked with fresh eyes as I surfaced from sleeping, I finally saw what we'd made.

WALLACE. What *you'd* made.

VALDEZ. What had *happened* between us, Wallace. What it *was*.

(*Brief pause.*)

WALLACE. What was it?

(*Brief pause.*)

VALDEZ. A button.

WALLACE. (*After a beat.*) A button.

VALDEZ. Yes. Worn into the stone was a button. A button with four small eyes. (*After a beat.*) How could she have known that?

WALLACE. Known what, Mister Valdez?

VALDEZ. How could she have known that my mother had told me, all those years ago, that a button could be a way to see the new world coming?

(*Brief pause.*)

Wallace? (*After a beat.*) Wallace? Are you there?

WALLACE. Yes, Mister Valdez. I'm here.

VALDEZ. Doesn't that seem like a sign?

(*Brief pause.*)

WALLACE. (*With mournful resignation.*) Yes, Mister Valdez. It does. In fact, that's rather, how shall I put it? Conclusive. Here all questions cease.

VALDEZ. Wouldn't that make you believe?

WALLACE. Yes. If it had happened to me, I suppose I might be inclined to believe. But it didn't.

VALDEZ. She never said anything like this to you?

WALLACE. Never! In fact, I came to the conclusion fairly early on, Mister Valdez, that whoever's in there, male or female, is, in the strictest sense of the term, an idiot. A mental deficient. Like someone deaf and blind from birth. For all intents and purposes an animal, and a rudimentary animal, at that.

VALDEZ. But you just heard all the things she's told me, Wallace, does that sound like an idiot to you?

WALLACE. No, Mister Valdez, not at all. Not at all. It sounds like the violently creative spurting of a highly pressurized mind.

VALDEZ. Hers?

WALLACE. Yours.

VALDEZ. You think I made all that up?

WALLACE. How shall I put this? Essentially.

VALDEZ. How could I make all that up?

WALLACE. I don't think you "made it all up," per se. I think you imagined it. I think that whoever's in there between us has tapped out an utterly random series of sounds over the past ten days that you, in your desperation, in your child-like hunger for hope, have arranged in your mind as a language. But you are seeing constellations, Mister Valdez, where there are, truly, only stars. And the fact that the most "convincing" piece of evidence in the case, so to speak, turns out to be one plucked straight from your childhood bedside only proves the whole affair is a massive misguided projection.

VALDEZ. No, Wallace. What is proves is that she *knows* each of *us* as our *selves!*

WALLACE. Or that *We* only *see* what we *Are!*

VALDEZ. That's not true.

WALLACE. Why doesn't she speak, Mister Valdez?

VALDEZ. What?

WALLACE. If so much is at stake in this matter of yours, if nothing short of the ultimate reversal of reality is waiting to be set into motion by this phantasm and her imaginary club of confederates, why doesn't she SPEAK OUT LOUD?

VALDEZ. But she does!

WALLACE. Taps and scratches?

VALDEZ. She speaks in a way we can hear what she's trying to say, Wallace! Some things can *only* be uttered in *code!* (*After a beat.*) How can you not believe what I'm telling you?

WALLACE. Because it's all absolutely impossible!

VALDEZ. But it's plain as day once you think about it! (*After a beat.*) Doesn't the world feel like that to you, Wallace? Like it's lined with secret tunnels? Like it's waiting to be radically changed!

WALLACE. No!

VALDEZ. But it's, it's all—it's plain as day!

WALLACE. NO! What's plain as day, Mister Valdez, the only thing that's plain as day, in fact, is that we have been brought here against our will—that, once here, we are continually tortured and starved—and that the only way we'll ever leave is by dying! THAT is what's plain as day! And anything else—everything else—is nothing but a bright idea!

VALDEZ. But the bright ideas are everything!

(*Buzzers and sounds break down. VALDEZ becomes concerned.*)

VALDEZ. Did you hear that Wallace?

WALLACE. Yes, Mister Valdez, I did.

VALDEZ. What do you think it means?

WALLACE. I no longer have the capacity to venture a guess.

(*Brief pause. The concern of* VALDEZ *deepens.*)

VALDEZ. My feeling, Wallace, my feeling…my feeling is gone. (*Calls out.*) Hello? Hello?

(SMASH *enters, agitated, and in a bit of a rush. He passes by* VALDEZ's *cell.*)

VALDEZ. Smash, what just happened?

SMASH. Don't call me that.

(SMASH *steps on a button in the floor. We hear* VALDEZ's *cell door open.*)

VALDEZ. Wallace! He just opened my cell!

(SMASH *walks to* WALLACE's *cell and opens it in the same manner.*)

WALLACE. Mister Smeija, what are you—

SMASH. (*To* WALLACE.) Get up. Get out. Get out!

(VALDEZ *stands at the entrance.* WALLACE *sits up.*)

WALLACE. Why?

SMASH. Because I fucking said so, what's the matter with you people, GO!

VALDEZ. What just happened?

SMASH. YOU'RE FREE, OKAY? YOU'RE FREE!

(SMASH *heads offstage past* WALLACE's *cell.*)

VALDEZ. (*Simultaneously.*) Why?

WALLACE. (*Simultaneously.*) Why?

(SMASH *stops.*)

SMASH. Because I can't take it anymore.

WALLACE. You can't take what anymore?

SMASH. The pain.

WALLACE. What pain?

SMASH. The pain of knowing there's pain.

(*Brief pause.*)

WALLACE. What happened, Mister Smeija?

SMASH. I don't know! (*After a beat.*) We were working him over. Nothing special.

VALDEZ. (*Baffled and concerned.*) Her?

SMASH. Him! (*After a beat.*) But when we put him under the faucet for, like, the fourth time, it was like his eyes opened up. Like they bloomed. It was like they were suddenly ten miles deep and he was looking up at me from this bottomless ocean of fear. Sorrow. Pain. Like he was scared and sad for *every-one, ever*. So I said to the other guys, "Stop, stop, we gotta stop!" I acted like something was wrong, like there'd been an infraction or something, and I sent 'em all outta the room. And then I unstrapped him from the board and tied him up in the chair, you know, and sat down. And he just sat there, looking at me with that face.

VALDEZ. Are you sure it was a man?

SMASH. Yes! (*After a beat.*) I started with the eyes. I slipped my thumbnails in past the corners and pushed. Felt them scrape past the backs of the sockets and out they came. Really easy. And I held them in my hands and looked at them. It was like my hands were staring up at me now, with all that misery, asking me what I'd just done. So I squished them to bits in my fists and they ran down my wrists and my arms like they'd never been anything but liquid. There was nothing but grease in my hands. And he's screaming. Begging for his mommy. Begging for his daddy. Begging and crying and, get this, *promising to be good.* I couldn't take it.

VALDEZ. He can talk?

SMASH. WOULD YOU PLEASE FUCKING SHUT THE FUCK UP?

WALLACE. So you took out his tongue.

SMASH. Yeah. I shoved two fingers deep down his throat, far back as my hand could go. So he's biting my wrist, you know? And I dug my nails down through his tongue, it was tough, but I pulled back his head as I did it to give myself leverage and then they popped through. I had blood spraying up in my face. And I pulled, and I pulled, like a hook, until it stretched and it tore out and his throat filled up with the blood. But he still kept on choking and screaming. So I went to the table and got the wrench and I pushed it all the way down his throat, you know, jammed it down through the vocal cords, down so hard that it straightened his throat and his head tilted back. But he wouldn't stop making, you know, sound! And his chest was pumping and there was piss and shit running out everywhere and his face was still twitch-ing and crying, he wouldn't fucking stop!

WALLACE. So what did—

SMASH. I set him on fire. And I sat there and watched while he burned. For a while, he even kept moving in the flames, so I couldn't tell when he was, you know, flailing and when he was falling apart. I couldn't tell what mattered. But I watched until the fire went out and I was sitting across from this thing. In a room full of wet stone and smoke. And the faucet had never stopped running. (*After a beat.*) But the knowing—it never got better. The knowing only got worse. It got deeper and wider until now I'm wrapped up inside it like I'll never get out. It's forever.

(*Brief pause.*)

I never meant to be this kind of person.

WALLACE. I know, Mister Smeija.

SMASH. I can't do this anymore.

(SMASH *goes to exit.*)

VALDEZ. Smash?

SMASH. What? What the fuck do you want? What?

VALDEZ. What was his name?

SMASH. (*After a baffled beat.*) Who?

VALDEZ. The person you just destroyed, the one in between us—

SMASH. The guy I just killed is not the one in between you!

VALDEZ. Oh. (*Suddenly relieved.*) Good.

SMASH. The one in between you is ME!

(*Brief pause. The bottom just dropped out completely.*)

VALDEZ. What?

(SMASH *knocks a few times.*)

SMASH. The one in between you is ME, dumbass!

VALDEZ. It's—you—?

SMASH. Yeah!

VALDEZ. (*After a beat.*) For the past ten days? You've been—

SMASH. Yeah.

VALDEZ. Why?

SMASH. Why do you think? You fucked up my party. I wanted to disappoint you like I was disappointed. I wanted to have some fun.

(*Brief pause.* VALDEZ *is completely destroyed.*)

Look. Get out while you can. At least from here. I can't make any guarantees about the, you know, the rest. But get out of here. Before they send someone else. (*After a beat.*) I'm sorry.

(SMASH *exits. Long pause.*)

WALLACE. Mister Valdez? (*After a beat.*) Mister Valdez?

(*Long pause.*)

VALDEZ. (*To himself.*) My feeling...

WALLACE. What, Mister Valdez?

VALDEZ. My feeling, Wallace. (*After a beat.*) What about my feeling?

WALLACE. What about it, Mister Valdez?

(*Brief pause.*)

VALDEZ. What was it? Where did it come from? If it wasn't from... (*After a beat, more lost than ever.*) What have I been doing? What's been happening to me?

WALLACE. I don't know, Mister Valdez. I don't know. (*After a beat.*) I feel like I don't know anything anymore.

(*Long pause while* VALDEZ *quietly cries.*)

Mister Valdez? (*After a beat.*) Mister Valdez?

VALDEZ. What?

WALLACE. The doors of our cells are open.

VALDEZ. I know.

WALLACE. Well... Perhaps we should...go...?

VALDEZ. (*After a long beat.*) It could be a trap.

WALLACE. I suppose.

VALDEZ. (*After a beat.*) The floor could be electrified.

WALLACE. It could be.

VALDEZ. (*After a beat.*) There could be some secret alarm.

WALLACE. It's possible.

VALDEZ. We could take one step outside and be instantly killed.

WALLACE. That's true. The buzzers have stopped, though, Mister Valdez. They seem to have, anyway. Things just might have fallen apart.

(*Brief pause.* VALDEZ *and* WALLACE *contemplate their hallways.*)

VALDEZ. Wallace?

WALLACE. What, Mister Valdez?

VALDEZ. I don't think I can do it.

WALLACE. You don't think you can do what, Mister Valdez?

VALDEZ. I don't think I can leave. I don't think I can step outside. (*After a beat.*) I'm scared. (*After a beat.*) I don't want to die.

WALLACE. I don't either, Mister Valdez. But to remain while the doors remain open seems counterproductive.

(*Long pause. Then* WALLACE *takes a step out of his cell and looks around.*)

WALLACE. Mister Valdez?

VALDEZ. Yes?

WALLACE. I can at least tell you, with empirical certainty, that the floor is not electrified.

VALDEZ. How do you know?

WALLACE. I'm standing on it.

(*Brief pause.* VALDEZ *steps out of his cell. Looks around. This takes as long as it wants to. Then, slowly, the two men take a few steps until they turn their respective corners and see each other. A long time passes.*)

VALDEZ. Wallace?

WALLACE. Mister Valdez?

VALDEZ. It's me.

(The two men walk slowly toward each other and take each other in.)

VALDEZ. You're not at all how I pictured you.

WALLACE. Neither are you.

(They look at each other.)

WALLACE. You know, I always half-wondered, Mister Valdez, whether you were just a voice in my head.

VALDEZ. I'm not.

WALLACE. No, you're not. This much...

(He touches VALDEZ's face. Brief pause.)

This much is certain.

(Brief pause. The circumference of the space begins to glow with a faint blue light. VALDEZ heaves a sigh, as if he might cry again.)

What, Mister Valdez? What's the matter?

VALDEZ. Nothing. *(After a beat.)* I was just thinking of that person Smash killed. *(After a beat, with great sadness.)* What an unfortunate human being.

(Brief pause.)

WALLACE. Yes. *(After a beat.)* What an unfortunate human being, indeed.

(Very long pause while they look around.)

VALDEZ. Which way are we going to go?

WALLACE. I don't know.

(They look around. Then at each other. WALLACE extends a hand.)

Here.

(VALDEZ takes his hand.)

Let's go.

(Brief pause. They take a few very cautious steps. Their focus is now on the world around them, not on each other.)

VALDEZ. I went to the ocean and I brought an apricot.

WALLACE. *(After a beat.)* I went to the ocean and I brought an apricot and a broken—

VALDEZ. Wallace?

WALLACE. What, Mister Valdez?

VALDEZ. Do you already have your X-word? In the back of your mind? Waiting?

WALLACE. *(After a beat.)* Yes.

VALDEZ. Is it one you've never used before?

WALLACE. Yes. It's one I've never used before.

VALDEZ. *(After a beat.)* You know, someday, you're going to run out.

WALLACE. I suppose you're right, Mister Valdez. Someday we will reach the end of the language.

(*Brief pause.*)

VALDEZ. Just so you know, it's okay with me if you want to repeat yourself. When we get there.

WALLACE. Thank you, Mister Valdez, for the kind thought. But I think I'd prefer to fall silent when that time comes.

VALDEZ. Alright. (*After a beat.*) That's still a little ways off, though, isn't it?

WALLACE. Yes. It's still a little ways off.

(*Brief pause.*)

VALDEZ. Good.

(*Brief pause. They head cautiously out. Lights begin to fade. Music rises.*)

WALLACE. I went to the ocean and I brought an apricot and a broken twig.

VALDEZ. I went to the ocean and I brought an apricot and a broken twig and a candle.

WALLACE. I went to the ocean and I brought an apricot and a broken twig and a candle and daisies.

VALDEZ. I went to the ocean and I brought an apricot and a broken twig and a candle and daisies and an experiment.

WALLACE. I went to the ocean and I brought an apricot and a broken twig and a candle and daisies and an experiment and a field…

(*They exit into the increasingly bright blue glow.*)

End of Play

THE OPEN ROAD ANTHOLOGY
by Constance Congdon, Kia Corthron, Michael John Garcés, Rolin Jones, A. Rey Pamatmat and Kathryn Walat with music by GrooveLily

BIOGRAPHIES

Constance Congdon has been called "one of the best playwrights our country and our language has ever produced" by playwright Tony Kushner in his introduction to her collection *Tales of the Lost Formicans and Other Plays.* That play and *No Mercy* received their first productions at Actors Theatre of Louisville's Humana Festival. Ms. Congdon's other plays include *Casanova, Dog Opera,* both produced at New York's Public Theater; *Losing Father's Body, Lips, Native American,* and *A Mother,* starring Olympia Dukakis, commissioned and produced by American Conservatory Theater in San Francisco. Her latest play, *Paradise Street,* is being developed at New York Theatre Workshop and her most recent production, at the Port Townsend Public Theater, was of *So Far: the children of the Elvi.* Her new verse version of *Tartuffe* will be included in the next Norton Anthology of Drama as well as in a single-volume edition.

Kia Corthron's plays include *Moot the Messenger* (2005 Humana Festival); *Light Raise the Roof; Snapshot Silhouette; Slide Glide the Slippery Slope* (2003 Humana Festival); *The Venus de Milo Is Armed; Breath, Boom; Force Continuum; Splash Hatch on the E Going Down; Seeking the Genesis; Digging Eleven;* and *Come Down Burning.* Ms. Corthron's plays have been produced at Actors Theatre's Humana Festival, New York Theatre Workshop, The Children's Theatre Company, The Mark Taper Forum, Alabama Shakespeare Festival, The Royal Court Theatre, Playwrights Horizons, Yale Repertory Theatre, Huntington Theatre Company, Atlantic Theater Company, New York Stage and Film, CenterStage, The Donmar Warehouse, Goodman Theatre, Manhattan Theatre Club, Hartford Stage, The American Place Theatre and others. Currently Ms. Corthron is developing *Tap the Leopard,* inspired by her Guthrie Theater-sponsored trip to Liberia. Ms. Corthron is a New Dramatists alumna.

Michael John Garcés' plays include *Los Illegals* (Cornerstone Theater Company); *points of departure* (INTAR Theatre); *Acts of Mercy* (Rattlestick Playwrights Theater); *audiovideo* (Drama League Director's Project); *agua ardiente* (The American Place Theatre); *caught (el sueño sueña al soñador)* (Peculiar Works Project); and *frag* (HERE). His collaboration with composer Alexandra Vrebalov, *Stations,* premiered in 2007 at the Rhode Island Civic Chorale and Orchestra. Mr. Garcés received the 2007 Princess Grace Statue Award and 2005 Alan Schneider Directing Award. At Actors Theatre: Director for *dark play, or stories for boys* (2007 Humana Festival), *Finer Noble Gases* (2002 Humana Festival) and *When the Sea Drowns in Sand* (2001 Humana Festival). He has worked in theaters regionally, internationally and in New York. Mr. Garcés is the

Artistic Director of Cornerstone Theater Company in Los Angeles and a resident playwright at New Dramatists.

GrooveLily inhabits that contemporary space where creative musicians ignore the boundaries laid down by words like rock, folk, jazz and pop. Intelligent, original songs with no shortage of wit connect lush musical textures and soaring vocals with the blazing six-string electric violin of Valerie Vigoda, the lightning-fingered piano of Brendan Milburn and the joyful drums of Gene Lewin. The three members of GrooveLily are making a new music that's all their own. Buoyed by the success of their critically acclaimed holiday concert-musical *Striking 12*, GrooveLily looks forward to making your acquaintance.

Rolin Jones' play *The Intelligent Design of Jenny Chow* was a finalist for the 2006 Pulitzer Prize in Drama and received the 2006 Obie Award for Excellence in Playwriting and the Elizabeth Osborne Award for Emerging Artist (American Theatre Critic's Association). His full-length play *The Jammer* received a Fringe First Award for Best New Writing at the 2004 Edinburgh Fringe Festival. Mr. Jones' ten-minute play, *Sovereignty*, was produced at Actors Theatre's 2006 Humana Festival. He currently writes for Showtime's award-winning original series *Weeds*. Mr. Jones is a Yale School of Drama graduate, class of 2004.

A. Rey Pamatmat recently completed a residency in Mabou Mines' 2005-06 Resident Artist Program/SUITE, developing his play *Beautiful Day*. In 2005, Vortex Theater Company presented his play *DEVIANT*, which was nominated for two New York Innovative Theatre Awards including Outstanding Full-Length Play. Mr. Pamatmat's short play *High/Limbo/High* was produced in the 2004 Queer @ HERE Festival. *Picture 24*, *DEVIANT* and *New* received workshops at Yale, and his pieces *High/Limbo/High* and *Baked, Bean & Fran* premiered at Yale Cabaret. His work has been developed at Playwrights Horizons; Ma-Yi Theater Company; Vortex Theater Company; New Dramatists, Inc.; and T. Schreiber Studio. Mr. Pamatmat is a resident playwright in The Ma-Yi's Writers' Lab and a Contributing Editor for Big Queer Blog.

Kathryn Walat's play *Victoria Martin: Math Team Queen* premiered Off-Broadway at the Women's Project, and is published by Samuel French and in *New Playwrights: The Best Plays of 2007*. Other plays include *Bleeding Kansas* (Hangar Theatre, Ithaca), *Know Dog* (Salvage Vanguard, Austin), *Johnny Hong Kong* (Perishable Theatre; Providence), and her latest play *Smile*. Her work has been developed at Manhattan Theatre Club; Playwrights Horizons; Ars

Nova; Bay Area Playwrights Festival; Boston Theatre Works; The Lark; New Georges, where she is an affiliated playwright; and MCC, as a member of their Playwrights Coalition. Ms. Walat received her B.A. from Brown University and her M.F.A. from the Yale School of Drama. She currently teaches playwriting at Marymount Manhattan College and Yale University, and lives in New York.

The Company
in *The Open Road Anthology*

31st Annual Humana Festival of New American Plays
Actors Theatre of Louisville, 2007
Photo by Harlan Taylor

ACKNOWLEDGMENTS

The Open Road Anthology premiered at the Humana Festival of New American Plays in March 2007. It was directed by Will MacAdams with the following cast and staff:

Open Roads, GrooveLily
Performed by the Company

the ride, Michael John Garcés
WYSS .... Zdenko Slobodnik
COUGHLIN .... Sean Andries
SALLY .... Eleanor Caudill

Quagmire Choir, Kia Corthron
MAN .... Timo Aker
WOMAN .... Ashley B. Spearman
PILOT .... Nicole Marquez

Ron Bobby Had Too Big a Heart, Rolin Jones
AMY .... Zarina Shea
ANYA .... Eleanor Caudill
CINDY DILLINGHAM .... Katie Barton

Live Through This (Are We There Yet?), GrooveLily
Performed by Timo Aker

on edge, Michael John Garcés
MARK .... Jeff Snodgrass
BLANCA .... Nicole Marquez
DAVE .... Rafael Jordan
STEVE .... Mark Stringham

Love Song without Metaphor, GrooveLily
SINGER .... Maurine Evans

Borough to Borough, Kathryn Walat
MELODY .... Biz Wells

Ain't Meat, A. Rey Pamatmat
WAITER .... Jake Millgard
CUSTOMER .... Loren Bidner

313

True North, Constance Congdon
HIM..Rafael Jordan
SHE.. Kristen B. Jackson

The Odometer Song, GrooveLily
Performed by the Company

Trade, Kia Corthron
WOMAN 1 ....Maurine Evans
WOMAN 2 .... Angela Sperazza

1260 Minute Life, A. Rey Pamatmat
CORA .... Jane Lee

Dunkin Amerika, Kathryn Walat
NICKI..Katie Barton
MICHELLE...................................... Emily Tate Frank
CUSTOMER ....Timo Aker

Rewind, GrooveLily
SINGER...Mark Stringham
VISITOR.. Sean Andries

The Mercury and the Magic, Rolin Jones
MIKE..................................Michael Judson Pace
JOE..Zachary Palamara

On the Road
Text and Lyrics by Constance Congdon
Music by Phil Pickens
MAN ....Phil Pickens

Live Through This (Are We There Yet?) (reprise), GrooveLily
Performed by the Company

MUSICIANS
Drums ....Timo Aker, Katie Barton, Mark Stringham
Keyboard ....Timo Aker, Jane Lee, Zachary Palamara
Acoustic Guitar ....Timo Aker, Phil Pickens,
                                    Zdenko Slobodnik, Jeff Snodgrass
Electric Guitar .... Phil Pickens, Zdenko Slobodnik
Bass Guitar.............................. Phil Pickens, Zdenko Slobodnik
Violin..Eleanor Caudill
Trumpet..Rafael Jordan

```
Saxophone ......................................................... Zachary Palamara
Trombone .............................................. Sean Andries, Biz Wells
Tambourine ............................................................ Zarina Shea
Soloists ............................................ Katie Barton, Maurine Evans,
                    Emily Tate Frank, Nicole Marquez, Jake Millgard,
                    Zachary Palamara, Zarina Shea, Ashley Spearman,
                    Angela Sperazza, Mark Stringham and Biz Wells

Scenic Designer ......................................................... Paul Owen
Costume Designer ................................................. Susan Neason
Lighting Designer ....................................................... Nick Dent
Sound Designer .................................................. Benjamin Marcum
Properties Designer ............................................... Mark Walston
Musical Supervisor/Arranger .............................. Brigid Kaelin
Stage Manager ...................................................... Melissa Miller
Dramaturgs ............... Adrien-Alice Hansel, Julie Felise Dubiner
Assistant Dramaturgs ................... Cara Pacifico, Diana Grisanti
Directing Assistant ................................. Gaye Taylor Upchurch
```

Commissioned by Actors Theatre of Louisville.

315

THE OPEN ROAD ANTHOLOGY

OPEN ROADS
by GrooveLily

Out where the highway sparkles like a treasure
And every exit sings a siren song
And the horizon stretches out forever
The road is open
And I am hopin'
That's where I belong

Drivin' in a car, there's feeling that I know I would feel
Underneath the stars, all alone, and my hands on the wheel
Free, free, free
And I'd never look back
Away from it all, I'm finally on the right track

Far as I can go, see the country that I never have seen
Out where life is slow, cars are fast and the breezes are clean
Free, free, free
From my little rat race
Away from it all, I'm feeling the sun on my face
Where the highway's not just a parking lot
And all I need are the things I got
And my life won't be just an afterthought
That's where I want to go

Where the highway sparkles like a treasure
And every exit sings a siren song
And the horizon stretches out forever
The road is open
And I am hopin'
That's where I belong

Anybody's guess what tomorrow's gonna bring it's all right
No return address, and I feel like a bird taking flight
Free, free, free, did I mention I'm free
Away from it all, exactly where I should be
And I'll say *au revoir* to the way things are
as the white lines shoot underneath my car
I'll go so fast and I'll go so far, I'll be there soon, I know

Where the highway sparkles like a treasure
And every exit sings a siren song
And the horizon stretches out forever
The road is open
And I am hopin'
That's where I belong

the ride
by Michael John Garcés

Characters:

john wyss
peter coughlin
sally pickett

*wyss and coughlin have known each other since before high school. way too old to
be acting this way. not geeks exactly, nothing that cool, just sort of awkward.
sally is the girl they've been speculating about since they were thirteen. not necessarily pretty (in fact better if she's not), but painfully sexy; she has always been
kind to them in a distant way, which makes it worse.*

wyss *and* coughlin *are hyped-up, jittery, an adolescent exuberance of
enthusiasm given an edge by a dawning adult sense of rising stakes and
diminishing time.*

wyss. so good.

coughlin. yeah?

wyss. so, so good.

coughlin. ok...

wyss. you trust me?

coughlin. yeah I trust you.

wyss. so good...

—

coughlin. what is that?

wyss. that? that, peter, that is a nineteen sixty-five eight cylinder two
hundred and ten horsepower homemade in the u.s.a. ford mustang stud,
guaranteed to put any female of the species within spitting distance into a
procreative frenzy, the supreme example of this great nation's automotive
imagination and ingenuity, an unholy souped-up synthesis of speed, sex and
style. that is what that is. car? come on, bro. this is a ride, man. this is your
ride.

coughlin. uh huh.

wyss. are you kidding me? uh huh? I'm sayin, bro, this is every red white and blue blooded american hombre's sweetest wettest dream.

coughlin. I haven't had a wet dream since I was eleven.

wyss. well I'm sorry for you.

coughlin. that is a beat-down hunk of steaming crap.

wyss. what—are you—what?

coughlin. what in that wildly overactive imagination whirring away in the tiny little atrophied organ that functions in place of your brain do you think we are going to do with—

wyss. what are you even talking about?

coughlin. what am I—what are we supposed to do with that…thing?

wyss. hit the road, I'm sayin, this is what we we talked about. the highways and byways of the great western plains and the mighty rocky mountain range, man.

coughlin. in that?

wyss. yeah, man. what? you wanted me to get a—a geo? a kia rio? huh? used? so we can look like someone's dad or, or their…grandmother. their high school principal. a guidance counselor car.

coughlin. oh, so, in that total heap of, of, of…of shit, john, of shit, you think we'll look like anything other than the monumental losers that we are, in that completely trashed pile of—

wyss. oh, man—what? you are so—no, man. that is a classic product of american engineering prowess and design artistry. what is wrong with you?

coughlin. does it even run?

wyss. look, man, I'm saying, that vehicle, that—that machine has all the self-esteem enhancement a man will ever need, bro.

coughlin. can…we…drive…it?

—

wyss. …not yet.

coughlin. right.

wyss. but it just…all we need to do is—

coughlin. fine.

wyss. where there's a will there's a—

coughlin. thanks Nietzsche.

wyss. just, just, a little puppy love and baby talk and that itty bitty kitty will purr like a—

coughlin. give it back.

wyss. back?

coughlin. to whoever talked you into that catastrophe.

wyss. give it—what? how? I don't even know where this guy—

coughlin. you don't know where—

wyss. no.

coughlin. I don't care how. get my money back.

wyss. I already bought it. I spent it. it's gone. this is a great deal, man, I took that dude for a ride, man, that rube, he had no idea what he had.

coughlin. in what?

wyss. huh?

coughlin. what did you take him for a ride in since that car hasn't gone anywhere since your mother lost it in the backseat to some pimple infested third string junior varsity waterboy who defied natural selection in more ways than one?

wyss. my mother?

coughlin. how much did you spend?

wyss. she's good to you man.

coughlin. how much?

wyss. I—what? how—how much of the, you mean—

coughlin. how much.

wyss. how—all of it.

coughlin. what?

wyss. do you have any idea what the blue book is on this model?

coughlin. all of it. you spent—

wyss. man—all of it? all of what? all of—ok, the money, your money, all of your money was barely enough to buy gas, man, what are you—pathetic is what you are, man—maybe some nineteen eighty-five vintage subaru or some—ugh. somebody's cousin's sister's old car with three generations of baby puke all over the backseat maybe. I'm sayin, you cannot, can not, drive historic route sixty-six from tulsa to l.a. in some subaru, man.

coughlin. we're not going anywhere in that—

wyss. no, man, all we have to do is—

coughlin. no, this is, this is my—how could I be so—so stupid, so—

wyss. what?

coughlin. you said trust me, I should know that when you say trust I should—

wyss. no, man, that hick had no idea, that car was in his backyard for—it's gold, we just fix it up and—

coughlin. how?

wyss. what?

coughlin. we don't have any money to fix anything.

wyss. man, why do you have to be like that?

—

fifty thousand dollars. that's how much that automotive triumph is worth. just a little bit of work. cherry apple red convertible classic—

sally. nice car.

coughlin. ...thanks.

sally. hi guys...

—

wyss. uh...

sally. what's up?

coughlin. uh, nothing.

wyss. hi, uh, sally.

sally. I heard you're maybe hitting the road?

coughlin. maybe.

wyss. yeah, maybe.

sally. california?

coughlin. maybe.

wyss. yeah.

sally. poppy.

—

wyss. ...what?

sally. poppy. that model didn't come in cherry.

wyss. oh.

sally. v-six?

wyss. v-eight.

sally. really?

coughlin. yeah. two hundred ten horsepower.

wyss. the hell do you know about—

coughlin. shut up, man.

sally. you got the super sonic sound option?

wyss. yeah. sure. yeah. super...sonic. yeah.

sally. stick?

coughlin. yes, I—think, yes.

sally. you think?

wyss. no, it is, yes. stick. uh huh. four speed.

sally. whose car?

coughlin. mine.

wyss. man...

coughlin. I just bought it.

sally. so you're gonna blow this town?

wyss. that's right.

coughlin. historic route sixty-six.

wyss. getting our kicks and all.

sally. huh.

coughlin. yup.

sally. I was maybe looking for a ride. west. if you're going my way, I'd go as far as you took me. leaving soon?

wyss. soon.

coughlin. yeah. this week. by...saturday?

sally. ok, well, you know, call me. 634-5789. maybe...

coughlin. ok.

wyss. yeah, ok.

coughlin. so, we'll call you.

wyss. soon.

coughlin. we'll call you soon.

—

wyss. so it's your car now huh.

coughlin. yeah it's mine.

wyss. or I could try to take it back, find that—

coughlin. no, it's good.

wyss. l.a.?

coughlin. sure. fun in the sun. yeah.

wyss. leaving this week?

coughlin. yup.

wyss. how?

coughlin. where there's a will...

wyss. ok, Nietzsche.

—

coughlin. kicks, man.

wyss. yeah. on sixty-six. ride, sally, ride. so good.

QUAGMIRE CHOIR
by Kia Corthron

Characters:

MAN, Native American

WOMAN, African-American

PILOT whose first language is Spanish

Missouri, the present.

A MAN *with a traveling backpack enters from one side of the stage, a* WOMAN *with a traveling backpack enters from the opposite side. Heads down, absorbed in thoughts, they bump into each other midstage. Stare at each other a moment, then.*

MAN. Are you familiar with the story of the north-going Zax and the south-going Zax?

WOMAN. I am well versed in all things Suess and, like the Zax, I never move to the side.

MAN. Let me tell you why *I* won't move to the side. My great-great-greats lived in Georgia since the time of *their* great-great-greats. Then, 1829, gold was discovered in Georgia, the first American gold rush, speculators popping up all over Cherokee land and Andrew Jackson ignores his lawful mandate to protect the Cherokee, instead he creates the Indian Removal Act, robbing Indians of all their Eastern land and pushing them west of the Mississippi. Chief John Ross fought the bullshit all the way but by 1838 he was broken down, thus began the Trail of Tears, the march starting in Georgia through Tennessee, Kentucky, Illinois, Missouri *here*, Arkansas, to end in Oklahoma. I have been following that trail since the beginning and I intend to see it through to the end. Fifteen thousand Cherokee, my ancestors, were in the march at its origin. Four thousand died along the way. Or eight thousand, the government wasn't keeping close records of Indian casualties.

(HE *takes a sandwich out of his pack. Bites. Chews.*)

WOMAN. Let me tell you why *I* won't move to the side. My great-greats poured into Oklahoma Territory at the end of the 19th Century and barely into the 20th oil was discovered in Oklahoma, attracting whites and blacks from across the country. Booker T. Washington dubbed Greenwood, the affluent black section of Tulsa, "the Negroes' Wall Street." You might imagine how the local whites felt about this. So when a young black man working his shoeshine on the white side goes to the only building with a colored bathroom and accidentally brushes against the young white female elevator operator, *well.* The whites burned down the black town, my great-grandmother hid and watching was three, thirty-five dead, unmarked graves and the Tulsa *Tribune* editorializes "In this old 'Niggertown' was a lot of bad niggers and a bad nigger is the lowest thing that walks on two feet." So my great-grandmother and what's left of her family pre-date the Great Migration of the '40s, I have been following their march in 1921 northeast from Oklahoma, through Kansas, Missouri *here*, to Chicago. I intend to see it through to the end.

(SHE *takes a sandwich out of* HER *pack. Bites. Chews.*)

MAN. That was Indian territory. Then they let you flood in.

WOMAN. Except the ones of us already there from the Indians who owned slaves.

(*They stare at each other, chew.*)

MAN. You fought with the American calvary against us.

(WOMAN *opens her mouth to answer, then finds she has none.*)

We adopted the whites' Christianity, we adapted the whites' "Amazing Grace." We took it with us on the Trail. (*He starts singing.*) *Ooh nay thla nah / Hee oo way gee' / E gah gwoo yah hay ee ...*

WOMAN. In the '60s we faced the fire hoses, refused to back down. (*Sings.*) *We shall not, We shall not be moved / We shall not, we shall not be moved ...*

WOMAN.	**MAN.** (*Resumes.*)
Just like a tree that's standing by the water	*Naw gwoo joe sah we you low say*
We shall not be moved	*E gah gwoo yah ho nah*

(*Suddenly the sound of a small plane coming down overhead. The* WOMAN *and* MAN *look up, following the sound down. In the distance the plane is heard sputtering to a stop. A* PILOT *appears wearing a backpack. All stare. Then.*)

PILOT. (*A thick accent.*) Land.

(*Pause.*)

WOMAN. You landed your plane?

PILOT. (*Nods.*) Land. (*Takes a sandwich (taco?) out of pack, bites. Mouth full.*) Lunch.

MAN. ¿*No ingles?*

(*The* PILOT *shakes her/his head no. Reconsiders. Nods.*)

PILOT. (*Sings.*) ¿*Amenece, lo veis / a la luz de la aurora?*

(*The* MAN *and* WOMAN *exchange glances.*)

WOMAN. That's not English!

MAN. That's the "Star-Spangled Banner"!

PILOT. (*Resumes.*) ¿*Lo que tanto aclamamos la noche al caer?* (*Uninterrupted as the* MAN *and* WOMAN *laugh.*) *Sus estrellas sus franjas / flotaban ayer*

MAN. (*Back to eating, irony.*)	**PILOT.**
You're not supposed to sing that	*En el fiero combate*
WOMAN. (*Back to eating, irony.*)	
You'll piss people off singing that.	*En señal de victoria*

(*The* PILOT *stops singing to take out of the backpack a little American flag, waving it as the* PILOT *resumes the song.*)

PILOT. *Fulgor de lucha,*
Al paso de la libertad,

(The WOMAN *and* MAN *exchange glances.)*

PILOT.		**WOMAN.**
Por la noche decían:		*We shall not, We shall not be moved*

PILOT.	**WOMAN.**	**MAN.**
"¡Se va defendiendo!"	*We shall not,*	*Ooh nay thla nah,*
¡Oh decid! ¿Despliega aún	*We shall not be moved*	*Hee oo way gee'.*
Su hermosura estrellada	*Just like a tree that's by*	*E gah gwoo yah hay ee.*

(The MAN *and* WOMAN *laughing, done eating, instinctively look for napkins and realize they have none. The* PILOT *tears the flag into thirds, offering the pieces. The* MAN *and* WOMAN *stare, confused. The* WOMAN *understands first, comes to take a piece, returns, using it as a napkin. The* MAN *then does the same. As they wipe their mouths, the* WOMAN *and* MAN *now realize that they had inadvertently switched places. They put their "napkins" into their backpacks, pick up the packs and walk in the direction of their original "Zax" paths. Just before they exit.)*

MAN. Hey.

(The PILOT *and* WOMAN *look at him.)*

Her people forced on the land. My people forced off the land. You? Free will?

(The PILOT *stares, then sings, most of the Spanish accent gone.)*

PILOT. *As I was walkin' / I saw a sign there*
And that sign said / No trespassin'
But on the other side / It didn't say nothin'
That side was made for you and me

(The MAN *and* WOMAN *stare at the* PILOT.*)*

They never like to sing that verse.

Ron Bobby Had Too Big a Heart
by Rolin Jones

Sweet, simple music.

Typical suburban two-car garage. A convertible. Two young women, AMY *and* ANYA. *They are wearing prom dresses.* ANYA *is packing up the car. A bulky laundry bag sits in the back seat. Amy carries a bright pink suitcase, her dress and face are, slightly…no… aggressively bloodied. She addresses the audience.*

AMY. You grow up in a small town, you don't dream big. You think you do, but you don't. You dream about college and marriage and what your breasts are gonna look like after you've had kids. You dream about living in a big house with a whirlpool bath and getting a job somewhere in the dental arts.

You dream your husband will be handsome and kind and manly and fix your breasts when they begin to sag. These are the things you dream of.

ANYA. Where's your dad keep his guns, Amy?

AMY. In the broom closet behind the Swiffer.

(ANYA *exits.*)

AMY. So you have small dreams. But until life asserts itself you don't know they're small. You just think that's all there is and all there ever will be. And more than anything when you're a young girl of age growing up in a small town, you dream about Prom.

(ANYA *enters with a bright yellow suitcase and a shotgun.*)

AMY. And when things don't go right at the Prom...

ANYA. They voted Cindy Dillingham Prom Queen.

(ANYA *tosses the suitcase in the car. Checks the shot gun for shells.*)

AMY. When things are rightfully yours and through coordinated sabotage, are given to the unqualified and undeserving...

ANYA. She caught Ron Bobby fingering Cindy Dillingham's junk after the coronation. Where's he keep the ammo?

AMY. Under the kitchen sink, next to the Liquid Tide.

(ANYA *puts the shotgun in the front seat and exits.*)

When you're a young girl of age and life reveals itself as unbearably and instantaneously cruel you see your town for what it truly is.

(ANYA *enters with a shovel and a box of shotgun shells.*)

ANYA. A four foot by six foot hole in the ground that rains non stop dirt.

ANYA. So go ahead. Take a picture.

ANYA. Record it while you can.

AMY. Cause we're ghosts.

ANYA. We're smoke.

AMY. Vapor.

ANYA. My best friend Amy.

AMY. My good friend Anya.

ANYA. The car.

AMY. The open road.

ANYA. The past.

AMY. The future.

ANYA. Ron Bobby's mix tape.

AMY. Ron Bobby.

ANYA. Ron Bobby.

(*We hear a moan coming from the laundry bag.* AMY *picks up the shotgun.*)

AMY. Shut up bitch. SHUT YOUR GOD DAMN LYING ASS UP!

(*She hits the laundry bag with the butt end of the shotgun.*)

BITCH IN THE LAUNDRY BAG. Uh.

ANYA. Too big a heart, he had.

AMY. Men should know better.

ANYA. You ready, Amy?

(AMY *holds up her suitcase.*)

AMY. Two sweaters. Thirty-one pair of cotton underwear. Girl's gotta breathe.

(AMY *throws her suitcase in the back seat.* ANYA *throws in the shovel. They get in the car.*)

ANYA. We drive.

AMY. We're drivers.

ANYA. Got ourselves early admissions to the university of Guam.

AMY. And we're driving all the way there.

(ANYA *starts up the car.*)

AMY & ANYA. Boo-ya.

ANYA. Listen to that bitch. We got Mickey over at the Jiffy Lube to hook us up.

AMY. Micky's a miracle worker if you give him a HJ. And I did.

ANYA. Gets eighty-three miles to the gallon. Cause while we might be re-morseless and entitled…

AMY. …and at this very moment understandably unlikable protagonists…

ANYA. We care about the environment.

AMY. That Al Gore scared the shit out of us.

ANYA. Where's your Dad keep the garage door opener?

AMY. Underneath the seat with his Trannie Porn.

(ANYA *searches for the garage door opener.*)

They wanted to barter us off. Marry one of us to the Sheriff's son. Bury us under the bleachers when we die. We will not be buried.

(ANYA *comes up with the garage door opener and some trannie porn.* THE BITCH IN THE LAUNDRY BAG *begins to wiggle her way loose.*)

ANYA. We're going west.

AMY. North.

ANYA. Southeast.

AMY. We're not telling you where we're going.

ANYA. You might know the Sheriff's son.

AMY. You might turn us in.

ANYA. Then we'd have to kill you.

AMY. With the lug wrench in the trunk.

ANYA. Or the butcher knife in the glove compartment.

AMY. Or the bottle of chloroform under my skirt.

BITCH IN THE LAUNDRY BAG. (*Delirious.*) Ron Bobby...
> (A *glimpse of a tiara from the laundry bag and another nearly involuntary smack to the head with the butt of the shotgun from* AMY.)

ANYA. We're prepared.

AMY. We're angry.

ANYA. That's Cindy Dillingham in the laundry bag.

AMY. Cindy thought she could fuck with my shit.

ANYA. Cindy got put in the laundry bag.

AMY. And Ron Bobby got his ass cut.

ANYA. And sliced.

AMY. And distributed.

ANYA. Lying-ass cheating boyfriends make great potting fertilizer.

AMY. The next heavy rain ought to bring flowers.

ANYA. Now in a couple days we're gonna drop the back door key in the mail...

AMY. So if you wouldn't mind getting the box at the curb in a couple of days, we had to duct tape Anya's parents to the furniture and while they're hateful people who chose physic torture over empathy, we still feel they should be fed.

ANYA. And the thought of your mother shitting on herself bothers me.

AMY. Bothers me too. She was a young girl of age once.

ANYA. Had herself some small easily attained dreams.

> (ANYA *hits the garage door opener. Cool lighting effect, brings the light of god onto the car.* AMY *reaches into the laundry and pulls out the tiara, crowns herself.*)

AMY. We dream big now.

ANYA. Pilates in Jerusalem?

AMY. Pilates in Jerusalem.

ANYA & AMY. Boo-ya.

> (ANYA *floors it.*)

on edge
by Michael John Garcés

Characters:

    mark—male, any race, no discernable accent or regionalism, 20s.

    blanca—latina female, texas accent, 20s.

    dave—latino male, no discernable accent or regionalism, adult, any
        age.

    steve—white male, texas accent, adult, any age.

south texas borderlands, night.
indeterminate night sounds resonate throughout, impossible to tell if they come
from miles or feet away.
two figures, walking like they've been going for a long time, dark against the
darkness of the highway.

mark. so we should get there soon, huh?

——

get...wherever, right? soon?

——

you don't talk much.

——

were you out here long?

blanca. thanks for picking me up.

mark. sure, no, I mean, sorry, ought to be something soon right? a store
or—

blanca. might be while.

mark. like, how long?

blanca. pray before day.

mark. at least then we could see.

blanca. the heat.

mark. right.

    (they are hit with bright light.)

hey —hel—hello?

blanca. wait, don't—mark don't—

mark. what?

blanca. don't move.

mark. what are you—are you—hello? hey? hey?

    (shots ring out.)

fuck—what the—fuck.

    (she's gone. another shot. he stands alone, squinting, off balance.)

jesus—fuck. hey don't—what the—

(then another. he breaks into an odd, jerky dance in place.)
hey shit hey uh, blanca, the fuck did you...?
(another. the dance turns frenzied.)
oh, fuck. fuck. blanca?
*(and another. then she's back, grabs him, pull him down and out of the light.
there is a pause, they breathe. he looks at her, she looks off. the light is abruptly
out.)*
they...they shot at us, they...
blanca. yeah.
mark. with guns, they—
blanca. they missed.
mark. what?
blanca. they missed.
—
mark. ...yeah?
blanca. shut up.
mark. what? why?
blanca. so they don't shoot at us again.
—
trying to scare us is all.
mark. how do you know?
blanca. you're still alive.
mark. well it worked. I'm scared.
blanca. I noticed.
mark. well I am.
blanca. that's how you survive. fear. someone shoots, you get scared, you
run. or I guess some people just stand there as if they were—
mark. well I guess my genes aren't suited for survival in texas.
blanca. you guess right.
mark. this is america, they can't just—
blanca. yeah this is america that's right, there's a war going on in case you
hadn't—
mark. war? what war? iraq, korea, not, this isn't—
blanca. texas. arizona. front line. florida. new mexico. what do you think
we're doing here?
mark. doing? nothing. walking. what are you doing?
blanca. me? I'm going to california.
mark. me, too. so?
blanca. why?

mark. what? why? because—

blanca. me too. get the hell out of some shit town, right? get a job, right? me too.

mark. so what the fuck?

blanca. they supposed to think? middle of the night middle of nowhere a mile from mexico no car no—

mark. wait, are you some kind of—of—

blanca. some kind of what?

mark. I mean, you're american.

blanca. kind of what?

mark. you talk like—I mean, even if you're not.

blanca. what?

mark. there is no war going on here.

blanca. yeah there is. right here. middle of nowhere. how wars are fought.

mark. what is?

blanca. how land is lost and won. america. the world.

mark. what are you—

blanca. not soldiers. people. you and me. moving. taking land.

mark. me?

blanca. uh huh. how the west was won. people.

mark. I don't see what this has to do with any—

blanca. multitudes untold come to live off the land, more and more poor desperate fucked up wretched castoff unwashed bodies, come west, like you.

mark. I'm not desperate.

blanca. that piece-of-shit van?

mark. you got in.

blanca. because I'm desperate. farmers and herders and trappers the army not soldiers. the more people came, the more they crowded the ones here first, fucking indians, fucking mexicans. they just kept—

mark. who?

blanca. you.

mark. me?

blanca. your people.

mark. what do you—

blanca. just kept coming and coming. paths into roads into train tracks into highways. your land, your law.

mark. nothing to do with me.

blanca. sure it does. when there are more of them than you, you're gonna be fucked. democracy, right?

mark. more of who?

blanca. they're coming. whose land is this?

mark. whoever owns it.

blanca. whoever's on it. israel, bosnia, sudan, same war. iraq too, you're right. but that ain't our war. yours and mine. this is.

mark. well, we're dying there.

blanca. I'm not dying there. are you?

mark. what are we even talking—

blanca. I'm dying here.

mark. so—then—we should—go for gas, or—or—

blanca. go ahead. I'll wait.

mark. for what?

blanca. sun.

mark. the heat?

blanca. that or get shot.

—

mark. they weren't shooting at us just for—some mistake—it's—just because—

blanca. population just hit three hundred million and they don't know if she was a brown baby born in east l.a. or a shit poor migrant scrambling over the edge but they do know she was most likely a mexican indian. there are more of them than there are of you, and they're coming.

mark. look, I got nothing against your people, I wasn't the one shooting at us, I picked you up, helped you out, so I don't know why you—

blanca. who?

mark. what?

blanca. against who?

mark. ...your people.

blanca. my people?

—

I don't want them to take my job.

mark. who?

blanca. anyone.

mark. you don't have one.

blanca. and when I finally get one anybody want to take it gonna have a problem.

mark. who would want to take your—

blanca. someone who don't have one. that's who.

—

maybe you.

mark. me? I don't want to take anything away from anyone.

blanca. and if they want to take from you what's yours?

mark. let's just—let's just figure out what we should do now, ok? just...

—

let's just do that?

—

this is too, this is—I think they're gone, ok? I think we should...
(he's alone in the dark.)
what do you think?

—

blanca?

—

where did you—

dave. don't move your hands. keep them away from your body. I said—don't move.

—

good. keep still.
(a man emerges from the blackness. dark colors, night vision goggles, binoculars, a pistol at his side.)

mark. who are you?

dave. just relax. steve?
(another man enters from another direction. dark combat fatigues, no insignia, dark green camouflage paint on his face, night vision goggles. carries a rifle with a scope. he pushes blanca *ahead of him.)*

steve. dave. I got her.

dave. I see some i.d.?

mark. who are you?

dave. question is, who are you?

mark. I don't have to—I don't—

steve. who's she?

mark. she's with—she's—

dave. doesn't talk?

mark. yeah she talks.

steve. they why don't she?

mark. ask her.

dave. we're asking you.

steve. i.d. now.

(mark *takes out his wallet.* steve *takes it from him.*)

dave. thank you.

steve. new york?

mark. yeah? so?

dave. how long have you known miss...? what's her name?

mark. ask her.

steve. not gonna say it again.

mark. tell them your name.

dave. should try spanish.

mark. I don't speak spanish.

steve. kind of inconvenient. language of love, huh?

mark. what do you mean by—

steve. fuck do you think I mean?

mark. hey—look, don't—

dave. we know how it goes. she bats her big brown eyes, looks sad, sexy, crawls into your car after a couple of beers, cuddles into your big strong shoulder, you just want to bring her home and keep her for your very own. right? pretty girl.

mark. no...I didn't...she...no.

steve. no? you don't think she's pretty? some kind of racist?

dave. trafficking in illegal human cargo over international borders is a federal offence.

mark. she's american, no accent, no—

steve. she don't act american. americans act like you, talk about their rights, not their wrongs, just like you.

mark. blanca, say something, why are you...look at the way she's dressed, she—

steve. you dolled her up real nice.

mark. me—I—I don't even know—I picked her up ten miles back, we ran out of—she looked alright, I didn't think—say...anything, what's wrong with you?

dave. miss, do you have something to say? anything? blanca?

—

passport? green card?

steve. no espeeki the english?

dave. visa?

(*she begins to laugh, quietly but then quickly her laughter rises and finally erupts into an incredibly loud piercing cry, almost a howl. just as quickly it subsides. the three men watch her, impassive.*)

take her.

>(steve *grabs her, she spits in his face, jerks away and tries to flee, he gets hold of her, shoves her roughly to the ground, pins and cuffs her.*)

mark. hey, don't—

>(dave *punches* mark *hard in the stomach. he falls to his knees, spasmodically retching.*)

mark. you can't just...you can't just...leave me here.

steve. you wanna come with?

—

mark. ...just...just say something to them...that's all they...all they want...

>(mark *is alone. he stands, off balance, takes an awkward step or two.*)

...you can't just...this is against...you can't...my motherfucking wallet, you can't...

>(*his voice, louder and louder, sounds weaker and weaker in the expanding darkness.*)

...you can't just, it's not...this...is...you can't...you can't.

>(*he wavers, legs akimbo. a funny little dance step or two. pause. the sun rises, glorious fire and raging heat. he is still, the sole standing object in the bright desert enormity.*)

LOVE SONG WITHOUT METAPHOR (I WANT YOU BACK)
by GrooveLily

I haven't gone outside today
It feels so long since you've been away
The sun is bright, the sky is blue
And I'm all right and I make do

The house is dark, the shades are drawn
I check for mail, I mow the lawn
I cannot sleep, I cannot dream
And it's enough to make me scream

I want you back and here with me
I don't care how, I'm too blind to see
I hurt so bad when you're away
I can't go through another day
Without you back and here with me

I wish that I could wish you well
But I can't pretend that life without you's not a living hell
I wouldn't waste a wish on that
I'd wish that wish to wish you back

I want you back and here with me
I don't care how, I'm too blind to see
I hurt so bad when you're away
I can't go through another day
Without you back and here with me

I'm alone and disenchanted
I've got lots of time to grieve
Have I taken you for granted?
And is that what made you leave?...

Well there it is, I've said my piece
This song won't bring you back but it may give me some release
I got no more words in my pen
I might as well sing it again

I want you back and here with me
I don't care how, I'm too blind to see
I hurt so bad when you're away
I can't go through another day
Without you back and here with me

BOROUGH TO BOROUGH
by Kathryn Walat

MELODY *is alone on stage, surrounded by people.*

MELODY. My feet are moving to save my life. My heart is racing, and sometime somewhere I'll stop, but not before I get to that— And the sidewalk under my feet pounds it back to me: step, step, step, step—*gone*, down the avenue, past the doormen thinking about smoking cigarettes or calling their honeys because here they are—here *we* are—working another Sunday night—move, move, move—while I wipe my just-washed-them-clean-of-you hands on my cater-waiter pants. Thinking of how many steps until rabbit hole, hop; subway ride, home.

Because there *is* something to save. Somewhere inside of me is Canary Island yellow, tube top hug to fit, caramel sundae on a Monday afternoon. I just need to find it, hanging out somewhere with that wasabi in the back of my refrigerator. Need to peel back the layers and layers of that *me* that made it through this day—because today? Is done.

I surrender. Night says, "No sweat, I'll take you on," without so much as a ripple. Just a little air on this skin that I *must* own, because here I am wearing it, and let me tell you, my shop-lifting days are done. Mud mask. That's what I need. Squeeze the last bit of clay from that tube. Put on the kettle. Pour the hot water into chipped bowl, mossy green towel over my head, breathing steam. I'm needing that: Breathing.

But now I'm passing fancy building after fancy building, and my mind moves on to fantasy. The one where I hold out my hand, catch a yellow car, and as we drive down long avenues—"Thanks, but I'll keep the windows open, sir"—and you talk on your hands-free phone in whatever tongue you choose, you drive this machine with an understanding that makes it more like flying—and me, I'll just sit back. Watch the cross streets go down, down, down. Until we cross a bridge, and I take my day and empty it out the window like my overturned pocketbook when I can't find my chewing gum. Letting it all fall, all over the water. And then look back over my shoulder like a tourist, looking at this island while I move away from it. Move towards home. Stop right in front of my door. "Keep the change," and I'm exhaling, halfway up five flights.

But back here on earth I'm down, down, down the subway steps. And the platform is hot, with the last bit of summer, just where you don't want it. And the train is cold, with air conditioning that they forgot to turn off. And my seat is just wide enough for my ass, and I'm thinking: If my ass were bigger, would I get a bigger seat?

My mouth is moving to save my life. But none of you know it. It's inside my head, this universal conversation—could be with any which one of you, but really it's just me here with my inexpressive face. Mask. Little girl at my side turns to look. Not *at* me, but past me, at the kids on the other end of the car. Everyone's looking, even the ones pretending to be inside their magazines. We can't help ourselves but hear the sound they're creating with their bodies inside this tube. Can't help but feel the rhythm they beat, beat, beat on the seats and the floor. Not for any audience, not for the spare change—but a Sunday night rhythm, for the love of being alive. That sound of people. Moving together as one. And I bite my lip, suck in air, and—

(*She exhales.*)

This is saving my life.

AIN'T MEAT
by A. Rey Pamatmat

A diner somewhere in the middle of the American Southwest. Let's say Arizona until we decide otherwise.

A CUSTOMER, *clueless.* A WAITER, *lascivious.*

WAITER. Chicken?

CUSTOMER. No.

WAITER. Chicken ain't meat. It's poultry.

CUSTOMER. I don't eat it.

WAITER. Fish? Fish ain't meat.

CUSTOMER. Fish is—

WAITER. Seafood. Don't like fish? Neither do I.

CUSTOMER. Meat. Fish is meat.

WAITER. Pork is meat. Beef. Not chicken or fish. My sister's a vegetarian, and she eats fish.

CUSTOMER. I don't.

WAITER. Grilled cheese.

CUSTOMER. Is there rennet in it?

WAITER. No, there's cheese in it. What's rennet?

CUSTOMER. If you don't know, then no, I cannot eat your grilled cheese.

WAITER. How the hell is cheese meat?

CUSTOMER. Rennet is made by boiling stomachs. Cheese is made with rennet.

WAITER. Shoot, you learn something everyday.

CUSTOMER. Look, 9 days. 2 driving up and over to Colorado. 3 hiking up. 2 hiking down. 2 more driving from the mountains to the desert. 9 days of trail mix, protein bars, apples, canned beans, and peanut butter and jelly sandwiches. And, even though it'll be another day or two before the rest of my body gets there, I could really use that feeling of home in my stomach. I could really use some hot food.

WAITER. Plenty of hot things here.

CUSTOMER. Vegetarian things?

WAITER. Meaty things. Telling me you never crave a hot, meaty thing?

CUSTOMER. No.

WAITER. Well, then: salad.

CUSTOMER. Not hot.

WAITER. That depends on what you like. I can toss your salad.

CUSTOMER. I would like something hot, without meat, that's not a salad.

WAITER. Where you from?

CUSTOMER. L.A.

WAITER. (*Yelling to people offstage.*) L.A.—I TOLD Y'ALL. VEGETARIAN, TOO.

CUSTOMER. Who're they?

WAITER. My regulars. Residents. They ain't really customers. Just sit here talking about what Dubya did today, who bombed what, and whether we're gonna get any rain. A traveler's the most exciting thing happened to us all week.

CUSTOMER. Can I get breakfast?

WAITER. At two p.m.? Lynette probably already put the grease away.

CUSTOMER. Grease?

WAITER. All our breakfast's cooked in bacon fat. BAM! Kicks it up a notch. You know, like that Portuguese guy? Lemme check. (*Yelling to the kitchen.*) LYNETTE! YOU EVEN BACK THERE, YOU GODDAMN METH MOMMA! LYNETTE!!!

CUSTOMER. Never mind. I can't eat it if it's cooked in grease.

WAITER. Grease ain't meat. It's fat, not flesh.

CUSTOMER. You killed a pig to get it.

WAITER. Looks like something hot just ain't in the cards for either of us today.

CUSTOMER. I really want—

WAITER. I keep offering you vegetarian things, but you keep telling me you can't eat 'em.

CUSTOMER. Grease is meat. Chicken, poultry, rennet, gelatin, flesh is meat. You're not a cow or pig, but this is meat.

(CUSTOMER *grabs* WAITER's *forearm.*)

WAITER. And I suppose you ain't gonna wrap your mouth around me?

CUSTOMER. No animals no matter what part or what kind.

WAITER. Don't they got no innuendo in L.A.?

CUSTOMER. What?

WAITER. You're never tempted to taste some sausage? Sink your teeth into a big ol' ham? I don't go for chicken myself. I'd rather get my mitts on a hot little piggy—

(CUSTOMER *bolts up.*)

I'm trying to help you.

CUSTOMER. By force-feeding me bacon or ham or whatever else your savage, evil, backwater mind can imagine shoving in my mouth?

WAITER. Evil? Listen here, Los Angeles. Not alla us can just get in cars or on planes and learn about other folk. We get by learning about what we got. And when what you got is sand, scrub grass, and Kenmores fulla meat, it maybe makes you a little ignorant about L.A. vegetarians and hot food that somehow doesn't include steak. I am good people, and I have spent the last five trying to help. And Jesus H. Christ himself, I'm trying to force feed you ME, not bacon. You're just real thick up there.

CUSTOMER. I... sorry.

WAITER. Making me play the fool, talking about meat and sausage and tossing salad.

CUSTOMER. All I can think about is home and hot food and until I eat something—

WAITER. What bread you got?

CUSTOMER. Wheat.

WAITER. Peanut butter?

CUSTOMER. Crunchy. Grape jelly.

WAITER. I got multi-grain, smooth p.b., bananas, and honey. So I am gonna fix you up a peanut butter and banana sandwich, I am gonna toast that puppy into a hot, crispy treat, and I'm not gonna make any jokes about bananas 'cause what would be the point, and I get outta here at four.

(CUSTOMER *passionately kisses the* WAITER *in gratitude. The* WAITER *melts, until he notices something over the* CUSTOMER's *shoulder.*)

WAITER. (*Yelling to the kitchen.*) LYNETTE, SNAP YOUR JAW SHUT, POP INTO THAT KITCHEN, AND SLICE ME A BANANA. SWEAR TO GOD, I WILL SEND YOU TO WEST HOLLYWOOD SO YOU CAN BE THE ONLY STRAIGHT WOMAN THERE FOR TWENTY-FIVE YEARS IF YOU SAY ONE GODDAMN THING ABOUT APPROPRIATE PUBLIC BEHAVIOR! SWEAR! TO! GOD!

(WAITER *kisses* CUSTOMER.)

WAITER. Four o'clock.

CUSTOMER. I'm camping.

WAITER. Don't you worry. I'll help you pitch that tent.

TRUE NORTH
by Constance Congdon
(A play for an African man and Original American woman.)

Daytime. On the Oregon Trail, somewhere near the Black Hills. After the Civil War and the Emancipation Proclamation. HIM, *a young Black man in parts of a Union uniform, puts a piece of hardtack in a cup of coffee and pushes it down, waiting for it to soften so he can eat it. He finds a couple of maggots, freed from the hardtack, in the coffee and takes them out and throws them on the ground, revolted.* HER, *a young Native American woman dressed in a "white woman's" cotton dress and shoes, enters and squats nearby.* HE, *not seeing her but feeling a presence, doesn't move.* SHE *makes a deep purring sound by trilling her tongue, then takes in a breath, loudly, then purrs again, then adds a deep chuffing sound, like big cats do to their young.* HE *is alert, still not moving. He puts his cup of hardtack and coffee down very quietly and then runs like hell offstage.* SHE *crosses quickly to the coffee and eats the hardtack in it, looking for the maggots he threw away. She finds them and eats them, too.* HE *re-enters slowly and stands near her. She shrieks at him, an aggressive act on the part of a predator, and runs off.* HE *runs after her, chasing her on and offstage a few times, until he stops, exhausted.*

HIM. JUST GIMMEE DA CUP!!

I don't get no dinner without it!!

(SHE *throws it onstage. He picks it up.*)

They be some maggots left! Come out or I'll be stepping all over 'em...

(SHE *enters slowly, squats, waits.*)

(HE *tosses her a maggot still in the cup.* SHE *picks it up and eats it. He gags.*)

HIM. You make me lose what I ate.

There's no more, so go ahead and get on your crazy way.

You dark like me. You got that good hair. You dressed pretty good.

(HE *crosses to her to touch her hair.*)

SHE. Don't you touch me, boy.

HIM. You got some fine hard English on you. Are you a house nigger?

SHE. I am a WIFE.

HIM. Where's your fine husband? He be somewheres eating up the garbage of the wagons? He a fly? Well, he be mighty peeved with you cause you just ate some of your own children.

Well, get on back to him. My cap'n be coming to fetch me. He let me eat by myself. He don't like eatin' with niggers. And I don't like eating with white bastard honky devils. So we work somethin' out. 'Cause we needs to be workin' something out on account of we be freed? You heard that, darkie girl? Niggers be free now. Except no one knows dat. Still pay a thousand dollars for me, some folk can't do nothing for theyselves so's needs black folk to do all they work, for free, too. Y'see we's all free. Niggers are freed and we still work for free. 'Cept those poor bastards didn't go into the army, they has to pay cash money to they former owners now. Can't live anywhere on dis land for free.

(*During this speech she is trying to stay awake and not pass out.*)

Lord have mercy don't be dying on me here. I'll get blamed f'sure. I'll get strung up.

(*He goes to her and starts shaking her.*)

Stay awake!! You got to stay awake!! And then you got to gets out of here or be strung up!! Your fly husband will come lookin' for you or someone from that wagon train and I'll get blamed and lynched!!

SHE. No one come looking for me.

HIM. Yeah, that's a damn shame. Don't all beat up women say that and then some big white bastard DO come looking for 'em. And whoever gots those womens, gets lynched.

SHE. My husband's mother wants me gone. She's starving me. Then she gonna tell John that I died on the trail.

HIM. You that wagon with the old lady? I never seed you.

SHE. You up front, riding with the Cap'n. You our guard, boy.

HIM. I ain't no boy and I'm gonna show you in a minute if you keep saying that I don't care if I get lynched. I'll run. I'll run out in the dark. Let the Indins get me and kill me! This is no kinda life. The war's over and I'm still eating hardtack. My stomach would be better off sitting in some slave cabin eating chitlins. So's I gots to stop lissenin to my stomach.

Lawsee!! It be dark in one shake of a mule's tail and I won't be seeing the hand in front of my face. Which way's the wagon train? You messed me up, chasing you, you, you—what in God's name are you?

SHE. I am Lakotah.

HIM. Is that some kind of Spanish?

SHE. I'm Sioux.

HIM. I'm Abednego.

SHE. What are those people?

HIM. Abednego was an Israelite. That's my given name.

SHE. You an Israelite?

HIM. Hell, now. They be people in the Bible. Live in Bible land for five thousand years.

SHE. Lakotah people been in this land longer. We been here forever.

HIM. Well, Sue. You sure be speaking like a white girl but you don't look like one.

SHE. Sue ain't my name. My name is Harriet. John named me when he married me.

HIM. You said you was Sue.

SHE. I said I was Lakota. White man call us "Sioux" but we're not.

HIM. YOU INDIN?

Then you can get us back. You can see in the dark.

SHE. No one can see in the dark.

HIM. What the hell kinda Indin are you?? I'm goin'. To hell with ya.

(*He exits. She gives in to her tiredness and starvation and lies down, passes out.*)

(*Light change, passage of time. SHE awakens suddenly and freezes, hearing something. She puts her ear against the ground and listens. Sits up, considers. Makes a decision, then relaxes and lies back down. Passage of time. HIM re-enters, on his hands and feet, his uniform dirty and his face and hands scraped, feeling his way in the pitch dark. SHE sits up, relaxed. She knows it's him.*)

SHE. Moonrise.

HIM. Where are you?? Where are you??

(*SHE reaches for him and he moves, with great relief and tiredness, to her.*)

Oh, Lord have mercy, dear Jesus, I ran into a tree and something fell on me—spiders, something.... (*He trembles with the memory.*) ...I turned and ran another way and fell down some gully and climbed out and I swear I heard a rattler...

SHE. Just a grasshopper. They go—

(SHE *makes a quick ticking with her tongue on the roof of her mouth.*) Only quicker.

(*The moonlight gives them some light. They really look at each other.*)

HIM. Sun be up—not too soon. They come lookin' I be dead. I be a dead man.

SHE. I don't think so.

HIM. What you know?

SHE. War party ride over that hill. The one you fell down from.

HIM. How you know that? Can't see nothin'.

SHE. But I hear. Many ponies with men on them. Indin ponies.

HIM. How can you tell that?

SHE. No tack. No saddle creaking. No horseshoes. Pony hooves being rode and the sound of willow shafts—a power of 'em.

HIM. What's that?

SHE. Arrows.

HIM. The wagon train?

(*Beat.*)

All those families?

SHE. Yes.

HIM. And the babies?

SHE. Might keep the ones not killed.

HIM. And your husband's mother? And my Cap'n?

SHE. Yup.

HIM. We be alright?

SHE. We?

HIM. I'm hopin' you'll keep me. If the Indins find us, I'm hopin' you'll spare me.

SHE. Those Indins won't find us. I'll be sure of that. They kill me as soon as look at me.

HIM. Why? You Indin, right?

SHE. My people and the Paiute don't get along. And I've been spoiled by a white man.

HIM. How can they know that?

SHE. I wear his clothes. I speak his language. And their women would know soon enough.

HIM. How?

SHE. I'm pregnant. I've got a redbone child inside me.

HIM. Look, you take me on. And I'll be protector to that chile. If we make it through this night and the terrible day ahead.

SHE. We'll go down to the wagon train after the massacre and get what supplies we can. What canteens are left. Any food. Couple of coats.

HIM. For headin' North.

SHE. We are North.

HIM. Not North enough. We'll follow the drinkin' gourd, jes' like the song.

>   (*Sings.*)

Follow the drinkin' gourd
Follow the drinkin' gourd
For the old man is a waitin'
For to take us all to freedom
If we follow the drinking gourd.

>   (*He points up at the sky.*)

There it is.

SHE. Where?

HIM. There. Can't you see it? There's the handle.

SHE. I can't see. Come down here.

>   (*They lie next to each other. He points up at the sky.*)

HIM. There's the gourd—see it? White folks call it the Big Dipper. But we's from a place where folks drink out of gourds.

SHE. I see it now. But that's just part of something else. See? It's the Great Bear. His legs there and the handle on your gourd is his tail. And over there is the Little Fisher.

>   (*Touches his hair.*)

You got nice hair. Like tatanka.

HIM. Tatanka?

SHE. Buffalo.

HIM. That mean you're keepin' me?

SHE. I'm thinkin' on it.

>   (*Back to the stars.*)

Now over there is—can you see it? That the Star Path. So many stars moving along wearing through that black of the sky, wearing a white trail so's other stars can find it and follow it, too.

HIM. Where they going those stars? Some place for me to be?

SHE. To the summer house. To the medicine wheel. They got to have one up there just like we do down here. Except that star. That star never move.

HIM. That the one. We go that way until we get free.

SHE. But for now we got to tuck ourselves into that halla over here. And stay quiet as can be. And no matter what kind of screamin' we hear. Even babies.

HIM. Babies just grow up and hate us, like all their kin.

SHE. You just remember that and hush now. Hush.

Because things are gonna get ugly, buffalo-man.

HIM. You keepin' me?

SHE. Seems like it.

HIM. I'm named for an Israelite who came through fire.

SHE. And then he came through dark and cold and silence.

(*They lie spoon-style.*)

THE ODOMETER SONG
by GrooveLily

Driving country I never seen
Spend all my money on gasoline
Never thinking of where I been
Sun go up and come down again
Come the night I go straight on through
Long enough, strong enough, counting down the miles till I get to you.

Highway night, I don't see no star
Only white lines shooting under my car
A.M. radio just broke down
And there ain't nobody for miles around
Only got one thing to do
That's see the road, be the road, counting down the miles till I get to you.

Since you left me, nothing runs right anymore
Steam is rising from the hood
Air conditioning is dripping on the floor
I try to shift my gear down, but it don't shift so good
Power lock is broken, I can't open the door
The engine is barely alive
Girl, I don't know how I can make you make it run like it did before
But I got to get to you now,
And I got a long, long, long, long, long, long,
long, long, long long way to drive.

Sun come up on a brand new day
And the road sign tell me I'm miles away
Say a prayer for my poor old car
If it will get me to where you are
I forget where I'm driving to
Long enough, strong enough,
See the road, be the road,
Turn the wheels, burn the wheels,
Counting down the miles till I get to you.

TRADE
by Kia Corthron

The D train to Coney Island, Brooklyn. The present.
A moving, elevated New York subway car. WOMAN 1 *in a bathing suit*
(one-piece or two) and shorts. WOMAN 2 *in a burka. Sudden darkness.*
Then lights back up.

WOMAN 1. God, that freaks me out! Weird when the train loses power! But I guess you're used to it. I'm a visitor, only been here two weeks. Not a tourist, not some damn seven-day excursion Statue of Liberty Empire State Building, I'm here for the whole summer, place in the Bronx. Wanted to spend some time in New York, my Bronx friend wanted to spend time in L.A., we traded! Traded places, my friend goes, "But wouldn't you rather be in Midtown? The East Village?" hell no! All the gentrification down in Chinatown to up in Harlem think they'll soon be changing the name from "Manhattan" to "Caucasian," I'll stick to my borough. Queens would have been even better, Queens considered the most ethnically diverse county in America. Jamaica Bay and the Russians, Latinos and Filipinos, forty-one thousand Native Americans in New York City in case you doubted there were urban Indians, and Indians! Queens boasts the largest concentration of Southeast Asians in the country where *you* from? (*No reply.*) Oh, I guess you can't talk under those things. Two weeks here and *love* it, but missed the beach. My friend goes, "Take the subway, all the way from the Bronx through Manhattan and Brooklyn, two hours, no transfers to Coney Island." Triple-digits again today, and no a.c., I looked forward to the long cool ride on the Brooklyn-bound D! And how many different people along the way? L.A. we got all kinds but everybody in their own car, L.A. you sure never find yourself sitting right next to a burka! (*Sudden outside light. Delight.*) Ah! Above ground!

(*A cell phone rings.* WOMAN 1 *looks around, confused.*)

WOMAN 2. Hello? (WOMAN 1 *eventually sees the cell phone is under* WOMAN 2's *burka.*) Subway. (*Pause.*) We came out of the tunnel, I got range now.

(*Pause.*) Where do I go *every* Friday? (*Pause.*) We're going back into the tunnel I have to hang up. (*Pause.*) I said We're going back into— Fuck you too!

(WOMAN 2 *has hung up and with irritation sticks a sucker into her mouth. Outside light disappears. After a moment,* WOMAN 2 *notices* WOMAN 1's *embarrassment.*)

WOMAN 2. My sister. (*Beat.*) We both committed to wearing them this week. Even at work. You know, as a protest.

WOMAN 1. Oh. (*Beat.*) Where's work?

WOMAN 2. We're barmaids.

WOMAN 1. Oh.

WOMAN 2. And before work this evening she thought it might be cool to stand on the Times Square army recruiting triangle, just a silent message, but she knows every Friday afternoon of the summer I go to Coney, I've done it since high school.

WOMAN 1. Uh huh. (*Beat.*) I did it too, back in L.A., hit the streets, bring the troops home! What the hell we doing in Iraq anyway?

WOMAN 2. It's not the only war we're in. (WOMAN 1 *is confused.*) I did *not* want us to bomb my parents' country but when it started, I thought, Well, at least we'll be free of the Taliban! My mom can go back if she wants, wear her blouse and skirt and teach high school lit again if she wants except they're coming back. Pakistan aiding the rebuilding of the Afghan Taliban and the U.S. turning the blind eye. There *are* still American troops in Afghanistan. They just aren't high on the Pentagon's priority list. But that wasn't my protest.

(WOMAN 2 *reaches from under her burka and pulls out a sign: a photo of a young man and the text "FREE SAYED LATIF."*)

He's my cousin. He's twenty-one now. Back in Afghanistan his family worked hard and stayed poor. But they picked him up off the street, no reason. The soldiers picked him up right after 9-11, he was sixteen, kidnapped him to Guantánamo, he's been there almost five years now, he could be in that little cage for the next *fifty* years, *die* there, no provision for a trial. His lawyer told our family he was once short-shackled to the floor, *hours.* His lawyer told us he was once taunted by a female American soldier who put her hand in her pants and pulled out red wet fingertips. His lawyer said he's done the hunger strikes and been force-fed, a tube rammed down his throat. Last week they found that twenty-one-year-old hanged himself, he'd also been there almost five years. We were relieved and grateful to find out the hanged boy wasn't Afghani, he was a Saudi. We were horrified to realize that we were relieved, and grateful, to find out the hanged boy wasn't Afghani. He was a Saudi.

(*Silence.*)

WOMAN 1. What's it like?

(WOMAN 2 *turns to* WOMAN 1, *who is glancing at* WOMAN 2's *burka. Sudden darkness. When lights are back up,* WOMAN 1 *wears the burka.* WOMAN 2 *wears shorts and a very American T-shirt, perhaps with a rap group pictured.*)

WOMAN 1. I can't see. Peripherally.

WOMAN 2. Uh huh. (*Outside light.*)

WOMAN 1. How can I walk if I can't see?

WOMAN 2. You'll learn.

CONDUCTOR ANNOUNCEMENT. Coney Island/Stillwell Avenue. Last stop, last stop: All passengers must exit the train.

WOMAN 1. (*Trying with confusion to take the burka off.*) We have to get off!

WOMAN 2. We can trade clothes back at the beach house. Come on.

WOMAN 1. The beach. It's only a couple of blocks, right? Not far?

WOMAN 2. Not for me.

(*From the handbag she had previously held under the burka,* WOMAN 2 *now pulls out a pair of sunglasses, puts them on.* WOMAN 1 *pulls out her own sunglasses, puts them on.* WOMAN 2 *takes* WOMAN 1's *arm, leads the way out the train exit.*)

1260 MINUTE LIFE
by A. Rey Pamatmat

The sound of a plane.

CORA, *32, Korean-American, sits alone in an airplane seat. In her lap is a small ceramic pig. She smiles an indecipherable smile.*

CORA. In five minutes, my life will end. I am seated in coach on the last of three flights from Seoul, Korea to Niamey, Niger. It's a journey of approximately 21 hours. 1260 minutes. I've flown between the cities twice each year for the past three years. Between my mother and my love.

(*Lights up on a Korean WOMAN in a white hospital robe, turned away from the audience. In her left fist, she clutches flowers to her chest (we don't see what kind); in her right, a handful of cooked corn kernels. They drip from between her fingers. Long black clumps of hair tumble reluctantly down her back.*)

I didn't plan these international journeys at six-month intervals, but my mom isn't one to be denied. And why would I? She's so gone now that when I go back to Korea, it doesn't matter what I've done or why I've been gone; I am always her dutiful daughter. I sit at her bedside reading Bible passages to her that she's marked with pink and lime green post-its. She tells me her mother's stories about empresses and monkeys, peasants and cranes. We eat gummy candies and watch shows with plots she remembers, because they're so twisted. Not like the endless, straightforward trajectory of her own life.

And I am again sixteen. In her less lucid moments she even asks, "Did you get into the International and Rural Development program at Cornell?" I get to be the little Cora, little Cho-Ann I would have remained if not for that one day…

(*Lights change as* CORA *stands.*)

Upstate New York. A classmate and I ditch our Social Networks and Social Processes class to go to a concert in Pennsylvania. Out the window disgusting strips of asphalt cut the American landscape—the highway system of which they are so proud slashing unsightly lines across beautiful views, engine roars displacing nature's sounds, pollution spreading as efficiently as an oil spill in an ocean current.

But then…our car breaks down. An hour of unreturned phone calls. A stranger stopping in an old clunker of a chariot, a 1980 Volkswagen Golf. A mathematics grad student who is also studying at Cornell, who tinkers with our engine. A moment that makes me understand the possibilities within those ugly tar ribbons of road. And I start down a new road. Away from a government post in Korea and toward a new home…

(*The* WOMAN *lowers the bouquet of flowers to her side. They are poppies. She drops them on the floor.*)

And now I go there. To my other home.

(*The "Fasten Seat Belt" light pings and brings us back onto the flight.*)

(CORA *stows the ceramic pig and sits. Her face changes. No more inscrutable smile. She is steel. Her soul is iron.*)

From Seoul to Paris. From Paris to Casablanca. From Casablanca to Niamey, Niger and my husband Aboubakar.

(*An African* MAN *and a chalkboard appear behind her in a well-cut but rumpled suit. His hands are covered in the powder of white chalk. He writes out a mathematical formula.*)

Humanitarian aid arrives in Niger through me. I shake American and European hands, grease bureaucratic wheels, and ensure that the right money gets to the right populations for the right reasons. In Niger I make the world go round and make the world come round to Niger.

With my husband the distinguished Dr. Aboubakar Sizwe, Chair of the Mathematics Department at L'Universite Abdou Moumouni, we lift up his native country, and it lifts us up. We no longer help out, we grant favors. We don't have space, we have distance. We've lost our friends and gained followers. People remind us daily that because of his education, my independence, and our marriage we are not one of them; we are a connection, a resource to fund their new initiative, to pull the strings that need pulling.

So to protect ourselves, our marriage has become a fortress, the height of whose walls are surpassed only by the ones protecting our hearts.

As I fly to Niger, my skin toughens, my heart slows to measure each beat, and my soul turns to iron. The African sun can't warm my steady, cold stare. Nothing penetrates the fortress we've built, until...

(*The* WOMAN *splatters the corn kernels against a wall.*)

Her need calls me home. And then...

(*The* MAN *flips the chalkboard over and scribbles more of the formula.*)

My life calls me home. And here I am again...

(CORA *grips the arms of her plane seat.*)

In a place that is no place: a sterile, anonymous cabin, an unmapped area above and between map points, a nowhere that hasn't been called somewhere in which I can be no one except the person I'll always be. An in between place where I am just enough of each Cora to be completely myself—when there are no bits and pieces of other existences dictating an identity: dutiful daughter or Iron Queen.

And maybe, here, I can choose. Maybe in these long hours that are really such a short period of time, maybe in this place and time outside of place and time, I can finally pick a life. Choose the me that is really me. See myself and stop—

(*A static speaker sound.*)

VOICE. (*Voicover.*) This is your captain speaking...

CORA. But 1260 minutes is very short when compared to the span of two lives. And before I can choose, my time is up, my life is over, my Self, again, is gone.

(*The rumbling of landing gear descending from beneath the steel belly of the plane, as the* WOMAN *and* MAN *disappear.* CORA *relaxes her grip, closes her eyes, and surrenders as lights fade.*)

DUNKIN AMERIKA
by Kathryn Walat

NICKI *and* MICHELLE, *just after the morning rush.*

NICKI. And what can I get you with that? OK. Well that's $1.15. Have a nice day!

(*Patron walks away.*)

NICKI. Freakin' idiot. I hope he spills that all over his crotch as soon as the train pulls out of the station, sizzles his little wienie.

MICHELLE. Totally.

NICKI. The train people—

MICHELLE. *So* much worse than the bus freaks.

NICKI. Like, just because he's riding Amtrak he thinks he's a cut above—

MICHELLE. Not above the "light 'n' sweet."

NICKI. He'll be back.

MICHELLE. Can't say no to *this* coffee.

NICKI. Even though he's—

MICHELLE. So not worthy.

NICKI. Totally.

(*For a moment they contemplate the powerful force that is caffeine.*)

MICHELLE. Hey, they in yet?

NICKI. Nope.

MICHELLE. You checked this morning's shipment?

NICKI. Yup.

MICHELLE. OK, but did you *unpack* the boxes, or did you sniff around the outside and leave them for me to do?

NICKI. Are you doubting my nose?

MICHELLE. Well last time your nose said *blueberry muffin*, they were *crullers*, and when Frankie stopped by for his afternoon fix and we turned him away cold—

NICKI. I had allergies then, and you know how I hate unpacking…

MICHELLE. You do remember I'm like an assistant manager now?

NICKI. I looked inside. Kinda felt around—usual stuff—it's still technically summer.

MICHELLE. *Late* summer. And I'm just—you know—*anticipation*.

NICKI. Michelle, the autumn-inspired donuts will be here before you know it.

MICHELLE. I just want to know what they're gonna be this year. I mean, pumpkin spice or maple glazed or what if they did something with squash? That's my own idea. Like a very special butternut squash bagel…

NICKI. You know, his whole freakin' summer, I didn't go anywhere.

MICHELLE. Do you think the managers know? Like, you think Larry's withholding that kind of information, and when I become manager I'll have my own private stash of pumpkin donuts by the Fourth of July?

NICKI. Don't you want something more than that?

MICHELLE. Hey, I am very into the pumpkin—pumpkin cookies, pumpkin soup—and you can *only* get in the fall—

NICKI. I mean, from life?

MICHELLE. Why is that?

NICKI. All these people come through here, and they're all *going* somewhere.

MICHELLE. OK, this is a *transportation hub*.

NICKI. I'm serious.

MICHELLE. Tell me this, Nicki—when's the last time you went to the toilet in the back of a Greyhound bus?

NICKI. I mean, like those two British girls backpacking?

MICHELLE. I saw one of them in the bathroom like putting benzoyl peroxide all over her T-zone, and I was like, *that* has got to suck. I mean, popping your pimples in the bus-slash-train terminal in Upstate New York— is that what you want?

NICKI. I want to look out the window and see something else besides the Applebee's and TJ Maxx across the parking lot. Those British girls—that could like be *us*, Michelle. You and me, we could travel around and stuff.

MICHELLE. I like TJ Maxx.

NICKI. I know, I don't mean...

MICHELLE. Did I show you that hottie two-piece bathing suit I got at the end-of-season sale for $7? With the little-boy shorts—

NICKI. So you don't have to shave your bikini zone...

MICHELLE. I mean, we have *cars*. That our parents let us drive. And even though you have to share with your sister, I still think that's better than carrying around all your stuff in a backpack and like taking a bus all over—I mean, why did those English girls even come here? What is it they expect to see?

NICKI. America.

MICHELLE. *This* is America?

NICKI. Well not all of it—

MICHELLE. How lame is that?

NICKI. Which is kinda my point. I mean, what have we seen? There's this whole country out there. Like the Rocky Mountains and New Orleans and that 12:07 train goes all the way to Chicago and I've never been to California. And there're like cornfields in Iowa and Elvis weddings in Vegas. And when's the last time either of us have *been* somewhere? Like, anywhere. I mean, I just want someone—some hottie guy—to come up to me, and we'll both be standing there, side by side, drinking our coffees and looking out over the horizon, and he'll ask me where I'm going and I'll just be like: Traveling. Traveling.... *Traveling*, Michelle.

MICHELLE. OK. OK, I get it. So—this is all about you wanting me to put in a good word for you with Larry so that he gives you some weekends off, isn't it? I mean, I *am* an assistant manager, Nicki, but that doesn't mean—

NICKI. Forget it.

MICHELLE. I do have more power, but, really—

NICKI. Summer's almost over anyway.

MICHELLE. Yeah.

(MICHELLE *is thinking about pumpkin donuts.* NICKI *knows it.*)

NICKI. They'll be here soon.

MICHELLE. I know. I'm just—*anticipation.*

NICKI. I should make some more decaf. That last guy, I just gave him regular.

MICHELLE. I'll do it. I know how you hate—

NICKI. You love the smell of this coffee don't you?

MICHELLE. Especially the hazelnut. Hazelnut *decaf*—I mean, when are we gonna get *that*?

REWIND
by GrooveLily
For robby0809, wherever and whenever you are

Calling all aliens
And time-traveling superfriends
Secretive scientists with secretive client lists
Calling all aliens
I know you've got this practical invention
To move a human through the fourth dimension
I need to get my hands on the remote control of my life
And press rewind
Rewind
Rewind
Rewind

I'm feeling paranoid
Hanging like Harold Lloyd
The clock face is dripping and my grip is slipping
I'm feeling paranoid
Ground control is tampering with my flight plan
Shortening and hampering my life span
I need to get my hands on the remote control of my life
And press rewind
Rewind
Rewind
Rewind

If I could rewind my life
If I could revise my ways
If I could rewrite my lines
If I could rerun some days

I'd take back all the ugly things I said
And all the people I misled
Would see me looking shiny new and clean
So
I'll give you lots of cash
If you take out my karmic trash
I will need proof, but I'll pay through the roof
I'll give you lots of cash
H.G. Wells me back to where I started
Please don't let me die here brokenhearted
I need to get my hands on the remote control of my life
And press rewind
Rewind
Rewind
Rewind

I am calling all aliens
I'm calling, I'm calling, I'm calling
Calling all aliens

THE MAGIC AND THE MERCURY
by Rolin Jones

We hear the sound of a dog barking. The sound of an owl. Crickets. JOE *and* MIKE *are crouched roadside, looking straight ahead. They have long, disturbing tails. They are possums.*

JOE. I've been having a lot of thoughts lately, Mike.

MIKE. Anything you want to talk about?

JOE. Not really.

MIKE. You sure?

JOE. I'm sure.

MIKE. Fine. It's not healthy though, Joe. Keeping your thoughts inside. Not a healthy thing.

JOE. I think I have seasonal depression.

MIKE. Seasonal what?

JOE. Depression. The winds come through the trees and the leaves fall to the ground and lake ices over and a void opens up inside you.... There's a void inside me, Mike.

MIKE. You don't have a void inside you, Joe.

JOE. Yes, I do.

MIKE. You don't have seasonal depression. You're a fucking possum. You eat garbage, you shit in the gutters, and when cars are really close and traveling at high speeds you cross in front of them. Don't be a pussy. Suck it up.

JOE. I'm having trouble justifying my existence.

MIKE. What's the fuck's that supposed to mean?

JOE. I'm just saying. This life we got here. It ain't right, Mike.

MIKE. What ain't right about it?

JOE. It's like you said. All we do is eat garbage, shit in the gutters, and run in front of cars.

MIKE. Sometimes we shit in a tool shed.

JOE. I'm not waking up every morning so's I can shit in a tool shed Mike. I'm sorry if that upsets you, but me, I think I've gotten all I can out of that activity thank you very much.

(*We hear the sound of a car in the distance.*)

MIKE. Car's coming.

JOE. I mean, I'm going through something here, Mike.

MIKE. Car's coming, Joe.

(*Car sound gets louder.*)

JOE. I don't even know who I am anymore.

MIKE. Time to focus, Joe.

(*Louder! Two headlights appear.*)

JOE. I'm dead inside.

MIKE. JOE!

(JOE *snaps to attention. He joins* MIKE *in making some godforsaken possum screetch. An actor holding two flashlights ("the car") runs across the stage.* JOE *and* MIKE *race out in front of it. The car swerves. Sound of skidding.*)

CAR. (*As car exits.*) Motherfucckkkeeeerrrrr!

MIKE. That's right bitch, this is my goddamn road! I OWN THIS SHIT!

(MIKE *rolls on his back.*)

MIKE. Suck my possum balls, Whoo-hooo.

(MIKE *gets up joins* JOE.)

MIKE. Any fucking cars wanna come through here, they gotta go through Mikey!

(*He holds out a fist for* JOE *to "dap." But there's no "dap" from* JOE.)

MIKE. Oh, it's like that now?

JOE. No.

MIKE. I see how it is.

JOE. I wish you did, Mike. I truly wish you did.

MIKE. You're beginning to piss me off.

(They resume their crouching posture, looking straight ahead again. We hear a dog bark.)

JOE. Look at Fred over there.

MIKE. The dog?

JOE. Yeah. Now there's a life.

MIKE. You got to be fucking kidding me.

JOE. A little doggie door. Food bowl. Taking a walk out in the light of day. Taking photographs with the family.

MIKE. D.T.S.

JOE. D.T.S?

MIKE. Dog taking a shit. You ever watch a dog take a shit with his owner.

(MIKE demonstrates.)

MIKE. All leashed up. His back all hunched up. His owner pulling out one of those blue bags. Where's the dignity I ask you?

JOE. They get to go on drives.

MIKE. So what?

JOE. Tell me you don't dream about that. Getting in the front seat, sitting in a warm lap, sticking your head out the window, the wind blowing back your jowls, all your regrets, the sheer terror of living, just flying off your face, falling away onto the open road.

MIKE. You want that life, Joe? Sniffing asses, licking your balls, playing fetch. What the fuck is fetch? Fred could play fetch till he fucking vomited. And then he'd eat the vomit, lick his balls and go play catch again. You want to know why, Joe? Because Fred is fucking retarded. Dream about taking a drive. Fuck you. Possum don't need to take drives. Possums own the road.

(We hear the sound of an owl hooting.)

JOE. What about Karl?

MIKE. What ABOUT Karl?

JOE. Karl can fly. Karl owns the sky.

MIKE. Karl's an asshole.

JOE. He looks down on us. He's got a barn. You're jealous.

MIKE. Jealous? Who sees Mikey snatch a Twinkie outta the McGiver's garbage then thinks to himself it's good idea to swoop down, dig his claws in Mikey's back and take me up…

JOE. Karl?

MIKE. Bit that asscracker right in the ankle before he even got me a foot off the ground. Try and take my Twinkie. SUCK MY DICK, KARL. YOU GOT THAT?!

(We hear KARL hoot.)

MIKE. Yeah, who's your fucking daddy?

(MIKE looks over at JOE.)

MIKE. What we got here, Joe? You shouldn't question it.

JOE. Well, that's what I'm doing, Mike. I'm asking the big questions. I'm engaging the universe.

MIKE. Engaging the universe? Seasonal depression? You're getting soft is what's going on here. You're disgracing yourself in front of your marsupial ancients.

JOE. You don't understand. You never will.

MIKE. Hmmm. Is that right?

(We hear the sound of a car in the distance.)

MIKE. I love that sound. Ain't it beautiful? In all that engaging of the universe you do, you ever ask yourself, why do we run in front of the car? That ever come up? Why do we run in front of the car, Joe? We run in front of the car because we can.

(The car gets louder.)

We run in front of the car, we run in front of Death, who comes robed in chrome, rubber, and steel, with his two shiny lights and his human puppet behind the wheel, because we choose to. While the rest of the world cowers in their warm corners, begging for food and love from anyone and anything, we grab life my the throat, wrestle it down to the ground, press our snouts right up against it and say, is that all you got bitch! We are possum. We are the mercury and the magic. And this godforsaken stretch of asphalt in front of us. This shit is ours.

(Louder! Two headlights appear.)

Who owns the road, Joe?!

JOE. Possum owns the road!

(They make their godforsaken possum screech. The car runs across the stage. JOE and MIKE race out in front of it. The car swerves. Sound of skidding.)

CAR. *(As car exits.)* Motherfucckkkeeeerrrrr!

MIKE AND JOE. Whoo-hooooo.

(MIKE and JOE roll on their backs.)

MIKE AND JOE. SUCK MY POSSUM BALLS!

(They stand up. They catch their breath. JOE feels reborn.)

JOE. Thanks Mike.

(MIKE holds out his fist for a dap. JOE daps.)

MIKE. I feel that taco moving…Let's hit the tool shed.

(They shuffle off.)

ON THE ROAD
by Constance Congdon

1933, heading out of Kansas.

MAN. Well, first thing I got to say—it's a great life if you don't weaken and nobody I knowed or was related to was weak. They's either alive and strong or they's dead. Nobody left but me and I'm heading my strong ass out to the West. There's no shame in trying and failin' and if we'd knowed what summer a '31 were gonna be like, we'd—we'd—well, hell—we'd done what we did. Which was to hunker down and wait it out. 'Cause there weren't nothin' to do but stay inside when it were blowin' around and then try to find sumpin' to eat when the sky's clear. Gettin' a blanket wet and then laying under it so's you can breathe cause dirt went everywhere. Open a jar of pickled beets and they's a layer of black dirt on top. And them jar's all sealed. Sand Plum Jelly—open up a jar and they's dirt on top. They's a lot of sad stories—some about babies who died with dirt in their lungs and they bellies and ears and eyes. But I'm gonna do my best to fergit those stories. Seems to me my people always been on some road or t'other. Walkin' out of Ireland and dying on the way, sailin' on a boat, coming to America, walkin' off the boat and movin' West, always West, lookin' for a new start, somethin' that will change things for the better. And now I'm going West, more West, until I find a place to settle that won't run me out. Oh, and my people always singing or telling stories. Queen Elizabeth, that evil hoor, put a price on the head of every Irish bard thinking that that will kill us off. But it didn't. And since we come to these shores, we picked up a few more walkin' people, from other places, other seas, and they have they own singers and storytellers, too. Some get on the radio. Some just on the road, like me. I figure that's my country, that's my history, this road here:
(*Sings:*) Woke up this morning,
Sky was full of dirt,
The land got up and left us,
Nothin; to eat but hurt.

We gotta move on, Mama,
You better lighten up your load
Pack you bag, sweet Mama,
'Cause we come to own the road.

I swear I saw my father
Travelin' by my side
Doesn't know he's passed on,
Still lookin' for a ride.

We gotta move on, Mama,

You better lighten up your load
Pack you bag, sweet Mama,
'Cause we come to own the road.

Behind me is the devil
Walking off his shoes
Dust got all the way to Hell
He's got those homeless blues.

We gotta move on, Mama,
You better lighten up your load
Pack you bag, sweet Mama,
'Cause we come to own the road.

Someday we all will settle
And find a place to be
Where the dirt will stay put
By a deep blue sea.

We gotta move on, Mama,
You better lighten up your load
Pack you bag, sweet Mama,
'Cause we come to own the road.

LIVE THROUGH THIS (ARE WE THERE YET?)
by GrooveLily

You ask me are we there yet
This road is harder than before
We've got to grin and bear it
We're not in Kansas anymore

But if we can live through this
We get everything we wanted
If we can live through this
We will find a house less haunted
If we can live through this
We will never feel so daunted
If we can live through

This used to be a party
This used to be like Sunday school
Those days are over darling
They crashed the planes and changed the rules

But if we can live through this
If we can hold out a little longer
If we can live through this

Surely things can't go much wronger
If we can live through this
What doesn't kill you makes you stronger
If we can live through this

Are we there yet?
Are we there yet?

We've all been suicidal
We've all been laid low with regret
We can't just sit here idle
We're not quite six feet under yet

But if we can live through this
We will come out into the sunshine
If we can live through this
We will be of one heart and one mind
If we can live through this
Maybe we'll get the cosmic punchline
If we can live through this

Are we there yet? Are we there yet? Are we there yet? Are we there yet?

End of Play

365 DAYS/365 PLAYS
by Suzan-Lori Parks

WHAT IS *365 DAYS/365 PLAYS?*

On November 13, 2002, Pulitzer-Prize winner Suzan-Lori Parks got an idea to write a play a day for a year. She began that day, and finished one year later. The resulting play cycle, called *365 Days/365 Plays*, is a daily meditation on an artistic life. Some plays are very short, less than a page. Others last forever.

At the 2007 Humana Festival, Actors participated in the rolling premiere of these plays by presenting eight plays from the first half of the cycle. After the first performance, we invited a panel of people involved with the national project to reflect, conjecture and dream about the meanings of the project thus far and into the future.

Panelists included Bonnie Metzger, Producer of *365 Plays/365 Days*; Rebecca Rugg, Festival Archivist and coordinator for the 365 University hub; Ralph Peña, Artistic Director of Ma-Yi Theater Company; Jessica Posner, who coordinated the *365 Days/365 Plays* week at Wesleyan University; Kathy Sova, editor of *365 Days/365 Plays*, published by TCG and 365 actor; and Freddie Ashley, Literary Manager at the Alliance Theater and co-coordinator of the 365 Atlanta hub.

BIOGRAPHY

Suzan-Lori Parks *365 Days/365 Plays* is a playwright, screenwriter and novelist whose plays include *Topdog/Underdog* (Public Theater), *Fucking A* (Public Theater), *Imperceptible Mutabilities in the Third Kingdom* (1990 Obie Award for Best New American Play), *The American Play* (Public Theater), *Venus* (Public Theater, 1996 Obie Award), *The Death Of The Last Black Man in the Whole Entire World* and *In The Blood* (Public Theater, 2002 Pulitzer Prize finalist), among others. Her work is the subject of the PBS Film *The Topdog/Underdog Diaries*. Her work for film and television includes *Girl 6* (directed by Spike Lee) and the adaptation of Zora Neale Hurston's *Their Eyes Were Watching God* for Oprah Winfrey Presents. Her first novel, *Getting Mother's Body*, is published by Random House. She is currently writing the book for the Ray Charles musical (for the film producers of *Ray*). A recipient of a MacArthur Foundation "Genius" Award, Ms. Parks received the 2002 Pulitzer Prize for Drama for her play *Topdog/Underdog*.

ACKNOWLEDGMENTS

Actors Theatre of Louisville staged the following *365 Days/365 Plays* at the Humana Festival of New American Plays in March 2007, as part of its rolling premiere. It was directed by Sean Daniels with the following cast:

Father Comes Home from the Wars (part 1), November 14
Father ....Lou Sumrall
Mother.. Jennifer Mendenhall

The Great Army in Disgrace, December 18
Jones...Tim Altmeyer
Smith ....Rafael Jordan
Soldiers...Ensemble

2 Marys, January 3
1st Woman .... Jana Robbins
2nd Woman...Kristen Fiorella
Man's Voice.. Marc Grapey

The Birth of Tragedy, January 6
Herald...Rafael Jordan
Tragedy ....Samuel Blackerby Weible
Chair-Man...Loren Bidner
Midwife .... Jane Lee
Cake-bearer .... Zarina Shea
Dignitaries & Crowd..Ensemble

If I had to Murder Me Somebody, January 31
Speaker.. Justin Huen

The Butcher's Daughter (For Bonnie), February 13 (Again)
Butcher...Lou Sumrall
Daughter.. Angela Sperazza
Stage Directions..Ensemble

A Play for the First Day of Spring Entitled, "How do you like the War?", March 21
Speakers ....Ensemble

George Bush Visits the Cheese & Olive, April 1
Small Man.................................... Matthew Stadelmann
Waitress... Zarina Shea
Wife .... Emily Tate Frank
SS Chorus .... Kristen B. Jackson, Ensemble

Ensemble..........................Tim Altmeyer, Heather Lea Anderson,
Loren Bidner, Kristen Fiorella, Emily Tate Frank,
Marc Grapey, Justin Huen, Kristen B. Jackson,
Rafael Jordan, Jane Lee, Jennifer Mendenhall,

Jana Robbins, Zarina Shea, Jeff Snodgrass,
Angela Sperazza, Matthew Stadelmann,
Lou Sumrall,Samuel Blackerby Weible
and the following production staff:

Scenic Designer .... Paul Owen
Costume Designer.. Susan Neason
Lighting Designer... Paul Werner
Sound Designer .... Paul L. Doyle
Properties Designer .... Mark Walston
Stage Managers .... Michael D. Domue, Debra Anne Gasper
Production Assistant.. Melissa Miller
Dramaturg .... Kyle J. Schmidt
Assistant Dramaturg... Cara Pacifico

WHAT IS THE 365 NATIONAL FESTIVAL?

Make Theater. Make History. The 365 National Festival invites every theatre
in the world to join a grassroots premiere of Suzan-Lori Parks' 365 Days/365
Plays. Over 600 theatres are producing the plays in Atlanta, Austin, Canada,
Chicago, Colorado, Greater Texas, Los Angeles, Minnesota, New York,
Northeast, San Francisco Bay Area, Seattle, Southeast, Washington DC Area,
Western U.S. and in universities (365U). And the festival is growing every
day.

To find out more, visit www.365days365plays.com.
Produced by Bonnie Metzgar and Suzan-Lori Parks
National Coordinator, David Myers
National Press Rep, Carol Fineman
365U Producer, Rebecca Rugg

The Company
of *365 Days/365 Plays*

31st Annual Humana Festival of New American Plays
Actors Theatre of Louisville, 2007
Photo by Harlan Taylor

The Panel Discussion

ADRIEN-ALICE HANSEL. This panel is the beginning of a conversation about a project that's halfway done about what may be the future of theater. We've got about 45 minutes to talk, and we'll likely run out of time to cover all of the interesting things that even these people on stage have done, much less really have a chance to start a larger conversation. So I encourage you to corner anyone up here over the course of the weekend, because we want to take advantage of all the thought and experience and conjecture that we have here in this theater right now.

BONNIE METZGER. Hi, everyone. My name is Bonnie Metzger, and I am the Producer of the 365 Festival, which is the simultaneous world premiere of this play cycle called *365 Days/365 Plays*. Most of what I've been doing is holding big recruitment town meetings around the country. The point of the meetings is to talk about what the project is going to be and how to participate in it. For anyone who's interested in joining, there are ways anyone can come on in any points of the process, and it'll be going on until November 2007.

But the point of this panel is to talk about this project, now that we've done 5 months of work. What is the project, and what, if anything, does it mean?

I'm just going to give a brief summary of the project to get us up to speed. Every theatre that is involved is engaged to do one week's worth of this 52-week cycle. So if you're in Atlanta at the Alliance, the Alliance would do seven plays or however many plays are written that week, and then like a relay race you'll pass it to Actors Express, the next theatre company in Atlanta. And in that way, in a region like that, you're going to do a whole 52-week cycle with at least 52 different companies there in their geographic region. That model is happening in 16 different networks simultaneously around the world, and many of them are defined regionally. New York City has its own; in the southeast, Actors Theatre is involved with ten states in that network; but there is also an international global component where we have American companies working side by side with companies from Italy and Africa and around the world.

Suzan-Lori wrote this play cycle from November 13, 2002 through November 12, 2003. These plays reflect what happened during that period of time: certain people died; we went to war. On each day she wrote a play, sometimes two, and those plays became part of that play cycle.

I read this piece and I was struck by a couple things: one, that each one felt like a daily prayer about what it is to be an artist. It made me think about the relationship between what we do as artists and our spiritual lives, and how that plays differently in all of our lives. And the other thing I noticed, as a producer, is that these plays beg questions of form. How does one render this form into the world? And so I was inspired by both the content as well as the form to begin asking questions about the producing model of this play. I went to Suzan-Lori and asked how we can think about breaking it into as many pieces as possible and give as many people as possible the opportunity to partake. And from there, we've talked to hundreds and hundreds of really smart people and we have come up with this grassroots model where we're all involved in simultaneously creating this world premiere together.

That's the basic idea of the festival. There are numerous guiding principles that I'm going to let emerge from the people who talk about it. But one thing that you should all know is that all the performances are free. I think lots of people have different intellectual reasons for liking that. It came from the gesture of wanting this play to be a gift. Also, the cycle hearkens back to medieval play cycles, before there was a consumer entertainment identity, before we thought about art as a transaction.

With that, I'm going to ask Ralph Peña to speak from Ma-Yi in New York. Ralph's had a couple of really interesting interactions with 365.

RALPH PEÑA. I remember my first meeting with you and Suzan-Lori Parks at the Public Theatre, and one of the things, knowing Suzan-Lori Parks's work, I immediately asked was: Do you realize we're Asians? *(laughter)* And she immediately said, "Yes! And that's great! And I want you to do it that way." And so that was my entry point, because looking at 365 and knowing its breadth, what I wanted to do for the company was take and make it culturally specific and not whitewash the experience for a general audience in New York. So I'm going to borrow my friend Alice Tuan's word, which is lens. I wanted to give it a specific lens, and Bonnie and Suzan jumped on board and said, "Yes, that's what we want to do!" So in fact what we're doing is translating all the pieces into four different languages, which would be Japanese, Chinese, Filipino and Korean, and performing them simultaneously every single night, because I wanted to be a bridge between these different things. I wanted to be messy, I wanted it to be as open and laterally wide as possible for unity, very specifically. And that can be the kind of fulcrum from which we reach out to other people so the approach here is that in being specific, we are in fact being universal

And then my second encounter with 365 was in Nairobi, Kenya, in January, where a group of US theatre artists went to attend the World Social Forum. Bonnie, being the impresario that she is, pulled myself and Lloyd Suh, who is an Asian-American writer, and an African performer who was in the middle of the room and said, "perform a play." And there were about 150 artists, non-artists, people we'd never met before, Africans from all over the continent who had never met each other before, artists from Europe, and we were all there solving the *365* rubric in this room in Nairobi in Kenya and to me, it was transformative, as I think it was for everyone, because the biggest take-away is that these plays are accessible. I didn't know how people would react. Most of the African artists there had not been exposed to her work, but you saw the audience beginning to buy into the experience. They were reacting to the show. And there was a word, I think, that was in Suzan-Lori Parks's play, which was garden gnomes.

REBECCA RUGG. So there's a garden gnome in the play and the African actor who we had asked to be in it was from Zimbabwe. His name was Sly—he told us we could call him Sly—and when we got to the part of the play with the garden gnome, he said, what is that? Is that like a porcupine? *(laughter)* I think you clarified.

BONNIE. I believe it's in a play called *The Wagon*, which is January 23rd, and not only does *The Wagon* refer to a garden gnome, it also refers to a troll. Trying to describe cross-culturally the difference between a garden gnome and a troll…

REBECCA. And he said, "Oh! It's like a bush baby!" And we didn't know what a bush baby was, so it was a great moment of translation.

RALPH. Yeah. And that's the take-away: that this is absolutely accessible, and you never make assumptions about your audience.

BONNIE. One of the things I want to say is that in listening to that kind of story where someone is handed pages of text and stands on their feet and just does these plays, that the huge range in production values of the festival is happening every day of the festival, and we felt it was very important that companies knew that. If folks wanted to invest the time that clearly Actors Theatre did for this kind of presentation that we saw, fantastic, but it's equally part of the festival to open the book and have whoever's selling Coke in the lobby read the plays out loud to whoever's coming to your play before whatever your show is. We really embrace all those different kinds of presentation models.

So one of the things all the companies do is participate in something called The Constants, where there are three little plays that everyone who participates does. One of them is called *Action in Inaction* and the other one is called *Inaction in Action*, and I still get confused which is which, but in one of them, the lights come up, an actor does 365 tasks, and at some point in the middle of that, the lights go down on them. And Jessica Posner was the producer of an extraordinary week-long event at Wesleyan University at Connecticut, where there were many more than 365 things happening, so she is going to enact *Action in Inaction* right now, and at some point I'm going to have to tell her to shut up, because there are so many things, she just can't talk about all of them right now. Go!

JESSICA POSNER. We performed the seven plays in our week over 52 times in campus coffee shops, the libraries, campus eateries, and the weight room of the gym, the cafeteria, the grocery store, at-risk after-school center, in classes, in faculty meetings, at a retirement home, in the middle of town restaurants, and on the roof of a dorm with a megaphone. We also created what we call the Write-on Play Festival, where we invited the community, for one week, to engage with this process and attempt to write a play a day for a week. So we had daily writers' sessions, and we received over 300 plays, of which we picked five and fully produced them. In the opening ceremonies, we invited Bonnie and Becca to come and talk about the project all over the country. A group of 20 students collaborated and wrote a 20-minute performance loop that reflected on tensions created by talking about race in the classroom. We had receptions every night to continue these conversations. Joseph Roach, of Yale's Oral Performance project, came to talk about what happened there. We wrote a play with 30 7 through 10-year-old at-risk students which featured Jerry Springer, though not in real life. We had a class that held their class onstage to have an open classroom, which reflected on the dynamics of performance in classroom environments. We invited Amiri Baraka, who came with his Blue Arc Septet, and performed for us, and we also performed for him. Stephen Sapp of Universes came and did a workshop about youth and personal experience as a starting point for art. We had a gala performance and reception at which he also performed the eight plays altogether.

Fifty students, poets, were walking around campus all week, just spitting their poetry verses as they went everywhere; over 30 student groups performed their activities for the campus. There were swing-dancing activities in the library lobby, open rallies, meetings, demonstrations; guerilla theatre happened all over the place. People went in mask walking around, and there was a procession with homemade instruments. There was a display in the library with a display of 365 things to do, and 365 things with which to do it. We performed the play, *Father Comes Home from the Wars* at an Army Recruitment headquarters. We had LED throwie lights, which we hung from the buildings, which said "365." We erected large frames all around the campus through which to view life as a staged picture. Our closing ceremonies we showed a documentary film that a student made which documented this whole process. *(Applause.)*

The Wesleyan student newspaper took a poll of the campus, trying to find out how many people were involved with or exposed to this, including the faculty and staff, and over 98% of the staff was somehow involved or exposed.

BONNIE. So this is an indication of a very, very active 365 University component, which is produced by Rebecca Rugg, who's on the panel with us. It features over 100 colleges. There are multiple colleges going every week, and one of the things that Becca is also doing as the project archivist, which is just completed, is an article in *Theatre* Magazine. There's a concept that we've started talking about which is called radical inclusion, in relation to the 365 Project, so I've asked Becca to talk to you guys a little bit about what that is.

REBECCA. Well, I think the best example of radical inclusion is Jessica's list here, which is just incredible. I'll give you some history of this term. Bonnie said that she and Suzan-Lori Parks went around the country last summer doing town meetings, mostly with communities of artists in different places talking to them about the festival. I was going around with them too, and at some point, there were questions like the ones Ralph described: Do you really want us involved in your festival, because we're all white people? Or, we're all this kind of person. And the answer was always, yes! Of course! We want you involved. And at a certain point, I think it was in the town meeting in Chicago Bonnie and Suzan-Lori started using this phrase, "radical inclusion." It sort of popped into the lexicon of the festival, that radical inclusion was a goal they were trying to reach, and in that context it meant that everyone is welcome to participate. The idea driving who could participate was one of radical inclusion: all parties were welcome to the table.

At first when I heard them saying that, I thought, "radical inclusion? That's kind of a hippie thing, I don't know." I'm from Santa Cruz, and I'm not always comfortable with those kinds of terms. But then they kept using it, and so I started thinking about it a little bit more, and they started to expand their usage of the term to different contexts, and Suzan-Lori now often talks about as a methodology for how she wrote these plays. Every morning, she woke up and waited for the idea to come and she couldn't be picky about what that idea was. She had to have a radically inclusive process whereby any idea, even if it seemed like it might be really stupid, she had to write it down. And so that's a way that she started to talk about her artistic process that I think is really interesting: radical inclusion of all things that come to the door of her mind and knock to be let in. She has to let them all in.

So I asked her, at a certain point this fall when I was writing this article, and I asked Bonnie, too: What's the difference between inclusion and radical inclusion? Because I wonder what's radical about it. And they both said that radical inclusion takes a lot of work, that it will require sweat, and it might be painful. I think Bonnie said that for her, radical inclusion means inclusion to the point of discomfort. Coming back to what that means in terms of who's invited to the table to be in this festival, I think what can be uncomfortable for Suzan-Lori is giving these plays out to companies whose work she's never seen before. So that begins to make sense to me: how it functions as a term about the writing process, that producing a festival with all different kinds of companies in it. Inclusion to the point of discomfort.

I've become interested in how it describes the dramaturgy of the plays themselves. It seems to me, in having seen a lot of these plays and having read them all, that there's a radical inclusion in terms of what kinds of characters are onstage. There are garbage men, ugly princesses—you just saw it, and that's a dramaturgy of radical inclusion. Many of the plays are very short and they tell the actor to write the words they will say onstage. So: "Begin a monologue with the phrase, 'I went down into the woods the other day' and continue for two minutes." When you see that monologue, done by different people, it's going to be a totally different monologue. That feels like a radically inclusive act for a writer, to share ownership in that way, especially when there are 600-plus companies doing it.

I also think that it challenges us as audience members to be radically inclusive about what we define as a play. Is what Jessica just did a play? It's certainly a version of this constant that Suzan-Lori wrote, in which a person does 365 tasks as fast as they can. That's an interesting way of thinking about radical inclusion.

In writing this article, I've found two other groups that seem to be using this term, because I became interested in where it came from. Did it just pop into your mind? Or is it something we've heard? And neither of them could remember. So I Googled it—this is research—and there are two other places that 'radical inclusion' is being used: in the theological community by people who are anti-radical inclusion, and say things like, "radical inclusion of homosexuals in the kingdom of God is heresy," and people who are pro-radical inclusion. There's a minister in Berkeley who's written a book called *Radical Inclusion* that's about how her ministry invites all people to the table up in Berkeley. So I think it's interesting that it's a term that she used in a spiritual community, because I feel like this festival and the plays themselves have a deep spiritual practice to them, and although it's not a specifically Christian practice, I think that it wants to reinfuse the idea of making art with what we know can be very spiritual about that.

The other place that the idea of radical inclusion surfaces is in the ten principles of the Burning Man festival: radical inclusion is their number one principal. And for those of you who don't know, Burning Man is a crazy artistic social party held in the desert in Nevada at the end of the summer. I think it shares some things in common with *365*: it's an ephemeral thing. Works of art get created at Burning Man that go away, and they're purposefully ephemeral: the man is burned every summer. It makes sense to me that that's one other place this phrase is being used, although they use a lot more drugs, probably, than we do, and maybe they're cooler, I'm not sure. Hard to say.

BONNIE. We're going to go to our resident burning man, Freddy—

FREDDY ASHLEY. Cool is in the eye of the beholder.

BONNIE. It was very important to us that we engaged theatre artists and theatre institutions that range from the huge, established regional theatre down to the perhaps non-existent prior to the application. And so Suzan-Lori and I went searching for our partners in leading institutions, and one of the first ones to jump on board was the Alliance Theatre in Atlanta, who helped us gain momentum behind the whole project, and Freddie was really one of the first ones that we talked to about doing the project. I wanted him to talk about what's in it for a big institution participating in a project like this.

FREDDY. Bonnie and Suzan-Lori came to us about a year ago and were really focusing on this sense of collaboration around the country and this sense of community, on how this project could translate into our own theatre community. Particularly, when you are on staff at the largest theatre in town, what does participating in this project mean in terms of how you interact with the artists where you live? So it was very important to us that the festival never be perceived as an Alliance Theatre Project, that we were deigning to allow smaller companies to participate in, because the arts ecology in Atlanta is very rich and complicated in terms of large institutions like the Alliance all the way across to small- or mid-sized companies that are doing great work on a day-to-day basis, to a huge network of non-professional amateur community theatres, to a large number of university departments that are very active around town. So to have these different organizations and collections of people involved that were very important, and we partnered with Emory University in part to share resources, but in part to send the message that we were not just imparting something on the community from the Big House, as we are often referred to.

That sense of real community collaboration started to take hold early on, and we started seeing people involved in creating these pieces that might not have collaborated together normally, or people in the same room that might not have been in the same room otherwise. When you are in the largest theatre in town, you have a responsibility. If you're going to call yourself a flagship theatre in a city, you damn well better be playing kind of a leadership role and putting your resources to good use. That was what was so exciting to us about the project, and what was even more exciting was when you started to see that sense of community spirit and collaboration have an impact on the aesthetics of the work itself, and how people were bringing the work to life. You had Southwest Art Center, which serves a radically underserved section of our city, bring in high school students and use Viewpoints to bring the work to life. Then you had a couple of Georgia State professors who took the work to subway stations in town and encountered people on the street videoing people reading from the work itself and it's actually posted on the web, and it's really something to behold. This project has really created a sense of community involvement in a city that's primed for that already, from the Naomi Wallace Festival a few years back to the Beckett Festival that has been all over the city for the past ten years. So it was really important to us to foster a sense of community, not just to use the words community collaboration as buzz words.

BONNIE. This video project that Freddy refers to is so extraordinary (www.atl365tracks.org). These two Georgia State professors, who I think are visual artists, went out into the city with video cameras and accosted people, and they got it on video. They said, "Do you want to be in a play?" and they would edit it and post it, but they would also post the unedited things, where people said, "Hell, no!" as if they were asked to sign a petition. And then you had other people who were in a crowd, and one person would say, "Yes! Yes yes!" and then her friend would say, "Are you kidding? We were supposed to meet so-and-so at the bar at two," and she'd say, "No! I want to be in a play!" and then they'd be in the play, and then they'd be interviewed afterwards, and especially for those of us who are practitioners, to listen to what these people say about theatre in their lives just being accosted in the street is so incredibly poetic and powerful as an act of affirming what we do and the impact we have on individual people. 365 gives us the opportunity to smack up against all these people we never would, and it's incredible to hear them tell that.

FREDDY. That particular project was a direct articulation of how democratic this project can really be; it was so exciting.

BONNIE. The dedication that those artists had where they went out that day, they edited it all, and by midnight, it was online. Those of us around the country could participate by going online and seeing what they had done that day. It was really extraordinary.

As a companion to that, I want to talk to Kathy Sova, who many of you know works at TCG and is Suzan-Lori's long-time editor of her work but was also hoodwinked into being in the plays in Marfa, Texas. I want her to discuss the impact of the project on a small community.

KATHY SOVA. I edit the theatre books and plays at TCG, and as Bonnie said, I have a long relationship with Suzan-Lori from editing her first book of plays in 1995. I want to talk about the book a little bit, and she really did write a play a day. It wasn't like if she missed a week, she went back and wrote seven plays. The way she thought about that material was that, you work with what's in front of you. She was travelling a lot that year for the book tour of her novel, and she had been on line in an airport and could have written a short description of somebody on line, or an impression that she had. As Bonnie said, people died that year, like Johnny Cash, and there's a play for him in there. And she might have added a play or two. Basically, all the plays you see that we published in a book for her are all the plays she did on that day.

And as she got close to launching that book with the start of the festival in November, she wanted to hear the material read, so Bonnie quickly organized some readings at the Public Theater in New York in August and September, and we needed to have that book out in November. So it was really kind of fast and furious, and there were some edits based on the way people read that material at the Public. But I will just say, if you sit and look through the book, just reading the text you can see her imagination, and it's unbelievable, the ideas that she would come up with on a daily basis. The littlest thing can actually be a play. And I think the thing that was so profound during those readings is that somebody would read the date and the title and we just kept going, on after another, and you really felt a day in the life of this great artist, but we could all think back to what we were doing on that particular day or how we all keep track of those details in our life. So you can see the kind of accessibility of material and the great humanity underneath all of these little plays, and longer plays, and stage directions, and there's an amazing power to this material.

Then there's the second part of my story, which is kind of a personal connection to her. I went to the small town of Marfa, Texas, where there are no professional actors or people with theatre backgrounds, but there are people who are able to access this material. In my long relationship with Suzan-Lori, I was lucky enough that she wrote a play for me in that cycle, and I have a friend who's co-artistic director of this great place out in Marfa, Texas called the Chinati Foundation, an art museum founded by Donald Judd in the nineties. It's a flat Texas landscape with these mountains in the background, but he wanted a sculpture of modern art to be shown in an open society where you can meander through these galleries and see the art in its own environment and not be constricted by the small gallery spaces. My friend from college is co-artistic director there, a director with a great appetite for theatre. Because Suzan-Lori had written a play for me, he decided to take on one of the weeks and I decided that I would go out and act in the play that she wrote for me. It was terrifying, because I haven't acted since college, but what was so wonderful was that they basically put an ad in the paper, and anybody who wanted could be in these plays. A lot of people from the town came, and I think he cast just about everybody there, and fit people based on their particular talents or fears or what they were able to do on the stage.

But it's a small place, and it's a very special community, and there are a lot of fine artists living out there. There are a lot of people who have gone to Big Bend National Park as kids and go back there as grown-ups to see that park again, and they kind of fall in love with Marfa and want to move there. So there are people there from all over the place. The woman who's a graphic designer did the costumes, a guy who's a lawyer did the lights, and they have this wonderful small little theatre.

Basically, the whole town then gets involved, and they painted the wall, *365 Days/365 Plays*, so you open the door to this great old wooden theatre, and there's a dedication to Suzan-Lori and the festival. She ended up coming out for it, and literally, everybody in the town was in it. The guy who edits the *Big Bend Sentinel* had a part. They had a band to play every night, and as Bonnie said before, one of the requirements is that you don't charge a fee, so every night there was a full house, and you had a hundred and thirty something people in this theatre. They had a potluck, so you had to bring a covered dish, and every night, there was Suzan-Lori, the writer, and all the actors and everybody sitting down and having dinner together, talking about the plays or anything else. It was a terrific experience of creating theatre with people who normally don't, and being able to sit around together at a table every night afterwards. It was fantastic to see a whole community focus on this one artistic endeavor, for one week.

BONNIE. I want to address Kathy's description of process, of putting together the plays. I think, to a lot of us, that would be the definition of community theatre. A lot of people want to engage with us about the issue of quality on this project. Suzan-Lori, who's seen lots and lots of these plays around the country, tells me this production of plays was among the highest quality of any that she's seen around the country, done with these people, many of whom are not actors, in the middle of nowhere in Marfa, Texas. I have to tell you that some of the best work has been done by companies some of us have never heard of, that we go and find throughout the country, and some of the worst work, also, is by companies you have never heard of, and the same is true of big theatres. Some great, incredible stuff is done and also some not very exciting stuff. I think that one of the reasons it was so important to us to have both the Marfa, Texases and the Alliance Theatres in this project is that some of those snobberies run both ways. And it doesn't, we find, line up with the quality of the work at all. It's one of those great experiments that's inside of this project, to break down a lot of that terminology we use to talk about our community, or to really look at what it is. And I would put the word 'quality' in amongst those words we should be taking to Burning Man and burning.

You can see, we're in process of this project. It continues until the middle of November, we're starting to see what it is, what the play cycle is, what we are learning about this grass roots model. It certainly brings up a lot of questions about the world premiere as we know it, and it's interesting for us to have that conversation here at Humana, where so many of us come in contact with work for the first time. One example I would tell you is that very first play you saw today, *Father Comes Home from the Wars*, where the father comes and the mother says, "Oh, I wasn't expecting you," comes from the first week of the cycle. We were fortunate enough to see it seven times, so this, tonight, was the eighth, and the thing that happens when you encounter so many artists working on the same texts at the same time it's being born is that it's not stamped with one vision. The text expands with having seen many different artists come in contact with that same text. It's an incredible gift to look at what a world premiere does. There are incredible benefits when you have so much emphasis put on the text by one group of artists, but also, it is stamped by that vision, especially when it's done in such a way that we all travel somewhere, and for those of us who are artistic staff members who are going and trying to choose plays to do, we go to see the world premiere or a play, it's stamped with that vision. One of the things we're learning is what happens when you get all the directors on the phone, as we did this Wednesday, all wrestling with the same dramaturgical questions, all talking with each other at the same time about the same text. It's extraordinary what happens, because you have multiple perspectives and interpretations on something that is being done for the first time. It brings up a lot of questions about the model that we use. Not that that in itself as 365 is some kind of answer, but it's bringing up a lot of questions about what we all do.